# MONITORING CHILD SOCIO-ECONOMIC RIGHTS IN SOUTH AFRICA: ACHIEVEMENTS AND CHALLENGES

Published by Idasa, 6 Spin St, Cape Town 8001

© Idasa

ISBN 1-919798-64-1

First published 2004

Copy editing by Moira Levy, Idasa Publishing Department
Cover design, book design and layout by Marise Groenewald, Logo Print
Cover photo by Robert J. Ross, Cape Photo Library

Bound and printed by Logo Print, Cape Town

# Monitoring child socio-economic rights in South Africa: Achievements and challenges

## Edited by
## Erika Coetzee and Judith Streak

## 2004

## About the Children's Budget Unit

The Children's Budget Unit (CBU) is part of the Budget Information Service (BIS) of the Institute for Democracy in South Africa (Idasa). The CBU was established in 1995 with the aim of conducting research and disseminating information on government's budgeting for children in South Africa. The work of the CBU has evolved over time. However, its objectives have essentially remained the same, as expressed in its most recent mission statement:

"To contribute to child rights realisation and child poverty reduction by conducting research, training and information dissemination on government's budget allocations and service delivery in relation to legal obligations."

## Previous books by the CBU

- *First call: The South African children's budget* (1997) edited by Linda Biersteker and Shirley Robinson.
- *Where poverty hits hardest* (1999) by Shirley Robinson and Mastoera Sadan.
- *Are poor children being put first? Child poverty and the Budget* (2000) by Shaamela Cassiem, Helen Perry, Mastoera Sadan and Judith Streak.
- *Budgeting for child socio-economic rights: Government obligations and the child's right to social security and education* (2001) by Shaamela Cassiem and Judith Streak.

# TABLE OF CONTENTS

# CHAPTER FOUR

## CHILDREN'S RIGHT TO HEALTH

*By Maylene Shung-King, Lori Michelson, Thokozani Kaime, Paula Proudlock,
Alexandra Vennekens-Poane & Nhlanhla Ndlovu*

# CHAPTER FIVE

## BUDGETING AND SERVICE DELIVERY IN PROGRAMMES TARGETED AT THE CHILD'S RIGHT TO SOCIAL SERVICES: THE CASE OF THE CHILD SUPPORT GRANT

*By Shaamela Cassiem & Lerato Kgamphe*

# CHAPTER SIX

## THE CHILD'S RIGHT TO BASIC EDUCATION

*By Mandla Seleoane*

# CONCLUSION

*By Judith Streak*

# INDEX

# LIST OF TABLES

## CHAPTER ONE: CHILD POVERTY

## CHAPTER TWO: MONITORING FRAMEWORK

## CHAPTER THREE: RIGHT TO BASIC NUTRITION

# CHAPTER FOUR: RIGHT TO HEALTH

# CHAPTER FIVE: RIGHT TO SOCIAL ASSISTANCE

## CHAPTER SIX: RIGHT TO BASIC EDUCATION

# Acronyms

| | |
|---|---|
| ACESS | Alliance for Children's Entitlement to Social Security |
| ACRWC | African Charter on the Rights and Welfare of the Child |
| AU | African Union |
| BOR | Bill of Rights |
| CBU | Children's Budget Unit |
| COSATU | Congress of South African Trade Unions |
| CRC | Convention on the Rights of the Child |
| CSIG | Child Support Implementation Grant |
| CSG | Child Support Grant |
| ECD | Early Childhood Development |
| ELSEN | Education for Learners with Special Education Needs |
| ES | Equitable share |
| FFC | Financial and Fiscal Commission |
| GEAR | Growth, Employment and Redistribution strategy |
| GET | General Education and Training |
| HRC | Human Rights Commission |
| HSRC | Human Sciences Research Council |
| ICESCR | International Covenant on Economic, Social and Cultural Rights |
| IDASA | Institute for Democracy in South Africa |
| IES | Income & Expenditure Survey |
| IFSS | Integrated Food Security Strategy |
| IMCI | Integrated Management of Childhood Illnesses |
| ISS | Independent School Subsidies (provincial budget programme) |
| MCWH | Maternal, Child & Women's Health |
| MTBPS | Medium-Term Budget Policy Statement |
| MTEF | Medium-Term Expenditure Framework |
| NCOP | National Council of Provinces |
| NFCS | National Food Consumption Survey |
| NPA | National Programme of Action for children |
| OAU | Organisation of African Unity |
| OHS | October Household Survey |
| PEM | Protein Energy Malnutrition |
| PMTCT | Prevention of Mother-to-Child Transmission (of HIV) programme |
| POS | Public Ordinary Schooling |
| PSFS | Primary School Feeding Scheme |
| RDA | Recommended Daily Allowance |
| RDP | Reconstruction and Development Programme |
| SSA | Statistics South Africa |
| SSE | Special School Education (provincial budget programme) |
| TAC | Treatment Action Campaign |
| UDHR | Universal Declaration of Human Rights |
| WHO | World Health Organisation |

# BIOGRAPHIES

**DANIE BRAND** lectures in public law at the University of Pretoria and is an associate researcher at the Centre for Human Rights, also at the University of Pretoria. His main research interests are human rights law, with a focus on socio-economic rights and administrative law.

**SHAAMELA CASSIEM** manages Idasa's Children's Budget Unit. She has a background in development practice including adult education and children's rights, and has an MPhil in development studies from the Institute of Development Studies at the University of Sussex. Shaamela has worked in the field of children's rights for several years — including advocacy and monitoring policy and legislation. At the Children's Budget Unit, she is responsible for the unit's capacity-building and support for child-focused budget work outside of South Africa. She is also concerned with monitoring the justice sector's commitment to improving its response to crimes by and against children and training development of the unit. Her particular area of interest is rights-based approaches to applied budget work.

**ERIKA COETZEE** is a freelance researcher and writer specialising in educational resources and plain language materials. She holds a Master's degree in political philosophy from the University of Stellenbosch. Erika has worked extensively in the areas of democracy education, youth development, curriculum design and organisational learning. She has written school materials for learners and teachers, popular booklets on a wide range of social, economic and political themes and training resources for youth and adults.

**LERATO KGAMPHE** is a research assistant for Idasa's Children's Budget Unit. Lerato holds an undergraduate degree majoring in Economics and Finance from the University of Cape Town. She is currently studying towards her Masters' degree in Financial Analysis and Portfolio Management.

**LORI MICHELSON** is a senior researcher within the Child Health Services Programme of the Children's Institute. She holds a Bachelor of Science Degree in Speech Pathology/Audiology and will soon have her MPhil in Maternal and Child Health. Her experience includes five years of work in community-based project management and the child health research policy arena.

**NHLANHLA NDLOVU** is chiefly responsible for the Children's Budget Unit's research on South African domestic public expenditure for HIV/AIDS at national and provincial levels. In addition, Nhlanhla monitors parliament's involvement in HIV/AIDS policy-making and service delivery. Moreover, he is also responsible for coordinating training undertaken by the Unit to contribute to capacity-building on budgeting issues for government officials, NGOs, parliamentarians, researchers and institutions involved in HIV/AIDS advocacy and research.

**PAULA PROUDLOCK** is the manager of the Child Rights Programme at the Children's Institute, University of Cape Town. She is a founding steering committee member of the Alliance for Children's Entitlement to Social Security (ACESS) and founding secretariate member of a national network on the Children's Bill (Children's Bill Working Group). She has a LLB from Stellenbosch University and is currently doing a Master's degree in Public Law at UCT.

**MANDLA SELEOANE** is campus Director at the Garankuwa campus of the Tshwane University of Technology. He previously worked as a research specialist at the HSRC, focusing on human rights studies. In addition, he has published and delivered material on socio-economic rights and human rights in general.

**MAYLENE SHUNG KING** is the deputy director and programme manager for the Health Services Programme of the Children's Institute. She is a medical doctor with post-graduate training in public health. Maylene has experience in the field of child health policy research and training and has been involved in several child health policy development processes with national and provincial departments of health.

**JUDITH STREAK** is senior researcher in Idasa's Children's Budget Unit. In this position she is responsible for leading the unit's research on government's budgeting for children. Judith has a background in history and economics (specialising in development economics). Her particular research interests are strategy options for the South African state to promote more rapid poverty reduction (particularly for children) and how to integrate the human rights approach into implementing and monitoring poverty reduction programmes in South Africa.

**GERALDINE VAN BUEREN** is Professor of International Human Rights Law at Queen Mary University of London and the University of Cape Town. She is one of the drafters of the Convention on the Rights of the Child and in 2003 was the recipient of the UNICEF Child Rights Lawyer Award.

**ALEXANDRA VENNEKENS-POANE** joined Idasa's Budget Information Service in 2002 as the health researcher in the Provincial Fiscal Analysis Unit. Since 2003, she has managed the Sector Budget Analysis Unit. Alexandra holds a Master of Science degree in Development Studies, has experience in socio-economic development and business research, and has developed training modules regarding civil society and legislature participation in the budget. She has done analyses of health budgets in the South African provinces and of provincial expenditure in the social and non-social sectors.

# FOREWORD

Geraldine Van Bueren

The twentieth century was the age of civil and political rights and this century will be the coming of age of economic, social and cultural rights. The essence of children's economic and social rights or social justice rights is transformation and redistribution. According to international law, children's social justice rights create a legitimate claim for children to benefit from an equal share in the state's resources. Yet even though a number of national constitutions expressly protect the social justice rights of children, including those of Brazil, Colombia, Croatia, Malawi and South Africa, and many constitutions include the right to health care and education as a general right of the population, these legally binding provisions have not been used to their maximum potential.

This is partly because lawyers and judges as well as a wide range of policy-makers are nervous about their potential and partly because these are often new areas for those making and challenging resource allocation decisions. They require new thinking and new tools for the effective measuring of implementation. Poverty of the imagination has been underestimated as a contributing factor to impoverishment.

*Monitoring Child Socio-Economic Rights in South Africa: Achievements and Challenges* deserves a wide readership because it provides policy-makers and the courts with invaluable data, disaggregating the resources expended on children's social justice rights. Without such data policy-makers and the courts are forced to rely on impressions and anecdotes. The data produced in this book seeks to analyse the content of each of the children's social justice rights and provides concrete evidence on precisely how much has been spent on their realisation and when. This can be fed directly both into the legislative policy-making stage and into any challenges to this policy through the courts.

The child rights budget is an essential new tool in alleviating poverty and assisting South Africa to meet its constitutional and treaty commitments. Courts have a duty to consider international law, which includes the progressive implementation of economic and social rights according to the maximum available resources or available resources. Terms such as progressive, maximum and available resources are terms of art requiring reliable statistical information to substantiate claims and counterclaims. Without such information the accurate assessment of the progress of government is at the very least difficult and probably impossible.

Progress towards social justice equity has been impeded not only because of the brutal legacy of apartheid but also because there is some fear of the potential of children's social justice rights protected in the Constitution. However, a textual analysis of the children's economic and social rights provisions in section 28 (1) does not support the floodgates argument. Each of the rights is qualified by minimum conditions – a right to basic nutrition, basic health care and basic social services – and although shelter is not qualified by basic, the concept of shelter itself is inherently basic.[1]

As the disaggregation of resources expended upon children reveals the floodgates fear is a false fear. Children's rights are inherently inclusive. There is an improvement in the lives of other sections of the community, as it is neither desirable nor possible to protect children's rights in isolation from their families and communities.

One of the inherent problems is how to distinguish between a government's inability to implement a specific right, nationally or provincially, and its unwillingness to do so. The court cannot order the government to do the impossible, but this is not the same as equality of access to national resources.

On becoming party to human rights treaties, a state's budget has to be tailored to meet its treaty commitments. As with other areas of executive responsibility, the sovereign act of becoming party to a treaty brings with it budgetary considerations, and states for the first time are now beginning to be held accountable.

In addition to the specific constitutional provisions on children, South Africa is also party to the United Nations Convention on the Rights of the Child (CRC) and the African Charter on the Rights and Welfare of the Child. Together these provisions move the borders for the state of what is political and what can be subject to a legal challenge in the courts, particularly in resource allocation and budgetary matters. The CRC and other international laws in effect narrow what were previously unfettered discretionary powers of governments.

In addition, where section 28 of the Constitution imports specific provisions of the CRC, the purposive approach of the Convention ought to be a factor, to be considered by the court, when reviewing the discretionary powers of the government in relation to each provision. In relation to children the dividing line separating such powers has moved as a matter of international law binding upon South Africa.

Governments can no longer plead unaffordability and hope to escape questioning. Hence the United Nations Committee on the Rights of the Child criticised Egypt and Indonesia on the proportion of their budget spent on defence, as compared to the proportion spent on children's social expenditure. It is the proportions that are of concern to the UN Committee, not the totals spent. An approach that focuses on proportions totally undermines the frequently heard government argument of non-affordability, and offers potential both for equitable resource distribution at a governmental level and through national litigation.

Children are not only the recipients of resource allocation. They are able to participate in the weighting of social justice priorities. It is frequently overlooked that children are citizens too, and have the rights of citizenship, including the freedom to make political choices together with the right to freedom of expression. The latter, enshrined both in the Constitution and in treaty law, is not limited to adults. In the allocation of resources, article 12 of the CRC is applicable, and therefore children have the right to be provided with an opportunity to participate in all decisions affecting their own destinies, including social justice priorities. The exercise of such a right is beneficial to the community as a whole.

The implementation of the social justice rights of children is still at a pioneering stage. Governments, courts and civil society are grappling with issues without the benefit of as much comparative jurisprudence as there is in the civil and political rights field. International law, particularly the General Comments emanating from the United Nations Committee on Economic, Social and Cultural Rights and from the United Nations Committee on the Rights of the Child, have helped establish clarity on the ambit of the rights and on different methods of protection. *Monitoring Child Socio-Economic Rights in South Africa: Achievements and Challenges* also provides essential analysis and data on what has been done and, just as importantly, what the Constitution requires to be done to help alleviate child poverty in South Africa.

---

1 See further Van Bueren, G.(2002) "No Turning Back – The Right to Housing is Justiciable". In H. Cheadle, D. Davis and N. Haysom, *South African Constitutional Law: The Bill of Rights*, Butterworths, commenting on the approach of the Constitutional Court in the *Grootboom* case.

# INTRODUCTION

Judith Streak

"We, the people of South Africa,
Recognise the injustices of our past;
Honour those who suffered for justice and freedom in our land; …..
We therefore, through our freely elected representatives, adopt this
Constitution as the supreme law of the Republic so as to:-
Heal the divisions of the past and establish a society based on democratic
values, social justice and fundamental human rights;
Lay the foundations for a democratic and open society in which government is
based on the will of the people and every citizen is equally protected by law;
*Improve the quality of life of all citizens and free the potential of each person…"*
*Preamble to the South African Constitution* (our emphasis added).

The objective of this publication is to contribute to the eradication of child poverty
and the realisation of children's socio-economic rights in South Africa. Towards this
end, the book uses research to monitor the measures taken by government to give
effect to the socio-economic rights given to children in the South African
Constitution (Act 108 of 1996, hereafter referred to as the Constitution).

The preamble to the South African Constitution commits South Africa to improve the
quality of life of all its citizens. Moreover, the Bill of Rights affords everyone a comprehensive set of justiciable socio-economic rights and gives children an additional set
of socio-economic rights. The rights afforded to everyone (in sections 26, 27 and 29)
relate to housing, health care, food, water, social security (including social assistance)
as well as basic and further education. The child-specific socio-economic rights are
contained in Section 28(1)(c). It states that every child has the right "to basic nutrition, shelter, basic health services and social services". The socio-economic rights in the
Constitution are designed to ensure that everyone, including children, gain sufficient
goods and services to have a quality of life consistent with dignity. These rights are also
formulated to include an element of progressive improvement over time.

The state and parents are the main players in translating the rights of children into
reality. However, parents have the primary responsibility: they fulfil this responsibility
by using their income to buy goods and services for children. When parents are unable
to fulfil the primary obligation (for example when parents are too poor to meet their
household's basic needs), the state's role becomes more prominent. The state is legally
obliged to provide for children's basic needs when their parents are unable to do so.
This obligation includes the socio-economic rights given only to children in section
28 and the right to basic education, given to everyone in section 29(1)(a). One
important way for the state to meet these obligations is by helping the market economy to create jobs. Another is by designing and implementing programmes that provide
effective services to poor children and their parents. These include programmes that
deliver basic education, social security, health, housing and basic nutrition. The state's
legal obligation to deliver these rights to children is of a higher level than its obligation to deliver the socio-economic rights given to everyone. This is because the obligation to give effect to everyone's socio-economic rights is qualified with reference to
progressive realisation, available resources and reasonable measures. There can be no
doubt that the child poverty situation in South Africa is at odds with the ideals
expressed in the Constitution pertaining to the quality of life of children (and their

families). Over the first decade of democracy, government has indeed made progress in rolling out basic services to poor people, including poor children. The analyses of service delivery in key programmes directed at poor children, as presented in this publication, are testimony to this. However after ten years, poverty amongst adults and children remains extensive and deep. Moreover and critically, the massive task of turning around the poverty crisis, left behind after the demise of apartheid, is still constrained by extensive structural unemployment. In this context, prospects for the market economy to create jobs for a larger portion of the poor continue to be bleak (see, for example, Department of Social Development 2002, Streak 2004 and Bhorat et al 2001). As a result, poor parents still struggle to earn an income that would allow them and their children to meet basic needs.

# AN EVOLVING APPROACH TO MONITORING

Against this background, it is clear that much still needs to be done to ensure that the quality of life experienced by South Africa's children is transformed in line with the ideals expressed in the Constitution. In order to inform and assist this process, there is a need to monitor, in an ongoing way, the achievements that have been gained thus far and to identify the critical areas in which progress is yet to be made. There are many institutions and actors with responsibilities in relation to constitutional child socio-economic rights. However, in the context of the extensive poverty that exists in South Africa, government's role is particularly important. This publication seeks to contribute to the process of achieving the child rights ideals in the Constitution by providing a monitoring perspective that links government's measures to give effect to children's socio-economic rights to its legal obligations in this regard.

The monitoring approach of the Children's Budget Unit (CBU) has evolved over several years and is itself the product of grappling with a number of strategic and methodological questions. From a strategic point of view, it seems essential for monitoring efforts to be designed in such a way as to generate findings that can be used constructively by activists, decision-makers and planners. It is also important for monitoring questions to be based partly on government's legal obligations in relation to child rights, as this provides a foundation for holding government accountable. The objective with child rights monitoring research is to produce information that suggests where government's measures may fall short of constitutional obligations, but also produces precise and concrete insights and recommendations for child rights activists and government policy-makers and implementers. As far as methodology is concerned, the challenge is three-fold:

- To try to establish what legal obligations government in fact has in relation to child socio-economic rights and to acquire knowledge about critical areas of interest for poor children, policy-makers and activists;
- To use this as a basis for deriving a rigorous monitoring method; and
- To decide which monitoring questions proposed by the method can be put into practice. For example, a key question that flows from the legal obligations is whether the budgets for government programmes targeted at realising child socio-economic rights, are sufficient in size. To answer this question requires technical and time-consuming research.

Establishing what government's obligations are in relation to constitutional child socio-economic rights is difficult, but important. It is difficult because there is not yet clarity around the scope and content of children's constitutional rights, nor therefore around the state's obligations to give effect to them. It is important because government cannot be left with the task of defining the scope and content of child rights, nor its obligations in relation to them. An important project for the advancement of children in South Africa is to generate consensus around the interpretation of the scope and content of children's constitutional socio-economic rights and associated with this, what we thus need to hold government accountable for. Another challenge is to develop better methods, data and capacity for monitoring government's measures to advance these rights.

The CBU has, since its inception in 1995, undergone many shifts in its journey towards developing an approach to monitoring that meets the needs outlined above. Over the first few years, the CBU found its feet by recording government's commitments to children (including those relating to the realisation of child rights and to poverty reduction), tracking budget allocations and policy developments for children and highlighting service delivery challenges in key government programmes providing services to children. There was no explicit attempt to link monitoring questions to the state's legal obligations to give effect to child rights. The first three monitoring publications of the CBU reflect this approach.

In 2001, a critical decision was made to try to base the monitoring method more on government's legal obligations to deliver child rights and hence to adopt an approach that holds government accountable for its legal obligations. This is not to say that the method adopted by the CBU is focused solely on an exploration into legal obligations (see chapter two). The CBU's fourth book - *Budgeting for child socio-economic rights: Government obligations and the child's right to social security and education* (2001) – was a product of this new direction in monitoring methodology.

In order to develop its methodological framework further, the CBU commissioned an evaluation of the monitoring method applied in the 2001 study. The evaluation team was led by Kenneth Creamer, an advocate and lecturer in economics, with expertise in public finance and socio-economic rights in South Africa. The team drew on inputs from several members, including Julia de Bruyn (National Treasury, but in her own capacity), Professor Charles Simkins (School of Economics, University of the Witwatersrand), Tseliso Thipanyane (South African Human Rights Commission), Danie Brand (Senior Lecturer in the Department of Public Law, University of Pretoria) and Geoff Budlender (Legal Resources Centre). The findings of this evaluation were summarised in a 2002 report by Creamer, titled *The impact of South Africa's evolving jurisprudence on children's socio-economic rights on budget analysis*. These insights are incorporated into the monitoring method developed in chapter two and used to guide the analyses in this publication.

# THE STRUCTURE OF THIS BOOK

This publication monitors the way government has conceptualised and implemented programmes aimed at delivering four of the socio-economic rights afforded to children in the Constitution. These are the rights to basic nutrition, basic health services, social services, set out in section 28(1)(c), and the right to basic education, contained in section 29(1)(a).

**CHAPTER ONE**, by Judith Streak, blends quantitative and qualitative research findings to provide a picture of the extent, nature and distribution of the child poverty crisis. It also uses the experiences of children living in difficult circumstances and/or in poverty to draw out inferences for government's poverty reduction strategy. The analysis of the extent and distribution of child poverty is based on two poverty indicators and on household survey data. The indicators are income and hunger. The household survey data derive from the 2000 Income and Expenditure Household Survey and the 1999 National Food Consumption Survey. The qualitative description of the child poverty crisis and the discussion of its policy implications are informed by a child participation study commissioned for this publication and conducted by Deborah Ewing.

**CHAPTER TWO**, by Joachim Wehner and Judith Streak, examines the socio-economic rights given to children in the Constitution and the associated obligations thereby placed on the state. It considers what implications these hold for how to go about monitoring government's measures to advance children's socio-economic rights. A related objective is to place in context the monitoring method that guides the enquiry in chapters three to six of the book. An important point that emerges is the importance of consensus-building in society around the question of what level of entitlements is implied by each of the rights and exactly what the state is obliged to do for poor children through service provision.

The monitoring approach introduced in chapter two is informed by the three-step logical sequence suggested by Creamer (2002:21), which draws from evolving jurisprudence on socio-economic rights in South Africa:

- First, develop an understanding of children's socio-economic rights;
- Second, identify which government programmes are being used as instruments to achieve these goals; and
- Third, analyse whether these programmes reasonably meet government's constitutional obligations to realise children's socio-economic rights.

Based on this approach, chapter two sets out the monitoring framework that guides the analyses in chapters three to six:

**STEP ONE:** To investigate the meaning and scope of the right and highlight the importance of reaching consensus and a clearer understanding of what which children are entitled to under the rights given only or primarily to children in the Constitution.

STEP TWO: To identify the key programmes in place and provide a broad description of each, focusing on the services the programme aims to provide, the beneficiaries it aims to reach and government's time-schedule for rolling out services.

STEP THREE: To investigate the sufficiency (not reasonableness) of one or more of the relevant key programmes by asking the following questions about programme conceptualisation and implementation:

i. Is the programme conceptualised in such a way that all children in need are targeted beneficiaries, that the most vulnerable children are specifically targeted and that services are to be rolled out as a matter of urgency and as quickly as administrative capacity seems to facilitate?

ii. How much has government budgeted for the programme (annually) since programme inception and what are the budgeted and estimated allocations for the MTEF period 2003/04 to 2005/06? What percentage of total expenditure planned for in the budget flowed to the programme in 2002/03 and is destined to flow to the programme over the MTEF period 2003/04 to 2005/06?

iii. Have funds allocated to the programme been spent or has there been wastage in the programme due to non-spending of budgets?

iv. Is programme implementation such that services are being rolled out to all children in need, particularly those whose needs are most urgent? Are services being rolled out as a matter of urgency and as quickly as administrative capacity permits?

v. What are the (financial and non-financial) problems that undermine the provision of programme services to all children in need (particularly to the most vulnerable)?

vi. What measures are being taken by government to overcome service delivery problems (particularly in the form of building administrative capacity)? What recommendations can be made about how these planned measures may be adjusted or improved?

Chapters three to six each give attention to a particular socio-economic right given only or primarily to children in the Constitution, as well as the corresponding government measures being used to give effect to this right. The chapters broadly follow the three steps of enquiry contained in the monitoring method outlined above. However, the different chapters give varying emphasis to each of the steps. In particular, the chapters differ considerably in analysing the sufficiency of the programmes selected for more detailed analysis (step three). Some chapters tackle most, if not all, of the research questions listed above under step three, while others address only some. This variation is partly due to discrepancies in the availability of programme data, as well as reflecting the natural diversity of different authors' expertise and styles of enquiry. In general, the time period considered in the publication is 1994 to 2003. However, the exact time period covered in the programme sufficiency analyses is dependent on when the programme was first introduced and on the availability of information.

**CHAPTER THREE**, by Danie Brand, monitors government's measures to give effect to the child's right to basic nutrition. The chapter focuses on the Primary School Feeding Scheme (PSFS) for step three of the monitoring method.

**CHAPTER FOUR** was prepared by Maylene Shung King, Lori Michelson, Thokozani Kaime, Paula Proudlock, Alexandra Vennekens-Poane and Nhlanhla Ndlovu. It monitors government measures to give effect to the child's right to health, focusing on the right to basic health services. The chapter applies step three of the monitoring method to the Prevention of Mother-to-Child Transmission (PMTCT) programme.

In **CHAPTER FIVE**, Shaamela Cassiem and Lerato Kgamphe monitor the measures taken by government to give effect to the right of children to social services. It gives specific attention to social assistance and the Child Support Grant (CSG) programme.

**CHAPTER SIX**, by Mandla Seleoane, monitors government's measures to give effect to the child's right to a basic education. The chapter focuses primarily on the legal meaning of the child's right to basic education and on government's budgeting to give effect to this right. Comments on the adequacy of three programmes – General Education and Training (GET), Early Childhood Development (ECD) and Education for Learners with Special Needs Programme (ELSEN) – are drawn from the legal and budgetary analysis.

The **CONCLUSION** to this publication summarises the main points that emerge across the chapters. It re-caps important aspects of the child poverty crisis from chapter one, including children's own perceptions of government efforts to realise their rights and how these can be improved. It then draws out the significant points that emerge from chapter two's investigation into the scope and content of children's unqualified constitutional socio-economic rights. It considers the associated state obligations and government strategies to realise child socio-economic rights between 1994 and 2003. In reviewing the main findings of chapters three to six, the conclusion highlights unresolved questions relating to the definition of the content of child socio-economic rights. Finally, it draws attention to current challenges in developing and implementing government programmes so that children's constitutional rights to basic nutrition, basic health care services, social services and a basic education can be realised more quickly.

# REFERENCES

Bhorat, H., M. Liebbrandt, M. Maziya, S. van der Berg & I. Woolard. (2001) *Fighting Poverty: Labour Markets and Inequality in South Africa.* Cape Town: University of Cape Town.

Creamer, K. (2002) *The impact of South Africa's evolving jurisprudence on children's socio-economic rights on budget analysis.* Report.

Department of Social Development. (2002) *Transforming the Present – Protecting the Future: Draft Consolidated Report of the Committee of Inquiry into a Comprehensive System of Social Security for South Africa.* Pretoria: Government Printer.

Republic of South Africa. (1996) *The Constitution of the Republic of South Africa.* Act 108 of 1996.

Streak, J. (2004) "The GEAR legacy: Did GEAR fail or move South Africa forward in development?". Forthcoming in *Development Southern Africa,* 21 (2), June.

# CHAPTER ONE

Child poverty in South Africa and implications for policy:
Using indicators and children's views to gain perspective

Judith Streak[1]

"We have electricity, which is illegally connected. We have lights and a radio but no stove, so we use an element to cook. It gives us electric shocks, so we wear rubber shoes when we use it."
*A boy, age 17, who lives with his sister and her one-year-old son in KwaZulu-Natal*

"We wear broken shoes and cannot wash every day."
*A child living on a farm outside Stellenbosch*

"Children are treated differently when they are poor."
*A child living on a farm outside Stellenbosch*

# INTRODUCTION

This chapter stands somewhat apart from the rest of the publication. The chapters that follow have a collective focus on monitoring the programmes government has put in place and the budget actions it has taken to realise four of the five socio-economic rights given only or primarily to children in the South African Constitution. As a preamble to this task, this first chapter attends to the broad context of the child poverty crisis in South Africa. It has two objectives:

- To describe the nature and extent of the child poverty crisis in South Africa in a way that captures both the scale and the real experiences of children living in poverty and/or difficult circumstances; and
- To use the insights of children living in poverty and/or difficult circumstances as a basis for drawing out policy inferences for government on how to use the state apparatus more effectively to reduce child poverty.

As Kanbur and Squire (1999:1) relate, there has been a progressive broadening of the definition of poverty. This broadening process shows a shift from focusing largely or exclusively on insufficient income towards the inclusion of other dimensions of living standards such as longevity, literacy, and healthiness, and most recently, to concerns with risk and vulnerability, exclusion and powerlessness (see Streak 2000:vii). The descriptions of child poverty quoted below come from two farm children experiencing economic hardship:

"It makes you feel like a lesser person."

"Children are treated differently when they are poor."

These descriptions remind us that child poverty is about more than the suffering associated with insufficient command over income and commodities, aspects that researchers have conventionally focused on. These forms of suffering include feelings of tiredness and hunger due to insufficient food, experiencing desperation due to an inability to attend school, feeling scared and cold due to inadequate shelter and clothing, as well as feeling dirty and/or sick due to difficulties associated with acquiring water. The evolving understanding of poverty now includes, in addition to the aspects above, attention to the psychological suffering associated with discrimination and the social exclusion that goes hand-in-hand with insufficient access to income and services.

The fact that child poverty is multi-faceted and includes subjective psychological elements makes it difficult to define and measure. This poses a challenge to realising the first objective of this chapter, namely to highlight the nature and scale of the child poverty crisis in South Africa. Traditionally, the description and measurement of poverty has concentrated on using quantitative data in the form of household survey data and money-metric measures. Thus, to describe the child poverty situation, the traditional approach involves choosing an income or expenditure poverty line and measuring how many children live below that line. Other indicators, such as access to schooling, access to health services and hunger – supported by quantitative data – may be added to the money-metric measurement and description.

Researchers have begun to try and meet the challenge of describing and measuring poverty in ways that more truly reflect its multi-faceted, experiential nature. To this end, more people-centred data-collection methodologies are emerging. With regard to child poverty, this involves "using children as informants through child participatory methods, rather than seeing their situation solely through the eyes of their care-givers and the economists who crunch the numbers" (Dawes 2003:personal correspondence). Qualitative child-centred data gathered from participatory research is important for providing in-depth information about what it means to be poor. As Ismail Serageldin has aptly pointed out (cited in Leibbrandt et al 2001:44), poverty statistics are "people with the tears wiped off". Too much of the reality of poverty gets lost in an approach that uses only quantitative data. At the same time, the use of quantitative-based indicators remains crucial to describing child poverty, as it helps to reveal the scale and distribution of child poverty. Therefore, in order not to lose the reality of the various forms of suffering that child poverty entails, quantitative-based indicators are best used in conjunction with qualitative data. Leibbrandt et al (Ibid) explain elegantly: "While objective measures are undoubtedly useful...qualitative data restores the reality that lies behind the rates and averages of poverty statistics". Participatory research provides a fuller and more holistic understanding of child poverty from the perspective of those who are poor and helps to fill gaps that are left by the statistics.

Following the emerging trend of using both qualitative and quantitative data to analyse poverty, this chapter adopts the following two-pronged approach to highlight the scale of the poverty crisis in South Africa and to deepen our understanding of the nature of the crisis. First, it uses two poverty indicators and quantitative data in the form of household survey data. The one indicator used in the research is income, the other is food insecurity (hunger). Secondly, the chapter makes use of qualitative data in the form of descriptions from children living in poverty and/or in difficult circumstances. These perspectives from children include views on their own personal experiences, their access to basic and social services, what their most important needs are and what they think government's budget priorities should be. The children's accounts help us understand child poverty as *it is lived* (Bray 2003:4). The qualitative analysis of child poverty is particularly important from a human rights perspective. From a rights point of view, we are not only interested in child poverty because of the scale of the problem. We are interested in, and want to highlight, the suffering of any *one* child (Bentley 2003); not even one child should have to live in poverty.

To generate the information needed for the income indicator view of the child poverty situation, the Children's Budget Unit (CBU) commissioned Dr Ingrid Woolard, a senior research specialist at the Human Sciences Research Council (HSRC). More specifically, the chapter presents new estimates by Woolard of the extent and regional distribution of child poverty, based on the 2000 *Income and Expenditure Survey* (IES 2000) of Statistics South Africa[2] and two absolute income poverty lines. The food insecurity indicator description of child poverty is based on questions asked in the *National Food Consumption Survey in Children Age 1-9 years: South Africa 1999* (NFCS 1999)[3], commissioned by the Department of Health (2000).

To gather the qualitative child poverty information, the CBU commissioned Deborah Ewing[4], a child participation expert, to conduct a child participation study. This study forms the source of the child poverty descriptions from the perspectives of poor and vulnerable children as presented in this chapter. It is also the source of the views from children on what their most urgent needs are and how they would prioritise government spending amongst these needs.

The profile of child poverty in this chapter is not intended to be comprehensive. However, it is of course important that in the process of doing any child poverty research, value is added to the existing body of work. What is new in this chapter? Firstly, the new measures of child poverty by Woolard give an updated perspective on the scale and distribution of the crisis. Another novelty is the blending of quantitative and qualitative data, as well as the policy inferences that emerge from the children's insights. A project for the future is to add other indicators — such as anthropomorphic indicators, access to shelter, health care and education services — to the two quantitative indicators presented here. This, together with the addition of more participatory research, will help to make our understanding of the extent and nature of child poverty more comprehensive.

The chapter proceeds as follows. Section one presents the indicator perspective of the child poverty situation. It has two parts. The first part of the analysis uses Woolard's measurement of poverty based on the IES 2000 and income poverty lines to present a picture of the extent and distribution of child poverty according to the income indicator. The second part uses the NFCS 1999 to illustrate the scale and distribution of child poverty according to the food insecurity indicator. Section two then presents the perspectives of poor and vulnerable children on what it means to be poor, what their most urgent needs are and what they think budget priorities should be. It also derives a collection of inferences for government policy on how to go about addressing child poverty. Section two has three parts. The first gives an overview of the child participation study Ewing conducted to gather the information from children. The second part provides the children's accounts of their experiences of poverty. The third part presents the results from Ewing's study relating to what children saw as their most important needs and what they thought government's budget priorities should be. In the course of presenting the children's views, inferences for government's child poverty reduction strategy are highlighted. The conclusion synthesises and summarises the chapter's most significant findings. It pays particular attention to the pointers for government's poverty reduction strategy emerging from the child participation research.

# 1. A QUANTITATIVE PERSPECTIVE ON CHILD POVERTY USING INDICATORS OF INCOME AND FOOD INSECURITY

## 1.1 LOOKING AT CHILD POVERTY THROUGH THE LENS OF INCOME

### 1.1.1 METHOD: CHOOSING A POVERTY LINE AND COUNTING POOR CHILDREN

It is difficult to decide where to set a poverty line to measure child poverty. The conventional approach to measuring poverty involves defining poverty in terms of "the inability to attain a minimum standard of living" and measuring it in terms of basic consumption needs. The challenge therefore lies in trying to set the poverty line at the level of income below which lack of income translates into an inability to consume the basic goods needed for a minimum standard of living (see World Bank 1990; Leibbrandt *et al* 2001:42).

What is "a minimum standard of living"? This is a difficult question to answer objectively. Even if there is consensus about the standard of living, it is still extremely difficult to work out how much income is needed by children with different initial income levels, physical needs and locations, faced with different transport costs and different prices of goods, in order to facilitate reaching this standard.

For the purposes of this chapter, the CBU decided to follow the conventional approach and identify absolute rather than relative income poverty lines for Woolard's money-metric measurement of child poverty. A relative poverty line defines poverty in relation to the situation of other members of the population. For example, using a relative definition of poverty and poverty line, poor households might be defined as those that fall within the poorest 40% of all households (when households are ranked according to their expenditure or income per individual). An absolute poverty line defines poverty in relation to certain fixed criteria. For example, following the conventional approach described above, poor households might be defined as those that do not have the level of income or expenditure (per individual) necessary to meet basic consumption needs and attain a minimum standard of living.

To set the two absolute income poverty lines used in Woolard's analysis, the CBU shied away from estimating the minimum level of income needed to meet basic consumption needs and ensure a decent standard of living for children. An amount of R215/month per capita (in 2000 rands) was chosen as a line for measuring the number of children living in deep poverty. In other words, it was chosen as a low poverty line to capture children living in dire poverty. R430/month per capita (in 2000 rands) was chosen as a higher poverty line. While the choice of both lines was guided by those used by other researchers in poverty measurement, they are open to scrutiny and need to be viewed in the light of those used by others. Table 1.1 below provides an overview of a range of per capita absolute poverty lines recently used by other researchers in their attempts to measure the extent of poverty, either amongst the whole population or specifically amongst children in South Africa. It also reveals the household survey data used in the research and the respective poverty rate findings (amongst the whole population or child population). The poverty lines are converted (in column three) to 2000 rands to facilitate easy comparison with our lines.[5] The purpose of the table is to provide a point of departure against which to compare the two income poverty lines chosen for this study and the results they generate.[6]

**TABLE 1.1  POVERTY LINES PER MONTH/CAPITA AND POVERTY RATES (GENERAL AND CHILD-SPECIFIC)**

| Research study | Poverty line | Poverty line in 2000 rands | Data used | Result |
|---|---|---|---|---|
| Studies of the general population | | | | Population poverty rate |
| Leibbrandt, Woolard & Bhorat (2001) | R149.50 (estimated amount of money required to achieve a per capita caloric intake of 8 500 kJ per day) | R244.28 | 1993 Project for Statistics on Living and Development (PSLSD) Survey | 40.4% |
| Leibbrandt, Woolard & Bhorat (2001) | Minimum and supplemental living levels per capita set by the Bureau of Market Research, University of South Africa: R220.10 (supplemental) R164.20 (minimum) | R359.64 R268.28 | 1993 Project for Statistics on Living and Development (PSLSD) Survey | 56.7% 44.7% |
| Child-specific studies | | | | Child poverty rate |
| Woolard (2002) | R200 in 1999 rands R400 in 1999 rands | R210.75 R421.50 | 1995 October Household Survey and 1995 Income and Expenditure Survey | 38.9% 64.7% |
| Woolard (2002) | R200 in 1999 rands R400 in 1999 rands | R210.75 R421.50 | 1999 October Household Survey | 58.1% 75.8% |
| Dieden & Gustafsson (2003) | R122.56 in 1995 rands (estimated equivalent of US$1 a day per capita) | R169.26 | 1995 October Household Survey and 1995 Income and Expenditure Survey | 28% |

**Note:**  The annual average CPI, as recorded by Statistics South Africa, and reported by Dr Ian Venter of the South African Reserve Bank (SARB) was used to inflate the poverty lines into 2000 rands.

**Sources:** Leibbrandt et al (2001:49) for the information on the studies for the population as a whole. Haarmann 1999; Woolard 2002 (cited in Streak 2001) and Dieden & Gustafsson 2003 for the studies that estimated poverty amongst the child population.

The information in Table 1.1 suggests that the two poverty lines chosen by CBU for the poverty measurement may be a little on the high side. As a line to be used to reflect extreme poverty, other researchers have chosen lines as low as R169.26 per month/capita (in 2000 rands). However, the question of whether the selected lines are too high requires further research. Before presenting the new estimates of child poverty based on the two selected poverty lines (the one relatively low and the other relatively high), Box 1.1 offers a brief description of the method used to estimate the child poverty rate from household survey data.

## BOX 1.1 OVERVIEW OF THE METHOD USED TO CALCULATE CHILD POVERTY RATES FROM HOUSEHOLD SURVEY DATA

1. Household survey data includes data on expenditure and income patterns for a sample of households in a country. This data is used to calculate the level of household expenditure or income for each household over a given period.

2. Researchers have to address the problem of households having different compositions and sizes before their level of well-being can be compared. For instance, if two households each spend R1000/month but one has three adults and the other two adults and one child, they are likely to have different levels of well-being. Similarly, if two households each spend R1000 per month but one has two individuals and the other five, the individuals are likely to experience different levels of well-being. There are two ways to address this problem:

   • One option is to calculate the expenditure per adult equivalent for each household. The expenditure per adult equivalent = total household expenditure/number of adults + 0.5 X number of children 0.9. The argument for counting children as half an adult is that they require less expenditure than an adult to obtain the same level of well-being as an adult. The argument for raising the denominator to the power of 0.9 is that while larger households do require more expenditure than smaller ones for the same level of well-being per individual, economies of scale in consumption ensure that the relationship is not linear.

   • Another option is to assume that adults and children need the same level of expenditure for the same level of well-being and to ignore economies of scale in consumption. Following this option, the researcher would simply divide household expenditure by the number of individuals in the household. Woolard followed option two and calculated per capita income.

3. A poverty line then needs to be selected to distinguish poor and non-poor households. This involves a choice between a relative or absolute concept of poverty. As already explained, for the purposes of this study, Woolard applied two absolute poverty lines, R215 and R430 per capita/month in 2000 rands.

4. Households that fall below the chosen poverty line are identified and the number of children in these households is then counted. Thus Woolard counted the number of households and children in them that fell below the two poverty lines of R215 and R430 per capita/month in 2000 rands.

5. To arrive at a child poverty rate, the number of poor children are divided by the total number of children in the sample and expressed as a percentage. The child poverty rate then tells us the percentage of the child population that is poor.

It is important to note from the method described in Box 1.1, that the approach to the measurement of child poverty adopted for this publication used the household as the primary unit of analysis. The researcher first determined whether the household was poor, and then classified all members in it (including children) as poor assuming that household income was equally distributed in the household. A household that was found to have less than the per capita poverty line times the number of household members, was found to be poor. So for example, the per capita poverty line of R430 per month/capita means that a household was counted as poor (and the children in it) if household income was less than R430 times the number of household members. To be classified as "non-poor" a child would for example have to live in a five-person household with an income of at least R2150 per month. An important implication of this method is that the accuracy of the results is undermined by a lack of knowledge about how income is actually allocated within the household and how much income children actually have access to. It would be much better to estimate child poverty using survey data that provided accurate data on how much income children actually have access to, rather than using household survey data and an assumption that income is equally distributed amongst household members. However, in the absence of the former, the latter is relied upon.

## 1.1.2 WOOLARD'S FINDINGS AND THEIR IMPLICATIONS

Table 1.2 below presents Woolard's estimates of the percentage and number of children (age 0 to 17) living below the poverty line of R430 per month/capita in each province using the IES 2000. The table also illustrates the provincial child poverty shares.

Thus using the IES 2000, the method described in Box 1.1 and an income poverty line of R430/month per capita (child) in 2000 rands, 74.8% of South Africa's children were found to be living in households where per capita income is less than R430 per month/capita. This translates into 13 million poor children, using Statistics South Africa's Census 2001 estimate of the number of children age 0 to 17. According to the 2000 survey data and the poverty line of R430/month per capita, three provinces (KwaZulu-Natal, the Eastern Cape and Limpopo) were home to 60% of our income poor children. Whilst the Northern Cape and Western Cape had large numbers in absolute terms, the data indicates that these two provinces had small shares of the total number of poor children in South Africa (2% and 5% respectively).

**TABLE 1.2 CHILD POVERTY RATES, NUMBERS OF POOR CHILDREN AND CHILD POVERTY SHARES (BASED ON IES 2000 AND AN INCOME POVERTY LINE OF R430/MONTH PER CAPITA), IN 2000 RANDS**

| Province | Child (0-17) poverty rate in 2000 | Estimated number of poor children (0-17) in 2000 | Child (0-17) poverty share in 2000 (%) |
|---|---|---|---|
| Western Cape | 46.95 | 670 973 | 5 |
| Eastern Cape | 85.69 | 2 707 592 | 20 |
| Northern Cape | 70.80 | 234 099 | 2 |
| Free State | 77.79 | 827 012 | 6 |
| KwaZulu-Natal | 78.98 | 3 002 813 | 22 |
| North West | 76.21 | 1 103 914 | 8 |
| Gauteng | 54.82 | 1 381 101 | 10 |
| Mpumalanga | 77.77 | 1 021 090 | 8 |
| Limpopo | 86.76 | 2 416 548 | 18 |
| **South Africa** | **74.87** | **13 365 142** | **100** |

**Source:** Woolard's 2003 analysis of Statistics South Africa's 2000 Income and Expenditure Survey.

Table 1.3 below presents the results of Woolard's analysis of the IES 2000 using the "ultra-poor poverty" line of R215/month per capita in 2000 rands. The table reveals that even when the much lower income poverty line was chosen, income poverty emerged as extensive. More precisely, Woolard found that 54% or about 9.5 million children were living in households where per capita income was less than R215 per month in 2000 rands. Again, these "ultra-poor" children were spread unevenly across the country, with a very large proportion (67%) living in the Eastern Cape, KwaZulu-Natal and Limpopo.

**TABLE 1.3: CHILD POVERTY RATES, NUMBERS OF POOR CHILDREN AND POVERTY SHARES (BASED ON IES 2000 AND AN INCOME POVERTY LINE OF R215/MONTH PER CAPITA), IN 2000 RANDS**

| Province | Child (0-17) poverty rate in 2000 | Estimated number of poor children (0-17) in 2000 | Child (0-17) poverty share in 2000 (%) |
|---|---|---|---|
| Western Cape | 19.69 | 281 357 | 3 |
| Eastern Cape | 72.23 | 2 282 069 | 24 |
| Northern Cape | 47.92 | 158 454 | 2 |
| Free State | 57.63 | 612 713 | 6 |
| KwaZulu-Natal | 59.87 | 2 276 256 | 23 |
| North West | 53.13 | 769 526 | 8 |
| Gauteng | 28.09 | 707 778 | 7 |
| Mpumalanga | 52.07 | 683 685 | 7 |
| Limpopo | 69.21 | 1 927 569 | 20 |
| **South Africa** | **54.34** | **9 699 407** | **100** |

**Source:** Woolard's 2003 analysis of Statistics South Africa's 2000 Income and Expenditure Survey.

As Bray (2003:6) points out, what we really want to capture when measuring child poverty – if we focus on the economic aspects of poverty[7] – is whether or not children have the ability to secure the basic necessities of life. In Bray's words, we are interested in "lived poverty" (Ibid). Clearly, measurements of child income poverty based on absolute income poverty lines and household survey data, such as those presented above, have limited power to accurately describe the child poverty situation in this sense. They do not give us a true picture of how many children actually have insufficient access to the resources they require to meet their basic needs.

As already pointed out, the accuracy of the estimates of the extent and distribution of child poverty in Tables 1.2 and 1.3 above are firstly affected by difficulties associated with choosing the "right" income poverty line. It is virtually impossible to select an income poverty line that adequately reflects how much income all children need to access basic necessities. It is suggested above that our two poverty lines – the one set to indicate ultra-poor children and the other all children suffering economic hardship – may be a little too high, but it is difficult to be sure about this.

A second problem with interpreting the accuracy of the new child poverty results based on the IES 2000 is that even if the poverty line chosen happens to be robust, the results are weakened by a lack of knowledge about intra-household income distribution. Again, as already indicated, the new estimates presented above – like the other child poverty estimates presented in Table 1.1 – are weakened by the assumption that household income is shared evenly amongst all members of the household, when this is probably not the case.

Finally, and very importantly, child poverty results are always only as good as the income survey data. Income is often under-reported in household surveys and this leads to measures of child poverty being too high. According to experts, the usefulness of both the IES 2000 and the October Household Survey (OHS) 1999 in reflecting the income position of South Africans is weakened by under-reporting of income (Simkins 2003; Woolard reported in Streak 2002). Therefore, it should be noted that these new child poverty rate estimates, like Woolard's results based on the OHS 1999, can reasonably be assumed to over-estimate the extent of child poverty because of under-reporting of income in the income data used.

In light of the problems identified above, perhaps the most accurate income indicators of child poverty currently available are those derived from Woolard's estimate of child poverty using the OHS & IES 1995. Using a poverty line of R200 per capita/month (in 1999 rands), she found 38.9% of children to be poor and using a line of R400/month per capita (in 1999 rands), she found 64.7% of children to be poor. However, the soundness of these measures is weakened by the probability that the escalation of unemployment in the years since 1995 and the impact of HIV/AIDS have increased child poverty since 1995.

It will never be possible to overcome all the problems associated with using money-metric measures of child poverty, based on household survey data, as a means to shed light on the extent and distribution of child poverty. However, this does not mean that this way of measuring child poverty should be discarded. On the contrary, it makes an important contribution in helping to reveal the scale and distribution of the problem. It is simply necessary to be cautious in the interpretation and application of this quantitative source of information. Policy-makers in particular need to be made aware of the limitations inherent in measures of child poverty based on household survey data and absolute income poverty lines.

The flaws in the measurement of child poverty based on absolute income poverty lines also requires that researchers and policy-makers focus on a wider spectrum of non-income indicators, which considered together have a stronger potential to reflect "lived child poverty". Towards this end, Bray (2003:7) suggests that there is a need to analyse and present the results of answers to the following types of questions:

> "In the last 12 months, how often have you or your family gone without these things: water, food, home safety, medical treatment, schooling, a cash income, home fuel and electricity: Was it often, sometimes, rarely, or never?"

While the weaknesses associated with the money-metric measurement of child poverty are thus acknowledged, the point remains that child poverty is extensive in South Africa, whichever income poverty lines and measurements in Table 1.1 are chosen. Child poverty is concentrated in three provinces, but it is extensive in all.

## 1.2 LOOKING AT CHILD POVERTY THROUGH THE LENS OF FOOD INSECURITY

In the face of the paucity of anthropometric, nutrient and food-intake data on children, the Department of Health commissioned a National Food Consumption Survey in Children Aged 1 to 9 years in South Africa.[8] The following section considers what the 1999 NFCS and the food insecurity indicator reveal about the extent and distribution of the child poverty crisis.

### 1.2.1 OVERVIEW OF THE NFCS METHOD FOR ESTIMATING CHILD FOOD INSECURITY

The National Food Consumption Survey was a cross-sectional survey in children aged 1 to 9 years. A nationally representative sample with provincial representation was drawn by Statistics South Africa using Census 1996 data. The stipulated number of children to be studied was originally 2200. However, in order to have a minimum of 50 observations per province and per urban/rural strata, the number of children to be studied was increased to 2440 children. The sample was further increased to 3050 children to over-represent children from high-risk areas. In order to ensure that this number of children (3050) would be studied, the total number of children to be included in the sample was further increased to 3120 children to allow for children who would not be at home at the time of the survey (Vitamin Information Centre 2001:1). A total of 156 randomly selected "enumerator areas" were included in the survey, 82 of which were urban and 72 non-urban. A qualifying household was defined as any household with at least one child aged between 1 and 9 years. If there was more than one child in the age range of 1 to 9 years in the same household, a "random numbers table" was used to select one child in a given household to be included in the survey.

The primary objectives of the survey were:

- to determine the usual food consumption of children aged 1 to 9 years;
- to assess the usual nutrient intake of 1- to 9-year-old children in South Africa;

- to identify factors impacting on food consumption; and
- to determine anthropometric status.

The secondary objectives of the survey were to use the data to identify appropriate foods for fortification and to develop nutrition education material (Ibid).

Collecting information on the food insecurity situation of children was not one of the specific objectives of the survey. However, in the process of collecting the information to realise the first two objectives of the survey, data on food insecurity was also generated. Moreover, within the design framework of the survey, it was deemed necessary to include a means of estimating hunger and food insecurity not only for the purpose of realising the first two objectives, "but also because no such data are available on children on a national basis" (Department of Health 2000:636). This section of the chapter has interest in using the estimation of hunger/food insecurity generated by the survey as a second indicator of the extent and distribution of child poverty in South Africa. It first considers the method through which the information on food insecurity was generated and classified. It then presents the results generated by the survey on food insecurity amongst children aged 1 to 9.[9]

The phenomenon loosely labelled "hunger" in the 1980s is now being discussed in terms of food security or insecurity. Food security is defined as access by all people at all times to enough food for an active healthy life. As a minimum, this includes:

- the ready availability of nutritionally adequate and safe foods; and
- the assured ability to acquire personally acceptable foods in a socially acceptable way (Department of Health 2000:636).

Food insecurity was defined by the survey to exist whenever food security was limited or uncertain. Briefly, the following method was used as a means to estimate food insecurity amongst children aged 1 to 9.

- A hunger questionnaire, referred to in the survey report as the "Hunger Scale Questionnaire" (HSQ) was used to collect data on food insecurity at the household level amongst children aged 1 to 9.

- The HSQ was based on a hunger index, derived from the Community Childhood Hunger Identification Project (CCHIP) and used in the United States.

- The CCHIP hunger index is a scale composed of eight questions that investigate whether the household, adults and children in the household are affected by food insecurity, food shortages, perceived food insufficiency or altered food intake due to constraints on resources. In addition, for each of the eight main questions, two sub-questions were asked in order to determine the extent of food insecurity over 30 days. These questions determine the temporal severity and periodicity of the hunger problem. Box 1.2 below lists the questions in the hunger scale questionnaire.

- A score of five or more (that is five affirmative (yes) responses out of the possible maximum of eight) was taken to indicate a food shortage problem affecting everyone in the household. These families (and the one child aged 1 to 9 in each household selected for inclusion in the survey) were classified as hungry or food insecure. A score of one to four was taken to indicate that the family (and the one child aged 1 to 9 in the family selected for inclusion in the survey) was "at risk of hunger" (see Department of Health 2000: 639).

## BOX 1.2 QUESTIONS USED IN THE NFCS TO MEASURE FOOD INSECURITY (HUNGER)

HOUSEHOLD LEVEL INSECURITY

*Food uncertainty component*

Q1. Does your household ever run out of money to buy food?
  a) In the past 30 days?
  b) 5 or more days in the past 30 days?

*Qualitative component*

Q2. Do you ever rely on a limited number of foods to feed your children because you are running out of money to buy food for a meal?
  a) In the past 30 days?
  b) 5 or more days in the past 30 days?

INDIVIDUAL LEVEL INSECURITY

*Quantitative component*

Q3. Do you ever cut the size of meals or skip because there is not enough money to buy food?
  a) In the past 30 days?
  b) 5 or more days in the past 30 days?

Q4. Do you ever eat less than you should because there is not enough money for food?
  a) In the past 30 days?
  b) 5 or more days in the past 30 days?

CHILD HUNGER

*Quantitative component*

Q5. Do your children ever eat less than you feel they should because there is not enough money to buy food?
  a) In the past 30 days?
  b) 5 or more days in the past 30 days?

Q6. Do your children ever say they are hungry because there is not enough food in the house?
  a) In the past 30 days?
  b) 5 or more days in the past 30 days?

Q7. Do you ever cut the size of your children's meals or do they ever skip meals because there is not enough money to buy food?

a) In the past 30 days?
b) 5 or more days in the past 30 days?

Q8. Do any of your children ever go to bed hungry because there is not enough money to buy food?
a) In the past 30 days?
b) 5 or more days in the past 30 days?

Source: Department of Health (2000:637-638).

## 1.2.2 THE NFCS RESULTS ON CHILD FOOD INSECURITY

The NFCS found that at the national level, 52% of children aged 1 to 9 years experienced hunger. A further 23% were at risk of hunger. Only 25% appeared to be food secure. Moreover, the survey found that in the rural areas, a significantly higher percentage (62%) of children experienced hunger than in urban areas. Households and children age 1 to 9 in informal urban and tribal areas, as well as on commercial farms, were the worst affected. There were significant differences in the prevalence of hunger across provinces (Ibid:640). Table 1.4 summarises the NFCS results on the incidence of hunger nationally and provincially in children aged 1 to 9. Table 1.5 derives the provincial shares of children aged 1 to 9 experiencing hunger and at risk of hunger.

**TABLE 1.4 HUNGER RISK CLASSIFICATION IN CHILDREN AGED 1 TO 9 YEARS, NATIONALLY AND BY PROVINCE (1999)**

| Province | Hunger risk classification (%) | | |
|---|---|---|---|
| | Experience hunger | At risk of hunger | Food secure |
| Eastern Cape | 83.2 | 12.6 | 4.3 |
| Free State | 37.8 | 16.8 | 45.5 |
| Gauteng | 41.8 | 21.5 | 36.7 |
| KwaZulu-Natal | 47.4 | 25.9 | 26.7 |
| Mpumalanga | 52.7 | 26.0 | 21.3 |
| Northern Cape | 63.2 | 23.6 | 13.2 |
| Northern Province | 54.5 | 26.2 | 19.3 |
| North West | 61.5 | 25.2 | 13.3 |
| Western Cape | 31.3 | 29.0 | 39.8 |
| **South Africa** | **52.2** | **22.9** | **25.0** |

**Source:** Department of Health (2000:692, Table 8.3).

The provincial shares of "hungry children" captured in Table 1.5 reveal that children experiencing hunger in 1999 were concentrated in the Eastern Cape, KwaZulu-Natal and Limpopo. Together, these three provinces were home to 50% of the children suffering from hunger. Gauteng was found to have the fourth largest share of children aged 1 to 9 experiencing hunger in 1999, with 12%. This distribution pattern of poor children is similar, but not identical, to that derived from the income indicator analysis in section 1.1 above. The income indicator analysis also found poor children to be concentrated in the Eastern Cape, KwaZulu-Natal and Limpopo. However, the concentration of child poverty in these three provinces was greater according to both the high- and low-income poverty lines and the IES 2000 (60% and 67% respectively).

In the hunger indicator analysis, Gauteng's share of poor children emerges as greater than it did in the income indicator analysis as does the Western Cape's.

**TABLE 1.5 PROVINCIAL SHARES OF CHILDREN AGED 1 TO 9 EXPERIENCING HUNGER AND AT RISK OF HUNGER (1999)**

| Province | Hunger risk classification (%) | |
|---|---|---|
| | **Experienced hunger** | **At risk of hunger** |
| Eastern Cape | 23 | 8 |
| Free State | 6 | 6 |
| Gauteng | 12 | 14 |
| KwaZulu-Natal | 17 | 22 |
| Mpumalanga | 6 | 6 |
| Northern Cape | 6 | 5 |
| Northern Province | 13 | 14 |
| North West | 10 | 9 |
| Western Cape | 8 | 16 |
| **South Africa** | **100** | **100** |

**Source:** Department of Health (2000:692, Table 8.3); and own calculations.

Table 1.6 illustrates that the prevalence of hunger or being at risk of hunger was similar in all households regardless of the age of the child.

**TABLE 1.6: HUNGER RISK CLASSIFICATION IN CHILDREN AGED 1 TO 9 YEARS, NATIONALLY AND BY AGE (1999)**

| Hunger risk classification | Age groups | | | |
|---|---|---|---|---|
| | **1-3 years** | **4-6 years** | **7-9 years** | **South Africa** |
| At risk of hunger | 22.5 | 22 | 27 | 23 |
| Experience hunger | 53 | 53 | 47 | 52 |

**Source:** Department of Health (2000:691).

**Note:** Chi-square test showed no significant difference among age groups.

The NFCS measure of food insecurity (hunger) showed that 52.2% of children aged 1 to 9 experienced hunger and that 22.9% were at risk of hunger in 1999. Like Woolard's new estimates of income poverty, these findings clearly indicate the scale and severity of the poverty crisis in South Africa. Even if only those actually experiencing hunger are classified as "poor", then the NFCS indicates that 52% of children aged 1 to 9 were poor in 1999. Applying this to the OHS 1999 estimate of the total number of children aged 1 to 9 in South Africa in 1999, this translated into 4.6 million children experiencing hunger in 1999. Adding children at risk of hunger to the classification of poverty, then the NFCS suggests, like Woolard's income measurement of child poverty based on the IES 2000, that 75% of South Africa's children suffer poverty.

What do the two indicators of child poverty reviewed in this section suggest about the numbers of poor children in South Africa today? The most recent estimate of the child population is from Statistics South Africa's 2001 Census. According to this source, there are 17 382 879 children aged 0 to 17 in the country. Taking this number as a point of departure:

- If 75% of children in South Africa are considered poor (as suggested by Woolard's analysis of the IES 2000 data and the high poverty line, together with the NFCS survey estimate of children experiencing hunger and at risk of hunger), this translates into 13 million poor children aged 0 to 17.[10]

- If 52% of children are considered poor (as implied by the NFCS measure of children experiencing hunger, which is very similar to Woolard's estimate of child poverty using the low income poverty line), this translates into 9 million poor children aged 0 to 17.

- If 64% of children are considered poor (the statistic arrived at by Woolard using the high poverty line of R400/month per capita and the OHS/IES1995, which is deemed to be more reliable than the IES 2000), then this translates into 11.1 million poor children aged 0 to 17.

# 2. A QUALITATIVE PERSPECTIVE ON CHILD POVERTY: CHILDREN'S VIEWS ON WHAT IT MEANS TO BE POOR

"The gap between policy on meeting child socio-economic rights and the reality is a pit of suffering for many of South Africa's children [and there are many] painful...obstacles to securing their basic rights...State agencies must listen very carefully to children's painful experiences of the obstacles to securing their basic rights. They must start to bridge the gap between policy and practice."
*Deborah Ewing (2004)*

In order to elicit the perspectives of children themselves on the child poverty situation and how government should respond, the CBU commissioned Deborah Ewing to conduct a child participation research study. Section 2.1 provides a broad overview of the study, focusing on its objectives, scope and method. Section 2.2 presents children's views on the poverty situation including their experiences of poverty and service delivery. Section 2.3 sets out the children's accounts of their most important needs and their perspectives on what government should prioritise in its budgets and policies. In the process of presenting children's views, inferences are drawn out to inform government's strategy for responding to the child poverty crisis and delivering children's socio-economic rights.

## 2.1 OVERVIEW OF THE CHILD PARTICIPATION RESEARCH[11]

### 2.1.1 OBJECTIVES

The objectives of the child participation research were linked to the objectives of this chapter, as set out in the introduction to the chapter. More specifically, the child participation research aimed:

- to involve children in describing and assessing their own socio-economic situations; and

- to facilitate a process for children to identify priorities (including government programme and budget priorities) for improving their quality of life as a basis for formulating  recommendations on how government can best meet its obligations to children.

### 2.1.2 SCOPE OF THE STUDY

The study investigated child poverty and the extent to which children's basic socio-economic rights — to food, water, shelter, clothing, education, health and welfare services — are being violated in particular communities. This included coverage of children's experiences of service delivery in the main programmes put in place by government to assist children in effecting child socio-economic rights. The study also sought to gather children's views of budget, programme and service delivery priorities and on what needs to be done (particularly by government) to reduce child poverty and improve the quality of their lives.

### 2.1.3 RESEARCH APPROACH AND PARTICIPATION GROUPS

In order to promote the principles of non-discrimination and equality in child poverty research (Bray 2003:5), the study focused on gathering information from groups of children who are marginalised or discriminated against for a variety of reasons.[12] The research thus targeted four groups of children because of their particular vulnerability and marginalisation.[13] Children were identified who were thought to be living in poverty and/or have difficulty in accessing services. Such difficulties in accessing services were in part due to their geographic or social isolation and/or the absence or inadequacy of the family and state support systems that children are assumed and entitled to depend on. The research targeted children aged 5 to 18, but in some instances the views of a minority of young people over 18 were included.[14] The four groups of children who participated in the research and whose perspectives are presented in sections 2.2 and 2.3 of this chapter, are briefly introduced below. In all, 177 participants took part in the research across all four groups.[15]

**GROUP 1** consisted of children living in traditional rural communities on the Msinga/Weenen district border in KwaZulu-Natal. This group comprised 13 boys and 12 girls. Msinga is one of the poorest districts in KwaZulu-Natal.  It has very little infrastructure, limited access to essential services such as health care, no piped water, hardly any income-earning opportunities and land that is only arable with irrigation and intensive labour. More than half of the households are headed by a single female, their husbands or partners having died or being absent 11 months of the year as migrant workers. Unemployment and under-employment levels are exceedingly high in Msinga. There is increasing mortality of parents due to HIV/AIDS.

**GROUP 2** included orphaned children living in households headed by children or under-21 year olds in and around the Pietermaritzburg area. This group was made up of 27 girls and 25 boys. All these children were living in communities struggling against poverty linked to high levels of unemployment and the impact of HIV/AIDS. They were invited to participate in this study by an NGO called the Thandanani Foundation. This organisation, operating out of Pietermaritzburg, offers support to children through emergency relief, developmental outreach and advocacy. The organisation targets orphaned, abandoned and other vulnerable children living in townships that form part of the Msunduzi municipality.

**GROUP 3** was made up of children of farm workers who live on farms in the Stellenbosch area in the Western Cape. This group included 36 boys and 46 girls. The children in this group came from four different areas close to Stellenbosch, each characterised by distinct socio-economic conditions. Some of the children lived on wine farms in Elsenburg. Their exact living conditions differed from farm to farm, but poverty and unemployment levels were reported to be high across the board. The second area represented by child participants was Kaapzicht wine estate. The housing conditions on this estate had been classified as so terrible that some of the farm workers and their children were not living on the farm at the time of the research. Some families had been relocated to a government housing scheme nearby in Kuilsriver. A third group of participants were from the Fine Farms and the De Rus farm in Grabouw. On the De Rus farm, a black economic empowerment and job creation project had been initiated by Paul Cluver, the owner of the farm. The children living on this farm were generally suffering less economic hardship than the rest of the research participants. Finally, children of full-time and seasonal farm workers in the Klapmuts community also took part in the study. As in Elsenburg and Kaapzicht, the economic living conditions of these children were considered dire. As Ewing (2004) relates, it is useful to bear in mind that the children of farm workers usually find themselves in households that are not destitute, but are locked into chronic poverty. This cycle of poverty is reinforced by the household's dependence on the limited security of a very low-paying job, coupled with (usually poor) accommodation and some services.

**GROUP 4** was composed of 18 girls living in a shelter in Woodstock, Cape Town in the Western Cape. The children from the shelter who participated in the study were all having their basic socio-economic rights met through the shelter. Being in a shelter also meant that they were gaining access to basic and other services, such as electricity, water, health and education.[16] However, these girls had all found their way to the shelter precisely because their families did not have the financial and/or social resources to provide for them. As such, they were at risk of ending up on the streets (Ewing 2004). According to the primary social worker at the shelter, all the girls in the shelter came from homes that were extremely poor in terms of income and living conditions. The shelter must therefore be seen as shielding these children from income poverty. The shelter is described as a second-stage shelter. This means that the girls were placed there not as an emergency measure, but as a short to medium-term alternative to living at home while efforts were made to investigate their return to their families. The children taking part in the interviews were thus not street children but children who were at risk of ending up on the streets without alternative care.

Deborah Ewing, with assistance from other researchers, conducted the interviews and workshops with all of the groups with the exception of the children of farm workers. The latter were conducted by the Women on Farms Project. This is an NGO that works on several fruit farms and wine estates in the Stellenbosch area. It offers advice, information and training to farm workers regarding their rights, working conditions and welfare, and engages in advocacy on behalf of farm workers and their families.

The research tools used for the study included workshops, questionnaires, focus group discussions, individual and household interviews, drawing and games, as well as participant observation. The tools were chosen depending on the circumstances of the children, their levels of literacy and confidence, and the environment in which the research took place. Photograph analysis was used with the two Western Cape groups of children as partner organisations had indicated that the children would be embarrassed to identify themselves as "poor" despite their clearly difficult home and/or living conditions. A drawing activity about "food on our plates" was used as an ice-breaker and to provide empirical information about diet and food security. Drawing activities were also used extensively with younger children and children with traumatic histories (orphans) to encourage them to express their feelings about positive and negative aspects of their lives. Discussions and games were facilitated to generate information on the children's wishes and ideas regarding budgeting. A "shopping list" group activity helped to ensure that the children understood the concept of budgeting in terms of prioritising spending on essentials and to reflect the level of food insecurity experienced by the children. Their views on how government should use its resources to address the needs of poor children were generated by means of group needs analyses, priority-setting and allocations of limited resources to priorities.

A challenge encountered in the child participation process was to conduct the research in a way that would allow children's voices to be heard. The research process intended to illicit the children's own views on what poverty means to them, what access they had to services and what policy priorities they thought government should have in place. At the same time, adult care-givers and facilitators had a role in helping to gather information from the children. It is essential to note, however, that it was the views of children, not those of the adult facilitators and care-givers, which formed the focus of the workshops and interviews, as well as the recording and analysis. The only exception in this regard was the information gathered from a small number of care-givers pertaining to the children's family backgrounds and access to support services. This was required in some instances to provide important contextual information that would allow a better understanding of children's perspectives and to support the views presented by the children. According to Ewing, the research process did facilitate drawing out the voices of children. In her opinion, the information gathered by the end of the process could be classified as 90% information from children and 10% from adults (care-givers, social workers and facilitators).

The following sections of the chapter now present the accounts derived from children through the participatory research process, regarding their experiences of the child poverty situation, their most urgent needs, as well as the policy and budget priorities they would like to see in place. All the opinions below are from the children themselves, unless specifically stated otherwise.[17]

## 2.2 CHILDREN'S EXPERIENCES OF POVERTY

### 2.2.1 THE PERSPECTIVES OF CHILDREN LIVING IN THE MSINGA/WEENEN DISTRICTS, KWAZULU-NATAL

"It took me two hours to walk to school and I was getting tired."
*A girl living in Msinga in KwaZulu-Natal*

The children and their care-givers (mostly mothers) were not reluctant to talk about the difficult economic circumstances in which they live. They said that their main problem was food. "Water is far but it's there; making a fire is time-consuming but there is still wood", said one woman. Basic (common) foodstuffs were described as mealie meal, samp, cabbage, spinach, sugar, beans, salt, flour, soup/stock, potatoes and seasoning. Meat (a favourite) was identified as a rarity in children's diets, being eaten as infrequently as once a month. The practice of *ukunana* (reciprocal borrowing of money and food) was highlighted as important for helping to meet food requirements. However, it was reported that there were still times when entire households, including children, go without food. Another key challenge noted by the Msinga children and their mothers was gaining access to adequate shelter and fuel.

Mothers and children talked about the problems associated with gaining access to basic services for children. According to the mothers, health services were not frequently available. This includes even the basic services that government theoretically provides free of charge to all children from birth to the age of six. The poor access to health care resulted in part from the suspension of the mobile clinic that was supposed to service the area (run by the Church of Scotland Hospital at Tugela Ferry), due to a lack of medical staff and drivers. This meant that anyone needing health services had to travel to the nearest hospital, requiring a return taxi fare of R26, which was unaffordable. Mothers also reported that it cost at least R20 for a doctor's consultation with a child over six years of age.

The mothers reported that there was a process underway to help all those eligible for social grants to access them. However, many residents were struggling to realise their own and their children's right to social assistance. This was due to bureaucratic difficulties – such as getting a birth certificate for a child before being able to access the Child Support Grant – and the hurdle of transport costs. To overcome the latter, community workers were planning to transport nine members of their beading project to the relevant application office every week until everyone eligible was covered.

Schooling was described both by mothers and children as a luxury, not a basic good. Many of the children interviewed were not attending school. According to the children and their care-givers, this was because of the distance that they would need to walk to get to school every day (about one to two hours for most children), the danger of assault en route and the lack of money to buy food, school uniforms and shoes. Tragically, a further reason sited for school non-attendance was that many children needed to use their time to earn money to support themselves and others. The tragedy of children having to trade their right to school in order to earn an income to meet the basic needs of themselves and others, is portrayed vividly in Box 1.3 below, a profile of a household maintained by child workers.

School fees were said to be about R20 to R30 a year. This cost was not identified as the primary obstacle to children realising their right to basic education. One group of out-of-school children reported that even if they did not have to pay fees or buy uniforms, they would be unable to attend school for lack of transport or taxi fares, or because they would have to go to school on an empty stomach (Ewing 2004). The description given by the Msinga/Weenen participants clearly outlines the interwoven set of obstacles that prevent many children from exercising their right to basic education. It elegantly highlights the inter-dependence that exists amongst the different basic socio-economic rights given to children in the Constitution.

The majority of the children from Msinga/Weenen who spoke about their experiences of poverty did not benefit from government's main programme directed at delivering nutrition services to poor children. This programme is the Primary School Feeding Scheme (PSFS). It aims to improve children's nutrition by providing a meal per child at targeted schools. Their failure to benefit was either due to an inability to attend school or because the school they attended did not have an operational nutrition scheme. (According to Deborah Ewing, the coverage of the PSFS in KwaZulu-Natal appears very erratic.)

On a positive note, interviews with children and their mothers in Msinga/Weenen revealed that government's Prevention of Mother-to-Child Transmission (PMTCT) of HIV programme was having a beneficial impact in the area. The nearest hospital was one of the pilot sites for the programme. It offered an outreach service through community health care workers to support women who were taking part in the programme. This has included the identification of households and children who are eligible for social assistance benefits, such as Child Support and Disability Grants. The outreach component of the programme also assisted women and children to apply for these grants.

Significantly, from a policy perspective, the accounts of the poverty situation that emerged from the Msinga/Weenen communities highlighted links between children's struggle to realise their basic socio-economic rights and the limited income-earning opportunities for adults in the area.

## BOX 1.3 A HOUSEHOLD MAINTAINED BY CHILD WORKERS IN MSINGA/WEENEN, KWAZULU-NATAL

Zama* is 15 years old. She lives in the Mashunka ward of the Mthembu Traditional Authority (part of Weenen). She lives with her mother, her four siblings, her late father's other wife and the latter's five children, and the father's two brothers and their wives. The only people working in the household are Zama, her 18-year-old brother and a 15-year-old orphan who has been taken in.

Zama's father was a migrant worker in Johannesburg who was shot dead in a fight years ago. Zama is the only one among the five children who has had any schooling. Her mother kept her in school for two years by selling firewood to pay her fees. School fees in the area are around R20 a year but when added to the cost of a uniform, shoes and food, the total expense is unmanageable for many families.

Zama is working in a bead project run by a community organisation. She can make up to R800 in two weeks if there are enough orders to work full-time, but the orders are erratic. Nearly all Zama's money goes on essentials for the family. If she has a good month, she sometimes buys herself a piece of clothing, or hair relaxer and black hair dye – short, wavy, shiny black hair is the current fashion in the district. Zama says she doesn't want to go back to school now: "It is better for the smaller children to go to school than me." On Saturdays she has time to play with her friends; the rest of the time she is working.

Musa is Zama's brother by their father's first wife. He is 18 years old. When his father was killed he was in Grade 2 and was taken out of school for lack of funds: "I had to come out because I had no shoes, no clothes and no fees." He has not been back to school since and none of his four younger brothers or sisters has ever been to school. Musa also does bead-work from home. He weaves *izinkamba* (bowls shaped like traditional clay pots) and lampshades from copper and beads which are sold to "people far away, from overseas". He can earn R800 to R900 a month if there are enough orders, but some months there are none. When there is no money, the family asks neighbours for food. "I am happy to do this work because I get money and because I don't know how else I could earn a living here. I would prefer to be a policeman or a teacher but with no education this is not possible." If Musa earns enough to buy groceries, he makes a budget: "Before anything else I buy 50kg of mealie meal for R200 and spend R150 on *isishebo* [that is tomatoes and onions, soup, beans or whatever can be eaten with the mealie meal]. My favourite food is meat but we normally have only one meal with meat a month, either beef or chicken."

"I can't save but if I earn R800 to R900 or more I might make it last for the month. Usually the groceries only last for 3 weeks. We all eat at the same time. In other families it is not like that – the worker usually eats better. But I don't, because I am not the head of the household."

The household gets its water from the river – about 40 minutes' walk away. They use paraffin for lighting and wood for the cooking fire. Their huts are leaking and Musa says sometimes he and his mother make and sell Zulu beer at the pension pay-out point, to get money for repairs: "It doesn't make me feel good because I should be at school but I am looking after the whole family". What could be done to improve his life and by whom? "The only thing I can think of is to get a better job so I can go to adult education while I am earning good money."

Musa has taken in a 15-year-old orphan. The boy stayed with his grandmother after his mother was fatally shot. Unfortunately, the family was then chased from their home because the granny was accused of stealing cows. He is also doing bead- and copper-work to pay his way. He only went to school for one year and was then taken out by his mother although at that time his parents were both working: "My mother said she didn't like to pay school fees". This boy has been very ill with sores on his back and buttocks. He didn't tell anyone because he didn't want to make a fuss and because he was frightened. Since he had no family and since he carried on working, no one noticed he was ill. He couldn't sit down and was working by lying on his stomach, just saying that it suited him. When he started to smell bad the community worker realised he was ill and arranged for him to be taken to the doctor for a course of injections.

*Names changed

## 2.2.2 THE PERSPECTIVES OF CHILDREN IN CHILD-HEADED HOUSEHOLDS IN THE PIETERMARITZBURG AREA, KWAZULU-NATAL

"The electricity is connected but there is no money to pay for lights and we have no stove so we only eat cooked food if it is given to us."
*A girl, aged 15, who lives with her sister, aged 18 and her three-year-old child*

Twenty-seven girls and 25 boys living in child-headed households in townships around Pietermaritzburg in KwaZulu-Natal were consulted to shed some light on the poverty situation from the perspective of children living in households without an adult caregiver.

The accounts of socio-economic living conditions and patterns of access to services emerging from the interviews with children in child-headed households were very similar to the picture painted by the children in the Msinga/Weenen districts. For the most part, the children lived in dilapidated informal housing and did not have electricity (due to insufficient cash to pay electricity accounts). Meeting the food needs of the household was a daily struggle.

Again it emerged that a large proportion of the children – about half – were not in school due to lack of money for fees, uniforms, shoes and food (Ewing 2004). The opinions of child care committee workers on children's access to services in the area were also canvassed in the research process (see section 2.1). They noted that discriminatory practices at certain schools also caused children to forego their right to education:

"Schools want documents [IDs]. otherwise they will not register children.

It differs from school to school but most are very strict…Also, children get thrown out of school for not having appropriate shoes or not having full school uniform…At one school [not named] it seems the principal is making up the rules on his own – even telling the security guard not to admit children without the correct uniform."

In general, the children taking part in the research stated that they had no access to state social assistance benefits. In order to survive, they had to rely on casual work, assistance from neighbours and relatives, begging, borrowing and donations from NGOs and welfare bodies.

There were a number of clear similarities between the living conditions of the group of orphans interviewed and the children living in the Msinga/Weenen communities. However, one main difference emerged: that the suffering associated with poverty was made worse by the children feeling lonely and missing their parents. The unhappiness and loneliness associated with the children's precarious living conditions was vividly illustrated when one girl spent most of the interview in tears, but said she did not want the researchers to go. She said she wanted to talk about her situation – it was just that she cried when thinking about her mother, as well as her own and her siblings' situation.

## BOX 1.4  A CHILD-HEADED HOUSEHOLD IN A TOWNSHIP OUTSIDE PIETERMARITZBURG IN KWAZULU-NATAL

Busi* is 15 and lives with her sister Lungi, aged 18, and Lungi's three-year-old child. Their father died in 1996 and when their mother died in 1998, they and their two sisters went to stay with an aunt. This arrangement didn't work out as the aunt was struggling to cope. The youngest child (now 12) still stays with the aunt and their 16-year-old sister stays with relatives in another township. Busi and Lungi and her child moved to the house where they are now staying in Edendale in January 2003. The aunt bought it for them. Their original family home was a mud structure that fell down soon after the mother died.

The aunt managed to obtain Foster Care Grants for the other two children. The youngest child is also receiving assistance with school fees and a uniform from the Thandanani Foundation. Busi should qualify for a Foster Care Grant but neither she nor Lungi has an ID. Currently it would not be possible for Lungi to obtain a grant for looking after her sister because she does not have an ID. Lungi has applied for an ID so that she can register her child for a Child Support Grant.

When Lungi's baby was born she was in Standard 6 and was told to leave school. She says, "I would love to go back but it's difficult, particularly because of money but also because there is no food at home. We survive by getting help from the neighbours. My sister is also not at school; she stopped schooling in 2001".

The children depend entirely on donations for food and clothing. They get water from a tap a few metres away. "The electricity is connected but there is no money to pay for lights and we have no stove so we only eat cooked food if it is given to us."

"I think the most urgent thing the government should do is to provide food and clothing to children who have nothing," says Lungi.

"And it should let us go back to school," says Busi.

Lungi spent most of the interview in tears. We offered to leave or to stop asking questions but she said she wanted us to stay and didn't mind talking. "It's just that I cry when I think of my mother and our situation."

*Names changed.

## 2.2.3 THE PERSPECTIVES OF CHILDREN LIVING ON FARMS IN THE STELLENBOSCH AREA

"[Being poor] makes you feel like a lesser person."
*A child of a farm worker*

How did the children of farmworkers describe their situation, including access to basic services? In general, the children were less inclined than those interviewed in KwaZulu-Natal to describe their situation as one of poverty. This was despite the fact that the living conditions they spoke of made it clear that most of the children were poor in the sense that they sometimes suffered hunger, lived in housing that offered little protection from the environment and had meagre clothing and other material goods (including bedding). A few children said they did not feel safe and/or warm where they slept because of holes in the windows and/or insufficient bedding. Acquiring water to wash every day was clearly a problem for a number of the children. The pride of the children and their desire not to be classified as poor was captured well by the following remark: "We might be poor but we are spiritually rich."

Children related that they found poverty extremely stigmatising. Furthermore, they were very uncomfortable with the knowledge that other people may see children on farms as poor or somehow inferior. The participants' comments about their circumstances made it clear that most children living on farms were suffering discrimination, social exclusion and trauma. The following statements by children are indicative of this:

"You feel shy because you are from the farm."

"*Hulle bly praat van 'die plaaskinders'.*"
("They always talk about 'the farm children'")

This group of children raised a social problem associated with poverty that was not apparent in the other groups' comments: their parents' dependence on alcohol and the impact that this has on children. One child said, "[p]eople on farms spend their money on wine and fight a lot". Another said, "[p]eople on farms do not look after their children because they let them drink wine". The children related that they experienced some difficulties with access to schooling and health services. However, they did

for the most part have access to these. Between a quarter and a third
said they had been sick in the six months before the workshops and
medical treatment and had recovered. At one farm, there was a bi-we
But the other children reported that their nearest clinic was between
away or "*baie ver*" (very far).

None of the children had a direct problem in exercising their right to access basic
schooling. However, two aspects of the schooling situation as described by the children are important to note from a rights perspective. The first is discrimination
against poor children: "More than half of the children said teachers (or other children) treated learners differently if they didn't pay school fees, or if they didn't have a
uniform, if they were sick, or if they were from the farm" (Ewing 2004). One child
commented, "[t]he teachers force you to pay. It makes you feel oppressed and afraid".
The second issue is corporal punishment. The group of children from Kaapzicht, in
particular, raised corporal punishment and harsh discipline at their school as something that makes them unhappy. One child said, "[t]he teacher slaps the children".
Another related that "the caretaker kicks the children and hits them with a pipe".

The children's comments revealed that awareness about and access to social grants
(including the Child Support Grant) was insufficient. Fewer than half of the children
on farms who were asked about social benefits said they were aware of the existence of
specific grants for children. Around half said they knew of someone in their household who was receiving some kind of grant and a minority said there were people at
home who they thought were eligible for a grant and didn't get one.

The participants' descriptions of their situation also indicated that coverage of the
Primary School Feeding Scheme was good in this part of the country. Most children
said they benefited from the programme. There were however complaints about the
type of benefit received from the programme: mainly peanut butter sandwiches, which
most of the children described as "chokers".

## 2.2.4 THE PERSPECTIVES OF GIRLS LIVING IN A SHELTER AND AT RISK OF LIVING ON THE STREETS IN CAPE TOWN

> "People don't even think we are children. They think we sleep with men; they
> shout at us. They don't think."
> *A young girl living in a shelter in the Western Cape*

Even more so than the children living on farms, the children from the shelter did not
want to be seen as poor. Moreover, they did not explicitly link their home problems to
the problem of poverty in the country. All of the girls (17 from the Cape Flats and
one from the Eastern Cape) said they were at the home because of "problems at
home". When probed about the economic conditions at home, they took the view that
"we are not rich or poor...we're all in between" (Ewing 2004). The following comments revealed the girls' level of concern about being branded as poor, as well as their
experiences of discrimination and the infringement of their dignity associated with
their living conditions:

"People pass by here and they think we are poor. They judge us: they give us old food, food they will never eat. We don't eat that; we just put it in the bin — we are not animals, we are human beings like them."

"They think we are poor because we stay in a shelter. They think we are staying on the streets or have come from the streets but we come from houses like they come from houses."

The child participants in this group were more interested in talking about their situation relative to others than their situation per se. In this sense, their perspective echoed those of the children living on farms and differed from the children in the Msinga/Weenen area and those living in child-headed households in Pietermaritzburg. Even when they did let slip that they may be in need of basic necessities such as clothes, they couched this in terms of their position relative to other children. For example, some of the girls — when asked what rights they should have — said that aside from "the right to be close to their families", they needed new clothes: "New clothes — sometimes we get clothes that people already wore; other children get clothes bought for them or new clothes donated by Woolworths."

A photo analysis session was used to tease out the girls' experiences and understanding of poverty. Their comments about why children in the pictures were poor or rich revealed a great deal about the extent and nature of their own suffering. It also highlighted how the deprivation of this group of children differed from (or was similar to) children in the other groups. Like the children in the other groups, the girls described poverty in a multi-faceted way. For example, they raised problems such as lack of access to basic services ("people wash in cold water" and "they go to the toilet in the bin") and insufficient income to meet basic needs ("they wear the same clothes every day" and "they have dirty clothes and no shoes"). However, more so than in the case of the children from Msinga/Weenen and the children living on farms, and similar to the children living in child-headed households, the girls highlighted the non-economic, psychological aspects of poverty. The following comments from the girls illustrate this point:

"You can see he is poor because he is lonely."

"This one is rich because he is flying ... it's about happiness."

The girls' description of their situation is a stark reminder of how important it is to work in an integral way in the delivery of child socio-economic and other child rights (including the right to a family life, to be protected and not be discriminated against). The girls in the shelter had all their basic socio-economic needs met, but this had come at the expense of their right to family life, which they all, without exception, saw as a terrible loss, despite the suffering they might have experienced at home (Ewing 2004).

## 2.3. APPEALING TO GOVERNMENT: MOST URGENT NEEDS AND BUDGET PRIORITIES IDENTIFIED BY CHILDREN

In the participatory research with children experiencing poverty and/or living in difficult circumstances, all the children were asked:

- what their most urgent needs were; and

- what it was most important for Trevor Manuel (South Africa's current Finance Minister) to spend tax-payers' money on.

In addition, the two groups of children in the Western Cape were asked what they thought President Mbeki should do to improve their lives. They answered this question through role-play activities and in the form of letters addressed to the President.

### 2.3.1 THE CHILDREN'S MOST IMPORTANT NEEDS

While the children had varying responses in identifying their most urgent needs, nearly all listed education as one of their top four needs. An exception to this trend were those children living in the girls' shelter, who already had access to school fees, uniforms, transport and books by virtue of their placement in the home (Ewing 2004). In talking about the need for education, children revealed that they saw the realisation of this right as linked to the realisation of other rights, such as sufficient income (to pay for transport) and basic nutrition. This once again highlighted that interventions targeted at any one right are only likely to realise their objectives if government simultaneously designs and implements measures to deliver, together, the entire set of basic child socio-economic rights in the Constitution.

The majority of the children – and in particular those from the Msinga/Weenen area and those living on farms – identified an improvement in the economic situation of their parents (or extended family) as one of their most important needs. In this vein, they spoke of the need for better wages and housing for their parents (on the part of some of the children living on farms) and employment opportunities (noted by children from Msinga/Weenen). Some of the children living in child-headed households and working to support themselves and their siblings identified higher wages for themselves as important for improving their situation. The way the children linked their own needs to their parents' economic status indicated that they were very aware of the difficulties their parents faced in trying to look after them and that they suffered in this knowledge. It also showed that children saw their needs and rights in relation to the ability of their care-givers to meet their needs.

This input from children is very significant as it highlights the need to view the violation of child rights in South Africa through a broad lens. Such a broad perspective must incorporate a view of the living conditions of parents (or alternative care-givers), as well as their capacity and potential to realise the socio-economic rights of their households. It also draws attention to the need for government to take a dual approach when designing budget and programme measures to give effect to child socio-economic rights. Children experience their poverty not in isolation, but as members of a household and society. As such, addressing child poverty requires measures directed at realising children's socio-economic rights while simultaneously measures are taken to improve the socio-economic conditions of their households.

The child participants in rural areas identified transport as a major issue, one that determines their access (or lack thereof) to most other services (and rights). Water and food were also listed within the top five urgent needs of children from rural areas (in the Msinga/Weenen districts, on farms outside Stellenbosch and communities outside Pietermaritzburg). The inference from this for policy is the importance of investment in infrastructure (such as roads) to facilitate the realisation of child socio-economic rights. In the context of the depth of the poverty crisis amongst adults and children, it also draws attention to the need for government interventions that bring services to the doorsteps of poor children. Alternatively interventions are needed that provide direct income support to parents or care-givers so that they are able to take children to services.

In addition to their material needs, the children in child-headed households highlighted an emotional need: "someone to talk to" (Ewing 2004). Not surprisingly, the girls in the shelter – whose basic socio-economic needs were being met but were separated from their families – also focused on non-material needs. These children worked in pairs or small groups to discuss and note their most urgent needs. The most common most urgent need they identified was "to be with my family". The second most urgent need emerging from the discussions was "to have a cell phone". When asked why, the children made it clear that this was also because they missed their families:

> "I need a cell phone to be like other children."

> "I want a cell phone to send a message home."

> "I need a phone to contact my family."

Other "most urgent" needs of the children living in the shelter included love, clothes, shoes and chocolate. The latter was the first-mentioned need of the youngest child in the group, who also wished to be safe from abuse and to live in her own house.

The emphasis on emotional needs by many of the children raised the importance of policy design for the delivery of child socio-economic rights to be sensitive to the danger of children being forced to trade socio-economic rights for other rights.

## 2.3.2 CHILDREN'S BUDGET PRIORITIES: "IF I WAS TREVOR MANUEL..." AND "PLEASE MR PRESIDENT..."

The children's budget priorities varied slightly depending on their own circumstances. However, the most common areas suggested for government prioritisation were:

- Education;
- Orphans/children on the streets;
- Pensions/grants;
- (Free) health care;
- Water;
- Food;

- Employment;
- Roads;
- Housing;
- Staff;
- Police stations.

Among the child-headed households, there was one group of five boys who said the top budget priority should be "mining" – of oil, coal and gold. They explained that this was because "we [South Africa] pay too much for oil and it affects the cost of transport and, therefore, the cost of food. So if we can get cheaper oil we will save on everything."

The children's views on budget priorities once again highlighted the need for a holistic strategy. In government budgeting such a strategy would involve giving equal and simultaneous priority to programmes that give effect to each of the basic socio-economic rights given to children in the Constitution. Most children found it difficult to trade one socio-economic right off against another when they compiled their lists of priorities. A stark example came from the work of one of the sub-groups of orphaned children in the budget allocation activity. When deciding how South Africa's current Minister of Finance should allocate taxpayers' money, they gave equal amounts to education and food "because you can't go to school on an empty stomach, so the two things go together".

Another important, albeit anticipated, point emerged out of the discussions with most of the children. This was how basic most of their needs were and hence the importance of government prioritising provision of basic services to children. This was illustrated most clearly in a focus group discussion facilitated by Ewing with the Msinga/Weenen group. Box 1.5 describes the focus group and presents their views about children's most urgent needs and what government should prioritise in its spending.

## Box 1.5: The views of children in Msinga/Weenen on children's most urgent needs and government budget priorities

Ten out-of-school children – 6 girls and 4 boys – living in a settlement above Nomoya took part in this focus group. They were interviewed at a place called The Station, a clearing in the bush at the top of a mountain. The children live about an hour's walk from where we met. The group met under a thorn tree. Tall grass, twigs and stones were cleared before everyone sat down. The children participating were aged 13 to 17. Of the 10 children, 5 were living with their mothers, 4 with their mothers and fathers and 1 with his or her father and grandmother. Seven of the children were from homes with some regular income. Six said there was a migrant worker sending money and one said the household relied on their grandmother's pension. Household size ranged from 4 to 10 members.

Children brainstormed in two self-chosen groups – male and female. They identified "the most important things children need". These were:

- Water – taps;
- Education;
- Clinics;
- Grants for orphans and older people;
- Roads;
- Food;
- Work.

We had to prompt the children to identify the last three needs. We knew they were important because several children had already said they could not get to school due to the absence of roads or transport. They had also spoken about a lack of income and food. But when they thought about "needs", they first identified services that they knew government was providing in other areas.

We asked the children to say what they thought were the priorities amongst the items listed. They all said:

- Education;
- Water;
- Roads;
- Jobs/work.

The children did not know what was meant by a budget. We explained the concept simply. The children were quite unused to being asked their opinions on anything and were extremely shy. We tried to initiate a discussion about what they thought government did spend and should spend money on, but all the children were clearly anxious about answering. We then asked them to identify spending priorities among the four needs. This was done by choosing objects to represent the four spending areas and then distributing sweets for each child to allocate to each of these areas. Each child was given ten sweets to divide amongst the needs to show what priority they gave it. They were asked to put the most sweets next to the area that was most important and the fewest sweets next to the area that they gave lowest priority. The children then added up the number of sweets allocated and reviewed the priorities. They then did a final count.

The boys' priorities were: Education, Water, Roads, Jobs. The girls' priorities were: Water, Education, Roads, Jobs. The difference reflected the fact that girls do most of the water collection, although some boys also do this. There are boreholes within 2km of the children's homes but for many months of the year, the water level is too low to make them effective.

The children living on farms raised the importance of money being spent to make sure that "children should not be taken away from their parents". A significant policy point flows from this. In designing strategies for improving the lives of South African children, there is a need for government measures that give effect to the children's socio-economic rights (as afforded in sections 28(1)(c) and 29(1)(a) of the Constitution) to be integrated with measures to secure the other rights given to children in section 28.

When told how government actually spent the national budget last year, many of the children felt it was not appropriate to spend so much on debt and defence when people are living in poverty. However it was notable that in the Msinga/Weenen area – where many households depend on borrowing to get through the month – the children agreed that debt was a budget priority. A 15-year-old girl from this group said, "Yes, that is right. We should pay our debts first, before we spend anything else."

In their role-plays and letters to the President, the two groups of children in the Western Cape made a number of requests. The requests of the children on farms included the following:

"There should be no poverty."

"Children should have clothes and shoes to wear."

"We want to have better homes with bathrooms."

"Our parents should earn more money."

"[We need] more money for food."

One of the letters written to President Mbeki sums up fairly eloquently the pleas of all the children in the shelter:

"Dear Mr President
I am Lettie, I am 14 years old. I wrote this letter to you, as we are children we ask you to help us to stay with our family. Help the children on the street, give them enough care and love. Can you please give our family money and give them jobs so that they can feed us enough food."

# 3. CONCLUSION

This chapter set out to raise awareness and provide information on the child poverty situation in South Africa in two ways. It made use of indicators and survey data to consider the extent, distribution and nature of the child poverty crisis. In the process, the analysis underlined how imperative it is for the state to meet its obligations regarding child socio-economic rights. The chapter also gathered the views of children living in poverty and/or in difficult circumstances as a means to enhance understanding of the nature of the child poverty crisis and derive inferences for government policy and budgeting in future. The primary findings of the chapter are summarised below.

As regards the extent, distribution and nature of child poverty based on quantitative data:
- Household survey data and two indicators – absolute income and food insecurity – were used to shed light on the extent and regional distribution of child poverty and to some extent, on the nature of child poverty.

- Two absolute income poverty lines were applied to the IES 2000 to measure the extent and distribution of child poverty, the one set to capture children living in dire poverty and the other to identify all poor children. The measurement of child poverty using the two income poverty lines was conducted by Woolard.

- In the income indicator analysis, methodological difficulties relating to the money-metric measurement of child poverty based on household income data were highlighted. These included problems associated with deciding what a "minimum standard of living" is, selecting the appropriate income poverty line to reflect this level, the assumption that household income is equally distributed across all members of a household, as well as weaknesses in the survey data (such as under-reporting of income).

- A consideration of absolute per capita poverty lines used by other researchers to measure poverty amongst the population and child population in South Africa led to the suggestion that the two poverty lines used in Woolard's money-metric measure may be slightly on the high side. However, more research is needed to be certain about this and to develop more robust child poverty lines to be used in measurement.

- Woolard's measurement using the high poverty line of R430/month per capita (child) found that 74.8% of South Africa's children were income poor in 2000, translating into 13 million poor children. Of these, 60% were living in one of three provinces, namely KwaZulu-Natal (22%), Eastern Cape (20%) and Limpopo (18%).

- The application of the lower poverty line of R215/month also found child poverty to be widespread and concentrated in the same provinces. With this poverty line, 9.5 million children (54.2%) emerged as income poor, with 24% in the Eastern Cape, 23% in KwaZulu-Natal and 20% in Limpopo.

- It was suggested that the 75% child poverty measure derived from Woolard's analysis may be a little on the high side. This is due to under-reporting of income in the IES 2000 survey (on which Woolard's most recent measurement of child poverty was based) and the consideration that a R430/month poverty line may be slightly too high. Woolard's measure of 64.7%, based on the same poverty line, but using the OHS/IES 1995, may be more accurate. However, the problem with using this estimate is that poverty is likely to have increased since 1995, given the escalation of unemployment over recent years and the impact of HIV/AIDS.

- The income indicator analysis concluded with the point that child poverty is extensive in South Africa, no matter which of the poverty lines and survey data are chosen. Moreover, child poverty is concentrated in three provinces, the Eastern Cape, KwaZulu-Natal and Limpopo.

- The picture of child poverty derived from the income indicator analysis was supplemented with a perspective based on the hunger indicator and the 1999 NFCS. Strictly speaking, the NFCS provided information on the food insecurity/hunger position of children only between the ages of 1 and 9. However, it also gives a good indication of hunger amongst the whole child population.

- The hunger indicator analysis supported the picture of child poverty emerging from the income indicator analysis. It similarly showed a concentration of poor children in the same three provinces, with the addition of Gauteng. The NFCS found that at the national level, 52% of children aged 1 to 9 years (4.6 million children) experienced hunger. A further 23% were at risk of hunger. Only 25% appeared food secure.

- It was pointed out that if poor children are classified as those experiencing hunger and at risk of hunger, the analysis from the NFCS survey suggests that 75% of South Africa's children are poor. This is similar to Woolard's analysis based on the IES 2000 and poverty line of R430/month per capita. Using the Census 2001 estimates of the number of children aged 0 to 17 in South Africa, this translates into 13 million poor children.

Of course it is impossible to understand what poverty is unless it is experienced. Listening to the views and perspectives of children living in poverty and/or difficult circumstances who took part in the child participation study, the following key issues emerged:

- All the child participants had a multi-dimensional view of poverty. Their descriptions of the conditions in which they live and how this makes them feel re-affirmed the point that poverty is not confined to hardship linked directly to insufficient command over commodities and services – such as hunger, fatigue, inadequate food and shelter or inability to attend school. However, these forms of deprivation still form the traditional focus of poverty analysis and policy.

- While the aspects of child poverty referred to above remain important, many of the children participating in the study related that they suffered from discriminatory practices, social exclusion and vulnerability linked to their economic situation. This included suffering due to the responses of other children to poverty and of adults to poor children. It also included discrimination and the violation of rights on the part of those officials (such as teachers) who are expected to deliver services to children (and particularly the most vulnerable of children!) so as to ensure that their rights are realised.

- The stigmatisation and the negative psychological impact associated with child poverty in South Africa came across most starkly with the children living in the shelter in Cape Town. They refused to judge themselves as poor and thought about poverty in relative, not absolute terms.

- The child participation study also illustrated that poor children, for the most part, understood that their situation was linked to the precarious economic situation of their parents (or alternative care-givers). Moreover, they were aware that this, in turn, is a product of limited job opportunities (high unemployment) or in the case of most farm workers, low wages.

- The children's perspectives on service delivery (or lack thereof) revealed that their inability to access certain services or meet some basic needs (such as schooling) was linked to their inability to meet other basic socio-economic needs (such as adequate nutrition and income to finance their transport). The child poverty situation is such that many children have to trade one basic economic right – such as schooling – for others. This was seen most starkly in the case of children who lived without adult care-givers and instead of going to school, had to work to earn income to meet the basic needs of entire households.

- Finally, the children's descriptions of their situations highlight how inappropriate it is to become too fixated on just one form of "child poverty". While there is no doubt a need to develop a deeper understanding of child poverty and its causes, it is essential to remember that all children experience poverty differently. This point was driven home by one of the boys in the focus group of children living on farms in the Stellenbosch area. Instead of focusing on the negative dimensions and in particular on social exclusion (which many of the others chose to do), he argued that even if they were poor, they were "spiritually rich".[18]

The indicator and child-centred analyses of the child poverty situation made it clear then that there is an urgent need for government to use the state apparatus to improve the living conditions – including the economic situation – of millions of South African children. Implementing the basic socio-economic rights given to children in the Constitution[19] should be high on the agenda of priorities for South Africa's developmental state. How can the views expressed by children in the participation study be used to inform the way government goes about conceptualising and implementing programmes to give effect to child socio-economic rights? The main pointers that emerged were as follows:

- In order to improve the lives of the millions of children in South Africa that suffer poverty, it is essential for government to continue with its set of programmes to deliver basic and other social services to children. Many of South Africa's children still say their most urgent needs are education, food and basic services such as water and electricity.

- Several factors prevent children from realising their socio-economic rights even when corresponding government programmes are in place, for example in the areas of education and health care. Foremost amongst these factors is a lack of income. The design of some government programmes is also such that certain children are excluded from the programme benefits (as is the case with the Primary School Feeding Scheme, Free Primary Health Care programme and the programmes offering social assistance to children). In these instances, there is a need to re-consider the relevant criteria so as to include all children in need. In addition, it is necessary to speed up the delivery of existing programmes and to ensure that discriminatory implementation practices are brought to an end.

- The children's perspectives revealed a need for government budgeting to continue prioritising expenditure on infrastructure in the form of roads.[20] Transport costs are one of the main obstacles poor children experience in accessing schools and health care. Alternatively, or in addition, cash transfers to poor households are needed to facilitate access to schooling and health services for poor children.

- Based on the perspectives of the children who participated in the study (and in particular those living in a shelter for girls in Cape Town), there is a need for government to develop and implement programmes that realise basic child socio-economic rights in tandem with programmes to realise the other rights given to children in section 28 of the Constitution. Children do not want to, and should not have to, trade the right to a family life for socio-economic rights.

- A further insight emanating from the study is that children living in households largely experience poverty as members of those households. Hence, government strategies to deliver children's socio-economic and other rights must be complemented with programmes directed at realising the socio-economic rights of poor children's parents (or alternative care-givers). This suggests that government will need to revisit options to create employment for unskilled labour and/or reconsider its stance on extending social assistance programmes for adults to ensure that there is greater coverage of those in need.

- The point above also calls for more thorough consideration of what minimum core rights are implied by the Constitution. Further to this, there is a corresponding need to unpack and interrogate what minimum services for everyone are implied by the socio-economic rights given to everyone in the Constitution and how to go about ensuring that the state makes them immediately available to everyone. The views of the children participating in this research study correspond with the verdict given by Judge Davis in the *Grootboom* case, which was heard in the Cape High Court in 1999. This judgment held that the delivery of socio-economic rights to children should be linked to the delivery of the non-socio-economic child-specific rights given in the Constitution and also to the delivery of adults' socio-economic rights.

Finally, this chapter concludes with another challenge in the struggle to realise children's basic socio-economic rights. Through the child participation study, Ewing pointed out that there is a need in South Africa to raise awareness amongst poor children and children living in difficult circumstances about what their basic child socio-economic rights are. Too few children know what their rights are, which in turn undermines their ability to claim their rights. For example, only around half of the children taking part in the study believed that they had a right to free education. Fewer than half the children on farms who were asked about social benefits were aware of the existence of specific grants for children, let alone their right to social assistance (to a minimum income) given to them in the Constitution.

# REFERENCES

Bentley, K. (2003) *Concepts and Standards of Children's Rights: Some Considerations of Relativity and Enforcement.* Paper prepared for presentation at the Seminar on Statistics and Human Rights, Brussels, Belgium, 27-29 November 2002.

Bray, R. (2003) *Working Summary of 'Review Paper 2'*. Prepared for Baseline Indicators Project planning meeting, July 17-18 2003.

Cape High Court. (1999) *Grootboom v Oostenberg Municipality and Others*. Case No.6826/99, BCLR 2000(3) 277.

Department of Health. (2000) *National Food Consumption Survey 1999*. Available at http://www.sahealthinfo.org/nutrition/foodconsumption.htm.

Department of Social Development. (2002) *Transforming the Present – Protecting the Future: Draft Consolidated Report of the Committee of Inquiry into a Comprehensive System of Social Security for South Africa*. Pretoria: Government Printer.

Dieden, S. & B. Gustafsson. (2003) "Child Poverty in South Africa: an assessment based on microdata for 1995". In *International Journal of Social Welfare*, 12: 326-338.

Ewing, D. (2004) *Report on the Children's Participation Component of Monitoring Child Socio-economic Rights in South Africa: Achievements and Challenges*. Cape Town: Idasa.

Ennew, J. (1997) "Monitoring Children's Rights: Indicators for Children's Rights Project". Available at www.childwatch.uio.no/cwi/projects/indicators/monitoring/monitoring.html.

Haarmann, D. (1999) *The Living Conditions of South Africa's Children,* Applied Fiscal Research Centre (AFREC), Research Monograph Series, 9. Cape Town: University of Cape Town.

Kanbur, R. & L. Squire. (1999) *The Evolution of Thinking about Poverty: Exploring the Interactions*. Washington: World Bank.

Leibbrandt, M., I. Woolard & H. Bhorat. (2001) *Measuring Poverty in South Africa. Chapter one in Fighting Poverty – Labour Markets and Inequality in South Africa*. Cape Town: University of Cape Town.

National Treasury. (2003) *Budget Review*. Pretoria: Government Printer.

Theis, J. (2003) *Rights-Based Monitoring and Evaluation: A Discussion Paper.* Working paper of Save the Children, available online at http://www.seapa.net/external/special/reports/first.htm.

Simkins, C. (2003) *A Critical Assessment of the 1995 and 2000 Income and Expenditure Surveys as Sources of Information on Incomes*. Working paper.

Streak, J. (2000) "The extent and provincial distribution of child poverty in South Africa". In Cassiem, S. & J. Streak, *Child Poverty and the Budget 2000 – Are poor children being put first?* Cape Town: Idasa.

Streak, J. (2001) "A framework for budget analysis based on government's obligations to deliver child socio-economic rights" in Cassiem, S. & J. Streak, *Budgeting for Child Socio-Economic Rights.* Cape Town: Idasa.

Streak, J. (2002) *Poverty Monitor.* Cape Town: Idasa Children's Budget Unit.

Streak, J. (2004) "The GEAR legacy: Did GEAR fail or move South Africa forward in development?". Forthcoming in *Development Southern Africa,* 21(2), June.

Vitamin Information Centre. (2001) *Medical Update,* 37, April.

Woolard, I. (2003) *Note on the results of analysis of child poverty based on income poverty lines of R430/month per capita and R215/month per capita in 2000 rands.* Conducted for the Children's Budget Unit.

World Bank. (1990) *World Development Report.* New York: Oxford University Press.

## PERSONAL COMMUNICATION

Mr Dawes, 2003.

# ENDNOTES

1     Thank you to Dr Ingrid Woolard, Dr Andy Dawes, Deborah Ewing and Christina Nomdo for comments on previous drafts of this chapter.

2     The *Income and Expenditure Survey* is conducted by Statistics South Africa every five years. It is piggy-backed by the Labour Force Survey (that is, the same households are visited for the two surveys). The last two editions of the *Income and Expenditure Survey* were in 1995 and 2000.

3     See also Vitamin Information Centre 2001.

4     Ewing is director of iMEDIATE Development Communications, a consultancy specialising in media, mediation, training and education. She has extensive experience in facilitating information-gathering and -sharing with children, particularly with poor children living in difficult circumstances. She has also researched and written extensively on the subject of child rights, particularly the child's right to protection in South Africa.

5     To convert all the lines to 2000 rands, the South African Reserve Bank CPI figures were used. Annual average CPI figures were used. Dr Ian Venter did the conversions for us.

6     Table 1.1 includes only studies that have used per capita absolute income poverty lines. It leaves out those that have used adult equivalent absolute income poverty lines and those using relative poverty lines. One study that used an adult equivalent poverty line is by Haarmann (1999). In the process of conducting a composite index measurement of child poverty based on the 1993 Project for Statistics on Living Standards, he estimated child poverty using R319/month per adult equivalent. He found 72% of children to be poor based on this absolute income poverty line. For an overview of studies estimating child population and

population poverty rates in South Africa using relative child poverty lines, see Streak (2000:5-7) and Streak (2001:20-23).

7    Traditionally, poverty measurers have focused on the economic dimensions of poverty because measuring this is more achievable in practical terms than trying to measure the psychological dimensions of poverty.

8    The survey design, implementation and analysis process was led by a team of nutrition experts including A. Dannhauser, D. Labadarios, U. MacIntyre and R. Swart. It was implemented nationally between February and July 1999.

9    The overview of the method is taken from the method section at the beginning of chapter eight in the final survey report. This chapter of the report focuses on the measure of hunger in the NFCS.
     See http://wwwsahealthinfo.org/nutrition/foodconsumption.htm.

10   Of course, using the statistic on the incidence of children experiencing hunger and at risk of hunger from the NFCS for children aged 1 to 9 and applying it to children in all categories, assumes that the incidence is similar across all age cohorts of children. According to the NFCS, this is a reasonable assumption (see Table 1.6).

11   The results of the study have been published by the Children's Budget Unit in a separate report which provides more detailed information on the study, including how it was conducted.

12   For more about a child rights perspective on research design and describing the child poverty situation, see Bray 2003; Bentley 2003; and Ennew 1997 at www.childwatch.uio.no/cwi/projects/indicators/monitoring/monitoring.html.

13   Children were invited to participate in the study based on their prior involvement with a partner or associate organisation. The partner organisations in KwaZulu-Natal were the CAP (Churches Agricultural Project) Farm Trust at Mdukatshani/Weenen and the Thandanani Foundation in Pietermaritzburg. In the Western Cape, the partnership organisations were the Women on Farms Project in Stellenbosch and the Ons Plek/Siviwe Girls' Homes in Cape Town. The involvement of partnership organisations was both to facilitate access to the children and also to ensure that the children would receive some support and/or follow-up, without creating expectations of needs being met through the research. Partner organisations were briefed on the aims and objectives of the study, and on how the information would be used. They were given outlines of the programmes and planned activities to comment on their suitability for and relevance to the different target groups. In each case, the research activities were integrated into the programme schedule of the partner organisation to avoid disruption to the children's lives and to avoid unnecessary expenditure on venues, transport and catering.

14   There were two reasons for the inclusion of a minority of young people over 18. First, although the United Nations definition of a child is 0 to 18 years, the legal age of majority in South Africa is 21. This has particular implications for orphans, since a young person aged over 18 but under 21 is generally not regarded as an adult in terms of access to services. Some of the child-headed households identified by the Thandanani Foundation in Pietermaritzburg were headed by young people then over the age of 18, but who had been heading their households for two or more years and had not been able to complete their schooling or access social benefits on behalf of younger siblings. Secondly, three of the partner

organisations contributing to the research had been working for several years with young people who were over the age of 18 but who attended workshops organised by the organisations as siblings of younger participants, or because they were still schooling and still needed the support that those under 18 receive from the organisation. It would have been insensitive to exclude these young people and, since they were few and this was a qualitative rather than a quantitative study, their input did not skew the findings. However, the views of the under-18s have been emphasised in the reporting.

15 The composition of the child participants in this study implies that the perspectives generated through the research process reflect the views of 74 boys and 103 girls.

16 All the children at the shelter have access to basic social services through the shelter. Seventeen of the 18 girls at the home were receiving schooling. At the time of the research, arrangements were being made to enrol the outstanding girl in school. They all have access to health services and receive regular medical and dental check-ups as well as emergency treatment and ongoing care for chronic conditions. The shelter receives subsidies from the Department of Social Development for the girls' basic accommodation, food and care and organises fundraisers to raise money and donations in kind, to meet other needs.

17 For example, the report on experiences of poverty in the Msinga/Weenen districts makes it explicit when information was derived from discussion amongst mothers and care-givers. Similarly, the text pertaining to children living in child-headed households specifically indicates when information on access to services was drawn from the comments of social workers.

18 This comment made by one of the boy children is open to interpretation in different ways. According to a facilitator working with the group in which the statement was made, it is not uncommon for parents in his community to teach their children to feel "spiritually rich", partly because they themselves are religious but also as a mechanism for coping with their inability to escape poverty. So the statement itself may reflect the child's real feeling or it could be a learned defence to being perceived as poor.

19 These rights are further protected by other legal instruments such as the Convention on the Rights of the Child, the International Covenant on Economic, Social and Cultural Rights and the African Charter on the Rights and Welfare of the Child.

20 For evidence of the prioritisation of transport in rural areas in government's current budgeting and development strategy, see chapter two of this publication; National Treasury 2003; and Streak 2004.

# CHAPTER TWO

Children's socio-economic rights in the South African Constitution: Towards a framework for monitoring implementation

Judith Streak and Joachim Wehner[1]

"If the socio-economic rights in the Constitution are to amount to more than paper promises, they must serve as useful tools in enabling people to gain access to the basic social services and resources needed to live a life consistent with human dignity."
*Sandra Liebenberg (2003:1-2)*

# INTRODUCTION

All children in South Africa have a comprehensive set of human rights, including socio-economic rights. These rights are enshrined in the South African Constitution[2] and in international and regional child rights treaties. The socio-economic rights set certain standards relating to the socio-economic conditions in which children in South Africa should live. A central aim of these rights is to create an environment in which all poor people and in particular, vulnerable groups such as children, have basic necessities — including adequate health care, education, water, shelter, sanitation, food and income. There is a dimension of progressive improvement in the enjoyment of the socio-economic rights given in the Constitution. Crucially, children's socio-economic rights create legal obligations on the state and on parents to give effect to these rights. The socio-economic rights in the Constitution are justiciable, which means that they are legally enforceable through the courts.

The socio-economic context in which most of South Africa's people (including children) live, is very different from the ideal advanced by the socio-economic rights in the Constitution. Child poverty remains extensive and deep. Literally millions of South African children often go to bed and wake up hungry, do not have the material means to go to school or to visit health clinics and find it impossible to live healthy and secure lives (see chapter one). The extent and depth of poverty in South Africa makes it very difficult for vast numbers of parents to fulfil their primary responsibility and meet the basic needs of their children. In this context, it is crucial for the state to respond effectively to its obligations to deliver socio-economic rights to children and their care-givers. In terms of state action targeted at realising these rights, it is furthermore particularly important for the executive branch of the state (government) to take the lead by implementing programmes that deliver basic services. Thus, if the state is to be able to fulfil its obligations in relation to child socio-economic rights, clarity is first required as to what exact services children are entitled to by virtue of the socio-economic rights in the Constitution.

It is essential for government to be held accountable for how it responds to its obligations in relation to child socio-economic rights. Research that monitors government's measures to give effect to these rights is one instrument that can be used to achieve this objective. The central purpose of this chapter is to review the socio-economic rights in sections 28(1)(c) and 29(1)(a) of the Constitution — as well as the obligations these place on the state — and then to consider what these imply about how to monitor government's measures to advance these rights. A related objective is to introduce and to place in context the research questions that guide the monitoring analysis in chapters three to six of this publication. Each of the latter chapters monitors a particular set of government measures aimed at realising one of the socio-economic rights given to children in the Constitution (see Box 2.1 below).

This chapter is divided into five sections:

- Section one describes the set of socio-economic rights given to South Africa's children, focusing on the rights in the Constitution and in particular, on those given only or primarily to children.

- Next, section two provides a brief overview of the role-players involved in translating child socio-economic rights into practice, distinguishing actors who have legal obligations (most notably the state and parents) from those who do not.

- Section three turns to the question of what obligations are placed on the state to deliver the rights given to children in sections 28(1)(c) and 29(1)(a) of the Constitution. It also identifies the channels through which government can work to fulfil its obligations.

- Section four sketches a broad picture of the strategy government has been using (since 1994) to deliver the child-specific and other socio-economic rights in the Constitution. This section identifies a range of public programmes related to child-specific socio-economic rights that have been introduced since 1994, and questions whether government has an effective process for directing and monitoring its budgeting and programming in relation to its obligations to deliver these rights. It also investigates whether government's socio-economic rights delivery strategy shows any recent shifts that may have significant impact on realising children's rights in future.

- In conclusion, section five draws together the inferences gathered through the course of the chapter and what these mean for monitoring government's measures to give effect to the socio-economic rights given to children in sections 28(1)(c) and 29(1)(a) of the Constitution. Against this background, it then introduces the monitoring questions that will guide the analyses in the chapters to follow.

# 1. WHAT ARE THE SOCIO-ECONOMIC RIGHTS OF SOUTH AFRICAN CHILDREN?

The rights of South African children (including socio-economic rights) are derived from the South African Constitution and from two child-specific human rights treaties (one international and the other regional), both of which have been ratified by the South African government. The relevant international rights treaty is the Convention on the Rights of the Child (CRC). The regional treaty is the African Charter on the Rights and Welfare of the Child (ACRWC).[3] In the South African Constitution and in both these rights treaties, a "child" is defined as a person under the age of 18 years.

## 1.1 CONSTITUTIONAL SOCIO-ECONOMIC RIGHTS

The South African Constitution was drafted in the context of a legacy of extensive and racially-biased poverty linked to apartheid and the coming to power of a democratic government deeply committed to poverty eradication. The Constitution – and the Bill of Rights (BOR) which forms its second chapter – is best understood in relation to the human rights abuses (political, social and economic) associated with the apartheid regime. The Constitution includes a particular set of values about the need to address poverty.[4] At the time of its drafting (1994-1996), there was a great deal of debate over whether to include justiciable socio-economic rights. The arguments in favour of their inclusion proved to be most convincing (Liebenberg & Pillay 2000:19-20).

As a result, the Constitution – in its BOR – gives everyone a comprehensive set of socio-economic rights relating to housing, health care, food, water, social security (including social assistance), as well as (basic and further) education. Within its catalogue of child rights (section 28), there are four socio-economic rights, namely the rights to basic nutrition, shelter, basic health care services and social services (section 28(1)(c)). Children are also the principle beneficiaries of another socio-economic right in the Constitution, the right to basic education (section 29(1)(a)). For the sake of brevity, the term "child-specific rights" is used in this publication to refer to those child socio-economic constitutional rights covered by the study (see Box 2.1 below). In the words of Liebenberg (2003:2), "socio-economic rights were included as justiciable rights in the Bill of Rights primarily to assist the poor to protect and advance their fundamental socio-economic needs and interests."

> **BOX 2.1: THE CHILD-SPECIFIC SOCIO-ECONOMIC RIGHTS COVERED IN THIS STUDY**
> 28. (1) Every child has the right...
>          (c) to basic nutrition, ... basic health care services and social services...
> 29. (1) Everyone has the right
>          (a) to a basic education...

Source: Constitution of the Republic of South Africa, 1996.

Crucially, the Constitution does not specify the exact content or scope of any of its socio-economic rights, including those given only or primarily to children in sections 28 and 29. Thus, as a number of rights experts have pointed out (Creamer 2002:19; Bentley 2003; Proudlock 2002; Liebenberg in personal correspondence), a critical issue that needs to be addressed is how to deal with the practical problem of clarifying the nature and scope of the obligations in relation to children's socio-economic rights. A lack of clarity around the level of entitlements implied by the rights is dangerous: it leaves room for government to arbitrarily decide on what level of services to provide to children in order to give effect to their rights. Social consensus on what standards of living are implied by the rights is obviously also important to facilitate rigorous monitoring of children's circumstances in relation to their rights. Bentley (2003) elegantly highlights the importance of clarifying the nature of the entitlements given to children as follows:

"It is difficult to deliver something if you don't know what it is. If asked to deliver for example, a piece of furniture, you would need to know its size, measurements, weight, and if it could be broken into separate pieces, before you could decide on the best method to deliver it. This is analogously true of the enforcement of human rights. In addition, we can't measure how well we have done our job of delivering something, if we don't know what it is, or indeed what it is for."

The socio-economic rights in the Constitution are coupled with particular state obligations. The Constitution obliges the state to "respect, protect, promote and fulfil" constitutional rights (section 7(2)). The drafting of the Constitution suggests that the rights given to children under sections 28(1)(c) and 29(1)(a) place a different, higher-level delivery obligation on the state (and on government), when compared to the socio-economic rights given to everyone in sections 26 and 27. This is because the latter sections of the BOR are formulated in a way that sets certain limitations on what is expected of government. For instance, everyone's right of access to health care, food, water and social security in section 27 is combined with the obligation that "the state must take reasonable legislative and other measures, within its available resources, to achieve the progressive realisation of each of these rights". This is not the case in the formulation of the child-specific rights in the Constitution: the state's delivery obligation is not made subject to any limitations.

A key question is whether all the unqualified socio-economic rights given to children in sections 28(1)(c) and 29(1)(a) are different from the socio-economic rights given to everyone in the sense that they only need to be met to a very basic level. It has been suggested by some (Brand and Creamer in Creamer 2002:6)[5] that this is the case – that is, that a distinction must be drawn in terms of the level of entitlements given to children in sections 28 and 29(1)(a) and those given to everyone in sections 26, 27 and 29. As argued by Creamer (2002:6, citing Brand):

"Even though there have been suggestions to the contrary, the entitlements of children under s28(1)(c) are only to a basic attenuated level of health care services, housing, nutrition and social services 'which is necessary for a dignified survival'... the unqualified right to basic education under s29(1)(a) will be similarly interpreted as a basic right."

Others, including Budlender (cited in Creamer 2002:27) caution against proclaiming with any confidence that the child socio-economic rights given in sections 28 and 29 are only basic rights, "except where the Constitution says so expressly".[6] It appears, therefore, as if the verdict is still out on whether all section 28(1)(c) and 29(1)(a) rights are basic rights. With regards to the child-specific socio-economic rights covered in this study, it can thus be presumed that the right to education given to children in section 29(1)(a) and the rights to health services and nutrition given in section 28(1)(c) are basic rights (as this is indicated expressly in the formulation of these rights in the Constitution). However, we cannot presume that the child's right to social services and shelter in section 28(1)(c) are basic rights.

The socio-economic rights in the Constitution give children (and others) a way of demanding that the state and other parties take actions to create the conditions in which their basic needs can be realised (Liebenberg & Pillay 2000:47).[7] However from the drafting of the Constitution, it is not clear exactly what children in need can claim from the state or how long they are expected to wait (in the face of real administrative constraints) for the delivery of services needed to meet their basic needs.[8] This theme will be discussed further in section three below.

It is important to note that the socio-economic rights in the Constitution need to be read together with the principle of non-discrimination. Section 9 of the Constitution guarantees equality before the law and prohibits discrimination in terms of race, gender, age, disability and other grounds (Liebenberg 2001:412). In terms of section 9, the socio-economic rights given to children in the Constitution are therefore guaranteed to every child without unfair discrimination. There is also a need to recognise the inter-dependence between the child-specific socio-economic rights contained in the Constitution. The delivery or non-delivery of any single socio-economic right to children impacts on their ability to realise other rights. Moreover, there is also an inter-dependence between the socio-economic rights given only to children in sections 28(1)(c) and 29(1)(a) and the socio-economic rights given to everyone in the Constitution. In other words, the extent to which socio-economic rights are realised amongst everyone (including poor and vulnerable children's parents and household members) influences how effectively children themselves can realise their own socio-economic rights. The views of children living in poverty and/or difficult circumstances, as presented in chapter one, illustrate how important it is to consider the inter-dependent relationship between these rights in both senses set out above.

## 1.2 CHILD SOCIO-ECONOMIC RIGHTS IN INTERNATIONAL RIGHTS TREATIES

The Convention on the Rights of the Child defines a holistic set of civil, political, economic, social, cultural and environmental child rights and also obliges state parties to take actions to give effect to these rights. State parties are obliged to undertake legislative, administrative and other measures for the implementation of the economic, social and cultural rights in the CRC. In this regard, article 4 stipulates:

> "State Parties shall undertake all appropriate legislative, administrative and other measures for the implementation of the rights recognised in the present Convention. With regard to economic, social and cultural rights, State Parties shall undertake such measures to the maximum extent of their available resources and, where needed, within the framework of international co-operation."

The CRC was adopted by the General Assembly of the United Nations in 1989 and it was ratified by the South African government in June 1995. The ratification of the CRC means that government is bound, through international legal obligation, to implement the socio-economic and other rights in the CRC. The socio-economic rights in the CRC include the right to a good enough standard of living (article 27), to health and health services (article 24), to benefit from social security (article 26), to education including free basic education (article 28), to be protected from harmful work practices and to be paid adequately for any work conducted (article 32). The CRC also includes a set of socio-economic rights specific to disabled children (article 23).

The African Charter on the Rights and Welfare of the Child (ACRWC) is a child rights treaty developed by the Organisation of African Unity (OAU) to set standards for child rights in Africa. It was adopted by the OAU in 1990 and ratified by South Africa in January 2000. The socio-economic rights afforded to South African children in terms of the ACRWC cover rights in relation to development (article 5.2), education (article 11), health and health services, as well as child labour and appropriate conditions of work (article 15). Unlike the CRC and the Constitution, the ACRWC makes no specific mention of the child's right to social assistance. However, article 20 calls on state parties to assist parents in carrying out their responsibility to take care of and promote the development of their children, including through material assistance. This article could thus be interpreted to include the right to social assistance. Like the CRC, the ACRWC has a specific article (article 13) that relates to the socio-economic rights of disabled children and the associated obligations on state parties to deliver them. This article also calls on state parties to assist parents in the provision of basic goods and services that are essential for the social integration and development of disabled children. This particular right is made "subject to available resources". The general article of the ACRWC on the obligations of state parties does not limit state obligations with reference to resource constraints.[9]

## BOX 2.2: THE INTERNATIONAL COVENANT ON ECONOMIC, SOCIAL AND CULTURAL RIGHTS (ICESCR)

The ICESCR is another important international treaty that includes child socio-economic rights. The ICESCR was developed, together with the International Covenant on Civil and Political Rights (ICCPR), from the Universal Declaration of Human Rights. The latter declaration emerged from the United Nations Charter of 1945. Both conventions were adopted by the United Nations on 16 December 1966 and came into force on 3 January 1976.

The ICESCR deals primarily with socio-economic and cultural rights pertaining to everyone. However, it does include a section (article 10(3)) which highlights children's socio-economic rights and suggests that special status should be given to children in the fulfilment of the rights listed in the convention.

The ICESCR (and CRC) influenced the design of the socio-economic rights in the South African Constitution, as well as the obligations placed on different actors to deliver them (Constitutional Court 2000; Liebenberg 2003:4). Moreover, the ICESCR and other United Nations treaties – together with the insights of the relevant committees' responsible for monitoring the implementation of these treaties – are used in the Constitutional Court in South Africa as a reference when interpreting socio-economic rights and the associated obligations. However, because the ICESCR has not yet been ratified by the South African government, it is not yet obliged to implement the child rights set out in this treaty. South African child rights activists are eager for the government to ratify the ICESCR, because the relevant United Nations supervisory committee pays particular attention to state parties' obligations to provide goods and services to implement a minimum essential element of each socio-economic right immediately (see *Comment Number 3* in the General Comments of the United Nations Committee on the International Convention on Economic, Social and Cultural Rights).

The South African Constitution, CRC and ACRWC constitute the starting points for understanding child socio-economic rights and the associated state obligations in South Africa. In monitoring the measures adopted by government to give effect to child socio-economic rights, this study focuses on the socio-economic rights contained in the Constitution – specifically those given only or primarily to children in sections 28(1)(c) and 29(1)(a). The decision to concentrate on constitutional child socio-economic rights is based on the Constitution's status as the supreme law of South Africa and the fact that, as litigation has proven, its socio-economic rights provisions are directly enforceable through the legal system (see sections two and three below). However, it is important to remember that the South African state is also under an obligation to implement the child socio-economic rights contained in the CRC and the ACRWC. Monitoring progress in this regard is essential. Moreover, the CRC and ACRWC have an important role to play in helping our society to define more precisely the entitlements given to children in sections 28 and 29 and the associated state obligations. For example, section 39 of the Constitution explicitly states that the socio-economic rights in the BOR must be interpreted in the light of our international obligations.[10] Thus the CRC and ACRWC are significant sources for child rights researchers and advocates to draw from as they attempt to define the nature and scope of the child rights in the Constitution, as well as the state's obligations to give effect to these rights.

Section three below places the spotlight on what obligations the South African state has to deliver the child socio-economic rights given only or primarily to children in the Constitution. Sections 4 and 5 then examine government's broad response to these obligations and consider how best to monitor government's actions in this regard, focusing on programme and budget measures. But first, section two below identifies the actors responsible for implementing child socio-economic rights in South Africa.

## 2. WHO TRANSLATES CHILD SOCIO-ECONOMIC RIGHTS INTO PRACTICE?

Rights that exist on paper must be translated into tangible benefits in order to be meaningful. Government, or the executive, is arguably the pivotal player in this regard. However, a range of other institutions and actors make valuable contributions to the delivery of socio-economic rights, including those of children. In South Africa and most likely elsewhere, it is possible to distinguish between actors that have a legal or constitutional obligation in translating these rights into practice and those who do not. This categorisation in itself does not automatically imply a difference in importance between these groups. However in the context of this discussion, this distinction is important. It implies that the efforts of the former set of actors should be measurable and subject to monitoring with reference to their legally defined obligations. This is a crucial point that underpins the development of the kind of monitoring systems explored in this publication. The two sets of actors identified by this distinction are discussed in turn below.

## 2.1 ACTORS WITH CONSTITUTIONAL OBLIGATIONS

The Constitution places an explicit obligation on the state to respect, protect, promote and fulfil the BOR (section 7). However, the Constitution is more precise than this: it also defines the roles of different components that make up the state, including the legislature, the executive, the judiciary and other organs of state.

**Parliament and provincial legislatures** can shape particular programmes or legal parameters through which socio-economic rights are made effective and monitor progress in delivery. At the national level, the Constitution empowers the National Assembly to do so "by passing legislation and by scrutinising and overseeing executive action" (section 42(3)).[11] For instance, Parliament has been involved in approving welfare laws and it receives reports from government departments regarding the administration of social services. Parliament also passes the annual Budget, which allocates funds to relevant programmes (section 77). It is entitled to draw on advice from the Financial and Fiscal Commission (FFC), an independent institution set up by the Constitution to advise Parliament on financial issues. In this way, members of parliament are expected to ensure that programmes are sufficiently funded and that funds are allocated to the levels and units of government that are charged with implementation (sections 214 and 220). Provinces participate in the national legislative process via the National Council of Provinces (NCOP), the second chamber of Parliament (section 42(4)). This is important when, for example, provincial governments will act as implementing agents for nationally-formulated policy (section 42(4)).

The Constitution implicitly calls for dynamic and continuous interaction between the legislative bodies and **national and provincial executives**. At the national level, executive authority is vested in the President (section 85), who exercises this power together with cabinet. Their responsibilities include the implementation of legislation (except where this is a provincial or local responsibility), the development and implementation of national policy, as well as the preparation and initiation of legislation. Part of this role is thus to develop and implement policy and legislation relating to the socio-economic rights in the Constitution. While the executive has to ensure the implementation of policy and legislation, this does not exclude the possibility of involving other actors in service delivery, such as the private sector or civil society. In the context of socio-economic rights in particular, responsibility for the delivery of relevant programmes often rests with provincial and sometimes local governments (refer to schedule 4 of the Constitution). When monitoring government's measures to give effect to child-specific constitutional socio-economic rights, this study focuses attention on national and provincial government.

The South African Constitution vests judicial authority in the **courts**, with the Constitutional Court at the apex (chapter 8). The Constitutional Court in particular has played a crucial role in checking the compliance of government with socio-economic rights obligations and in ordering appropriate remedial action (more in this regard in section 3 below). In a recent case, the Constitutional Court explicitly affirmed its power and duty not only to assess whether a right has been breached, but also to ensure "appropriate relief" when necessary (Constitutional Court 2002:106).

The Constitution assigns a role to **parents** in the fulfilment of child socio-economic rights. More specifically, "every child has the right…to family care or parental care, or to appropriate alternative care when removed from the family environment" (section 28(1)(b)). Extensive poverty in South Africa makes it impossible for millions of parents to fulfil their obligations towards their children. In this context, the court and others have gone some way towards defining when parents should be seen as unable to fulfil their obligations and hence, when and how the state is to step in (Sloth-Nielson 2001; Cape High Court 1999; Constitutional Court 2000 & 2002; Creamer 2002). As will be illustrated below however, there is still no full clarity on the relative roles of poor parents and the state in giving effect children's socio-economic rights (Creamer 2002; Proudlock 2002).

Finally, the Constitution establishes a range of "state institutions supporting constitutional democracy", commonly referred to as "chapter nine institutions".[12] These include the **Human Rights Commission** (HRC), which has powers to monitor the observance of human rights and the relevant measures taken by organs of state to realise socio-economic rights. The South African HRC also has powers to take steps in order to secure redress in cases where socio-economic rights have been violated (see Box 2.3; also refer to Liebenberg 2001).

## BOX 2.3: FUNCTIONS OF THE HUMAN RIGHTS COMMISSION

184. (1) The Human Rights Commission must
    (a) promote respect for human rights and a culture of human rights;
    (b) promote the protection, development and attainment of human rights; and
    (c) monitor and assess the observance of human rights in the Republic.

  (2) The Human Rights Commission has the powers, as regulated by national legislation, necessary to perform its functions, including the power
    (a) to investigate and to report on the observance of human rights;
    (b) to take steps to secure appropriate redress where human rights have been violated;
    (c) to carry out research; and
    (d) to educate.

  (3) Each year, the Human Rights Commission must require relevant organs of state to provide the Commission with information on the measures that they have taken towards the realisation of the rights in the Bill of Rights concerning housing, health care, food, water, social security, education and the environment.

(4) The Human Rights Commission has the additional powers and functions prescribed by national legislation.

Source: Constitution of the Republic of South Africa, 1996.

## 2.2 OTHER ACTORS

A range of other actors also contribute to the translation of child socio-economic rights into practice, even if their role is not defined (or at least not as explicitly defined) in the Constitution. These include the private sector, rights-bearers themselves, civil society, the media and international bodies. There may well be others that prove crucial in particular instances.

For many people **private sector** employment generates the income necessary to enjoy the benefits of socio-economic rights without further support by the state. The state's primary obligation is then to those who do not fall within this fortunate category. The exact nature of measures to be taken by the state to realise socio-economic rights is crucially dependent on the socio-economic context, in particular the prevalence and depth of poverty. For instance, the higher employment levels are, the more rights-related benefits — such as shelter or nutrition, and to some extent health and education — can be purchased by individuals using income derived from employment. Thus in a situation of full employment, access to rights-related benefits would largely be facilitated via the market. (Of course even in this scenario, the state would still have an important regulatory role to play in the protection of socio-economic rights and in the provision of education and health services). The necessity for the state to intervene in order to safeguard and fulfil socio-economic rights is correspondingly far greater in the context of widespread income poverty, which deprives many individuals of shelter, adequate nutrition and the like (World Bank 1990; Annand & Ravallion 1993).

**Rights-bearers** are not automatic **beneficiaries.** The former have to claim their rights and create demand on the state to extend the benefits or entitlements of relevant programmes to them. In this regard, individual rights-bearers can indeed have considerable impact. For example, it was the grievances of one individual that gave rise to South Africa's watershed Constitutional Court ruling on socio-economic rights — the *Grootboom* case (Constitutional Court 2000). Rights-bearers are also frequently expected to catalyse access to specific rights. For instance, no social assistance grant will be paid out without the person entitled to the grant making an application. However, in the case of child rights-bearers and particularly in the context of extensive poverty, it is unrealistic to expect children themselves to be in a position to actively claim their rights. Pro-active programmes are needed when poor children are involved. For example, in order to be effective in the provision of the child's right to social assistance, there is a need for the state to *reach out* towards potential beneficiaries — by creating one-stop centres, mobile clinics and removing unnecessary bureaucracy.

Not all rights-bearers will know exactly what they are entitled to, where they must go to apply, or how to obtain the relevant documentation needed to do so. Raising awareness and facilitating access calls for information campaigns on the part of the state and advocacy from the side of civil society. The electronic and print **media** provide pivotal fora for activism, government information campaigns and the exchange of views in general.

Rights-bearers might need support in order to access or protect their rights, in particular when the state falls short with regard to delivery. South Africa has a strong tradition of **civil society** activism. On different levels, non-governmental and community-based organisations can contribute to the realisation of socio-economic rights by, for instance, assisting in the delivery of services and lobbying government to design necessary programmes or to upgrade the benefits of certain programmes. In South Africa, civil society activism played a crucial role in putting pressure on government to increase the initial benefit level of the Child Support Grant before it was introduced in 1998. Social movements, such as the Treatment Action Campaign (TAC) in particular, have helped to enforce socio-economic rights. Civil society organisations have supported individuals in claiming the benefits of their socio-economic rights through the legal system, for instance in the *Grootboom* case.

In addition to advocacy, civil society research that monitors government's actions in relation to its legal obligations can act as a powerful tool for the advancement of child-specific socio-economic rights. The impact of such research depends on its capacity to prompt government into improving its measures aimed at realising rights. This highlights how important it is for civil society research findings to be disseminated effectively and used by the media, parliamentarians, advocacy groups and government officials.

Finally, the important contribution of **international bodies** must be recognised. For instance, the South African government is obliged to record the progress it is making with the implementation of the CRC. It is also expected to make submissions on this progress to the United Nations Committee on the Convention on the Right of the Child, which triggers a formal response. In many countries, international donors also play a crucial role in monitoring and supporting the delivery of socio-economic rights through a variety of measures. These may include funding the work of civil society organisations, financial contributions to relevant government programmes or technical advice. Regional structures such as the African Union can also safeguard and promote human rights.

# 3. OBLIGATIONS ON THE STATE TO REALISE SECTION 28(1)(C) AND 29(1)(A) RIGHTS

Section one of this chapter pointed out that the Constitution obliges the state to "respect, protect, promote and fulfil" all constitutional rights (section 7(2)). It also noted that section 28(1)(c) and 29(1)(a) rights are not qualified with reference to resource constraints, reasonable measures and progressive realisation, whereas those socio-economic rights given to everyone are qualified as such. This absence of qualification suggests a higher level of state obligation in relation to the child-specific rights.

This section enquires more precisely after exactly what higher level obligations are placed on the state to give effect to the unqualified socio-economic rights of children.

This is not an easy task. It has already been pointed out that definition is still being given to the level of entitlements implied by the socio-economic rights given to children in sections 28(1)(c) and 29(1)(a) of the Constitution. Similarly, the precise nature of the obligations on the state in relation to these rights remains unclear. The matter is open to interpretation and ongoing dialogue in society. Because these rights are enforceable through the legal system, the Constitutional Court has a crucial role to play in this process through evolving jurisprudence. The details of the obligation on the state to deliver the rights given to children in sections 28(1)(c) and 29(1)(a) – and the content of these rights – is being developed over time, directed by broad dialogue in society, led by jurisprudence and informed by expert opinion. Unfortunately to date, the evolving Constitutional Court jurisprudence (see Constitutional Court 1997, 2000 & 2002)[13] has been focused on defining the state's obligations in relation to the qualified socio-economic rights given to everyone in sections 26 and 27. It has also, to some extent, addressed the question of the scope of the rights given to children in sections 28(1)(c) and 29(1)(a). Critically however, the court has to date not taken a decision about government's fulfilment of its obligations based on the unqualified socio-economic rights given to children. As such, it has largely avoided defining state obligations in relation to these rights.[14] Pending further clarification from the Constitutional Court, our current understanding of the state's obligations to deliver child socio-economic rights can largely only be based on the court's interpretation pertaining to section 26 and 27 rights and on expert opinion. Section 3.2 below draws on Constitutional Court jurisprudence and expert opinion to put forward the current tentative understanding of the state's obligations in relation to section 28(1)(c) and 29(1)(a) rights. The focus is on the *Grootboom* and *TAC* cases because these two cases, more so than the *Soobramony* case, are helpful in understanding the nature of the state's obligations to deliver the child-specific socio-economic rights given to children in the Constitution. To provide the necessary context, section 3.1 first gives an overview of the channels through which the state works to fulfil socio-economic rights.

## 3.1 CHANNELS THROUGH WHICH THE STATE CAN FULFIL ITS RIGHTS OBLIGATIONS

The state has two main channels through which to fulfil its obligations in relation to the child-specific and other socio-economic rights contained in the Constitution. Firstly, it does so by creating an economic environment in which the private sector can provide opportunities for parents to obtain the income necessary to meet their primary obligation. For example, government's Growth, Employment and Redistribution (GEAR) strategy had as one of its primary aims to create an environment in which the private sector would offer more jobs to the poor – so that more parents have the income necessary to meet the basic needs of their children. This can be described as the "indirect channel" for delivering socio-economic rights. Secondly, government also needs to advance socio-economic rights through direct measures such as policy development, legal reform and enforcement, as well as the design and implementation of relevant programmes. For instance, as a means to give effect to the child's right to social assistance[15], government reviewed its existing policy and decided to replace the State Maintenance Grant with the Child Support Grant. National government designed a five-year implementation plan to roll this grant out to all eligible children, while provinces had to finance and implement the new programme (Streak & Wehner 2002). Government is also currently contemplating further legal reforms in relation to this right and is conducting a review of the Social Assistance and Child Care Acts.

Government thus uses both direct and indirect measures to pursue the delivery of socio-economic rights. The extent to which government must undertake the challenge of using direct measures is highly dependent on its success in using the indirect mechanism. The more successful government is in helping the private sector to create jobs, the less it has to do by way of developing and implementing programmes to meet its obligations. The Constitution does not prescribe the exact balance that should be struck between indirect and direct measures, nor have the courts pronounced on this matter. The Constitution does recognise that the socio-economic rights of children and of everyone make demands on the total aggregate fiscal envelope. It places a duty on government to set aside a substantial yet sustainable proportion of total public funds for direct measures (including programme implementation) to fulfil socio-economic rights. However, the Constitution does not prescribe an exact aggregate amount or proportion that has to be spent on direct measures, including those direct measures giving effect to child socio-economic rights. Thus when it comes to defining exactly how and to what extent government is obliged to use direct measures to realise children's constitutional socio-economic rights, many unanswered questions remain. Given the limited income prospects for the poor in the market economy, it becomes all the more imperative to grapple seriously with these questions.

## 3.2 THE UNCLEAR VIEW ON THE SCOPE AND NATURE OF STATE OBLIGATIONS

In the *Grootboom* case, the Constitutional Court conducted its first review of government's measures to give effect to everyone's right to have access to adequate housing (section 26). Importantly in this case, the court confirmed that the Constitution does not prescribe any *particular* measures to government. In the words of Judge Yacoob: "The precise contours and content of the measures to be adopted are primarily a matter for the Legislature and the Executive" (Constitutional Court 2000:41). At the same time, the court offered guidance on what the state is required to do by way of direct measures. This guidance came in the form of a "reasonable measures test", which the court applied in order to decide whether government's programmes to give effect to section 26 rights complied with constitutional requirements. The reasonable measures test was subsequently applied in the later *TAC* case in the Constitutional Court (2002). Creamer (2002:11, based on Budlender) summarises the test of reasonableness emerging from jurisprudence, as set out in Box 2.4 (pg 65).

## BOX 2.4: THE REASONABLE MEASURES TEST

A government programme seeking to deliver socio-economic rights may be considered a *reasonable measure* if:

- the programme is reasonable both in its inception and in its implementation;
- the programme is balanced and flexible;
- it makes appropriate provision for crises and gives attention to short-, medium- and long-term needs;
- the programme does not exclude a significant segment of society; and
- the programme takes into account the degree and extent of the denial of the right it is trying to realise. It does not ignore those whose needs are most urgent.

For the purposes of this study, the judgment of the Constitutional Court in the *Grootboom* case is valuable for its introduction of the reasonable measures paradigm. However, it is also important for what the court said specifically about the scope of section 28(1)(c) rights and the state's obligations in relation to these rights. The *Grootboom* dispute was first heard in the Cape High Court before it went on appeal in the Constitutional Court. The Constitutional Court argument on the scope of section 28(1)(c) rights and the associated state obligations is best understood in the context of the High Court's judgment in this regard.

In the High Court decision, Judge Davis adopted a broad and progressive interpretation of the scope of section 28(1)(c) rights and the state's associated obligations. He argued that the right to shelter in section 28(1)(c) entitled children to an immediate and direct claim against the state to provide services to meet their need for shelter. Moreover, that "parents enjoyed a derivative right to be accommodated with their children in the aforesaid shelter, based on a joint reading of sections 28(1)(b), 28(1)(c) and 28(2). According to Davis J. it would not be in the children's best interests to break up the family unit without justification" (cited in Liebenberg 2003:12). The court granted a supervisory jurisdiction, ordering the respondents to report back to it on the implementation of the order and giving the applicants an opportunity to deliver commentary on the state's report. The court refrained from being prescriptive as to the exact services to be provided, but provisionally indicated what basic services would constitute the bare minimum.

In the *Grootboom* judgment, the Constitutional Court rejected the argument that all children in need of shelter and their parents have a direct claim against the state for the realisation of the right to shelter in section 28. Instead, the court suggested that only children physically removed from their family environment are entitled to a direct claim against the state under section 28(1)(c). The court argued that the primary duty to fulfil a child's socio-economic rights rests on that child's parents or family: "[T]he obligation...is imposed primarily on the parents or family and only alternatively on the State" (Constitutional Court 2000:77). Moreover, it held that that while the state does have obligations under section 28(1)(c), these are limited to:

- firstly, providing the legal and administrative infrastructure necessary to ensure that children enjoy the protection afforded in section 28; and

- secondly, fulfilling the qualified obligations in sections 25, 26 and 27 (Constitutional Court 2002:G at 78).

In the wake of the *Grootboom* judgment, this view of the scope of section 28(1)(c) rights was criticised. This is because it implied that poor children living with their families are not entitled to claim anything tangible from the state for the realisation of their section 28 rights, even when parents are prevented by material destitution to provide the level of care required to fulfil their primary obligation.

The later judgment of the Constitutional Court in the *Treatment Action Campaign* case (2002) has been cited as suggesting a wider interpretation of the scope of section 28 rights (see for example Creamer 2002:9). Such a wider interpretation would place an obligation on the state to provide for the socio-economic rights not only of children physically removed from their parents, but also of all children living in indigent households. With reference to section 28, the court (2002:79) held as follows:

> "The state is obliged to ensure that children are accorded the protection con-templated by section 28 that arises when the implementation of the right to parental or family care is lacking. Here we are concerned with children born in public hospitals and clinics to mothers who are for the most part indigent and unable to gain access to private medical treatment which is beyond their means. They and their children are in the main dependent upon the state to make health care services available to them."

This wider interpretation regarding which children have a direct claim against the state for the realisation of their section 28(1)(c) and 29(1)(a) socio-economic rights, would accord well with Budlender's view on the relative responsibilities of parents and the state. Using the example of health care services, he argues (in Creamer 2002:31):

> "1. Parents have the primary duty to care for their children, and to meet their needs. They must therefore ensure that their children obtain the basic health care services which are their right.
>
> 2. The primary duties of the state in this regard are to: create and enforce a legal framework which places those legal duties on the parents, and take progressive measures in terms of section 27 (1)(a) and (2) which will enable the parents to fulfil their duties.
>
> 3. In the nature of things, parents cannot be the health care service providers. Their duty is to do what they can to ensure that their children obtain these services. If they can afford to pay for the services, they must do so. If they cannot pay, the parents must ensure that their children are taken to state clin-ics etc., for treatment.
>
> 4. The state must provide and pay for the services for those children whose par-ents cannot provide for them..."

In the *TAC* case, it is important that the Constitutional Court appears to broaden its view of the scope of section 28(1)(c) rights, as Liebenberg (2003 and personal correspondence) points out. However, with the exception of certain references to the *Grootboom* case, the *TAC* judgment did not go any further in defining exactly what entitlements indigent children can claim from the state under section 28(1)(c). Nor did it argue that all indigent children have a direct entitlement to Nevirapine by virtue of their rights under this section. Although children were seen as dependent on the state to make health care services available to them, the court defined the state's duties in terms of the qualified section 27 obligations, not in terms of individual rights to direct entitlements under section 28(1)(c). Using the reasonable measures test, it found that government's programme to prevent mother-to-child transmission of HIV violated the rights of children and their mothers to health services under section 27.

The *TAC* case thus did little to clarify the issue of the nature of the state's obligations under section 28(1)(c) and by implication, section 29(1)(a). Taking a collective view on the Constitutional Court's decisions regarding socio-economic rights thus far, the scope and nature of the state's obligations under section 28(1)(c) and 29(1)(a) remain unclear. Box 2.5 provides a summary of the main points that have emerged thus far from Constitutional Court jurisprudence regarding the nature and scope of state obligations to deliver unqualified child socio-economic rights.

---

**BOX 2.5: INFERENCES FROM CONSTITUTIONAL COURT JURISPRUDENCE THUS FAR ON THE NATURE AND SCOPE OF STATE OBLIGATIONS TO GIVE EFFECT TO UNQUALIFIED CHILD SOCIO-ECONOMIC RIGHTS**

- In *Grootboom*, the court took a conservative view of the scope of section 28 rights and the state's obligations in relation to these rights. It rejected the view that all children in need plus their parents have direct entitlements against the state for section 28(1)(c) and 29(1)(a) rights. Only children without parental care were seen to have such a claim against the state.

- In the *TAC* case, the scope of the application of section 28(1)(c) and 29(1)(a) rights seems to have been broadened, to include all indigent children.

- Critically however, the question of what children are entitled to claim from the state under sections 28(1)(c) and 29(1)(a) has been left hanging.

---

In reviewing and defining the state's obligations in relation to section 26 and 27 rights, the court chose to adopt the reasonableness review paradigm. It used the reasonable measures test set out in Box 2.4 to decide whether government was meeting its obligations. The court rejected the minimum core argument, according to which poor people would be seen as entitled to an immediate claim against the state for tangible services to give effect to a basic level of the rights given in sections 26 and 27 (see Liebenberg 2003). In explaining what the reasonable measures test requires of government, the court has largely refrained from commenting on the speed at which services have to be delivered to give effect to socio-economic rights. In *Grootboom* however, it was made clear that the Constitution at least obligates the state to *build sufficient* financial and administrative capacity to give effect to socio-economic rights.[16]

In the context of such uncertainty, Creamer (2002) has drawn on input from Budlender and Brand to present a useful proposal about how the Constitutional Court may be expected to review government's measures to give effect to section 28(1)(c) and 29(1)(a) socio-economic rights. It suggests, firstly, that the Constitution can be seen to impose an obligation on government to absolutely prioritise the basic rights of children set out in sections 28 and 29 (Brand and Creamer in Creamer 2002:5). Further to this, the scope of these rights should be understood to cover all children in need (Creamer 2002:9). Secondly, it can be taken as unlikely that the Constitutional Court, in making a judgment based on the rights of children in sections 28(1)(c) and 29(1)(a), would use the existing reasonableness review paradigm. But, because of the unqualified nature of the state's obligations in relation to these rights, the court would be likely to apply a *higher standard* of reasonableness in assessing programmes for the advancement of these rights:

> "Such higher standard would impact on both the speed and scope of the programmes...In particular, criteria are likely to include the requirement for rapid implementation of such programmes and the requirement that programmes are effectively constructed to reach all children in need...the reasonable time period which should be regarded as concomitant with the state's obligation to absolutely prioritise these rights, will be measured in terms of the time period required for the urgent marshalling of real administrative capacity, rather than any delay being justified in terms of a constraint of financial resources" (Creamer 2002:14, 27).

There is particular significance in this view of how the Constitutional Court would interpret the unqualified obligation on the state to deliver section 28(1)(c) and 29(1)(a) rights and apply the reasonable measures test to assess programmes designed to advance these rights. It suggests that the state should be held accountable for putting in place, as a matter of priority, programmes to realise the socio-economic rights given to children in sections 28(1)(c) and 29(1)(a). Moreover, government in this view also has the obligation to cater for *all children in need* in such programmes and to roll out services from relevant programmes as a matter of urgency and as quickly *as the building of administrative capacity permits* (irrespective of financial considerations).[17]

It must be stressed that this argument about how the Constitutional Court would interpret the state's obligations under section 28(1)(c) and 29(1)(a) has the status of a recommendation (Budlender, cited in Creamer 2002:9; Liebenberg & Creamer in comments on this chapter). It is not certain, for example, whether the court would in fact accept that the unqualified nature of the state's obligations in relation to these rights means that financial resources only have a limited role in determining the pace of rolling out corresponding programmes (Budlender, cited in Creamer 2002:9). Likewise, it cannot be predicted whether the court might in fact adopt a more progressive approach than that suggested by Creamer. For instance, it might adopt the view that the rights in sections 28(1)(c) and 29(1)(a) entitle all children in need to a direct claim against the state for the immediate provision of commodities that will allow them to meet their basic needs (see Liebenberg 2003).

Liebenberg (2003 and in comments on this chapter) has stressed that even if Creamer's recommendation is accepted as reasonable and its implied view of state obligations is allowed to inform the monitoring of government actions, it remains important to consider and highlight its negative implications for poor children. In this regard, it should be noted that Creamer's interpretation of Constitutional Court jurisprudence implies that poor children are unable to claim anything tangible from the state under section 28(1)(c) and 29(1)(a). All a child in need would be entitled to claim is a reasonable programme (that passes the higher level reasonable measures test), one that may or may not (in the face of real world administrative constraints) result in the short-term realisation of his or her relevant basic rights. Another problem is that it is very difficult and time-consuming to prove, through litigation, that government is not fulfilling its obligations to a particular child or group of children if the obligation on government is to implement a programme that passes the higher standard reasonable measures test (see Liebenberg 2003). These are strong reasons to advocate for the more progressive interpretation of the state's obligation to realise the unqualified socio-economic rights given to children in the Constitution.

It remains to be seen whether the Constitutional Court will interpret the state's obligation as one of having to implement a reasonable programme or as a duty to immediately provide services to give effect to each of the unqualified socio-economic rights given to children. Even so, the fact remains that in practice the rate of delivery will depend on programme delivery capacity. Thus, it is critically important to advocate for the building of state institutional capacity to deliver services to poor children as one dimension of what is needed to facilitate the fulfilment of government's obligations in relation to child socio-economic rights.

# 4. GOVERNMENT STRATEGIES TO MEET ITS SOCIO-ECONOMIC RIGHTS OBLIGATIONS, 1994 TO 2003

"In order to reverse the rising debt trend, we have been prudent about overall spending, putting the emphasis firmly on reprioritisation and better quality of expenditure. Now we can reinforce public service delivery without threatening fiscal sustainability, and our children and grandchildren can look forward to a future unencumbered by debt... So that the tree bears not the bitter but the sweet fruit of liberty."
*Finance Minister Trevor Manuel (National Treasury 2001a:6)*

Two leading development strategy statements have largely framed the budgetary and programming measures government has taken since 1994 to reduce poverty and give effect to the child-specific and other socio-economic rights in the Constitution. The first of these is the *Reconstruction and Development Programme* (RDP) of 1994.[18] The second is the *Growth, Employment and Redistribution* (GEAR) Strategy, released by the Department of Finance in 1996 (Streak & Wehner 2002:6). The implementation period of GEAR was from 1996 to 2000 (this is the period for which predictions of key economic variables were made). These two leading development strategy statements were designed to achieve the central goals of reducing poverty and inequality in South Africa. As such, they were not explicitly formulated in terms of delivering the child-specific or general socio-economic rights contained in the Constitution. Clearly however, a close correlation can be drawn between the reduction of poverty and the realisation of children's socio-economic rights. Thus the arguments in these strategy documents about how to reduce poverty are reflective of government's approach to advancing child socio-economic rights, including child-specific constitutional rights.

GEAR is yet to be replaced officially by another policy document outlining post-GEAR development strategy. However, since the end of 2000 (the end of the GEAR implementation period), government's approach shows important new aspects, most of these favourable from a child socio-economic rights perspective. The new aspects of government's development strategy (which is discussed further below) can be seen to emerge in the *State of the Nation Addresses, Medium-Term Budget Policy Statements, Budget Speeches* and *Budget Reviews* from 2001 to 2003.

Up until November 2002, the key speeches made by the Minister of Finance follow the RDP and GEAR in having poverty reduction and redistribution, rather than the realisation of socio-economic rights, as their central objective. However, in the November 2002 *Medium-Term Policy Statement* (MTBPS), the socio-economic rights in the Constitution were mentioned (for the first time) in government's explanation of its plans to promote development.[19] In the 2003 *Budget Speech* and *Budget Review*, the realisation of socio-economic rights is moved even further into the centre stage as an objective of government's budget and development strategy. For example, the *Budget Review* (National Treasury 2003b:14) states:

> "The underlying objectives of the medium term expenditure framework are growth and development and the progressive realisation of the social and economic rights of our people."

## 4.1 OVERVIEW OF THE RDP APPROACH TO POVERTY REDUCTION

The *RDP Base Document* is rooted firmly in post-Keynesian economics. It was ambitious and optimistic about the potential for government to use the budget and the broader state apparatus to reduce poverty quickly by allocating public resources to and implementing a wide range of programmes targeted at delivering social services to the poor. The key message of the *RDP Base Document* was that an ANC-led government would rapidly reduce poverty and inequality through large-scale government investment in and implementation of a range of public sector programmes and projects that would create jobs and extend services to the poor.

The subsequent *RDP White Paper* reveals the same essence as the *RDP Base Document*: government would lead poverty reduction by spending heavily on public programmes that would deliver services to the poor. However in the *RDP White Paper*, government embraced a number of more orthodox arguments about what needs to be done to ensure sustainable poverty reduction. Most notably, it argued that the objectives of redistribution and poverty reduction could only be met in the long term by adopting fiscal prudence and reducing the high levels of debt accumulated before 1994 (Republic of South Africa 1994:21). The public programmes put forward in the RDP as a means to meet basic needs reflected a prioritisation of children, particularly young children.

## 4.2 OVERVIEW OF THE **GEAR** APPROACH TO POVERTY REDUCTION

The GEAR strategy was somewhat more firmly rooted in a neo-liberal economic paradigm. GEAR acknowledged the important role of spending on and implementing social programmes (including programmes relating to social assistance, health, welfare[20], public works and micro-economic finance) as one of the means to reducing poverty. Spending on and implementing programmes to provide basic services to the poor was thus identified as a crucial part of what had to be done in South Africa to alleviate poverty and give effect to the socio-economic rights in the Constitution. However, this mechanism played second fiddle to employment-creation through private investment. More specifically, the GEAR strategy identified and presented economic growth, led by private sector investment, as the most important vehicle for reducing poverty. The mechanism for translating economic growth into poverty reduction was job creation, led by private sector investment (Michie & Padayachee 1998:628).[21]

Critically, the GEAR strategy drew a link between poverty reduction and conservative economic policy, in the form of budget deficit reduction and restrictive monetary policy. Very low levels of budget deficits and inflation were presented as crucial to facilitate growth, employment and poverty reduction by generating lower interest rates, building confidence and igniting the private sector investment engine (Weeks 1999:801; Streak 2004:4-5).[22] The GEAR strategy showed greater awareness of potential government failure (for example inefficiency arising from corruption, poor communication systems, lack of human and administrative capacity). Hence it emphasised the need to build the state's capacity to deliver and linked this to spending on programmes that provide services to the poor. A key argument of the GEAR strategy was that rapid poverty reduction would require increases in the efficiency of public spending, or budget reform.

## 4.3 GOVERNMENT PROGRAMMING TO ADVANCE CHILD SOCIO-ECONOMIC RIGHTS

Under the RDP and particularly the GEAR strategy, government's approach to delivering constitutional socio-economic rights (including child-specific socio-economic rights) has involved a heavy reliance on the market (the indirect channel of delivery). At the same time however, it has used an extensive array of direct measures. These have included various legal reform initiatives and most importantly in this context, the financing and implementation of a broad range of programmes aimed at giving the poor (including poor children) services to meet their basic needs. Some of the programmes used by government after 1994 as a means to deliver child socio-economic rights were simply carried over from the previous administration. However, government also extended some existing programmes and implemented a range of new programmes. The plethora of programmes giving effect to the child-specific socio-economic rights in the Constitution includes those targeted only at children, as well as more general programmes targeted at poor families or households. A comprehensive list of the relevant programmes is too long for this chapter. In the monitoring chapters to follow, more details are provided on the range and content of the different programmes in place to advance child socio-economic rights. The list below is confined to the main government programmes giving effect to child-specific constitutional socio-economic rights, focusing only on those targeted specifically at children:

- Social assistance programmes transfer income to the care-gives of eligible children. These programmes include the Child Support Grant, the Care Dependency Grant and the Foster Care Grant (see chapters three and five).

- The Primary School Feeding Scheme provides children in targeted schools with a meal per school day as a means to improve nutrition and education outcomes. In principle, this programme provides an early morning nutritious supplementary meal comprising not less than 25% of the recommended daily allowance of energy for 7 to 10 year olds and not less than 20% of recommended daily allowance of energy for 11 to 14 year olds (see chapter three).

- Various programmes provide free health services to poor children (see chapter four).

- Programmes relating to Early Childhood Development, General Education and Training, as well as Education for Learners with Special Needs provide basic education to children (see chapter six).[23]

In the early 1990s, government also put in place a National Programme of Action for Children, an umbrella co-ordinating programme that aims to ensure that children and child rights are prioritised in policy, budgets and service delivery (see Box 2.6 below). However, it is crucial to note that there is as yet, in practice, no systematic process for prioritising child-specific and other socio-economic rights in government's policy formulation, budget allocation process or programme implementation (see Creamer 2002:19-20). Even though the Constitution's socio-economic rights should be used as a benchmark to direct government programming for children, there is as yet no effective process linking, tracking and evaluating government's programme development, budget allocations and service delivery in relation to the child socio-economic rights obligations in the Constitution. It is worth quoting Brand and Creamer on this point:

> "The pith of socio-economic rights is the fact that they determine the goals, also the goals according to which the state must budget...The choice of exact allocation, to particular items and needs is the state's to make, as long as it moves within the bounds of reasonableness when doing so...But what the goals

of allocation are, is not something that can be decided in a vacuum by the state" (Brand in Creamer 2002:20).

"....nowhere in the budget process are government's socio-economic rights obligations in general, or its socio-economic rights obligations to children in particular, explicitly taken into account and planned for" (Creamer 2002:20).

## BOX 2.6 THE NATIONAL PROGRAMME OF ACTION FOR CHILDREN

The NPA was developed by government and a broad spectrum of civil society organisations in the early 1990s to advance child rights in South Africa. It was formally launched on 16 June 1994 when President Mandela was presented with the outline of the NPA at Orlando Stadium in Soweto (Cassiem & Streak 2001:54). The NPA is currently located in and managed by the Office on the Status of the Child, within the Presidency.

According to the policy statements of the NPA, its objective is to advance child rights by helping to ensure that children are prioritised in policy making, budget allocations and public service delivery. Its mission is articulated in the statement "Put children first" (Republic of South Africa 2000). As a means to realise this objective and mission, the NPA engages in four main activities, referred to in NPA policy documents as "the main project groups". These are:

- communication and information-sharing relating to child rights;

- advocacy, participation and mobilisation for child rights realisation;

- research, policy review, reporting and evaluation on child rights implementation; and

- child rights data-collection and monitoring (Ibid).

Three main government structures are tasked with the effective implementation of the NPA. Firstly, the National Programme of Action Steering Committee is tasked with the overall co-ordination and monitoring of NPA activities. Secondly, Provincial Programmes of Action (PPAs) have responsibility for carrying out NPA activities at the provincial level. Thirdly, there are eight "priority area groups" that focus on the cross-cutting "special issues" of HIV/AIDS, gender and disability but also on one of the following: special protection measures, education, early childhood development, child and maternal health, nutrition, leisure and recreation, as well as peace and non-violence (Ibid).

It is important to make two final points about government's programming to give effect to child socio-economic rights. Firstly, for policy design and monitoring purposes, the programmes targeted specifically at children must be viewed as a holistic package. The inter-dependence between the realisation of the different child socio-economic rights means that even if a programme is targeted primarily at one particular child socio-economic right, it can have positive spin-offs in terms of helping to realise other child socio-economic rights. For example, programmes providing income to the parents of poor children are directed primarily at giving effect to the right to social assistance. However, the income transfers are also important for helping to deliver the right to basic education and health services because insufficient income is often an obstacle to accessing the latter services. Chapter one offers more discussion on the inter-linkages between programmes giving affect to different child-specific socio-economic rights. Secondly, when looking into the way government works to advance child socio-economic rights, it is important also to consider programmes giving effect to the rights of poor children's parents. As confirmed by the views of poor children presented in chapter one, the realisation of child socio-economic rights is tightly wound up with the poverty and rights situation of parents.

## 4.4 THE GEAR LEGACY AND EMERGING "POST-GEAR" STRATEGY

There has been a great deal of debate over the success of government's poverty reduction strategy as expressed in GEAR.[24] The debate has taken place in the context of failure in meeting the targets for employment-creation, economic growth and private sector investment as presented in the GEAR strategy, but success in realising the targets set for debt and interest rate reduction. The performance of the economy in the implementation period of GEAR is summarised in Tables 2.1 and 2.2 below.

**TABLE 2.1 GEAR PREDICTIONS FOR KEY VARIABLES (1996 TO 2000)**

|  | 1996 | 1997 | 1998 | 1999 | 2000 | Average 1996-2000 |
|---|---|---|---|---|---|---|
| GDP growth (real) | 3.5 | 2.9 | 3.8 | 4.9 | 6.1 | 4.2 |
| Inflation (CPI) | 8.0 | 9.7 | 8.1 | 7.7 | 7.6 | 8.2 |
| Fiscal deficit | -5.1 | -4.0 | -3.5 | -3.0 | -3.0 | -3.7 |
| Employment growth | 1.3 | 3.0 | 2.7 | 3.5 | 4.3 | 2.9 |
| Private sector investment growth | 9.3 | 9.1 | 9.3 | 13.9 | 17.0 | 11.7 |

**Source:** Department of Finance 1996.

**TABLE 2.2 ACTUAL OUTCOMES FOR GEAR PERIOD (1996 - 2000 AND 2001)**

|  | 1996 | 1997 | 1998 | 1999 | 2000 | 2001 | Average 1996-2000 |
|---|---|---|---|---|---|---|---|
| GDP growth (real) | 4.2 | 2.5 | 0.8 | 2.1 | 3.4 | 2.2 | 2.5 |
| Inflation (CPI)* | 7.4 | 8.6 | 6.9 | 5.2 | 5.3 | 6.6 | 6.6 |
| Fiscal deficit** | -4.6 | -3.8 | -2.3 | -2.0 | -2.0 | -1.4 | -2.9 |
| Employment growth | -0.6 | -1.7 | -3.4 | -2 | -2.7 |  | -2.0 |
| Private sector investment growth | 7.7 | 4.8 | -1.8 | -3.3 | 6.4 | 5.3 | 2.7 |

**Source:** Streak 2004: Table 2.

**Notes:**

i. CPIX had to be used to indicate inflation in 2001, as CPI for that year was omitted in the 2002 *Budget Review*.

ii. The data on the fiscal deficit as a percentage of GDP use the main budget deficit and is for financial years.

This publication does not tackle the question of whether GEAR was a success or failure. For the purposes of this study, it is more useful to put the spotlight on the critical challenges and opportunities left by GEAR, as well as the changes in government's strategy for delivering child socio-economic rights and reducing child poverty in the post-GEAR implementation period.

The first important aspect of the GEAR legacy worth noting is that poverty remains extensive and deep in South Africa (see chapter one). Moreover, the rapid reduction of poverty and the concomitant realisation of socio-economic rights will depend heavily on government developing more direct measures in the near future (such as job-creation projects and new social security programmes). Despite favourable conditions for attracting private sector investment, critics in the debate over the success of GEAR (see footnote 26) have pointed out that a surge in private sector investment cannot be relied on to generate many jobs for the poor (Bhorat et al 2001:9; Streak 2004:19; Department of Social Development 2002:70).

Secondly, it is important to note that the public sector debt reduction and budget reform initiatives implemented in the late 1990s under the auspices of GEAR, have placed government in a better position to facilitate the realisation of socio-economic rights through direct measures as we move into the future. There are still complex administrative and human resource capacity constraints in the public sector. However, public sector administrative capacity has seen improvement and government's financial position is more conducive to raising the level of government spending. The state now has more resource power, in our Finance Minister's words, to facilitate the enjoyment of the "sweet fruit of liberty" (National Treasury 2001a:5).

The third important aspect of the GEAR legacy is that, in the context of government's improved fiscal position, it is now more inclined towards using direct measures to help alleviate poverty and deliver child socio-economic rights.

How has development strategy changed in the wake of the GEAR implementation period? One shift – one that has been much noted – is an increased emphasis on micro-economic as opposed to macro-economic reform as a means to facilitate more rapid development (see Samson 2002; Streak 2004). Another shift – even more important in this context – is a more expansionary (yet still prudent) fiscal stance (adopted since Budget 2001), with prioritisation being given to infrastructure and basic services for the poor (particularly for children) in the allocation of new spending (Idasa 2002; National Treasury 2003b; Streak 2003). The following summary of the Medium-Term Expenditure Framework for 2003/04 to 2005/06 in the 2002 MTBPS (National Treasury 2002c:6) illustrates this new expansionary pro-poor stance in fiscal policy:

> "Building on the focus on poverty reduction and infrastructure investments in the 2001 and 2002 Budgets, next year's MTEF will allocate substantial additional resources to social security, health, education and the provision of basic water, electricity and other household services."

The 2003 Budget revealed even further evidence of a more expansionary fiscal stance, with government giving priority to investment in programmes delivering services to the poor (particularly poor children). In this, National Treasury presented an MTEF framework that incorporated a large increase in government expenditure, substantial tax relief and an increase in the planned budget deficit to GDP ratio (See National Treasury 2003b; Idasa 2003; Streak 2003).[25] In the distribution of new government investment, the prioritised sectors included welfare, health and community services. At the programme level, particularly large investments were made in social assistance (most notably the Child Support Grant) and basic services delivered by municipalities.

Attached to government's more expansionary fiscal stance, the "post-GEAR" development strategy reflects a greater focus on investigating the more effective use of direct measures to create jobs and deliver basic services to the poor. The latter trend can be seen, for example, in the government's appointment of the Taylor Committee, which was tasked to examine the social security system in South Africa with a view to extending it (Department of Social Development 2002). Government has also extended two of its leading programmes offering services to realise child socio-economic rights, namely the Child Support Grant programme and the Primary School Feeding Scheme. The exact details of these extensions are covered in the chapters dealing with the rights to social services (chapter five) and basic nutrition (chapter three).

# 5. Conclusion: Deriving a monitoring framework

How can the discussion above be translated into a method for monitoring the measures taken by government to give effect to child specific socio-economic rights? The broad monitoring approach adopted in this publication is guided by (though not exclusively based on) the three-step logical sequence suggested by Creamer (2002:21). He has argued that this sequence best reflects the current interpretation of the Constitutional Court in its evolving jurisprudence on socio-economic rights:

- First, develop an understanding of children's socio-economic rights, as these are the constitutionally-prescribed goals of government policy;

- Secondly, identify which government programmes are being used as instruments for the achievement of these goals; and

- Thirdly, analyse whether these programmes reasonably meet government's constitutional obligations to realise children's socio-economic rights.

There are four chapters in this publication that monitor government's measures in relation to child socio-economic rights. Each covers a different socio-economic right given only or primarily to children in the Constitution. Chapters three, four and five focus on the rights given to children in section 28(1)(c). They monitor, respectively, government's measures to give effect to the right to basic nutrition, basic health care services and social services.[26] Chapter six monitors government's measures to give effect to the right to basic education as stipulated in section 29(1)(a). Box 2.7 sets out the generic mode of enquiry that guides the analysis in all four chapters.

## BOX 2.7 MODE OF ENQUIRY GUIDING THE ANALYSIS IN CHAPTERS THREE TO SIX

- **Step one:** The chapter first investigates the meaning and scope of the right in question. In the process, this section highlights why it is so important to reach a consensus and a clearer understanding of what (which) children are entitled to under the rights given only or primarily to children in the Constitution.

- **Step two:** The chapter then identifies the key programmes in place to give effect to the right under the spotlight. It provides a broad description of these programmes, focusing on the services the programme aims to provide, the beneficiaries it aims to reach and government's time-schedule for rolling out services.

- **Step three:** Finally, the chapter interrogates the sufficiency (not reasonableness) of some of the key relevant programmes by asking and answering the following questions about programme conceptualisation and implementation:

  i. Is the *conceptualisation* of the programme such that all children in need are targeted beneficiaries, that the most vulnerable children are specifically targeted and that services are to be rolled out as a matter of urgency and as quickly as administrative capacity seems to facilitate?

  ii. How much has government budgeted for the programme (annually) since programme inception and what are the budgeted and estimated allocations for the MTEF period 2003/04 to 2005/06? What percentage of total expenditure budgeted for in the budget flowed to the programme in 2002/03 and is destined to flow to the programme over the MTEF period 2003/04 to 2005/06?

  iii. Have funds allocated to the programme been spent or has there been wastage in the programme due to non-spending of budgets?

  iv. Is programme *implementation* such that services are being rolled out to all children in need, particularly those whose needs are most urgent? Are services being rolled out as a matter of urgency and as quickly as administrative capacity permits?

  v. What are the (financial and non-financial) problems that undermine the provision of programme services to all children in need (and particularly to the most vulnerable)?

  vi. What measures are being taken by government to overcome service delivery problems (particularly in the form of building administrative capacity)? What recommendations can be made regarding proposed adjustments and improvements to government's planned measures?

A central challenge in deriving an appropriate monitoring method for this publication was to develop the set of research questions for interrogating the sufficiency of government's programmes. It was essential for these questions to be rigorous and useful, as well as lending themselves to analysis that could be undertaken in practice (step three).

In trying to meet this challenge, the Constitutional Court's reasonable measures test offered some guidance. This came largely from the set of broad questions, derived by Creamer from the reasonable measures test, pertaining to government programmes that aim to give effect to the unqualified rights given to children in the Constitution (refer to the reasonable measures test and its suggested extension in section 3 of this chapter). The test itself, as outlined by the court, only has limited usefulness for the purposes of developing the kind of monitoring method required in this study. The test cannot easily be taken out of the context in which it arose, namely of the Constitutional Court pronouncing on the assessment of government programmes. The bullet points below explain why the court's reasonable measures test cannot readily be translated into an adequate benchmark, to be used by child rights activists and researchers for monitoring government's programmes. The following problems make it difficult to operationalise the set of questions flowing from the reasonable measures test in a rigorous way:

- First, the way the test is formulated means that it requires further interpretation before application. The Constitutional Court can apply the test to various sets of circumstances by constructing its exact meaning from the specifics of a case before it. Researchers concerned with monitoring do not have this advantage. They can try to extrapolate from existing jurisprudence how the court might concretise these terms in the light of their own research objectives, but this exercise remains to a large extent speculative and subjectivity is bound to creep in. By way of example, in monitoring work, questions need to be formulated to assess exactly under what circumstances a programme is being reasonably implemented. It would seem logical here that researchers would need to ask whether the size of budgets is sufficient to roll out services rapidly to all children in need, and whether administrative procedures facilitate access for all children, especially those most in need. They would also need to assess whether the tangible level and quality of the service provided by a programme to a child beneficiary is sufficient for the delivery of a right. However, it cannot be claimed for certain that these are the questions that the reasonable measures test calls on researchers to ask in their attempt to shed light on the sufficiency of government's programmes to give effect to a particular child socio-economic right. It is also not clear – and this is a crucial point – what level of services children are entitled to under each right, or for that matter, what level they *should* be entitled to in order to facilitate the realisation of that right.

- Secondly, there are data obstacles associated with addressing the questions that the test suggests we ask of government programmes. For instance, survey data are too dated to establish with certainty the current number of children in South Africa, let alone to establish the target beneficiaries for programmes such as the Child Support Grant (CSG) and the Primary School Feeding Scheme (PSFS).

While government is improving its beneficiary data (for example by providing output targets in budget documentation) it often remains difficult to obtain data on how many children are actually receiving benefits from key programmes. A classic example here is the Home- and Community-Based Care and Support programme.

- Thirdly, there are time and capacity constraints associated with implementing the questions raised by the test. For example, it may typically take in excess of two years for a researcher to cost the implementation of just a single child rights programme.[27] At the same time, the costing of implementation makes only one small contribution to answering just one of the questions asked by the reasonable measures test. As another example, consider what would be involved in answering whether the level of service provided is such that a programme "does not leave out of account the degree and extent of the denial of the right it endeavours to realise". This would involve establishing whether the range and level of services provided by the Primary Health Services programme, for instance, is such that it generates a benefit sufficient to meet the right to basic health services of many children with different health needs. Here researchers would initially be confronted with the challenge of having to establish the exact content of children's right to basic health services. Next they would have to tackle the exceedingly difficult task of establishing what the different needs of children are that government needs to fill, and through which services, in order to assess whether the standard set by the content of the right is met for each child.

Against this background, it is clear that the questions suggested by the reasonable measures test cannot mechanistically and rigorously be applied by researchers to monitor government's performance. However, it is important to make explicit how the questions contained in step three of the monitoring framework described above relate to the reasonable measures test.

The development of the monitoring framework started from the premise that it would be impossible to use the test rigorously to assess whether a programme passes constitutional muster (and this is a function only the Constitutional Court can fulfil). Yet it was important to draw on the test to decide how to interrogate the sufficiency of government's programmes. After all, the test provides a set of broad questions that helps identify key features of government programmes to focus attention on. In addition, building some synergy with the test was seen to add to the credibility and hence the impact of the information generated in this study. In order to make an effective contribution, research efforts emanating from civil society must engage with the legal debate and with evolving Constitutional Court jurisprudence. It is hoped that this will ultimately lead to the Constitutional Court clarifying the exact nature of state obligations and how best to monitor them. However at the same time, there was a clear need to steer clear of pursuing the impossible task of trying to address all the questions raised by the test and mechanistically generating an answer to whether programmes are reasonable or not. Furthermore, this study makes no attempt to address some very difficult (in the sense of time and data constraints), if critical, questions raised by the test. For example, it does not consider whether the amount budgeted for relevant programmes is sufficient to facilitate the roll-out of services to all children in need as rapidly as administrative capacity permits. Instead, two of the questions suggested by the test were selected and included in step three of the monitoring method (listed as i and iv above). These two questions are not only important; they are also the ones offering the best chance of being answered.[28] In addition, four further questions make up the sufficiency analysis of government's programme measures (listed as questions ii, iii, v and vi in Box 2.7). Their inclusion rests on the view that child rights researchers need not be limited to questions derived from the law and jurisprudence. To the contrary, there was a clear need to include questions that would generate information that would be useful to child rights advocates and/or would result in informed recommendations to assist government in improving its measures.

# REFERENCES

Adelzadeh, A. (1997) "From the RDP to GEAR: the gradual embracing of neo-liberalism in economic policy". In *Transformation*, 31: 66-95.

Annand, A. & M. Ravallion. (1993) "Human development in poor countries: On the role of private incomes and public services". In *Journal of Economic Perspectives*, 7(1): 133-150.

Bentley, K. (2003) *Concepts and Standards of Children's Rights: Some Considerations of Relativity and Enforcement.* Paper prepared for the Seminar on Statistics and Human Rights, Brussels, Belgium 27-29 November 2002.

Bhorat, H., M. Liebbrandt, M. Maziya, S. van der Berg & I. Woolard. (2001) *Fighting Poverty: Labour Markets and Inequality in South Africa.* Cape Town: University of Cape Town.

Cape High Court. (1999) *Grootboom v Oostenberg Municipality and Others.* Case No.6826/99, BCLR 2000(3) 277.

Cassiem, S. & J. Streak. (2001) *Budgeting for Child Socio-economic Rights: Government Obligations and the Child's Right to Social Security and Education.* Cape Town: Idasa.

Constitutional Court of South Africa. (1997) *Soobramoney v Minister of Health, KwaZulu-Natal.* 1998 (1) SA 765 (CC); 1997 (12) BCLR 1696 (CC).

Constitutional Court of South Africa. (2000) *Government of the Republic of South Africa and Others v Grootboom and Others.* 2001 (1) SA 46 (CC); 2000 (11) BCLR 1169 (CC).

Constitutional Court of South Africa. (2002) *Minister of Health and Others v Treatment Action Campaign and Others.* 2002 (5) SA 721, 2002 (10) BCLR 1033 (CC).

Creamer, K. (2002) *The Impact of South Africa's Evolving Jurisprudence on Children's Socio-Economic Rights on Budget Analysis.* Occasional Paper, December. Cape Town: Idasa Budget Information Service.[29]

Department of Finance. (1996) *Growth, Employment and Redistribution: A Macro-economic*

*Strategy.* Pretoria: Government Printer.

Department of Social Development. (2002) *Transforming the Present — Protecting the Future: Draft Consolidated Report of the Committee of Inquiry into a Comprehensive System of Social Security for South Africa.* Pretoria: Government Printer.

Institute for Democracy in South Africa. (2001) *Budget Information Service response to Budget 2001.* Submission to the Portfolio Committee on Finance and printed in *Budget Brief,* 59. Cape Town: Idasa.

Institute for Democracy in South Africa. (2002) *Response to Budget 2002: "A missed opportunity to alleviate the poverty crisis".* Submission to the Portfolio Committee on Finance.

Institute for Democracy in South Africa. (2003) *Idasa Statement on Budget 2003 — Great but the poor need more.* 27 February.

Liebenberg, S. & K. Pillay. (2000) *Socio-economic Rights in South Africa: A Resource Book.* Cape Town: Community Law Centre.

Liebenberg, S. (2001) "Violations of Socio-economic Rights: The Role of the South African Human Rights Commission". In P. Andrews & S. Ellmann (eds), *The Post-Apartheid Constitutions:* 405-443. Johannesburg: Witwatersrand University Press.

Liebenberg, S. (2003) "South Africa's Evolving Jurisprudence on Socio-economic Rights: An Effective Tool in Challenging Poverty?". Forthcoming in *Law, Democracy and Development.*

Manuel, T. & M. Ramos. (2002) *Presentation on Budget 2002 to the Portfolio Committee on Finance.* 21 February.

Michie, J. & V. Padayachee. (1998) "Three years after apartheid: growth, employment and redistribution?". In *Cambridge Journal of Economics,* 22: 623-635.

National Treasury. (2001a) *Budget Speech.* Pretoria: Government Printer.

National Treasury. (2001b) *Budget Review.* Pretoria: Government Printer.

National Treasury. (2001c) *Medium-Term Budget Policy Statement.* Pretoria: Government Printer.

National Treasury. (2002a) *Budget Speech.* Pretoria: Government Printer.

National Treasury. (2002b) *Budget Review.* Pretoria: Government Printer.

National Treasury. (2002c) *Medium-Term Budget Policy Statement.* Pretoria: Government Printer.

National Treasury. (2002d) *Minister Trevor Manuel's Address to the National Assembly on the*

*Introduction of the 2002 Medium-Term Budget Policy Statement and the 2002/03 Adjustments Appropriation Bill.* Pretoria: Government Printer.

National Treasury. (2003a) *Budget Speech.* Pretoria: Government Printer.

National Treasury. (2003b) *Budget Review.* Pretoria: Government Printer.

Proudlock, P. (2002) "Children's Socio-economic Rights: Do they have a right to special protection?". In *ESR Review,* 3 (2):6-8.

Republic of South Africa. (1994) *White Paper on Reconstruction and Development: Government's Strategy for Fundamental Transformation.* Pretoria: Government Printer.

Republic of South Africa. (1996) *The Constitution of the Republic of South Africa.* Act 108 of 1996.

Republic of South Africa. (2000) *National Programme of Action: 2000 & Beyond – An Assessment of the NPA and the Way Forward.* Pretoria: Presidency, Office on the Status of the Child.

Samson, M. (2002) "What can the Growth and Development Summit deliver?". In *Budget Watch,* April: 2.

Sloth-Nielsen, J. (2001) "The child's right to social services, the right to social security, and primary prevention of child abuse: Some conclusions in the aftermath of Grootboom". In *South African Journal of Human Rights,* 17(2):210-231.

Streak, J. (1997) "The Counter-counterrevolution in Development Theory on the Role of the State in Development: Inferences for South Africa?". In *Development Southern Africa,* 14(3), October.

Streak, J. (2003) "Child poverty, child rights and Budget 2003 – The right thing or a small step in the right direction?". In *Budget Brief,* 125. Cape Town: Idasa.

Streak, J. (2004) "The GEAR legacy: Did GEAR fail or move South Africa forward in development?". Forthcoming in *Development Southern Africa,* 21(2), June.

Streak, J. & J. Wehner. (2002) *Budgeting for Socio-Economic Rights in South Africa.* Applied Fiscal Research Centre (AFReC) Research Monograph, 24. Cape Town: AFReC, University of Cape Town.

Weeks, J. (1999) "Stuck in low GEAR? Macro-Economic Policy in South Africa, 1996-1998". In *Cambridge Journal of Economics,* 23:795-811.

World Bank. (1990) *World Development Report: The State in a Changing World.* New York: Oxford University Press.

# ENDNOTES

1   The authors would like to thank Christina Murray, Sandra Liebenberg, Kenneth Creamer, Shaamela Cassiem and Albert Van Zyl for their useful comments on early drafts of this chapter.

2   Act 108 of 1996 (hereafter referred to as the Constitution).

3   The full text of the CRC can be found on the internet at http://www.unicef.org/crc/crc.htm. The full text of the ACRWC is available at http://www.itcilo.it/english/actrav/telearn/global/ilo/law/afchild.htm.

4   The preamble to the Constitution states a commitment to "improve the quality of life of all citizens and free the potential of each person". In the words of Liebenberg (2001:408-409), "the Constitution establishes a framework of norms and institutions for the achievement of substantive (real and effective) human dignity, equality and freedom for the people of South Africa".

5   Liebenberg (2001) argues that the Constitution includes three categories of socio-economic rights. The first she refers to as a set of "basic rights" consisting of children's socio-economic rights given in section 28, the right of everyone to basic education and the socio-economic rights of detained persons, including sentenced prisoners.

6   Budlender (in Creamer 2002:27) stresses the need to note that in the *Grootboom* case, "the Constitutional Court appeared to decide otherwise".

7   This source was written before the *Grootboom* matter was heard.

8   Understandably, the Constitution says nothing explicit about the time schedule according to which these conditions have to be created. However, in this regard it is recognised that the socio-economic rights in the Constitution (including those in sections 28 and 29) do not give children the right to demand that the state provides houses and other material gains to realise their socio-economic rights overnight (see Brand and Creamer in Creamer 2002:14-15).

9   Article 1 of the ACRWC, on the obligations of state parties says: "Member States of the Organization of African Unity, Parties to the present Charter shall recognise the rights, freedoms and duties enshrined in this Charter and shall undertake the necessary steps, in accordance with their Constitutional processes and with the provisions of the present Charter, to adopt such legislative or other measures as may be necessary to give effect to the provisions of the Charter".

10  Section 39, titled Interpretation of the Bill of Rights, says:
    "(1) When interpreting the Bill of Rights, a court, tribunal or forum –
    a) must promote the values that underlie an open and democratic society based on human dignity, equality and freedom;
    b) must consider international law; and
    c) may consider foreign law."

11  The National Council of Provinces (NCOP) also represents provinces in the legislative process.

12  The institutions are commonly named after the chapter of the Constitution containing the provisions relating to their establishment, powers and functions.

13  Thus far, the Constitutional Court has dealt with three cases involving claims of non-delivery of socio-economic rights. In *Soobramoney*, the Court found that the state was not in breach of its obligations as set out under section 27 by denying

the provision of renal dialysis to a chronically ill patient. It argued that limited resources at times require "a holistic approach to the larger needs of society rather than to focus on the specific needs of particular individuals within society" (Constitutional Court 1997:31). The *Grootboom* case involved a group of homeless people demanding that government provide access to housing and shelter under sections 26 and 28 of the Constitution (Constitutional Court 2000). This claim was upheld on the basis that the state's housing policy, in this instance, failed to make reasonable provision within its available resources for people in that area who had no access to land, nor a roof over their heads, and were living in intolerable conditions. Most recently, the Treatment Action Campaign (TAC) and others challenged the government over the reasonableness of its programme to provide anti-retroviral drugs to pregnant mothers to prevent mother-to-child transmission of the human immuno-deficiency virus (HIV). This action was brought in terms of sections 27 and 28 of the Constitution. The court found in favour of the applicants on two grounds. Firstly, it held that government had unreasonably restricted the provision of the anti-retroviral drug Nevirapine to a limited number of pilot sites, when latent capacity already existed elsewhere for administering the drug. Secondly, the court found that government had not sufficiently provided for a broadening of the prerequisite programme capacity (Constitutional Court 2002:135). The analysis of Constitutional Court jurisprudence in this chapter only considers the *Grootboom* and TAC cases. The arguments of the court in these two cases have the most significant bearing on how to interpret the state's obligations to deliver child socio-economic rights and how to monitor the implementation of child socio-economic rights.

14  The court did offer some interpretation of the scope and meaning of section 28(1)(c) rights in the *Grootboom* Constitutional Court case.

15  The drafting of the BOR does not explicitly clarify whether social assistance is included under the right to social services given to children in section 28(1)(c). This question remains unresolved (see section one in chapter five for a more detailed discussion of this topic).

16  In *Grootboom*, the Constitutional Court (2000: paragraph 39) held as follows: "A reasonable program must…ensure that the appropriate financial and human resources are available".

17  This expert argument put forth by Creamer about the nature of the state's obligations to give effect to the rights in section 28(1)(c) and 29(1)(a) is a convincing one. However, Budlender (in Creamer 2002:9) and Proudlock (2002) warn that it should be kept in mind that the Constitutional Court itself has not yet given its view on "whether such rights must be realised progressively" (Budlender in Creamer 2002:9). Nor has it indicated whether the availability of financial resources has only a limited role to play in determining the rate at which government is obliged to deliver services to give effect to these rights.

18  The RDP programme was initially developed from the election manifesto of the liberation alliance under the banner of the African National Congress (ANC), also referred to as the RDP Base Document. After the electoral victory of the ANC, an RDP White Paper was released in September 1994 (Republic of South Africa 1994).

19  For example, the MTBPS stated: "…let us remain mindful of the Constitutional mandate that is the bedrock on which our strategy rests – the progressive realisa-

tion of social and economic rights, within secure and sustainable fiscal policy foundations" (National Treasury 2002d:7).

20    It is now more common to use the term 'social development' rather than 'welfare'. For the purposes of this discussion, no differentiation is made.

21    Economic theory and historical evidence suggest that when it comes to sustainable reductions in poverty, it may well be valid to assume that economic growth is more important than government provision of services through programmes. However, it is debatable whether the private sector can lead the process of poverty-reducing growth in a developing country like South Africa (See Streak 1997 & 2004; Michie & Padayachee 1998).

22    As noted by Michie and Padyachee (1998:628), when GEAR is compared to the RDP, it amounts to a down-playing of the role of government in initiating development and ensuring that private sector-led growth actually improves income opportunities for the poor.

23    The Early Childhood Development and General Education and Training programmes, together with Education for Learners with Special Needs, collectively provide a good proxy for "basic education" to children. As illustrated in chapter six, there are strong arguments to consider "basic education" as extending up to the age of 15 or the end of Grade 9, whichever comes first. However, it is important to note that the latter two programmes above also advance the education rights of children above the age of 15, or enrolled in grades 10 to 12.

24    On the one hand, government and a number of leading private sector economists argue that GEAR was a big success. Because GEAR was conducive to maintaining private sector investment and improving the efficiency of public sector spending, the argument is made that the trend in unemployment and poverty (including child poverty) in the late 1990s (see Streak 2004) would have been worse without it. Attention is also drawn to the way GEAR reduced high levels of government debt to very low levels, created a low and stable inflation rate and facilitated a drop in real interest rates. These factors, it is argued, created the macro-economic conditions necessary for sustainable poverty reduction in the future (see for example National Treasury 2001a:6 and Manuel & Ramos 2002). On the other hand, the trade union umbrella body Cosatu and some independent economists argue that GEAR failed dismally. Instead of leading to employment creation, growth, redistribution and poverty reduction, these commentators argue that it left the economy with slow rates of growth and failed to impact on income inequality, poverty or the employment crisis (see Streak 2004). These critics argue moreover that it is not surprising that GEAR failed as a poverty reduction (socio-economic rights realisation) strategy. In their opinion, it relied too much on indirect stimuli (deficit reduction and "sound macro-fundamentals") leading to poverty reduction through private sector employment creation, and too little on government directly reducing poverty and delivering socio-economic rights (for instance via public works and social assistance).

25    More specifically, the MTEF in Budget 2003 had aggregate non-interest government expenditure growing by 6.1% in 2003/04 and at an annual average of 5.4% over the period 2002/03-2005/06. In per capita terms, there was real growth in non-interest government expenditure of 5.0% in 2003/04 and an annual average of 4.3% between 2002/03 and 2005/06. The expansionary fiscal policy has not come at the expense of fiscal discipline and does not threaten to undermine the sustainability of poverty reduction in future.

26  In the analysis of government's measures to give effect to the right to social services, it is assumed that this right includes the right to social assistance. The chapter focuses on programmes to give effect to the latter. However, as has been pointed out by Liebenberg (personal correspondence) and Budlender (in Creamer 2002), whether or not the right to social services given in section 28(1)(c) includes social assistance has not been clarified.

27  The exception is probably social assistance programmes, where costing is less time-consuming, although also far from simple (Streak & Wehner 2002).

28  Due to the data problems, some researchers experienced difficulties even in answering these two chosen questions, particularly question iv. There is therefore still a need to advocate for better data and the building of capacity to improve monitoring in future.

29  For further information on this Occasional Paper contact judith@idasact.org.za or shaamela@idasact.org.za.

# CHAPTER THREE

Budgeting and service delivery in programmes
targeted at the child's right to basic nutrition

Danie Brand

# INTRODUCTION: CHILDREN'S NUTRITIONAL STATUS – AN ENDEMIC CRISIS

Even a cursory glance at the available figures shows that far too many South Africans, and particularly far too many South African children, regularly suffer what Constitutional Court Justice Tolakele Madala once called "the daily terrorism of hunger".[1]

Roughly 14 million South Africans are food insecure.[2] Thus approximately 37% of our population does not have regular and sustainable access to enough food of a good enough nutritional quality, that is both safe to eat and culturally acceptable to them (Mgijima 1999:60). This fact shows in food consumption patterns. A 1999 survey, for example, found that one in two children ingest less than half the recommended daily amounts of energy, vitamins A and C, iron, zinc and calcium (Labadarios 1999:242).[3] It also shows in what people have to say about their own lives. In 1998, 45% of the population in rural areas and 26% in metropolitan areas reported that they go hungry at least a few times a month. 17% of people living in rural areas reported going hungry at least once a week and 5% of those living in urban and semi-urban areas go hungry every day (CASE 1998:63).[4] Finally, it is also demonstrated by studies on the resources that South Africans can command to gain access to food through exchange. A recent study indicates that 42.6% of households in South Africa marshal so small an income that they are in "food poverty", unable to afford regularly even a basic subsistence diet (Caelers *et al* 2001:1).

The wide-spread lack of access to sufficient food experienced by South Africans has a clear and debilitating physical effect on children. 16% of South African babies are born underweight and amongst children under nine, 21.6% are stunted, 10.3% are underweight and 3.7% experience wasting (Labadarios 1999:167-169).[5] Micro-nutrient deficiencies are also prevalent amongst South African children. In 1994, of children between the ages of 6 and 72 months, 33% were vitamin A deficient (Labadarios & Van Middelkoop 1995:1), 10.6% were iodine deficient (Steyn & Labadarios 2002:330) and 10% were iron deficient (Labadarios & Van Middelkoop 1995:1).[6]

The broader impact of this malnutrition on children's ability to participate in the processes and privileges of society is more difficult to quantify and trace, but it is potentially devastating. The link, for instance, between nutrition on the one hand and children's ability to participate effectively in education and their general cognitive development on the other, is well documented. Improved nutritional status is therefore widely regarded as an important aspect of an optimal educational environment (McCoy *et al* 1997:8-9).

The point is that South Africa generally, but specifically with regard to its children, faces and has faced for a long time, a food crisis. The figures cited above show that the nutritional status of a significant number of South African children is not simply inadequate – it is desperate, or in crisis. That is, many South African children experience full-blown *nutritional deprivation,* rather than only *under-nourishment,* as they don't even meet *basic essential levels of access* to food.[7] This crisis situation requires a crisis response: it seems to indicate that a substantial component of state measures aimed at addressing children's nutritional needs should focus on the direct transfer of food to the many desperately deprived children to immediately improve their food entitlement. In addition, there is also a need to focus on longer-term capacity-building initiatives that will gradually and indirectly improve their food entitlement.

Against the background sketched above, this chapter reviews government measures aimed at providing basic nutrition to children and so realising their right to basic nutrition. Section one starts by describing the scope and content of the child's right to basic nutrition and the child-specific duties that this right imposes on the state. Section two then provides an overview of the range of different government measures related to the child's food and nutritional needs. This section considers whether government's general policy framework adequately provides for the nutritional needs of children and highlights certain constraints. Finally, section three places the spotlight on one of government's child-specific nutritional policy measures, the national Department of Health's Primary School Feeding Scheme (PSFS), focusing on its conceptualisation and implementation. Section three asks whether (and if so, how) this programme makes an important contribution to the realisation of the child's right to basic nutrition. It also identifies problems that undermine the potential effect of the PSFS as a nutritional intervention.

# 1. THE MEANING AND SCOPE OF THE CHILD'S RIGHT TO BASIC NUTRITION

## 1.1 THE SCOPE OF CHILDREN'S CONSTITUTIONAL RIGHT TO BASIC NUTRITION IN SOUTH AFRICA

In terms of section 28(1)(c) of the Constitution, every child has a right to basic nutrition. In addition, in terms of section 27(1)(b) children, like everyone else in South Africa, have the right to have access to sufficient food. The latter is a right that the state, through reasonable measures, must realise progressively, within its available resources.[8]

These two rights confer on children a range of different entitlements that intersect and overlap with each other. Section 27(1)(b) entitles children to require the state to take measures that are reasonably capable, within the resources that are available, which will allow them to gain access to food over time. This entitlement is limited. In other words, children cannot, in terms of section 27(1)(b), claim that the state must provide them with immediate and direct access to food. They can only require the state to take reasonable steps to attain this goal in future, to the extent that its available resources allow.[9] The Constitutional Court has held that this, first and most obviously, means that the state must indeed institute measures to realise all aspects of this right over time. It also means that these measures must be rational, comprehensive and coherent, inclusive of all significantly "at risk" groups in society, co-ordinated, flexible enough to respond to both short- and longer-term needs, effectively implemented and transparent.[10]

The entitlements engendered by section 28(1)(c) are much less attenuated. In broad terms, children's right to basic nutrition entitles them to require of the state to ensure that they receive at least that level of nutrition that enables dignified survival and basic physical and mental development. This imposes two sets of constitutional duties on the state. First, the state must take steps, regulatory and otherwise, to ensure that those parents or family members who are able to care for their children in fact provide for their nutritional needs. These steps include legal measures to ensure that parents meet their constitutional duties towards their children, as well as measures to support parents so that they are in fact able to do so. Second, the state must itself provide for the nutritional needs of those children whose parents or family members are unable to care for them, either because they are absent, or for reasons of poverty or other forms of incapacity. The state must meet this latter duty both by supporting parents and family members in their efforts to provide for the nutritional needs of their children and, in appropriate cases, by providing food directly to children.[11]

The precise scope and contours of the nutritional duties placed on the state by section 28(1)(c) are not yet entirely clear. The Constitution appears unambiguous in its implication that section 28(1)(c), as compared to section 27(1)(b), places duties of heightened intensity on the state. Section 28(1)(c) is formulated in direct terms as a right to basic nutrition, whereas section 27(1)(b) confers only a right to have access to sufficient food. Section 28(1)(c) is also not self-limited by the qualifier that the state can only be required to take reasonable measures, within available resources to realise nutritional rights progressively, as section 27(1)(b) is. Furthermore, the fact that section 28(1)(c) only promises basic nutrition, whereas section 27(1)(b) guarantees access to sufficient food, points in this direction. The idea seems to have been that, if the state's duty toward children is limited so that it is only required to provide a very basic level of nutrition, then it can realistically be bound to provide that basic level directly to children in need.[12]

It would be impractical to assume that this means that children are entitled to demand the provision of basic nutrition when they are in need, irrespective of resource constraints. As suggested in the introduction and chapter two of this publication, what this does most probably mean is that the state has a heightened duty of justification to show that its nutritional policies in fact prioritise the basic needs of children, both on paper and in terms of budgetary allocations and implementation measures (see section three of chapter two). The requirement that children's nutritional needs be prioritised requires in the first place that their basic survival nutritional needs be given precedence over other broader societal, economic and political demands. Also, and perhaps more controversially, it does seem to mean that at least children's basic survival nutritional needs should be given precedence over the food needs of other people.

## 1.2 THE CONTENT OF CHILDREN'S RIGHT TO BASIC NUTRITION AND TO FOOD

The content of the duties engendered by the right to basic nutrition has been described in quite some detail in international law.[13] The content that has, at international level, been attributed to the right to food provides an important guide to the interpretation of the right to food and children's right to basic nutrition in the South African Constitution.[14] Broadly speaking, although the law does not prescribe to policy-makers the specific measures that they must take, the state must engage in two areas of activity to meet its obligations in terms of the right to basic nutrition: it must ensure both the *availability* of food, as well as access, or *actual entitlement*, to food.

Availability of food connotes the idea that the state, through appropriate food production and trade policies and practices, must ensure that a sufficient supply of food exists nationally to meet the nutritional demands of the people of the country. Availability of food is therefore related to the idea of *national food security*. The state must also ensure that this supply of food is geographically distributed, nutritionally adequate and safe.

The accessibility of – or entitlement to – food refers to the idea that people must actually be able to access the food that is available. Sufficient entitlement to food results in household food security. In practical terms the duty to ensure access or entitlement to food – or put differently, the duty to ensure *household food security* – is almost always the most important food-related duty of the state. Malnutrition and hunger are almost never caused by a lack in the national food supply (by national food insecurity), but almost always by failures in entitlement to food (by household food insecurity) (Sen 1981:1).[15]

To meet its duty of creating actual entitlement to food, the state must first simply facilitate access to food to make it possible for reasonably self-sufficient people to obtain food for themselves. This it can do in a variety of different ways, ranging from the regulation of the price of basic food-stuffs to making it more affordable (tax zero-rating of basic food-stuffs, food-price monitoring, market regulation, subsidisation or actual price control). Other measures may include the provision of assistance to people who produce food for own use (education or actual material assistance to small and subsistence farmers) or enhancing the ability of people to access food for themselves. Children are not self-sufficient and therefore this facilitative element of the duty to engender entitlement to food does not apply to them directly. However, the extent to which the state succeeds or fails in this duty obviously affects children, as they usually gain access to food through their parents or families.

In addition, to meet its duty of creating entitlement to food, the state must, under some circumstances, directly provide food or the resources with which to acquire food to those who are unable to make use of existing access to food. Again, there are many different ways in which the state can meet this duty. It can directly provide food, institute food stamp programmes or enable people to buy food through social assistance programmes. This duty is obviously directly relevant to children, as they are never reasonably self-sufficient, and very often in South Africa cannot depend on parents or family to provide for their needs.

The state must of course also take steps to ensure that existing entitlement to food is in fact effective. In other words, it must institute policies to ensure that, when people gain access to food, that food is of a good enough nutritional quality and safe enough (free of toxins and adverse substances) to maintain an adequate nutritional status.

Again, this can be done in a variety of different ways. For example, it may institute educational programmes that teach people how to prepare and store food in such a way that they will derive the optimum nutritional benefit from it. The state can also regulate food production, requiring food to be demonstrably free of adverse substances and/or calling for the micro-nutrient fortification of food.

Finally, food rights require the state to have appropriate monitoring systems in place so that it can be aware of the food security situation in the country and able to adapt its policies to deal with problems as they arise. These would include systems to monitor food production and trade, systems to monitor entitlement (food prices and so forth) and systems to monitor actual nutritional status.

In summary then, children's nutritional rights are derived from two constitutional provisions – section 27(1)(b) and section 28(1)(c). The former requires the state to institute measures, progressively and within its available resources, to make adequate food accessible to everyone, including children. The latter requires the state to be able to show that the measures it institutes to meet its section 27(1)(b) duty prioritises the basic survival food needs of children over other needs. Whatever measures the state institutes must be reasonable. That means in the first place that they must be comprehensive in the sense that they address all aspects of the right to food. They must in some way be capable of ensuring the availability of food (national food security, requiring appropriate trade and production policies) and entitlement to food (household food security, requiring facilitation of entitlement, provision of entitlement and measures to make entitlement effective). They must also include appropriate measures to monitor the food security situation in the country so as to inform policy development. Reasonableness also requires that the state's measures to realise food rights are rational, coherent, inclusive, co-ordinated, flexible, effectively implemented and transparent.

## 2. GOVERNMENT PROGRAMMES GIVING EFFECT TO CHILDREN'S RIGHT TO BASIC NUTRITION

Policies relating to access to food and household food security are currently co-ordinated and managed in terms of a cross-departmental policy framework, the Integrated Food Security Strategy for South Africa (IFSS).[16] This document sets out a broad policy framework for measures aimed at enhancing food security in South Africa. The IFSS does not itself create nutritional programmes. It is intended to "streamline, harmonise and integrate diverse food security sub-programmes in South Africa" and to serve as a guiding framework within which existing policies can be co-ordinated and expanded and new policies can be developed (Department of Agriculture 2002a:11). To this end, the IFSS calls for a cross-departmental and cross-sectoral management structure.[17] It also identifies a number of key focus areas for policy development and implementation.[18]

The Department of Agriculture is the lead department driving the IFSS. Together with the Departments of Social Development, Health and to a lesser degree Public Works, it also currently runs the most important projects aimed at enhancing access to food.

This chapter does not attempt to provide an overview of all projects and programmes that contribute to the realisation of the right to food. For a variety of reasons, such an overview would be impossible within a single chapter in any useful degree of detail. First, it remains a difficult task simply to identify the different programmes and policies that either directly or indirectly contribute to food security in South Africa. Until recently, no single overarching policy framework dealing with the right to food existed in South Africa. No specific government department at national, provincial or local level focuses in the first instance on the right to food in the way that, for instance, the Department of Health is dedicated primarily to realising the right to have access to health care services. Food-related policy has developed in a piece-meal fashion, with different aspects – and sometimes the same aspects – of nutritional policy addressed by different departments.[19] Despite the recent introduction of the IFSS, any attempt to provide a full overview would be confounded by the difficulty of making overall sense of a loose patchwork of policies and programmes.[20]

Secondly, as pointed out in section one above, the realisation of the right to food requires measures that ensure both the availability of food (creating and maintaining national food security by ensuring that an adequate supply of safe and nutritious food exists nationally) and actual access, or entitlement to food (creating and maintaining household food security). A complete overview of all policies relating to the realisation of the right to food would therefore require a focus on agricultural and trade policies that are intended to secure and maintain an adequate national food supply, as well as the wide range of policies that are meant to engender entitlement to food. This represents an extremely broad focus.

Thirdly, the extent to which the right to food is realised itself depends on the fulfilment of a number of other rights. People usually gain access to food by producing it for themselves or by acquiring it through exchange. The ability to produce food or to acquire it through exchange thus depends on the realisation of such rights as the right to have access to land, the right to education and in some instances the right to have access to social security and assistance. Furthermore, a person's ability to be nourished by food physically acquired and ingested "depends crucially on…characteristics of a person that are influenced by such non-food factors as medical attention, health services, basic education, sanitary arrangements, provision of clean water [and the] eradication of infectious epidemics…" (Drëze & Sen 1998:13, 177). A person suffering from a simple disease such as diarrhoea, caused by contaminated water, is unable to properly ingest the nutrients and calories of the food he or she eats. A person who is insufficiently educated would possibly not derive the full nutritional benefit from food acquired because he or she may not be aware how to store or prepare that food optimally. As a result, providing a comprehensive overview of policies that contribute to the full realisation of food rights would therefore also entail a review of a host of programmes and policies that are not expressly intended to address nutritional problems, but that impact indirectly on the right to food.

To deal with these problems of scope, this overview is restricted to a focus on those policies and programmes that are *directly* engaged in fostering *entitlement* to food. Thus it reviews only those policies and programmes that are expressly intended to facilitate or to provide access or entitlement to food and those that are expressly meant to improve the effectiveness of entitlement to food (those intended to enhance nutritional status).[21] Consequently, this section does not consider those policies that indirectly contribute to food security, nor does it examine those policies that are aimed at maintaining national food security.

Although the aim of this section is to review policies that are intended to realise *children's* right to basic nutrition, it does not only focus on programmes that are specifically targeted at children. It also considers policies that are intended to realise food rights for everyone, as these policies both directly and indirectly also benefit children.

The overview below is structured as follows. Section 2.1 begins by reviewing government's general policy response to the nutritional needs of its people. Thereafter, section 2.2 briefly recounts the partly temporary emergency response occasioned by the drastic rise in the prices of basic food-stuffs during the course of 2002. Finally, section 2.3 provides a brief critique of both these aspects of government's food-related policies.

## 2.1 PROGRAMME OVERVIEW

### 2.1.1 PROGRAMMES THAT AIM TO BUILD CAPACITY TO PRODUCE OR ACQUIRE FOOD

As pointed out in section one above, food rights impose a duty on the state to facilitate access to food: to make it possible for reasonably self-sufficient people to gain access to food for themselves by building their capacity to produce or acquire food. This category of programmes includes those that seek to enable household food production, income-generation and job-creation. The IFSS identifies the Agriculture and Public Works Departments as lead agencies in this area. Apart from these two, the Departments of Health, Social Development and Land Affairs also presently run programmes aimed at facilitating access to food. A number of these projects encourage household food production with the idea that this enables food-insecure households to provide for their own food needs, to generate income for other needs by selling food and to contribute to broader food production in South Africa. Other projects in this area focus on job-creation and other forms of income-generation that would enable people to acquire food through exchange (Department of Agriculture 2002a:28). Table 3.1 lists and describes the most important such projects.

**TABLE 3.1 PROGRAMMES AIMED AT BUILDING CAPACITY IN ORDER TO FACILITATE ACCESS TO FOOD**

| Responsible department | Programme title | Services offered | Targeted beneficiaries | Implementation time-frame |
|---|---|---|---|---|
| Agriculture | Food Security and Rural Development | Agricultural starter-packs and information packs to enable food production for own consumption. | Food insecure rural households | N/A |

| Responsible department | Programme title | Services offered | Targeted beneficiaries | Implementation time-frame |
|---|---|---|---|---|
| Agriculture in partnership with Land Affairs | Land Redistribution for Agricultural Development (LRAD) | Financial support for farmers to enable them to buy land and agricultural implements. | Small farmers from previously disadvantaged communities | 669 000 hectares of state-owned land was disposed of by 2003. |
| Public Works | Community-Based Public Works Programme | Job-creation through involvement of poor communities in public works projects. | Poor rural households | Since 1998, 76 000 people were employed temporarily, 6 300 sustainable jobs were created by 2002. |
| Social Development | Poverty Relief Programme | Rural food production clusters (food gardens, poultry houses, pig units). | Poor rural and urban house holds | 30 000 beneficiaries were reached in 2001/02. MTEF 2002/03-2004/05 target: 61 200 in total over 3 years. |
| | | Urban renewal, providing skills development and job opportunities to youth. | Poor urban youth | 3 000 beneficiaries were reached in 2001/02. MTEF 2002/03-2004/05 target: 6 000 in total over 3 years. |
| | | Local economic development projects for women generating income. | Poor rural women | 5 000 beneficiaries were reached in 2001/02. MTEF 2002/03-2004/05 target: 10 400 in total over 3 years. |
| Health | Integrated Nutrition Programme | Contribution to household food security through funding of various poverty relief projects. | | N/A |

**Sources:** Department of Health 2002; Department of Agriculture 2003a & 2001; Department of Social Development 2002a: 37-97; Department of Public Works 2001.

## 2.1.2 PROGRAMMES THAT AIM TO ENHANCE NUTRITION AND FOOD SAFETY

Food rights also enjoin the state to take steps to enhance the effectiveness of whatever entitlement to food exists. In other words, the state has a duty to make sure that food is of a good enough quality and safe enough and that people are sufficiently educated about food preparation and storage to gain the maximum possible nutritional benefit from the food that they have access to. The IFSS identifies the Department of Health as the lead agency in this area (Department of Agriculture 2002a:31). Table 3.2 lists and describes the most important projects in this area.

**TABLE 3.2 PROGRAMMES AIMED AT ENHANCING NUTRITION AND FOOD SAFETY**

| Responsible department | Programme title | Service offered | Targeted beneficiaries | Implementation time-frame |
|---|---|---|---|---|
| Health | Integrated Nutrition Programme: nutrition education, promotion and advocacy | Development of educational materials and guidelines on nutrition. | General public, with particular focus on children | Achieved by 2003: <br>• Breastfeeding policy/guidelines for health workers; <br>• Nutritional guidelines for people with TB, HIV/AIDS and other debilitating diseases; <br>• Vitamin A supplementation information for health workers and care-givers; <br>• Guidelines for intervention at health facilities to prevent/manage child malnutrition; <br>• Educational materials on iodine deficiency disorder; <br>• Public communication strategy on the importance of micro-nutrients and food fortification; and <br>• Primary school nutrition education programme |
| Health | Integrated Nutrition Programme: micro-nutrient malnutrition control | Micro-nutrient fortification of staple foods and micro-nutrient sup-plementation. | General public with particular focus on children | Achieved by 2003: <br>• Vitamin A supplementation programme; <br>• Fortification of maize and wheat flour with vitamin A, thiamin, niacin, pyridoxine, folate, riboflavin, iron and zinc; and <br>• Salt iodisation |

**Sources:** Department of Health 2002a; Department of Health 1998; Steyn & Labadarios 2002:327, 343-345.

## 2.1.3 PROGRAMMES THAT AIM TO PROVIDE ACCESS TO FOOD

As pointed out in the preceding section, government is required to create entitlement to food not only by facilitating access to food, but also by providing food, or the means with which to acquire food, to those who are unable to make use of available access opportunities. This duty can be met in a variety of possible ways: either through the direct provision of food, or through a range of different social assistance grants such as food stamps, food vouchers or cash grants. Government currently provides food directly in a certain number of limited instances. It also provides the means with which to acquire food through a relatively extensive system of social assistance cash grants. Significantly, all these programmes are special needs-based. In other words, they accrue only to certain groups who are, for some or other reason, regarded as especially vulnerable to failures in food security. Table 3.3 lists and describes the most important of these programmes.

TABLE 3.3 PROGRAMMES AIMED AT PROVIDING ACCESS TO FOOD

| Responsible department | Programme title | Services offered | Targeted beneficiaries | Implementation time-frame |
|---|---|---|---|---|
| Health* | Primary School Feeding Scheme | Early morning nutritious supple-mentary meal com-prising not less than 25% of RDA of energy for 7-10 year olds and not less than 20% of RDA of energy for 11-14 year olds. | Primary school learners from poor households. The programme targets schools in areas with the highest poverty levels, rural schools, farm schools and schools in informal settlements. | Implemented 1 September 1994. Up to March 2002, an average of 5 million learners from 15 000 schools have drawn benefit from the scheme (47% of all primary school learners). |
| Health | Programme for the in-patient management of acute, severe Protein Energy Malnutrition (PEM) | Provision of in-patient primary and secondary nutritional inter-ventions to child-ren hospitalised for severe, acute PEM. | Children suffering from acute, severe PEM | Guidelines deve-loped in 2000, piloted in Eastern Cape in 2001. Mortality rates for malnourished children at pilot facilities dropped from 18% to 14%. Extended to all nine provinces in 2002. |
| Social Development | Child Support Grant | R160 per month per child (as at 1 April 2003). | Children under 9 years of age (to be extended to children under 14 by 2005) whose care-givers meet a means test. | Number of beneficiaries: 04/2000:348 532 04/2001:1 078 884 04/2002:1 810 977 02/2003:2 517 021 |
| Social Development | Foster Care Grant | R500 per month per child (as at 1 April 2003). | Children in foster care whose care-givers pass a means test. | Number of beneficiaries: 04/2000:49 843 04/2001:61 268 04/2002:69 423 02/2003:133 400 |
| Social Development | Care Dependency Grant | R700 per child per month (as at 1 April 2003). | Disabled children under 18 years of age whose care-givers meet a means test. | Number of beneficiaries: 04/2000:22 789 04/2001:30 269 04/2002:36 065 02/2003:56 173 |

| Responsible department | Programme title | Services offered | Targeted beneficiaries | Implementation time-frame |
|---|---|---|---|---|
| Social Development | State Old Age Pension | R700 per beneficiary per month. | Men of 65 years or older, women of 60 years or older. If married, the beneficiary's spouse must meet a means test. | Number of beneficiaries: 04/2000:1 848 726 04/2001:1 882 188 04/2002:1 903 085 02/2003:2 002 320 |
| Social Development | Disability Grant | R700 per beneficiary per month. | Disabled persons | Number of beneficiaries: 04/2000:607 537 04/2001:631 758 04/2002:707 920 02/2003:895 937 |
| Social Development | War Veteran's Grant | R718 per beneficiary per month. | Veterans of war | Number of beneficiaries: 04/2000:7 908 04/2001:6 062 04/2002:5 243 02/2003:3 670 |
| Social Development | Grant in Aid | R150 per beneficiary per month. | Additional grant for those receiving Old Age/Disability/War Veteran's grant, who are unable to care for themselves. | Number of beneficiaries: 04/2000:22 789 04/2001:30 269 04/2002:36 065 02/2003:56 173 |
| Social Development | Social Relief of Distress | Temporary assistance (of varying nature) for people in such dire need that they cannot meet the basic needs of themselves or their families. | On condition that they do not receive another social assistance grant or assistance from any other organisation, this grant is targeted at persons: • awaiting permanent aid; • appealing the suspension of an existing other grant; • found medically unfit to work for a period less than 6 months; • in families with bread-winners deceased, with insufficient means; or • affected by disaster where their area has not yet been declared a disaster area. | N/A |

**Sources:** Department of Social Development 2003a; Department of Social Development 2003b; Department of Social Development 2002b.

**\* Note:** Responsibility for this programme is to transfer to the Department of Education in April 2004 (Kloka 2003: personal communication).

## 2.2 TEMPORARY CRISIS RESPONSE TO FOOD INSECURITY

During 2002, the prices of basic food-stuffs such as maize and potatoes rose dramatically, due to a combination of economic factors.[22] The price increases placed basic food-stuffs far out of the financial reach of a large portion of the population and led to a public outcry. On 9 October 2002 government responded, announcing a package of measures outside the scope of its existing policy framework relating to food, designed to alleviate the crisis (Department of Agriculture 2002b). This package of measures, as then announced, contained the following:

*Immediate to short-term measures:*

- Increases in the scope of coverage and the monetary amounts of social assistance grants;

- Agreements with producers and marketers of basic food-stuffs to provide food at special low prices for the poor;

- Investigation into the feasibility of a programme of food stamps/vouchers; and

- Provision to poor families of food parcels and agricultural starter-packs.

*Medium- to long-term-measures:*

- Investigation into the re-establishment of strategic grain reserves as "buffer stocks" in times of food crises;

- The lowering of tariffs within the SADC as an incentive for increased food production in the region;

- Support for co-operative milling in local areas, with the benefit of such milling to accrue to the local communities; and

- The establishment of a Food Pricing Committee to monitor the food production and supply chain and its effect on food prices, so as to advise government on steps to take to avoid dramatic fluctuations in food prices.

Since the 2002 announcement, a number of these measures have in fact been implemented:

- The Child Support Grant was increased first from R130 to R140 per month in October 2002 and again from R140 to R160 in April 2003. Its coverage was also extended so that, by April 2005, all needy children up to 14 years of age will qualify for the grant (Department of Social Development 2003c).[23] The State Old Age Pension was increased from R620 to R640 per month, the Foster Care Grant from R450 to R460 per month and the Care Dependency Grant from R620 to R640 per month.

- Government reached an agreement with food retailers Premier Foods, Metro, the farming group Agri Corporation and other donors who agreed to provide 1 400 tonnes of maize every month for three months (until the end of January 2003) at a recommended price of R25.99 per 12.5kg bag, compared to the normal rate of R43.

- At the end of October 2002, in its Medium-Term Budget Policy Statement, government announced that it had set aside R400 million to be used over the following three years for food relief. Of this R400 million, R170 million was intended for food aid through the Food and Agriculture Organisation to other southern African countries. The bulk of the allocation, R230 million, was to be used to provide food parcels and agricultural starter-packs once a month for three months during 2003 to 240 000 poor households across South Africa with no income and who spend a maximum of R200 on food per month.[24] The first phase of this programme has since been implemented in all nine provinces, beginning with a launch in February 2003 in the Eastern Cape. Food parcels and starter-packs were distributed to 249 000 households during this phase. A further R800 million has been allocated for the continuation of the programme through 2004 and 2005 (Morongwa 2003:personal communication).

- On 8 January 2003, in terms of section 7 of the *Marketing of Agricultural Products Act* (47 of 1996), the Minister of Agriculture appointed the National Food Pricing Monitoring Committee, to operate for a period of one year (Madima 2003:personal communication).[25] The Committee's terms of reference are:

  * to monitor the pricing of basic food-stuffs;
  * to investigate any sharp or unjustified food price increases;
  * to determine the competitiveness of food production operations;
  * to investigate food price formation mechanisms within the value chain of basic food-stuffs;
  * to recommend required food productivity improvements;
  * to investigate collusive, discriminatory or unfair business practices in the basic food value chain;
  * to investigate and make recommendations on food market inefficiencies and distortions; and
  * to investigate incidents of predatory food pricing and monopolistic tendencies.

## 2.3 COMMENTARY ON GOVERNMENT'S FOOD ENTITLEMENT MEASURES

The brief overview above shows that, at least on paper, government has policies in place to meet all the duties imposed on it by the right to food generally and children's right to basic nutrition specifically.

As demonstrated by the tables in section 2.1, government has instituted a range of programmes intended to engender entitlement to food – that is, to ensure household food security. A number of different departments run programmes intended to facilitate access to food, to make it possible for reasonably self-sufficient people to gain access to food for themselves (see Table 3.1). There are also a variety of programmes in place that aim to provide access to food to those who cannot access food for themselves (see Table 3.3). The bulk of these programmes take the form of special needs-based social assistance cash grants, which enable certain especially vulnerable groups of people to acquire food. Amongst these, two programmes specifically aimed at children provide food and nutrition directly to beneficiaries. These are the Primary School Feeding Scheme (PSFS) and the programme targeting children with acute Protein Energy Malnutrition (the PEM programme), both managed by the Department of Health. In 2002, government also introduced a short-term crisis response to rising food prices in the form of a programme to provide food parcels and agricultural starter packs to destitute families (to run for three years). In addition, government has programmes in place that seek to ensure the effectiveness and safety of access to food: most importantly the Department of Health's Integrated Nutrition Programme, in terms of which nutritional education is provided and micro-nutrient deficiencies in food-stuffs are addressed (see Table 3.2).

Over and beyond the programmes reviewed in this chapter, government has also instituted or maintained policies that help it to meet other duties imposed by food rights. The Department of Agriculture (through appropriate production policies) and the Department of Trade and Industry (through appropriate food import strategies) have programmes in place and currently manage to maintain an adequate national food supply and so ensure national food security.[26] Different departments and institutions within government also run programmes to monitor different aspects of national and household food security in South Africa and to enhance nutritional status through nutritional education and the micro-nutrient fortification of food-stuffs. An important recent addition to these programmes is the appointment of the Department of Agriculture's National Food Pricing Monitoring Committee (for a period of one year) to investigate and advise government on food prices in South Africa.

The impact of this broad approach to dealing with poverty and the concomitant food insecurity should not be underestimated. In particular, the link between social assistance cash grants and poverty reduction has been well documented.[27] However, despite its seeming comprehensiveness, this policy scheme poses certain definite problems, both of a conceptual and a practical nature. Although many of these are by now almost trite, they are briefly repeated below.

First, and as always, there are practical problems of implementation. Despite significant annual growth in programme outputs, government's existing programmes aimed at facilitating access to food are clearly insufficient to address poverty and the resultant household food insecurity in a comprehensive way. The numbers of beneficiaries reached through government's various capacity-building programmes – a rough figure of 120 300 by 2001 (see Table 3.1) – is only a very small percentage of the nutritionally needy in South Africa. The same can be said of government's efforts to provide food or the means through which to acquire food. The take-up rate of the different social assistance grants, despite significant annual gains, remains relatively poor. The Child Support Grant, for instance, currently has only about 2.5 million children beneficiaries (see Table 3.3). However, there are an estimated 6.1 million children between the ages of 6 and 15 alone who live below the poverty line and therefore presumably require social assistance. (See chapter five for more on the limited reach of government's social assistance programmes for children.) In addition, the levels of certain grants, despite recent increases, remain out of touch with the actual cost of living.[28] Even government's recent emergency food parcel scheme comes nowhere near to the kind of coverage that is required.[29]

Perhaps more importantly, there are also conceptual problems with government's current approach to food entitlement. In its assessment of government's programmes to address poverty, the report of the Taylor Committee[30] (Department of Social Development: 2002b) indicated that the poverty situation in South Africa requires, in addition to long- and medium-term programmes aimed at addressing asset and capability poverty, significant programmes aimed at the immediate alleviation of income poverty. The committee argued convincingly that government's range of poverty relief projects will have little impact unless "urgent steps [are taken] to provide the basic means to enable the poor to access" the benefits these projects offer (Ibid: 56). The same can be said about the food security situation in South Africa. Programmes aimed at engendering the capability to produce or acquire food for oneself are laudable as they will contribute to "sustained human development and economic growth" (Ibid). At the same time, however, there is also a need for significant programmes that directly provide food or the means with which to acquire food. In the absence of such programmes, initiatives aimed merely at facilitating access to food will remain ineffectual, as people's basic food needs go unmet and they are thus unable to make use of opportunities created for them. This is particularly true in a situation such as ours, where a significant portion of the population, including many children, suffer from full-blown nutritional deprivation, rather than simply from inadequate nutrition.

Government's food policy scheme of course makes quite substantial provision for such direct transfer of food, or the means with which to acquire food, through the PSFS, the PEM programme and the various social assistance grants. However, all of these efforts are in some way targeted to special needs. The PSFS benefits only children at primary school. The PEM programme benefits only severely malnourished children treated at public health facilities. The Child Support Grant currently only benefits children under 9, the State Old Age Pension only men older than 65 and women older than 60 and the Disability Grant only disabled persons. The result is that if you are older than 9 years of age and younger than 60 (for women) or 65 (for men), physically and mentally able, not in foster care and not a war veteran, however bad your nutritional situation is, there is no regular state assistance to meet even the most basic of your food needs.[31] The only state assistance that is available for such persons is the Social Relief of Distress grant and the current food parcel programme. Both these programmes provide only temporary relief: Social Relief of Distress is provided monthly for a maximum of three months, while food parcels are handed out for three months in any given year and the programme is only in place until 2005. In addition, the coverage of both these programmes is very low.[32]

Government might argue that the special needs-based nature of its policies that aim to provide entitlement to food is an example of the kind of prioritisation of children's basic needs that the Constitution requires (see section one of this chapter). However, such a view fails to take account of the fact that government is in the first place obliged to make it possible for care-givers to provide for the needs of their children, before it steps in to do so. In addition, as section three below shows, the nutritional benefits of the programmes targeted specifically at children, such as the PSFS and the

CSG, are severely mitigated by the absence of effective assistance to children's families. Children who gain nutritionally from the PSFS lose that benefit when they do not have access to sufficient food in their own homes outside of school. Similarly, children whose lives are saved through nutritional intervention in terms of the PEM programme, often re-appear at hospitals because there is no food at home to sustain the benefit gained from state assistance (Chopra *et al* 2001/02).

# 3. ANALYSIS OF A KEY PROGRAMME: THE PRIMARY SCHOOL FEEDING SCHEME

This section provides an analysis of the conceptualisation and implementation of one programme that is (at least partly) intended to realise children's right to basic nutrition and to food: the Department of Health's PSFS. The PSFS is examined in more detail here because it is really the only programme that is explicitly (even if only partly) intended to directly advance children's right to basic nutrition. More importantly, apart from the various social assistance grants outlined in Table 3.3, it is the only relatively comprehensive programme in terms of which government provides children with access to food. In other words, it is one of the few programmes that directly addresses the food crisis outlined in the introduction to this chapter. Finally, the PSFS has been studied and evaluated quite extensively, so that information about its implementation is readily available.[33] However, as the analysis of the PSFS will show, it is important to keep in mind from the outset that it forms part of an inter-linked and mutually supporting range of policy measures. All of these have to function well for the PSFS to have its optimal effect.

## 3.1 PROGRAMME CONCEPTUALISATION

### 3.1.1 BACKGROUND

The PSFS was introduced in September 1994 as part of the Primary School Nutrition Programme (PSNP), one of then President Nelson Mandela's Presidential Lead Projects. It has enjoyed an uninterrupted run since then. The PSNP was intended to be a comprehensive nutritional enhancement programme involving, apart from school feeding, also nutritional education projects, parasite control and micro-nutrient supplementation programmes in primary schools (Kloka 2003:2). In 1997, the PSNP was incorporated into and subsumed by the Integrated Nutrition Programme (INP).[34] Since then the PSFS has been a sub-programme of the INP, located within its focus area of Contribution to Household Food Security (Ibid:2-3)

### 3.1.2 SERVICE PROVIDED

The PSFS provides an early morning meal to primary school learners at targeted schools every school day. This meal is meant to be sufficiently nutritious to provide not less than 25% of the recommended daily allowance (RDA) of energy for 7 to 10 year olds and not less than 20% of the RDA of energy for 11 to 14 year olds.

## 3.1.3 AIMS

The aim of the PSFS is to minimise the impact of malnutrition and short-term hunger on the ability of primary school learners to participate in and derive benefit from education.[35] The primary aim of the PSFS is therefore to bring about improvement in the quality of primary education, rather than general improvement in the nutritional status of primary school learners. Nevertheless, the undoubted impact of the programme on the nutritional status of those children who benefit from it is acknowledged as a secondary aim (Kloka 2003:4-5).[36]

## 3.1.4 INSTITUTIONAL MATTERS

At national level, the PSFS is currently managed jointly by the Departments of Health and Education. In practice, the Department of Health takes responsibility for the health and nutritional aspects of school feeding and the Department of Education for the educational aspects (Ibid:9). On the basis of recommendations made in the latest evaluation of the PSFS, the management of the PSFS will, in April 2004, shift to the Department of Education alone (Kloka 2003: personal communication).

At provincial level, provincial health and education departments generally collaborate in the management of the programme. The PSFS is implemented at local level by a variety of different institutions: school project committees, school governing bodies, community-based organisations and non-governmental organisations (Ibid).

## 3.1.5 TARGETING

The PSFS is intended to address short-term hunger that is the direct result of poverty. As a result, the programme is meant to target only needy schools, as opposed to covering as many schools and children as possible (Ibid:11). The Department of Health has developed targeting criteria at national level to guide the implementation of the PSFS at provincial and local level. In addition, provinces have developed their own targeting strategies.

The national targeting guidelines require provinces to select schools where the PSFS will be implemented on the basis of need. They are supposed to do so first by identifying the poorest geographical areas, then prioritising the selected geographical areas according to severity of need, and then selecting, according to the geographical prioritisation, needy schools from within the selected areas, focusing particularly on rural schools, farm schools and schools in informal settlements. In addition, the National Department of Health (Ibid:11-12) recommends that provinces:

- avoid targeting individual needy children in targeted schools and that they should rather feed all children in targeted schools;
- give priority to Grade R learners;
- determine the maximum number of learners that could be fed by applying the following formula: PSFS budget/number of feeding days/cost per learner = maximum number of learners that could be fed; and
- focus on quality rather than numbers, by targeting only really needy schools and

children, while providing them with an adequate quantity and quality of food, with different menu options on as many school days as possible, rather than trying to feed as many children as possible.

As the latest evaluation of the PSFS also indicated in 2001, these national targeting criteria and guidelines are not strictly followed in the provinces (Louw *et al* 2001:49).[37] A number of provinces follow their own targeting practices that broadly accord with the underlying principle of targeting needy schools first. So for example, the Northern Cape's provincial Department of Health reports that it follows the national targeting guidelines in principle. In practice however, it applies a rule of thumb in terms of which former Model C schools are excluded from the PSFS and other schools are included. Within selected schools, individual targeting is also still applied, to ensure that the benefits of the programme reach only needy children (Le Roux 2003:personal communication). The Western Cape Department of Health selects schools for the PSFS by using a Poverty Index List, provided to them by the national Department of Education. This list grades schools on a scale of 0-1 according to the poverty levels of their learners (1 representing the poorest schools). All schools that fall above 0.6 on the Poverty Index List are selected. In addition, as in the Northern Cape, individual targeting is still applied within the selected schools (Titus 2003:personal communication). The Free State Department of Health, in co-operation with the provincial Department of Education, seems to follow the national targeting guidelines quite closely, and is the only province canvassed that does not apply individual targeting within selected schools (Pretorius 2003:personal communication).

In general, it seems that the provinces are currently not adding many new schools to the ones already targeted for placement in the PSFS. Rather, the focus appears to be on ensuring that the PSFS can be implemented more effectively at schools that are already targeted. As Table 3.9 in section 3.4 below shows, this means that the number of schools across the country targeted annually has tapered off from a high of 20 110 in 1995/96 to 16 685 in 2002/03. At the same time, the percentage of those targeted schools actually reached has shown an overall increase.

## 3.1.6 PLACEMENT PROCEDURE

No procedure for the placement of schools is prescribed from national level. Accordingly, different provinces place schools within the PSFS programme in different ways. In the Northern Cape, the provincial Department of Education annually identifies schools that have not yet been placed on the programme. The provincial Department of Health then sends application forms to these schools, so that they can apply for admission to the PSFS. In practice, this application process is followed more in form than in substance: the applications of all schools except former model C schools are automatically accepted. In addition, because the vast majority of such eligible schools (and generally speaking, of the primary schools in the province) are already on the programme, very few new applications are processed annually by the province (Le Roux 2003:personal communication). In the Western Cape, the initiative to place new schools on the PSFS lies with the Department of Health. Upon receipt of the Poverty Index List from the national Department of Education, it simply identifies those schools that are eligible and includes them in the programme (Titus

2003:personal communication). The Department of Health in KwaZulu-Natal applies a combination of these two processes. It first selects a pool of schools according to the nationally prescribed criteria and then allows schools from that pool to apply for admission to the programme (Ncqobo 2003:personal communication). The Free State Department of Health indicated that, as there are a large number of schools already on the programme, only a small number of additional schools are admitted every year, according to the availability of funds. The Department of Health, in co-operation with community health structures, annually identifies needy schools not yet on the PSFS. Then, together with the Department of Health, it applies the national criteria to decide which of the additional schools to take on board (Pretorius 2003:personal communication).

In general, all the provinces canvassed indicated that there are currently very few new schools being admitted to the programme, as most schools that meet the selection criteria already benefit from the PSFS.

## 3.2 BUDGETING FOR THE PSFS

Since its inception in 1994/95, the PSFS – then a sub-programme of the PSNP – received an earmarked RDP allocation. This arrangement lasted up to the 1997/98 financial year. In 1997, the PSFS was incorporated into the INP, which is funded through a conditional grant (the INP conditional grant). Consequently, since the 1998/99 financial year, the PSFS has been funded through a portion of the INP conditional grant.

The national Department of Health distributes the INP conditional grant amongst the different provinces in terms of a particular distribution formula, which takes into account the average poverty gap and the number of young children (in age group 5 to 14 years) in each province.[38] Provincial health departments, together with provincial education departments, then allocate funds for school feeding from their allocation of the INP conditional grant. The budget for the PSFS at provincial level is further augmented by ordinary budget allocations.

It is clear that the PSFS by far accounts for the bulk of provincial spending on nutrition. The national Department of Health indicates that, since 1998/99 and up to and including 2002/03, the PSFS was on average allocated 86% of the INP conditional grant at provincial level. In addition, an average of 4.8% of normal budget allocations was used to augment PSFS funds over the same five-year period.

Tables 3.4 to 3.7 summarise the most important information regarding budget allocations for the PSFS. Table 3.4 lists the budget allocations (across provinces) for the PSFS from the year of its inception (1994/95) up to and including 2001/02. The figures (allocations and percentages) are for the total annual budget allocations to the PSFS from the INP conditional grant, as well as from ordinary budgets. Table 3.5 lists the projected programme budgets for the MTEF period 2003/04 to 2005/06, converting them to percentages of the consolidated national and provincial expenditure. The allocations provided here are the total allocations for the INP (the total INP conditional grants), rather than the specific allocations to the PSFS from within the conditional grant, as the latter information for the period 2003/04 to 2005/06 was not yet available. Table 3.6 shows the real annual growth rates in PSFS allocations for the period 1999/00 to 2001/02. Finally, Table 3.7 lists the projected real annual growth in the PSFS budget for the period 2003/04 to 2005/06, converted into a percentage of average real annual growth. Again the figures provided here are the projected INP conditional grants *in toto,* as the percentages of the conditional grant allocated by the provinces particularly for the PSFS for the period 2003/04 to 2005/06 are not yet available.

### TABLE 3.4  PSFS PROGRAMME BUDGET (1994/95 - 2001/02)

| Year | Amount | Percentage of INP conditional grant and ordinary budgets |
|---|---|---|
| 1994/95 | R472 840 000 | N/A |
| 1995/96 | R500 000 000 | N/A |
| 1996/97 | R500 000 000 | N/A |
| 1997/98 | R496 000 000 | N/A |
| 1998/99 | R477 443 132 | 72% |
| 1999/00 | R457 945 362 | 69% |
| 2000/01 | R489 577 960 | 61% |
| 2001/02 | R496 665 565 | 76% |

**Source:** Kloka (2003:10-11).

### TABLE 3.5  PSFS PROGRAMME BUDGETS (2002/03 & MTEF 2003/04 - 2005/06)

| | 2002/03 | MTEF | | |
|---|---|---|---|---|
| | (dedicated PSFS budget as allocation from INP conditional grant) | 2003/04 (total INP conditional grant) | 2004/05 (total INP conditional grant) | 2005/06 (total INP conditional grant) |
| Programme budget | R534 744 493 | R808 660 000 | R950 418 000 | R1 041 543 000 |
| Consolidated national and provincial expenditure | R291 823 000 000 | R333 965 000 000 | R363 345 000 000 | R395 606 000 000 |
| Programme budget as a % of consolidated provincial and national allocated expenditure | 0.2% | 0.2% | 0.3% | 0.3% |

**Sources:** Kloka (2003:10-11); National Treasury (2003).

### TABLE 3.6  REAL ANNUAL GROWTH RATES IN PSFS PROGRAMME BUDGET (1999/00 - 2001/02)

| 1999/00 | 2000/01 | 2001/02 |
|---|---|---|
| -9.6% | -0.8% | -5.6% |

**Source:** Table 3.4 above

**Note:** 1998/99 is the base year.

**TABLE 3.7  REAL ANNUAL GROWTH AND REAL ANNUAL AVERAGE GROWTH IN PSFS PROGRAMME BUDGET (2002/03 - 2005/06)**

| 2003/04 (growth in total INP conditional grant) | 2004/05 (growth in total INP conditional grant) | 2005/06 (growth in total INP conditional grant) | 2002/03-2005/06 (annual average) |
|---|---|---|---|
| 28% | 12% | 4% | 15% |

**Sources:** Kloka (2003:10-11); National Treasury 2003.
**Note:** 2002/03 is the base year.

The overview of budgetary information above shows clearly that the PSFS is regarded as a priority programme within the INP. On average, 86% of the INP conditional grant and approximately 70% of the total budget available for the INP (the conditional grant together with other ordinary budget sources) is allocated by provinces to the PSFS.

The annual allocations to the PSFS are substantial and will increase even more substantially over the next three financial years. Up to and including the 2002/03 financial year, the programme generally showed negative real budget growth, on average − 5.3%. In fact, on a number of occasions over this period, the programme has also seen negative nominal growth.[39] However, the PSFS will see an average annual real growth of 15% in budget allocations over the next three years. This marked increase is consistent with a 2002 Cabinet decision (taken after an intensive review of the PSFS) not only to continue with the programme but, in the light of rising food prices and incidences of mal- and under-nutrition, to expand the programme

## 3.3  SUCCESS OR FAILURE IN EXPENDITURE?

Since the inception of the PSFS, there has been significant annual under-spending by provinces of money allocated to the PSFS. Table 3.8 shows the percentage of budget allocation actually spent annually.

Since the inception of the PSFS in 1994, the average annual expenditure on the programme has been 74% of allocated budgets. Overall under-spending on the programme amounts to R1 182 448 727 over the nine years of its operation. In addition, the PSFS has not once managed to spend all the money allocated to it.

However, expenditure has shown a gradual and eventually a marked improvement. The first three years of the PSFS's operation account for R699 917 037 or 59% of the total under-spending to date. In fact, 28% of the total under-spending (an amount of R338 016 214) occurred in the first year (1994/95). This was largely because an amount was allocated to the PSFS for that full financial year, while the programme was only implemented in the last six months of the year. Clearly therefore, the bulk of the overall under-spending comes from the first three years after the inception of the PSFS. By contrast, the average percentage of budget allocations spent annually over the years 2000/01 to 2002/03 is 89%. Over these years a total amount of R206 574 000 was under-spent, representing only 17% of the total amount under-spent over the nine years of the programme's existence.

**TABLE 3.8 ALLOCATED VERSUS ACTUAL EXPENDITURE ON THE PSFS (1998/99 - 2002/03)**

| Year | Actual budget allocation (budgeted expenditure) | Estimated expenditure | Estimated expenditure as % of budgeted expenditure |
|---|---|---|---|
| 1994/95 | R472 840 000 | R134 823 786 | 29% |
| 1995/96 | R500 000 000 | R312 478 000 | 62% |
| 1996/97 | R500 000 000 | R325 621 177 | 65% |
| 1997/98 | R496 000 000 | R399 376 266 | 81% |
| 1998/99 | R477 443 132 | R399 909 093 | 86% |
| 1999/00 | R457 945 362 | R356 145 445 | 78% |
| 2000/01 | R588 411 000* | R533 772 000 | 91% |
| 2001/02 | R613 630 000* | R488 732 000 | 80% |
| 2002/03 | R672 411 000* | R645 374 000 | 96% |

**Source:** Ms Dianne Kloka, Department of Health, personal communication, 27 October 2003

\* The budgeted expenditure reflected in this table for the years 2000/01, 2001/02 and 2002/03 is that for the total INP conditional grant, with roll-over funds from the respective previous years added, and not the specific amount allocated from the INP conditional grant for the PSFS. The estimated expenditure is therefore that of this total amount and not the estimated expenditure for the PSFS specifically, as the latter figures were not available nationally. Still, seeing that the PSFS has annually on average been allocated 86% of the INP conditional grant, these global figures give a strong indication of expenditure trends regarding the PSFS specifically.

## 3.4 SUCCESS OR FAILURE IN PROVIDING SERVICES?

Different criteria can be used to assess the success or failure in the implementation of the PSFS. Firstly and most obviously, it would be possible to simply consider the reach of the programme and assess it according to the number of schools and children it reaches. According to this quantitative criterion, the more schools and children have been reached, the better the programme has performed. Although this basic criterion is obviously important, it can obscure – if used alone – the really important qualitative question: whether the programme is cost-effective in the sense that it expends its resources to reach only those children who are really in need. To assess the programme's performance in light of the latter question, it is necessary to consider the extent to which it is successfully targeted at children in need, and the extent to which children who are indeed targeted, are reached through the programme. Finally, of course, the implementation of the programme also has to be assessed according to other criteria, such as the number of school days on which food was actually provided to children during the year, and the nutritional quality and safety of the food provided to children.

With regard to the first of the criteria raised above, the figures indicate that the PSFS has quantitatively been successfully implemented. In 2001/02, the programme reached 85% of all primary schools in South Africa. Since its inception and until 2001/02, the programme reached an average of 14 746 primary schools per year. If compared with the number of primary schools in South Africa in 2001/02 (17 254), this also translates into an annual average of 85% of primary schools in the country reached. In 2001/02, the PSFS also reached 47% of all primary school *learners* in the country.

Turning to the second of the two criteria, the targeting of the programme, the picture is also encouraging. After an initial sharp rise from 1994/95 to 1995/96, both the number of schools and the number of children targeted for the PSFS have shown a slight but steady annual decline. At the same time, the percentage of targeted schools actually reached annually has shown a marked increase, while the percentage of targeted children actually reached has shown a similar, if somewhat less impressive, increase. These trends seem to indicate that the targeting of the programme has become progressively more precise and that delivery to those children identified as in need has become progressively more effective. The implication is that the programme has progressively been implemented in an increasingly cost-effective manner. Tables 3.9 and 3.10 illustrate these trends. Table 3.9 shows the number of schools targeted annually and actually reached through the PSFS, and the percentage of actual coverage of targeted schools nationally. Table 3.10 provides the percentages of those children who were targeted for purposes of the PSFS, who were actually reached through the programme, both per province (where available) and on national average.

**TABLE 3.9  NUMBER OF PRIMARY SCHOOLS TARGETED AND ACTUALLY REACHED BY THE PSFS, WITH PERCENTAGE OF COVERAGE (1994/95 – 2002/03)**

| Financial year | Schools targeted | Schools reached | % of targeted schools reached |
|---|---|---|---|
| 1994/95 | 15 911 | 13 167 | 83 |
| 1995/96 | 20 110 | 15 894 | 79 |
| 1996/97 | 17 025 | 13 061 | 77 |
| 1997/98 | 17 945 | 14 549 | 81 |
| 1998/99 | 17 500 | 15 776 | 90 |
| 1999/00 | 16 087 | 15 428 | 96 |
| 2000/01 | 16 087 | 15 428 | 96 |
| 2001/02 | 16 000 | 14 667 | 91 |
| 2002/03 | 16 441 | 15 653 | 95 |
| 2003/04 | 16 962 | | |

**Source:** Kloka (2003:12).

**TABLE 3.10 PERCENTAGE OF ELIGIBLE (TARGETED) CHILDREN ACCESSING PSFS SERVICES, PROVINCIAL FIGURES AND NATIONAL AVERAGES, (1994/95 - 2002/03)**

| Province | 1994/95 | 1995/96 | 1996/97 | 1997/98 | 1998/99 | 1999/00 | 2000/01 | 2001/02 | 2002/03 |
|---|---|---|---|---|---|---|---|---|---|
| Eastern Cape | N/A | N/A | N/A | 88 | 89 | 99.7 | | | |
| Gauteng | N/A | N/A | N/A | 100 | 100 | 94 | | | |
| Free State | N/A | N/A | N/A | 93.7 | 97.4 | 89.6 | | | |
| KwaZulu-Natal | N/A | N/A | N/A | 50.3 | 86.9 | 85.9 | | | |
| Limpopo | N/A | N/A | N/A | 95.3 | 72 | 81 | | | |
| Mpumalanga | N/A | N/A | N/A | 95.7 | 100 | 100 | | | |
| Northern Cape | N/A | N/A | N/A | 100 | 99.4 | 100 | | | |
| North West | N/A | N/A | N/A | 100 | 100 | 70.9 | | | |
| Western Cape | N/A | N/A | N/A | 99.5 | 88.2 | 69.2 | | | |
| **National averages** | | | | | | | | | |
| **Number targeted** | 6 293 626 | 6 877 175 | 6 075 356 | 6024773 | 5 574 305 | 5 422 204 | 5 422 204 | 5 400 000 | 4 830 600 |
| **Number reached** | 5 628 320 | 5 567 644 | 4 880 266 | 5021575 | 4 830 098 | 4 719 489 | 4 719 489 | 4 700 000 | 4 595 452 |
| **% of targeted children reached** | 89 | 81 | 80 | 83 | 87 | 87 | 87 | 87 | 95 |

**Source:** Kloka (2003:12).

In 2003/04, the PSFS targeted 65% of all primary schools learners in South Africa (7 284 845 children). In 2002/03, 66% of all primary school learners and 95% of those learners targeted by the PSFS actually benefited from it.

As noted in section 3.1, the Department of Health sees the primary aim of the PSFS as the enhancement of children's ability to participate in education by alleviating short-term hunger. Given this objective, it is obviously important for school feeding to take place in targeted schools on as many school days as possible so that the children, whenever they are at school, can exhibit the enhanced concentration and other educational abilities that the PSFS intends to engender. A 2001 survey and evaluation of the PSFS identified the inconsistency and irregularity with which feeding is provided as one of the problems of the programme. While more recent figures are not available, Table 3.11 shows those for the 2000 calendar year. It presents the number of school days selected by provinces on which to provide school feeding at targeted schools, the number of days on which feeding was actually provided and translates these figures into percentages of the total number of school days in that calendar year. The table shows that on average, 83% of available school days were targeted for feeding and feeding actually took place on 71% of all available school days.

TABLE 3.11 PSFS COVERAGE OF SCHOOL DAYS (2000 CALENDAR YEAR)

| Province | Number of school days selected for feeding | % of all school days selected for feeding | Number of selected days missed | Number of actual feeding days | % of selected feeding days on which actually fed | % of all school days on which actually fed |
|---|---|---|---|---|---|---|
| Eastern Cape | 143 | 73 | 29 | 114 | 80 | 58 |
| Free State | 197 | 100 | 71 | 126 | 64 | 64 |
| Gauteng | 186 | 94 | 4 | 182 | 98 | 92 |
| KwaZulu-Natal | 152 | 77 | 11 | 141 | 93 | 72 |
| Mpumalanga | 116 | 59 | 4 | 112 | 97 | 57 |
| Northern Cape | 129 | 65 | 26 | 103 | 80 | 52 |
| Northern Province | 196 | 99 | 44 | 152 | 78 | 77 |
| North West | 197 | 100 | 23 | 174 | 88 | 88 |
| Western Cape | 163 | 83 | 5 | 158 | 97 | 80 |

**Source:** Louw *et al* (2001:57-60).

A final criterion according to which the success in implementation of the programme can be evaluated is the quality and safety of food actually provided to children. It is of course very difficult to determine on an empirical basis what quality of food children ingested through the PSFS. The most useful indication available is the objective adequacy of the nationally prescribed nutritional criteria for school feeding menus in the provinces, and the extent to which the implementation agencies in the different provinces managed to comply with the nationally prescribed criteria. This question was exhaustively researched during the latest evaluation of the PSFS, for the 2000 calendar year (Louw *et al* 2001:69-115). At that time, the national criteria prescribed in broad terms that provincial menus should provide at least 25% of the RDA of energy for 7 to 10 year olds and at least 20% of the RDA of energy for the 11 to 14 year olds. In addition, it was recommended that:

- the overall nutrient content of foods, apart from their energy content, should also be considered;

- certain specified food-stuffs (non-dairy creamers, other dairy imitations and certain commercial foods such as cool-drinks and biscuits) not be used, because of inferior nutritional quality, because the use of such foods can undermine efforts to educate children about good nutritional habits, because such foods seldom fit in with local eating habits and because their use does not encourage community involvement in providing food; and that

- food be used that is readily available, culturally acceptable and commonly eaten in the particular area.

Provinces were expected to formulate their own menu's according to these criteria. In 2000, it was found that:

- not one of the menus formulated by provinces fully met the national criteria;

- contrary to the national recommendation, commercial foods such as energy cool-drinks and biscuits were used in most provinces;

- the nutritional specifications developed by provinces, with which food-stuffs had to comply, were inadequate and incomplete (in fact, in one province no such specifications existed); and that

- in some provinces, food not listed on the provincial menu lists were routinely served to children.

In addition, the national nutritional guidelines were found to be impractical and unclear (Ibid:111-114).

## 3.5 PROBLEMS RELATING TO THE CONCEPTUALISATION AND IMPLEMENTATION OF THE PSFS

On the basis of the conceptual, budgetary and implementation overview of the PSFS above, a number of problems related to the conceptualisation and the implementation of the programme can be highlighted.

As for the implementation of the programme, there have been problems related to the precision of targeting. Initially, the respective provinces developed their own targeting guidelines. The result was that for political reasons, most provinces simply sought to cover as many schools and learners as possible within available resources, often compromising on the quality and quantity of food provided to learners in the process and often making no real attempt to target the benefits of the programme at needy children (Louw *et al* 2001:53). Once national targeting criteria were established, the problem became that few of the provinces actually applied the national criteria. In addition, the national criteria were not sufficiently clear and practical, making it difficult for provinces to follow them (Ibid). However, whatever targeting was in fact applied, it was acted upon relatively effectively. On average over the last nine years, the PSFS reached 86% of the children it targeted. This figure has also gradually increased over the years – the percentage for 2002/03 is 95%. To place these percentages in context, in 2001/02 the PSFS reached 77% of the 6.1 million children between the ages of 6 and 15 who live below the poverty line – in other words 77% of those children that, in broad terms, it is supposed to be reaching. Although not yet available, the number for 2002/03 is likely to be substantially higher.

As for the quality of the service that the PSFS provides to those children that it actually reaches, there have also been a variety of problems over the years. Measured against an ideal of providing food to targeted children on all school days, the performance of the PSFS has been troubling. As noted above, the PSFS in 2000 managed on average to provide food to targeted children on only 71% of the school days available in that year and on only 34% of the total number of days in the year. This undermines both the educational and the nutritional benefits of the programme. There have also been some question marks over the nutritional quality and safety of the food provided to children. The 2000 survey showed both that the national criteria in this regard were in some respects vague and impractical, and that none of the provinces actually applied these criteria fully (Ibid).

Conceptually, the PSFS is sound. It is important that the PSFS is seen to aim first at enhancing the quality of education by combating short-term hunger and low energy levels amongst children at school and only secondarily as a nutritional programme, aimed at enhancing the nutritional status of the children involved. The PSFS certainly has a significant nutritional impact, but it cannot be construed as government's pre-mier nutritional programme regarding children. For this to be the case, the service it provides is too intermittent and covers too small a portion of the calendar year, even if it manages to cover all the school days in a year. Its secondary nutritional aims can only be fulfilled properly if it is seen and operated as a component of a broader social assistance programme, in terms of which food or the means with which to acquire food is transferred directly to needy children and their care-givers also in other ways.

## 3.6 GOVERNMENT'S PLANS TO ADDRESS PROBLEMS WITH THE PSFS: OVERVIEW AND RECOMMENDATIONS

In reaction to the 2001 evaluation of the PSFS and the recommendations resulting from it, the national Department of Health has gone to considerable effort to stream-line and generally improve the implementation of the PSFS. The national department revised and refined its targeting guidelines to ensure that they indeed focus the PSFS on the problem of school children experiencing short-term hunger that is the direct result of poverty. The Department is currently in the process of further refining and updating the guidelines (Kloka 2003:12) and this action has already had some effect. A brief survey conducted for the purposes of this chapter showed that, although most provinces still did not follow the national criteria to the letter (some, for instance, still targeting the programme individually at needy children within schools), there was a pervasive attentiveness to the importance of proper targeting. In addition, all of the provinces canvassed had developed their own methods of targeting that accorded with the broad terms of the national guidelines. The renewed efforts to improve targeting have had a desired impact in practice. After an initial surge in the number of schools targeted between 1994/95 to 1998/99, the number of schools targeted dropped sig-nificantly and then leveled off in the period 1999/00 to 2003/04. In addition, the percentage of targeted schools actually reached, as well as the percentage of targeted children actually reached, has shown a gradual but steady overall increase from 1997 onwards.

Again on the basis of the recommendations resulting from the 2001 evaluation, the Department of Health has taken steps to improve both the regularity with which the services of the PSFS are provided and the quality of those services. First, the national department now requires provinces to provide school feeding on a minimum of 156 school days a year (80% of the available school days). In 2002, the following provinces had already implemented this requirement, feeding on more than 80% of available school days (Ibid:21):

- Western Cape (170 days – 86%);
- North West Province (160 days – 81%);
- Free State (186 days – 94%);

- Limpopo (156 days – 80%); and
- Gauteng (186 days – 94%).

Secondly, to ensure that food of an adequate and uniform nutritional standard is served in the different provinces, the department has moved away from its previous guidelines, within which provinces had to develop their own menus for school feeding. It now requires provinces to use four basic standardised menu options, which give expression to the department's erstwhile guidelines (Ibid:13-15).

In addition to these specific practical measures designed to improve the implementation of the PSFS, the Department of Health managed to obtain political recommitment to the programme from Cabinet in 2002. The decision was made not only to continue with the PSFS, but also to expand it. This political commitment has been translated into budgetary measures. As indicated above, up to 2002/03, the PSFS programme budget had shown an average real growth of –5.4%. Yet over the subsequent three financial years, the INP conditional grant from which the PSFS is funded (on average 85% of the grant is allocated to the PSFS) will show an average real growth of 15% (28% for 2003/04). This is a very significant increase and should be welcomed. However, it does raise some question marks. First, the negative growth rate shown by the PSFS budgets up to and including 2002/03 was to some extent a function of the progressively more cost-effective implementation of the programme. During this time, the programme was being targeted more and more precisely. As indicated above, the number of schools and children targeted for the PSFS showed a gradual decrease, whilst the number of children targeted that was actually reached increased steadily and markedly. In addition, the provincial governments were progressively managing to close the gap between allocated budgets and actual expenditure (managing to spend 96% of the INP conditional grant in 2002/03). In this light, it is not clear how to interpret the expansion of the PSFS that is implied by the substantial budget increases. The two areas where most improvement is probably still required are in the coverage of available school days and the quality, quantity and safety of the food provided.

The substantial budget increases envisaged over the next three years are also somewhat troubling from a conceptual perspective. As indicated above, the PSFS has always, and rightly so, been conceptualised as an educational programme with nutritional spin-offs, rather than as a nutritional programme in the first place. Although the PSFS undoubtedly makes an important contribution to children's nutritional status and so to the realisation of their right to basic nutrition, it cannot be the primary vehicle through which government meets its constitutional duty to provide food to needy children. At best, it can be an important supplement to other more pervasive social assistance measures that have this as their central purpose. If the budget increases are to be interpreted as an indication that government indeed sees the PSFS as its premier nutritional transfer programme for children, this would be troubling.[40] The budgetary focus of realising children's right to basic nutrition should perhaps be located elsewhere.

# 4. CONCLUSIONS

This chapter has aimed to uncover and evaluate those steps that government has taken to meet its constitutional duties in terms of children's right to basic nutrition. In light of the fact that South Africa faces a problem of relatively wide-spread nutritional deprivation, particularly amongst its children, the specific question throughout has been to consider whether government meets its duty to provide food directly to children who are nutritionally deprived.

With regard to government's general policy framework regarding the right to food, it was found that, specifically as regards children, the framework was sufficient on paper. However, various problems relating to scope and application meant that it was insufficient in practice. Particularly, those programmes intended to provide food – or the means with which to acquire food – directly to children were found to be lacking in this regard. In addition, because the general policy framework is based on special needs, it excludes from its scope many South Africans in a desperate nutritional situation, who do not qualify for any of the special needs-based programmes. This is bound to have a negative effect on the nutritional rights of children, as they are largely dependent on care-givers who often receive no or little nutritional support from the state.

The PSFS was analysed in more detail as it represents the only programme in terms of which the state provides food directly to children on a large scale. This section of the chapter showed that within its conceptual bounds, the PSFS is effectively implemented and adequately funded. Despite several problems relating particularly to the coverage of the programme and the quality of the service provided, the PSFS makes close to as significant a contribution as it can, on its own, to enhance the nutritional status of poor children.

However, it was also noted that the nutritional contribution that the PSFS can make is necessarily limited. Because only school-going children benefit from it and because they only receive food from the PSFS on school days (and only some), the programme has to function in co-operation with other more extensive and regular programmes providing direct access to food for children, such as social assistance grants in particular. The unfortunate problems relating to the coverage, scope and the take-up of social security grants, specifically the Child Support Grant, are well known (see for example, chapter five in this publication). The impact that these problems can have on the effectiveness of nutritional programmes such as the PSFS, has recently been illustrated in studies conducted on the impact of the Department of Health's Programme for the in-patient management of severe Protein-Energy Malnutrition (the PEM programme).

The PEM programme provides treatment in hospitals and clinics to severely malnourished children and discharges them when they have recovered. In its pilot phase in rural areas in the Eastern Cape, the programme showed remarkable success in reducing fatality rates amongst young children admitted for severe malnutrition (Chopra *et al* 2001/02:16). However, the improvement in the children's nutritional status that was achieved while they were in the hospitals could not be sustained once they left. The study involved 30 children, none of whom gained weight once they had left the hospital (as would be expected) and hospitals in the focus area reported a large number of re-admissions of children who had been treated before (Ibid:17). The study conclusively found that the cause of this regression in the children's nutritional status was poverty. For all 30 children studied, there was simply not enough food at home to sustain their nutritional gains (Ibid). Most significantly, the study found that all 30 children studied were entitled to receive the Child Support Grant, but that only one of them did (Ibid:16). Clearly, if the social assistance to which these children were entitled was in fact available to them, it would be possible to sustain the successes achieved in their treatment via the PEM programme.

This lesson can also be applied to the PSFS. Although the PSFS itself is relatively successful in achieving its own nutritional aims, this success is mitigated by the lack of proper functioning in those programmes that are supposed to sustain its gains.

# REFERENCES

Boyle, D. (2002) "Government steps in to feed poor". Accessed from *News24.com* at www.news24.com/contentDisplay/level4Article/0,1113,2-1134_1269972,00.html, on 10/22/2002.

Caelers, D., E. Sylvester & E. Gano. (2001) "Quarter of Western Cape families starving". *In Cape Argus,* May 28:1.

Chopra, M., N. Sogaula, D. Jackson, D. Sanders, N. Karaolis, A. Ashworth & D. McCoy. (2001/02) "Poverty Wipes out Health Care Gains". In *ChildrenFirst,* 6 (4): 16-18.

Community Agency for Social Enquiry (CASE). (1998) *Monitoring Socio-economic rights in South Africa: public perceptions.* Johannesburg: CASE

Constitutional Court of South Africa. (1997) *Soobramoney v Minister of Health, KwaZulu-Natal.* 1998 (1) SA 765 (CC); 1997 (12) BCLR 1696 (CC).

Constitutional Court of South Africa. (2000) *Government of the Republic of South Africa and Others v Grootboom and Others.* 2001 (1) SA 46 (CC); 2000 (11) BCLR 1169 (CC).

Constitutional Court of South Africa. (2002) *Minister of Health and Others v Treatment Action Campaign and Others.* 2002 (5) SA 721, 2002 (10) BCLR 1033 (CC).

Department of Agriculture. (2001) *Land Redistribution for Agricultural Development.* Accessed at http://www.nda.agric.za/docs/LRAD/LRAD_E.htm on 27/08/2003.

Department of Agriculture. (2002a) *Integrated Food Security Strategy for South Africa.* Pretoria: Government Printer.

Department of Agriculture. (2002b) *Cabinet statement on measures to address high food prices.* 10 October. Accessed at http://www.nda.agric.za/docs/cabinet foodprices.htm on 25/06/2003.

Department of Agriculture. (2003a) *Strategic Plan for the Department of Agriculture.* Accessed at http://www.nda.agric.za/docs/pfma/default.htm on 27/08/2003.

Department of Agriculture. (2003b) "Food pricing committee asks public to help". In *AgriNews*, January/February: 2.

Department of Health. (1998) *Integrated Nutrition Programme: A Foundation for Life.* Accessed at http://www.doh.gov.za/programmes/nutrition.html on 25/06/2003.

Department of Health. (2002) *Annual Report 2001/02.* Accessed at http://www.doh.gov.za/docs/reports/annal/2001-02.html on 18/07/2003.

Department of Public Works. (2001) *The Community-Based Public Works Programme (Ilima/Letsima).* Accessed at http://www.publicworks.gov.za/programmes/cbpwp.htm on 23/08/2003.

Department of Social Development. (2002a) *Annual Report 2001-2002.* Pretoria: Government Printer.

Department of Social Development. (2002b) *Transforming the present – Protecting the future: Report of the Commission of Enquiry into a Comprehensive System of Social Security for South Africa.* Accessed at http://www.welfare.gov.za/documents/2002/2002.htm on 22/10/2002.

Department of Social Development. (2003a) *Fact Sheet: Social Grants Beneficiaries.* Accessed at http://www.welfare.gov.za/Documents/2003/Budget%20Vote/Fact%20Sheets/benf.pdf on 25/07/2003.

Department of Social Development. (2003b) *You and Your Grants.* Accessed at http://www.welfare.gov.za/Services/serv01.htm on 25/07/2003.

Department of Social Development. (2003c) *Budget vote speech by Dr Zola Skweyiya, Minister of Social Development, to the National Assembly, 27 March 2003.* Accessed at http://www.welfare.gov.za/Statements/2003/March/votesp.htm on 25/06/2003.

Drëze, J & A. Sen. (1998) *Hunger and Public Action.* Oxford: Clarendon Press.

Eide, A. (1995) "The right to an adequate standard of living including the right to food". In Eide, A., C. Krause & A. Rosas (eds), *Economic, social and cultural rights: a textbook.* Dordrecht: Marthinus Nijhoff.

Eide, A. (1999) "Overview". In *International consultative conference on food security and nutrition as human rights.* Johannesburg: South African Human Rights Commission.

Health Systems Trust. (2002) "Health status indicators". In *South African Health Review*. Accessed at http://new.hst.org.za/indic/index.php?indtype_id=003007 on 18/07/2003.

Immelman, E. & L. Bamford. (2000) *Implementing an Integrated Nutrition Programme: A Situation Analysis of Progress in the Lower Orange Region of the Northern Cape.* Northern Cape ISDS Technical Report (4).

International Labour Research and Information Group (ILRIG). (2003) "Food inflation". In *Workers World News,* 27, July.

Kloka, D. (2003) *Integrated Nutrition Programme: School Feeding.* Background document for Cabinet briefing. Pretoria: Department of Health.

Künneman, R. (2002) "The right to adequate food: Violations related to its minimum core content". In Brand, D. & S. Russel (eds), *Exploring the core content of socio-economic rights: South African and international perspectives.* Pretoria: Protea Book House.

Labadarios, D (ed). (1999) *The national food consumption survey.* Pretoria: Department of Health.

Labadarios, D. & M. van Middelkoop. (1995) *Children aged 6-71 months in South Africa, 1994: Their anthropometric, vitamin A, iron and immunisation coverage status.* Isando: South African Vitamin A Consultative Group.

Louw, R., E. Bekker & E. Wentzel-Viljoen. (2001) *An External Evaluation of Certain Aspects of Primary School Feeding.* Pretoria: Department of Health.

McCoy, D., P. Barron & A. Wigton (eds). (1997) *An Evaluation of South Africa's Primary School Nutrition Programme.* Report prepared on behalf of the Child Health Unit of the University of Cape Town, for the Department of Health. Durban: Health Systems Trust.

Mgijima, C. (1999) "South African Government: Department of Health". In *International consultative conference on food security and nutrition as human rights.* Johannesburg: South African Human Rights Commission.

National Treasury. (2003) *National Medium-Term Expenditure Estimates 2003.* Accessed at www.treasury.gov.za.

Ravindran, R. & A. Blyberg (eds). (2000) *A circle of rights. Economic, social and cultural rights activism: A training resource.* New York: International Human Rights Internship Programme/Asian Forum for Human Rights and Development.

Reuters. (2002) "Cosatu hails food help, but..." Accessed from *News24.com* at www.news24.com/contentDisplay/level4Article/0,1113,2-1134_1270080,00.html on 10/10/2003.

Sapa. (2003) "Not enough funds for food relief". Accessed from *News24.com* at http://www.news24.com/News24/South_Africa/Politics/0,,2-7-12_1372887,00.html on 18/06/2003.

Sen, A. (1981) *Poverty and famines: An essay on entitlement and deprivation.* Oxford: Oxford University Press.

South African Institute for Medical Research. (2000) *Report of the South African Institute for Medical Research on the Iodine Deficiency Disorder (IDD) Survey of Primary School Learners for the Department of Health, South Africa.* Pretoria: SAIMR.

Steyn, N. & D. Labadarios. (2002) "Nutrition policy implementation". In *South African Health Review 2002.* Health Systems Trust.

United Nations Committee on Economic, Social and Cultural Rights. (1999) *General Comment No. 12. Substantive issues arising in the implementation of the International Covenant on Economic, Social and Cultural Rights: The right to adequate food (article 11 of the Covenant).* Geneva: United Nations.

Van Marle, K. (2002) "'No last word' – Reflections on the imaginary domain, dignity and intrinsic worth". In *Stellenbosch Law Review/Regstydskrif,* 13(2):299-308.

## PERSONAL COMMUNICATION

The following people provided information through personal communications:

Ms Rebecca Mamabolo, Department of Agriculture, 28 August 2003.

Ms Diane Kloka, Department of Health, August to October 2003.

Ms Morongwa, Department of Social Development, 22 September 2003.

Mr T.M. Madima, National Agricultural Marketing Council, 22 September 2003.

Ms M. Le Roux, Northern Cape Department of Health, 14 October 2003.

Mr S. Titus, Western Cape Department of Health, 14 October 2003.

Ms N. Ncqobo, KwaZulu-Natal Department of Health, 14 October 2003.

Ms F. Pretorius, Free State Department of Health, 15 October 2003.

# ENDNOTES

1   This description derives from an address by Justice Tolakele Madala during the *International Right to Food Seminar,* Centre for Human Rights, University of Pretoria, Pretoria, 27-29 January 2002.

2   Food security has been defined as: "[A]ccess for all, at all times, to adequate food which is nutritionally adequate, safe, and in the best interest of the consumer, and where the food supply and access is sustainable" (Eide 1999:8). This situation exists despite the fact that there is, and has been for the past 20 years, suffi-

cient food available in South Africa to feed our population adequately (Department of Agriculture 2002a:19-20).

3   The study focused on children aged between one and nine years. For a useful summary of this survey and its findings, see Steyn & Labadarios (2002:336-341).

4   See also Department of Social Development (2002b:29), which indicates that in 1999, 21.9% of households nationally reported going hungry.

5   *Underweight* indicates a weight-for-age ratio under two standard deviations from the norm. *Stunting* indicates a height-for-age ratio under two standard deviations from the norm. *Wasting* indicates a weight-for-height ratio under two standard deviations from the norm. It is an indicator of severe current under-nutrition.

6   More recent studies are consistent with these 1994 figures, showing that, for instance, 69% of children between 4 and 6 years old have an intake of vitamin A less than two-thirds of RDA and 62% of the same age group have an intake of iron less than two-thirds of RDA (Labadarios 1999:242-245).

7   *Nutritional deprivation* indicates a condition of not receiving enough nutritional input to avoid stunting, wasting, being underweight and other serious health risks. *Under-nourishment* indicates a condition of not receiving enough nutritional input to live a normal, active working life, without however facing serious and long-term health risks (Drëze & Sen 1998:35). Any such categorisation of nutritional need, whether between "simple" inadequacy on the one hand, and desperation – or crisis – on the other, or between *under-nourishment* and full-blown *nutritional deprivation,* is scientifically somewhat crude and also politically and ethically very problematic. It is scientifically crude both because it is difficult to draw context-sensitive basic standards against which to measure data and because, once such standards have been set, it is difficult to test whether they are being met, due to problems of measurement. The extent to which the right to food is being realised can be measured in two ways: through analysing input or output data. Both these approaches have their problems. The daily calorific and other nutrient intake of a person as measured against predetermined nutritional requirements is not an entirely accurate measurement of actual nutritional capability. This is because, among other things, the actual nutritional requirements of a person are determined individually by his or her height, weight and basal metabolism. Also, the ability of a person to be nourished by food actually ingested is determined by certain non-food factors such as existing disease and even climate. Measuring a person's status in relation to realising his or her right to food through anthropometric indicators is flawed for the same reason: stunting, being underweight and wasting are also partly caused by non-food factors, not the least social factors (see, in general, Drëze & Sen 1998:35–45). Nutritional activists further resist these kinds of distinctions on a political basis because they might be interpreted as trivialising the very real and very urgent needs of those who are not nutritionally deprived, but "only" under-nourished. The conceptual and ethical difficulties of distinguishing and then prioritising categories of need have also often been pointed out (see Van Marle 2002:307). Nevertheless, for policy purposes it does seem to make sense to distinguish, even if only roughly, between desperate and inadequate nutritional status.

8   Children's nutritional rights are also protected by the Convention on the Rights of the Child, 1989 (see articles 24 and 27) and the African Charter on the Rights and Welfare of the Child, 1990 (see articles 14 and 20). South Africa is a

state party to both these treaties and as such, is legally bound to the duties they create.

9   This is borne out in the judgments of three Constitutional Court cases, popularly refered to as *Soobramoney* (1997), *Grootboom* (2000) and the *Treatment Action Campaign* (TAC) case (2002). For more on the limited entitlements created by section 27(1)(b) rights, the full legal citations are as follows: *Soobramoney v Minister of Health, KwaZulu-Natal* 1998 (1) SA 765, 1997 (12) BCLR 1696 (CC) (hereinafter '*Soobramoney*'), paragraph [11] at 771G/H – I; *Government of the Republic of South Africa v Grootboom* 2001 (1) SA 46, 2000 (11) BCLR 1169 (CC) (hereinafter '*Grootboom*'), paragraph [34] at 66F/G – H/I and paragraph [38] at 67G/H – I/J; *Minister of Health v Treatment Action Campaign* 2002 (5) SA 721, 2002 (10) BCLR 1033 (CC) (hereinafter '*TAC*'), paragraph [23] at 736A/B – B/C and in particular paragraphs [29] – [32] at 738E/F – 739D.

10  *Grootboom*, paragraphs [39]–[44].

11  See *Grootboom* supra note 8, paragraphs [76] – [79], at 81F/G – 82H; TAC supra note 8, paragraphs [75] – [77], at 749D – G/H.

12  Section 28(1)(c) reads as follows:
    "(1) Every child *has the right* to –
        (c) *basic* nutrition, shelter, basic health care services and social services"
        (emphasis added).
    Section 27 in turn reads as follows:
    "(1) Everyone has the right to have access to –
        (b) *sufficient* food and water...
        (2) The state must take *reasonable* legislative and other measures, *within its available resources,* to achieve the *progressive realisation* of [this right]"
        (emphasis added).

13  See for instance United Nations Committee on Economic, Social and Cultural Rights 1999; Künneman 2002.

14  Section 39(1) of the Constitution requires courts to take heed of international law, including international human rights law, when interpreting the rights in the Bill of Rights.

15  See also Eide (1995:94-95); Ravindran & Blyberg (2000:222).

16  Published by the Department of Agriculture on 17 July 2002 and approved by Cabinet (Mamabolo 2003: personal communication).

17  The IFSS is headed at political level by an Inter-Ministerial Committee, chaired by the Minister of Agriculture. It is managed and implemented by a National Co-ordinating Unit, with corollaries at provincial level (Provincial Co-ordinating Units), which oversee the work of District Food Security Officers and, at local level, Food Security Officers. The IFSS also envisages the establishment of a National Food Security Forum (NFSF), with membership drawn from the public sector, the private sector and civil society and with corollaries at provincial level (Provincial Food Security Forums), at district level (District Food Security Forums) and local level (Local Food Security Action Groups). The role of the NFSF is to provide "strategic leadership and advisory services on food security" and to set standards and recommend policy options (Department of Agriculture 2002a:34).

18  These are: Increasing household food production and trading; improving income-generation and job-creation; improving nutrition and food safety; increasing safety nets and food emergency systems; improving analysis and information manage-

ment systems; providing capacity-building; and facilitating stakeholder dialogue (Department of Agriculture 2002a:6).

19 This fact has been acknowledged by government (see Department of Agriculture 2002a:11).

20 Partly in response to these problems of co-ordination and coherence, Cabinet requested the Department of Agriculture to draft an over-arching policy framework that would co-ordinate and draw together the activities of the different departments. This policy was published on 17 July 2002, as the *Integrated Food Security Strategy for South Africa*, discussed in section two of the chapter. A right-to-food framework law, which would create and empower co-ordinating policy bodies and set basic standards, has also been in the pipe-line since the end of 2001.

21 A focus on the facilitation, provision and enhancement of entitlement is apt for a number of reasons. Entitlement, rather than availability, is manifestly where the problem in South Africa lies. Despite the fact that an adequate national food supply is currently available (and that South Africa has been nationally food secure for the past 20 years), malnutrition and hunger persist in South Africa due to failures in access to food (Department of Agriculture 2002a:19-20). Furthermore, if the purpose here is to review the extent to which the state is meeting its *legal duties* relating to the provision of food to its people, then a focus on entitlement is apt, as entitlement is much more clearly a legal issue than is the availability of food. Food availability and national food security is mostly determined by natural and macro-economic factors, things that the law can do little to control and shape. Access to food, on the other hand, is determined largely by social and political factors. It depends on the ability "to establish command over food, using the entitlement relations operating in...society depending on its legal, economic, political and social characteristics..." (Sen 1981:165). The law can do a great deal to control and shape these factors. Amartya Sen puts it thus: '[T]he focus on entitlement has the effect of emphasising legal rights. Other relevant factors, for example market forces, can be seen as operating through a system of legal relations (ownership rights, contractual obligations, legal exchanges, etc). The law stands between food availability and food entitlement." (Ibid:166).

22 Food prices rose by an average 18.2% over the first eight months of the year. Staple grain prices rose by a stunning 44% (Boyle 2002). The food price index rose by 11.4% in 2001 (as opposed to an increase in items other than food of only 3% for that year) and 21% in 2002 (ILRIG 2003:7). The cause of these rises in food prices has been a matter of some dispute. Those linked to the food industry point to fluctuations in the value of the rand, rising production prices and rising world food prices as the major causes. Trade unions, food security NGOs and other social movements in turn blame "defects in the market caused mainly by speculative pricing and concentration of ownership" (Ibid). Government has focused its energies on trying to trace a combination of possible causes, listing rising world food prices, low regional food production, lack of competition in the food supply chain beyond the initial food production stage, depreciation of the rand, rising oil prices and possible "opportunistic pricing behaviour" as culprits (Department of Agriculture 2003b:3).

23 The extension of coverage is phased in as follows. From 1 April 2003, all eligible children under 9 years of age could be registered. At the same time those who turned 7 and would under the old coverage have fallen off the system, simply

remained registered and continued receiving their grants. From 1 April 2004, coverage is extended to the 9 to 10 year age cohort, and finally, by April 2005 to the 11 to 13 year age cohort.

24    The money was allocated per province in the following manner:

| Province | Number of households targeted | Amounts (in R million) |
|---|---|---|
| Eastern Cape | 35 000 | 31.5 |
| Free State | 30 000 | 27 |
| KwaZulu-Natal | 30 390 | 27.4 |
| Northern Cape | 4 670 | 4.2 |
| North West | 72 000 | 64.8 |
| Limpopo | 50 890 | 45.8 |
| Mpumalanga | 12 000 | 10.8 |
| Gauteng | 5 000 | 4.5 |
| Western Cape | 5 000 | 4.5 |
| **Total** | **244 950** | **73.5 per month for 3 months = 220.5** |

25    The committee is chaired by Prof Johann Kirsten of the University of Pretoria and its members are Ms Fikile Mazibuko (Deputy Chairperson), Prof Johann Potgieter, Prof Sbu Nkomo, Ms Josephine Hlophe-Nhlapo, Prof Herman van Schalkwyk, Mr Lumkile Mondi and Ms Nonia Rampomane.

26    Although current production of most basic food-stuffs equal and even significantly outstrip current consumption, projections show that agricultural production of basic food-stuffs will not be able to keep up with consumption in future. So for instance, wheat consumption will exceed wheat production by at least 60% by 2010 if current production trends continue (Department of Agriculture 2002a:20).

27    It has been estimated that social assistance grants close the "poverty gap" (the gap between household income and the subsistence income line) by an average of 23% (Department of Social Development 2002b:59).

28    Cosatu, for instance, has pointed out that the increases in social assistance grants were not increases in real terms, as they only just kept up with general inflation and did not nearly keep up with food price inflation (see Reuters 2002). The same can be said of the scope of beneficiaries eligible for some of the social assistance grants. So for example, it is still unsatisfactory that the Child Support Grant should eventually only accrue to children under 14 years of age.

29    The Minister of Social Development recently admitted as much in Parliament, saying that the money allocated for the food package scheme was not enough to provide for the needs of all people affected by rising food prices (Sapa 2003).

30    The Taylor Commission is officially known as the Committee of Enquiry into a Comprehensive Social Security System for South Africa, appointed under the auspices of the Department of Social Development.

31    People thus excluded from existing special needs-targeted social assistance programmes, according to the Taylor Commission, translates into more than half of poor South Africans, or 11 840 597 people (Department of Social Development 2002b:59).

32    For example, at the time of writing this chapter, legal action was pending against the North West provincial government for its failure to take any steps to implement Social Relief of Distress grants.

33  The PSFS has been rigorously evaluated since its inception. This section relies extensively on three such evaluations/studies: McCoy *et al* 1997; Immelman & Bamford 2000; and Louw *et al* 2001. Full reference details are provided in the reference list at the end of this chapter.

34  The integration of the PSNP into the INP occurred as part of a general consolidation of nutrition-related policies in 1997, mandated by the *White Paper for the Transformation of the Health System in South Africa*, 1997 (Kloka 2003:2).

35  The effect that malnutrition and short-term hunger has on children's learning capacity is well documented. (see McCoy *et al* 1997:8-9 and the sources cited by them; Louw *et al* 2001:1). The PSFS is intended to foster better quality education by enhancing children's active learning capacity, alleviating short-term hunger, providing an incentive for children to attend school regularly and punctually and addressing certain micro-nutrient deficiencies (Louw *et al* 2001:2; Kloka 2003:5).

36  From the outset, the programme was conceptualised as primarily an educational intervention, aimed in the first place at addressing children's ability to learn. This choice of goal was largely motivated by the fact that school feeding schemes have generally proven to be an ineffective and costly means to improve the nutritional status of children, amongst other reasons because of the multiplicity of factors causing malnutrition, the relatively small contribution that a school feeding programme can make to a child's daily nutritional requirements and logistical problems related to large-scale implementation. The most recent evaluation of the PSFS recommended that it should be re-conceptualised as a nutritional programme (Louw *et al* 2001:244) It is not clear whether the Department of Health has adopted this shift in focus (Kloka 2003:3).

37  Of those provinces that were available and also willing to provide information, only KwaZulu-Natal seemed to follow the national guidelines. They targeted farm schools, rural schools and schools in informal settlements. From this group, the most needy schools are then selected for targeting according to an application process (Ncqobo 2003).

38  The formula uses an index with two indicators: the average poverty gap (counts 60%) and the number of young children (counts 40%) in a province (Kloka 2003:10).

39  Negative nominal growth is, in itself, of course not necessarily problematic. An important indicator of the successful implementation of the PSFS is the extent to which it is cost-effective in the sense that it successfully targets only those children who are sufficiently in need and then effectively delivers services to them. In light of this criterion, a decline in the number of children targeted, coupled with a rise in the percentage of those targeted who are in fact reached, would indicate the success rather than failure of the programme. Against this background, a slight real decline in budget allocations for the PSFS is not cause for concern, particularly in light of the fact that the provinces have not once managed to spend their full allocations for the programme.

40  There are indeed indications that government may be viewing the PSFS increasingly as a vehicle for delivering children's food rights. In the Medium-Term Expenditure Estimates for 2003, "the impact of escalating food prices" is listed as one motivation for the increase in funding for the PSFS (National Treasury 2003:328).

# CHAPTER FOUR

## Children's right to health

Maylene Shung-King, Lori Michelson,
Thokozani Kaime, Paula Proudlock
Alexandra Vennekens-Poane and Nhlanhla Ndlovu

# INTRODUCTION:
# CHILDREN'S HEALTH STATUS IN SOUTH AFRICA

In its most recent definition, the World Health Organisation (WHO) defines health as "a dynamic state of physical, mental and social well-being and not merely the absence of disease or infirmity". This contextualises health as a state that encompasses all aspects of an individual's life and well-being.[1] For children, this means the development and protection of all dimensions of their lives and demands a comprehensive inter-sectoral approach to ensuring that children's health rights and needs are met.

Regular and accurate monitoring and reflection on children's health status would provide the ultimate indication of whether and to what extent children's health rights have been met. Very specific and methodologically sound health evaluations are required in order to follow the thread from rights to services to resources to child health status. Such evaluations have not yet been carried out in South Africa, making the connection between a commitment to child rights and child health outcomes difficult to assess. This introduction aims to highlight the current health status of South African children in an attempt to draw attention to the challenges that the country still faces in meeting and responding to children's constitutional health rights.

Available information on child health in South Africa mainly takes the form of indicators of survival, such as child death and child morbidity rates. These indicators are not able to provide a comprehensive insight into the multiplicity of factors that impact on child health, nor on the many other dimensions of child health and well-being. Some aspects of child health are still poorly understood. For example, no regular information exists as to the psycho-social and mental health challenges that children face in a context of poverty and devastating epidemics such as HIV, trauma and violence. Morbidity and mortality indicators nevertheless provide a crude, albeit incomplete, measure of the extent to which children's health rights are being met. Boxes 4.1 and 4.2 set out the most recent information on child morbidity and mortality amongst South African children.

The most recently available national estimates of the leading contributors to the burden of disease for children were released by the Medical Research Council, in their brief entitled *Initial estimates from the South African National Burden of Disease Study, 2000* (Bradshaw 2003). Two other sources are used together with this study to provide a picture of children's health status and the key child health challenges.

## BOX 4.1  CHILD MORTALITY

In the Burden of Disease for South Africa study, the national infant mortality rate for 2000 was estimated to be 59 deaths per 1000 live births, while the under-five mortality was estimated at 95 deaths per 1000 live births. This is significantly higher than that estimated by the 1998 *South African Demographic and Health Survey*, in which the estimates for national infant mortality stood at 45 and that for under-five mortality at 59. These figures show that infant mortality and under-five mortality have increased significantly from 1998 to 2000 and that concerted measures are required to reverse this upward trend. HIV/AIDS is cited as the major cause for the increase in child deaths.

For children between the ages of 5 and 19, trauma remains the number one cause of death. Motor vehicle accidents are the predominant killers of children in the 5 to 15 year age group, while homicides due to fire-arm injuries are the major killer of boys in the age group 15 to 19. This has been a consistent trend over the past five years. There is no current national policy or programme effort that focuses on the prevention of child deaths due to trauma and violence, apart from sporadic local initiatives. Thus while motor vehicle accidents are the number one killer of younger children and firearms the number one killer of adolescent boys, neither the Departments of Transport nor Safety and Security have any significant prevention programmes to reduce child deaths due to these factors. This illustrates the need to view the realisation of children's health rights as an inter-sectoral challenge and not just a health responsibility.

## Box 4.2  Child morbidity

The epidemiology of childhood illnesses is not monitored on a routine basis, except for the statutory-required notifiable diseases. The extent of most health conditions in children is thus likely to be under-estimated. Nonetheless, the most common conditions in children are still those that are integrally linked to poverty. Diarrhoeal disease due to a lack of access to safe clean water remains the number one health challenge in young children. Malnutrition, due to a lack of access to food, affects one in every ten children in the short term, while chronic malnutrition due to a sustained lack of food affects one in every five children. Vitamin A deficiency in children, an easily remediable nutritional deficiency, is prevalent in all of the country's nine provinces. The highest prevalence is in Limpopo, where a third of children under 6 are Vitamin A deficient (Department of Health 1998b). Preventable conditions such as tuberculosis (TB) and malaria affect thousands of children annually. Children constitute one-fifth of all reported TB cases annually, totalling more than 12 000 cases per year (Department of Health 1999). The prevalence of TB is increasing due to the HIV epidemic.

An estimated one in every ten children has a chronic disease or disability, this being a health condition lasting one year or longer. The rising HIV epidemic is contributing significantly to this figure. An estimated 100 000 babies per annum are born with HIV infection, thus increasing the pool of children with chronic health conditions. The majority will die before their second birthday unless they have access to anti-retroviral therapy and the required supportive treatment.

This brief overview indicates the dire and indeed worsening overall health status of South African children. It demonstrates an urgent need for health and related sectors to understand and fulfil their constitutional obligations towards children and to muster an urgent and sustained response towards improving children's right to health and to basic health care services.

As a number of other rights are dealt with in parallel chapters of this book, this chapter focuses exclusively on the right to health as embodied in Section 28 (I) (c) of the South African Constitution. The purpose of this chapter is to shed some light on government's budgeting and programming for child health services and in so doing, to examine its commitment to children's section 28 health rights. This undertaking is not without its own constraints, as will become clear in section one.

Given the enormous public health implications of the HIV epidemic, as well as the significant contribution of HIV/AIDS to child mortality and morbidity, this chapter focuses specific attention on the Prevention of Mother-to-Child Transmission of HIV (PMTCT) programme. The success or failure of this programme has vast implications for children and society as a whole. It is also worthy of attention due to the high international and national profile of the AIDS epidemic, the significant tensions between government and civil society in this regard, as well as the recent Constitutional Court ruling regarding the implementation of the programme.

The structure of this chapter is briefly outlined below:

- Section one considers the international and national context of children's right to health. It also examines the current interpretation of the meaning and scope of the right and the associated state obligations, using recent interpretations of children's health rights by the Constitutional Court.

- Section two provides a synopsis of government's legislative response to the child's right to health care in South Africa. It then gives an overview of government's health programming for children since 1994.

- Section three puts the spotlight on the PMTCT programme. More specifically, this section seeks to answer, in as far as available information allows, the following questions:
  * The extent to which the programme conceptualisation targets children in need;
  * Whether the programme plans allow for roll-out as a matter of priority and as quickly as administrative capacity permits;
  * Whether programme implementation has been rolled out quickly and if all children, especially the most vulnerable, have been catered for;
  * What problems impede access and/or service delivery in this programme;
  * Whether the budgetary framework and allocations to the programme adequately support implementation; and
  * Government's plan to deal with any current shortcomings in the coverage and overall delivery of the programmes.

- The conclusion offers a set of recommendations relating to future evaluations of this nature and to government's budgetary and implementation plans for child health programmes.

# 1. SOUTH AFRICA'S OBLIGATIONS IN RELATION TO CHILDREN'S RIGHT TO HEALTH

South Africa has made significant progress with regards to the signing and ratification of key international human rights treaties that promote and protect health rights. South Africa has also taken the important step of enshrining everyone's right to have access to health care services and children's right to basic health care services in the Bill of Rights.

Despite this progress, children's health status indicators suggest that these rights are not being realised in practice. This can be partly attributed to a lack of understanding of the exact meaning and implications of the obligations and duties created by the rights. The Constitutional Court has yet to provide clear guidance on South Africa's obligations in respect of children's socio-economic rights. In the absence of such guidance, various experts have ventured opinions, which are briefly outlined in section 1.2 below.

## 1.1 THE INTERNATIONAL FRAMEWORK FOR CHILDREN'S RIGHT TO HEALTH

The right to health is recognised in a number of international human rights instruments (Hendricks 1999:225, 227). It forms the preamble to the constitution of the World Health Organisation (1981)[2] and is also included in article 25 of the Universal Declaration of Human Rights.[3] The latter states that "everyone has the right to a standard of living adequate for the health and well-being of her/himself and her/his family, including food, clothing, housing and medical care and necessary social services".

Child health has been prioritised globally, as evidenced by the prominence given to children's health rights in a number of international processes and instruments. Children's health rights are protected through child-specific treaties and instruments, as well as in treaties and instruments that recognise health as a basic human right for all. Furthermore, child health indices such as infant mortality are used as markers of the social and economic development of countries and of whether a signatory to a human rights treaty is adhering to its obligations.

International treaties which South Africa has signed and/or ratified, such as the International Covenant on Economic, Social and Cultural Rights (ICESCR)[4], affirms the universal right to health. The ICESCR calls upon state parties "to recognise the right of everyone to the highest attainable standard of physical and mental health...to the maximum extent of [their] available resources with a view to achieving progressively the full realisation" of the right to health. It further calls upon all state parties to adopt "special measures of protection and assistance on behalf of all children and young people without any discrimination".

At a regional level, the African Charter on Human and People's Rights (hereafter referred to as the African Charter)[5] provides that governments shall "take the necessary measures to protect the health of their people and to ensure that they receive medical attention when they are sick".

The Convention on the Rights of the Child (CRC)[6] confers on all children the right to "the enjoyment of the highest attainable standard of health" and calls upon governments to progressively work towards the full realisation of this right. In line with the CRC, the African Charter on the Rights and Welfare of the Child (ACRWC)[7] proclaims that "every child shall have the right to enjoy the best attainable state of physical, mental and spiritual health".

Article 24 of the CRC is the predominant health article in the convention that provides the foundation for governments as to the specific responsibilities that they have towards meeting children's health rights. It is a composite article that contains a number of specific requirements to ensure that the chief provision of ensuring "the child's right to the highest level of health possible" is met. Article 24 requires signatory countries to pay particular attention to all the provisions it contains, including:

- the right to access to health services;
- the duty to diminish infant and child mortality;
- the duty to provide medical assistance and health care to all children with emphasis on the development of primary health care;
- the duty to ensure the provision of adequate nutritious foods and clean drinking water and to consider the danger and risks of environmental pollution;
- the duty to provide pre- and post-natal care for mothers;
- the duty to ensure that parents and children have information and are supported in the use of basic knowledge relating to child health and nutrition, breastfeeding, hygiene, environmental sanitation and accident prevention; and finally
- the duty to develop preventive health care guidance for parents, family planning education and services.

The CRC thus provides a useful framework for considering what each country is responsible for in terms of basic health care obligations to children.

However, the realisation of children's health rights also depends on the fulfilment of a number of additional rights that do not directly fall under the jurisdiction of the health sector. This is because multiple factors, over and above specific health interventions and services, impact on the health of individuals and communities. Using the comprehensive WHO definition of health, at least ten additional CRC articles embody rights that either directly or indirectly impact on the "right to the highest level of health possible". These include the right to care and protection, the right to social security, ensuring that facilities and services are to an agreed standard, the right to education and the right to play, amongst others. While specific interventions within the health sector play a major role in the attainment of children's right to health, the non-fulfilment of basic rights and related interventions within other sectors play an equally important part in promoting or hindering the fulfilment of this right.

The overall responsibility currently lies with government to ensure that children's right to health is met. Government is obliged to report back to the United Nations in terms of progress made towards the fulfilment of the CRC in South Africa. It is therefore paramount to ascertain whether and to what extent government has promoted and protected children's health rights.

## 1.2 CHILDREN'S HEALTH RIGHT IN THE SOUTH AFRICAN CONSTITUTION

As a signatory to the CRC, South Africa's most significant commitment to the fulfilment of this right is the embodiment of health as a fundamental right of children in section 28(1)(c) of the South African Constitution. This constitutional commitment to children's right to health is expressed as children having a right to basic health care services. This section looks at expert opinion on the possible meaning of section 28(1)(c) rights and at recent Constitutional Court interpretations in this regard.

Children's constitutional right to health is founded upon two platforms. Firstly, it is sourced from section 27 of the Constitution, which is a general provision guaranteeing everyone various socio-economic rights including health care, food, water and social security. The relevant part of the provision reads:

> "(1) Everyone has the right to have access to health care services, including reproductive health care...
>
> (2) The state must take reasonable legislative and other measures, within its available resources, to achieve the progressive realisation of each of these rights."

Secondly, section 28(1)(c) provides additional and child-specific protection by pronouncing that:

> "(1) Every child has the right -...
> (c) to basic nutrition, shelter, *basic health care services* and social services"
> (authors' emphasis).

The challenge currently lies in interpreting what the differences are between the section 27 and section 28 provisions and what the judicial and practical applications of such differences mean. Key issues that have been clarified to an extent and some that still require clarification include:

- What are the implications of children having a "right to basic health care services", in comparison with the right of everyone "to have access to health care services"?

- Who bears the duty to ensure that the object of the right (basic health care services) is provided to children?

- What constitutes "basic health care services" as stipulated in section 28(1)(c)?

- What is the nature of this duty and is it qualified by the "progressive realisation within available resources" clause that relates to the right of everyone in section 27(2)?

- Finally, if the qualification is applicable to the children's right, will the Constitutional Court apply a different test and standard if it is asked to interpret the qualification in relation to section 28(1)(c)?

Expert opinions, recent Constitutional Court rulings and various interpretations of these rulings shed some light on the questions above, although much debate is still required to provide clear and unambiguous direction for policy-makers, service providers and civil society. Some key interpretations are outlined below.

## 1.2.1 THE RIGHT TO BASIC HEALTH CARE SERVICES VS THE RIGHT OF ACCESS TO HEALTH CARE SERVICES

The child health right in section 28(1)(c) is not an access right but rather an entitlement to basic health care services. This can be deduced from the textual difference between the section 27(1) and section 28(1)(c) rights. A "right to" is generally considered to place a clear positive duty to provide the entitlement that follows the words "right to". However, the Constitutional Court has not yet applied its mind to the implications of this crucial textual difference. Expert opinion has also concentrated more on the implications of the absence of the "progressive realisation within available resources" clause, with little reference to the implications of this textual difference.

## 1.2.2 THE DUTY TO REALISE CHILDREN'S RIGHT TO HEALTH

The duty to fulfil the rights in section 28(1)(c) rests primarily with the parents and care-givers of the child. However, if the parents or primary care-givers are absent or are unable to provide the minimum level of care required (for example, because the parents are too poor), the obligation falls on the state. Two Constitutional Court judgments are relevant in this regard. Firstly, the *Grootboom* judgment (Constitutional Court 2000) could be narrowly interpreted to mean that the duty only falls upon the state when the child is not in the care of his or her family. However, in the *Treatment Action Campaign (TAC)* case (Constitutional Court 2002), the court's judgment can be interpreted to say that the duty falls upon the state if the care is lacking, and that care can be considered to be lacking in circumstances where the child is living with their parents but the parents are poor and unable to provide the care required. This latter judgment has provided much needed guidance with regards to who bears the obligation to provide children's health rights.

In the *TAC* judgment, the court also said that the very nature of health care services is such that a parent cannot directly provide the service. Instead, parents or care-givers have the duty to facilitate the child obtaining access to the service, by for instance taking the child to the clinic and paying for the service. However, where the parent cannot pay for the service due to being poor, the state has the obligation to provide the service free of charge. If this interpretation of the *TAC* judgment is accepted, then what remains to be determined is what services government is obliged to provide? In other words, what falls within the ambit of "basic health care services"?

## 1.2.3 WHAT ARE BASIC HEALTH SERVICES?

If the duty is to deliver basic health care services, what falls within the package of "basic" services? The Constitutional Court has not yet pronounced on the meaning of the word "basic" and government has not yet defined the concept in law or policy.

In health policy documents, emphasis is placed on the concept of primary health care. In practice, the primary health care policy aims to provide everyone with free services at clinics and day hospitals (Department of Health 2000). However, expert opinion suggests that the term "basic" is broader than the term "primary" and includes services that are not currently provided for in the primary health care package (Proudlock & Shung-King 2003).

In terms of national policy and now also the National Health Act (passed by Parliament in 2003), children under six and pregnant women who are not on medical aid, besides being entitled to free primary health care services at clinics and day hospitals, are also entitled to free "health care services". In practice, this means that they can access these services free of charge at any level of care, as long as they have accessed the system at the level of a clinic or day hospital and have been referred to a higher level of care. However, there are clear provincial variations in the package of "health care services" that pregnant women and children under six are provided with at these various levels of service and a lack of clarity exists as to what exactly the package of care consists of.

Furthermore, with regards to children above six years of age, it is not clear what obligations fall on the state with regards to aspects of health services that do not fall within the package of primary health care services, but may be considered to fall into the concept of "basic" health care services. For example, the management and treatment of certain chronic illnesses, such as asthma and HIV, can be managed and treated at a primary level of care such as a clinic or day hospital. In some areas within the more wealthy provinces, clinics and day hospitals have the resources, staff and equipment to manage and treat children with chronic illnesses. On the other hand, primary level service providers in the poorer provinces tend to refer all chronic illness cases to secondary and tertiary hospitals, which are often far away and where services are subject to fees. While a means testing system is applied and poor people are exempted from fees or charged a nominal fee, they still need to supply the required transport costs and suffer the inconvenience of travelling often long distances to receive what should be a "free" primary level of care.

There is therefore a need for further research and deliberation at policy and legislative level to establish clarity on the question of what falls within the package of "basic" health care services.

## 1.2.4 CAN THE HEALTH RIGHT OF CHILDREN BE REALISED PROGRESSIVELY WITHIN THE LIMITS OF AVAILABLE RESOURCES?

It remains to be clarified whether and to what extent section 28(1)(c) is qualified by the "progressive realisation within available resources" clause, which appears in section

27(2). If the state is obliged to provide basic health care services to children in state care and poor children, free of charge, is it obliged to do so immediately or can it rely on the "progressive realisation within available resources" qualification to justify a lack of delivery to vast numbers of children?

The Constitutional Court has been presented with two opportunities to resolve this question. In the *Grootboom* case (Cape High Court 1999; Constitutional Court 2000), the respondents were rendered homeless as a result of their eviction from informal homes situated on private land set aside for low-cost housing. They applied to the Cape High Court for an order requiring the government to provide them with adequate basic shelter or housing until they obtained permanent accommodation. The respondents' claim was based on section 26 of the Constitution, which provides that everyone has the right to adequate housing. As is the case with section 27 rights, section 26(2) imposes an obligation on the state to take reasonable legislative and other measures to ensure the progressive realisation of this right within its available resources. The respondents also based their claim on section 28(1)(c) of the Constitution, which provides that children have the right to shelter.

At High Court level, the judgment in the *Grootboom* matter drew a distinction between section 26 and 28(1)(c) rights. The court held that section 26 of the Constitution did not impose an obligation on the state to provide housing on demand, but that the state had to take reasonable legislative and other measures within available resources to provide housing. As regards section 28(1)(c), the court held that the provision created an obligation on the state to provide rudimentary shelter to children and their parents, if parents are unable to provide shelter for their children.

On appeal to the Constitutional Court, it was held that the High Court had erred in making a distinction between the right to housing in section 26 and the right to shelter in section 28(1)(c). It argued that such reasoning would produce an anomalous result, in that people who have children would have a direct enforceable right to housing in terms of section 28, while others who have no children would not be entitled to housing under that section even though they may be old or disabled. Yacoob J stated that section 28(1)(c) does not create an obligation on the state to provide shelter on demand to children nor through them, to their parents.

The judgment in *Grootboom* would, therefore, seem to suggest that the right to basic health care services in section 28(1)(c) adds nothing to the general provision of the right of access to health care services in section 27(1)(a).

In the *TAC* case (Constitutional Court 2002), the court again had the opportunity to pronounce on the nature of the state's duty in section 28(1)(c). This time, the Constitutional Court stated that government is obliged to ensure that children are accorded the protection contemplated by section 28, which arises when family or parental care is lacking. It further held that it was possible for such care to be lacking even where the child was being cared for by his or her parents. However, the court did not go on to discuss whether the obligation to ensure the protection envisaged by section 28 imposed immediate positive obligations on the state. It also did not clarify whether this protection is subject to the same qualifications as those placed on the general socio-economic rights in section 27.

Expert opinion provides some guidance with respect to this issue. After *Grootboom*, legal experts Liebenberg (2002) and Sloth-Nielson (2001) expressed the view that children who are not in family care have an immediate and direct claim against the state to be provided with the services listed in section 28(1)(c). Since the *TAC* case has clarified that the state is also responsible for providing health care services for children who are living with their parents but who lack care due to poverty, this opinion could be extrapolated to include such children also having a direct and immediate claim against the state. However, Brand (in Creamer 2002) suggested that if the court were to accept the notion of an unqualified right for children, it would most likely interpret this as conferring a duty upon the state to provide the services and goods which comprise the right as a matter of "absolute priority". Brand believes that an interpretation that placed an immediate claim upon the state is unlikely as "a right cannot place a duty on the state to do what is practically impossible". Budlender (in Creamer 2002) has described this question as a "fundamental unresolved issue".

Further clarification from the Constitutional Court is thus direly needed. In the meantime, this chapter takes as a point of departure that, at the very least, children's basic needs should be receiving priority attention within government's programming and budgetary procedures and that this is not happening at present. The right of children to basic health care services in section 28(1)(c) was included in the Constitution for a purpose. When this provision is read in a way that subordinates it to the general provision on everyone's right of access to health care services, this negates the special protection envisaged by section 28(1)(c). In resolving the tension between sections 27 and 28, preference should thus be shown for a purposive interpretation that favours the promotion and protection of children's rights. In addition, clear legislation is required that further interprets the constitutional provisions on children's right to health so as to ensure that specific child health interests are protected through the law. Such responses fit well with the CRC requirement that "in all actions concerning the child, the best interests of the child must be the primary concern." They also echo the recognition that there must be a first call for children (Creamer 2002).

In summary then, the practical application of the child's right to health as outlined in section 28(1)(c) and what it means in terms of the responsibilities of government and civil society, has yet to be defined conclusively. There is currently no clear definition of what constitutes "basic" health care services. Aside from the absence of the progressive realisation clause in section 28, it is also not certain whether the two sections granting children health rights provide a fundamentally different protection to children. Clear guidelines are needed on how to interpret this distinction. Against this background, it remains a challenge to develop robust monitoring and evaluation systems to track the link between rights, response and resources in South Africa. In the absence of a conclusive understanding of government's exact obligations as regards section 28(1)(c) rights, it remains difficult to assess the follow-through from constitutional provision, to programme and service response, to concomitant resource allocation for sufficient, equitable, good quality health services for children.

# 2. GOVERNMENT'S RESPONSE TO CHILDREN'S HEALTH RIGHT

## 2.1 LEGISLATIVE MEASURES

It is unfortunate that at this crucial point in South African policy and legislative reform, there is as yet no comprehensive legislation on child health. The National Health Act (passed by Parliament in August 2003) gives some recognition to children as a group deserving of special attention. However, it fails to provide a clear legislative framework for health services, health managers and service providers in terms of their responsibilities and roles to ensure that children's health rights are met.

The various drafts of the National Health Bill oscillated between completely excluding children as a group deserving of special attention, to recognising children's health rights in two lines of the preamble, to the current approach of giving children some specific recognition as one of various vulnerable groups. Yet the bill still leaves considerable aspects of child-specific requirements in health services with no clear legislative direction. This is despite the establishment of an unambiguous foundation for a child-specific approach in post-1994 health policy and management, as well as years of dialogue between child health service providers, child policy researchers, child rights organisations and the drafters of the legislation.

The National Health Act makes specific provision for free health care to children under six at primary level health care services and includes some general provisions for vulnerable groups that include children. The act does not provide for mechanisms that would ensure the statutory creation and prioritisation of child health management and service structures such as Maternal, Child and Women's Health Directorates, nor does it include mechanisms aimed at ensuring the adequate planning and resourcing of key child health priorities and programmes. It also does not address crucial aspects of child health service delivery such as consent, confidentiality, participation, access to information and the leeway to treat children that live without adult care-givers (and therefore have to seek health care on their own). These issues are currently addressed, in part, in the draft Children's Bill.

It is of concern that this opportunity has been missed to entrench health gains for children through legislative reform and thus provide a clear legislative framework for all health issues relating to children and their specific health needs. It emphasises the key theme that re-emerges time and again across the chapters of this publication: that there is an urgent need for all sectors of society to unequivocally define and understand their obligations towards children and children's health rights in terms of section 28(1)(c) of the Constitution, the CRC and the ACRWC.

## 2.2 POLICY AND PROGRAMME MEASURES

Aside from the constitutional and legislative responses to children's health needs, a number of governmental policies, plans and programmes have been formulated to address the health needs of children and give effect to children's right to health and basic health care services. Earlier initiatives include the African National Congress's National Health Plan for South Africa (ANC 1994), the Reconstruction and Development Plan (Republic of South Africa 1994) and the *White Paper for the Transformation of the Health System in South Africa* (Department of Health 1997). All of these documents prioritised specific programmes and interventions for children. Some of the specific health priorities for children in the afore-mentioned documents included:

- Free health care for children under six and for pregnant women;
- Immunisation;
- Reduction in morbidity and mortality from common conditions; and
- Improved nutrition.

Specific responses by the Department of Health included the establishment of a national and nine provincial directorates of Maternal, Child and Women's Health (MCWH), with specific sub-directorates for child health. Child health programmes were emphasised in key departmental initiatives, such as the Department of Health's five-year strategic framework and the Primary Health Care Service Package (Department of Health 2000).

In an attempt to give effect to children's health rights as set out in the international frameworks and the Constitution, the Department of Health has also developed a number of child-specific policies and programmes since 1994. It is noteworthy that in the majority of these programmes and policies, the preamble recognises children's health rights and cites this as a basis for the development of the policy and/or programme.

This section focuses primarily on national child-specific policies and programmes that have been introduced since 1994. These are summarised in Table 4.1. The table provides a list as well as a brief description of the policies and programmes that address various aspects of child health care, including the services each aims to deliver, to whom and within what time-frames. While the table mainly contains programmes that are specifically targeted at children, it also includes a few select programmes that are targeted at the general population but that have very prominent child-directed components.

**TABLE 4.1  NATIONAL GOVERNMENT CHILD HEALTH PROGRAMMES**

| Programme title and inception date | Targeted beneficiaries | Services provided by the programme | Implementation time-frame, coverage and service targets |
|---|---|---|---|
| GENERAL POLICIES AND PROGRAMMES | | | |
| Primary health care service package | The entire population, but specific services for children are explicitly out-lined in the package. | The package requires that all districts must implement the package in its entirety as a minimum level of service delivery to the population residing within that district. It makes provision for the following basic services for children:<br>• health promotion and prevention activities;<br>• immunisation;<br>• developmental and genetic screening;<br>• growth monitoring;<br>• school health services; and<br>• acute curative care using approved protocols such as the Integrated Management of Child-hood Illnesses (IMCI).<br>The package makes little mention specifically of chil-dren with chronic conditions (this includes children with HIV infection and AIDS), or victims of sexual abuse and violence. While it does address these areas in a general way, more thought is required into the specific needs of children affected by these conditions. | The package has to be universally implemented by 2006. Districts have a five-year time-frame in which to roll out the package. |
| Free health care for children (announced in 1994) | Children under six years and pregnant women, not covered by a medical sche-me and using public sector health facilities. | This programme refers to all health services provided by state health facilities, with an emphasis on the primary level of care. | Coverage was to be universal. |
| Free primary level care for all (announced in 1996) | The entire population not covered by a medical scheme and using public sector facilities. | This programme refers only to health services offered at the primary level of care and requires co-payment at higher levels of care. | Roll-out was to be universal. |
| Free health care for all persons with disabilities (announced in July 2003) | Adults and children with moderate to severe dis-abilities, not covered by a medical scheme and using public sector facilities. | This programme refers to a specified range of services, including the provision of assistive devices. A set of inclusion criteria is provided. The difficulty with assessing persons in terms of eligibility has not yet been addressed. | Presumably this programme is with immediate effect and for universal roll-out. Further clarity is required. |

| Programme title and inception date | Targeted beneficiaries | Services provided by the programme | Implementation time-frame, coverage and service targets |
|---|---|---|---|
| PROGRAMMES ADDRESSING HUNGER & MALNUTRITION | | | |
| Food security, nutrition & health campaign | The general population is targeted for this programme. | The campaign promotes healthy eating practices, the production of micro-nutrient-rich foods, stimulates household food security and income generation, using food gardens as entry points. | See Table 3.1 in chapter 3. |
| Protein-Energy Malnutrition (PEM) programme | All undernourished pre-school children visiting health facilities. | The programme provides a food-supplement to children who are malnourished and fit the criteria for the programme. | Roll-out was to be universal. |
| Primary School Feeding Scheme (PSFS). Initially known as the Primary School Nutrition Programme (announced in May 1994) | Primary school learners at targeted schools. | The PSFS addresses short-term hunger by providing a daily meal to children on the days that they attend school. The goal is to improve learners' ability to participate in education by improving their nutritional intake. | The initial objective was to reach 50% of all primary school children, but this was replaced by provincially-determined targets, based on criteria of need. This programme is being transferred from the Department of Health to Education in April of 2004 and thus might undergo revision. |
| Vitamin A Supplementation Programme (released for implementation in April 2000) | The programme targets children at risk of malnutrition and childhood infections. | Supply of vitamin A at all public health sector facilities. Routine administration: 6 – 60 months, additional supplementation to children vulnerable to malnutrition, childhood infections and chronic conditions like HIV/AIDS. | No specific roll-out plan was initially indicated, but the programme was meant to be universally available. More recent targets (Goga 2003: personal communication) specify that vitamin A deficiency should be reduced from 33% to 19% nationally by 2005, thus giving provinces a two-year period in which to achieve this. |

| POLICIES AND PROGRAMMES AIMED AT REDUCING CHILDHOOD INFECTIONS | | | |
|---|---|---|---|
| **Programme title and inception date** | **Targeted beneficiaries** | **Services provided by the programme** | **Implementation time-frame, coverage and service targets** |
| Expanded Programme for Immunisation (EPI), a global pro-gramme for tetanus, measles, Hepatitis B and Haemophilus (initiated in 1974) | Children between birth and five years of age. | The programme undertakes the routine administration of vaccines against measles, TB, diphtheria, pertussis, influenza. | Implementation is meant to be universal. |
| Integrated Manage-ment of Childhood Illnesses (IMCI) (introduced in 1997) | Children primarily under five years that present with specific acute illnesses. The guidelines are constantly updated and expanded to include additional clinical conditions. | This strategy includes the standard case management of priority child health conditions, including diarrhoea, acute respiratory infections, measles, childhood emergency medical conditions and HIV. Interventions are targeted at health facilities, households and communities. | A phased implementation plan accompanied the IMCI, with provinces first having to put a training programme in place and then roll out the IMCI programme accordingly. |
| Policy framework for non-communicable chronic conditions in children (currently being discussed within national health struc-tures preceding official acceptance) | Children with non-communi-cable chronic conditions – that is conditions that last longer than one year and are not infectious. | The policy aims to define basic health services and responsibilities at each level of health service and the relationships between each level. It also aims to delineate support services required to sustain the programme. | Policy not yet officially approved. |
| POLICIES AIMED AT CHILDREN & YOUTH OF SCHOOL-GOING AGE | | | |
| Health-promoting schools policy | Learners, educators, the school community and the broader community in which the school is located. | This policy is aimed at collaborative efforts to address children's health needs in a holistic manner, using schools as nodes of health promotion activities. For example, under this policy, hunger needs may be addressed through food gardens kept at schools. | Policy guidelines are being drafted by the Health Promotion Directorate in the Department of Health. |
| School health policy (adopted in May 2003) | Children of school-going age who are in formal learning sites. Children not in formal learning sites must be covered through programmes such as those within the Youth and Adolescent Health policy. | This policy is intended to deliver health promotion and education activities in schools. It also aims to identify health barriers to learning in the Grade 0 /Grade 1 children who have not been identified through the primary level services before. | Implementation was planned to progress in a phased manner from September 2003. Full implementation in all districts is to be achieved by 2007. |

| Programme title and inception date | Targeted beneficiaries | Services provided by the programme | Implementation time-frame, coverage and service targets |
|---|---|---|---|
| Policy guidelines on youth and adolescent health (initiated in 1999 and officially issued in 2002) | Children and youth aged 10 to 24 years old. | This initiative aims to promote the healthy development of all adolescents and youth. The policy guidelines focus on preventing and responding to health problems in youth, including sexual and reproductive health, mental health, substance abuse, violence, unintentional injuries and nutrition. | Some aspects of the policy guidelines had already been implemented in 2001. |
| Policy guidelines on child and youth mental health services | | These guidelines pertain to youth mental health care services envisaged at all levels health care. | |
| PROGRAMMES FOR CHILDREN AFFECTED AND INFECTED BY HIV/AIDS | | | |
| The National Integrated Plan for Children Infected and Affected by HIV/AIDS: Social cluster, 1999 | All children infected with and affected by HIV/AIDS. | The plan is meant to be an integrated effort between the health, social development and education sectors. It makes provision for a number of interventions at individual patient, home, community and service level. | The plan is still being finalised and specific intervention strategies are also being further developed and researched. |
| Prevention of Mother-to-Child Transmission (PMTCT) Programme | Covers HIV-positive pregnant mothers and their newborn babies that use public sector facilities. | The programme provides for the administration of anti-retroviral therapy to HIV-infected mothers before, during and after labour, as well as to the newborn baby. | See section three of this chapter for more on implementation. |
| POLICIES AND PROGRAMMES AIMED AT CHILDHOOD DISABILITY | | | |
| Integrated national disability strategy | General disabled population. No specific mention of children with disabilities. | This strategy calls for the equalisation of opportunities and the full participation of disabled persons in societal life. | |
| Policy guidelines for the management and prevention of genetic disorders, birth defects and disabilities | Priority conditions: Down's syndrome, albinism, foetal alcohol syndrome. | The guidelines deal with what genetic services should be offered prior to conception, during pregnancy, at birth, in infancy and childhood, as well as adolescence and adulthood. | The guidelines have been adopted by provincial health departments. |

144

The information presented in Table 4.1 clearly illustrates that many commendable programmes have been developed and implemented through the Department of Health in an attempt to improve the health and well-being of children. A multitude of other clinical initiatives also exist, too many to include in a publication of this nature. The key challenge thus remains to effectively implement the array of programmes put in place to give effect to children's right to health in South Africa.

While a number of the programmes and policies presented in Table 4.1 are worthy of in-depth analysis for the purposes of monitoring the extent to which government is meeting its obligations in relation to child health rights, due to data and time constraints only one programme has been selected for further discussion in section three below.

# 3. ANALYSIS OF THE PREVENTION OF MOTHER-TO-CHILD TRANSMISSION PROGRAMME

## 3.1 BACKGROUND

The Prevention of Mother-to-Child Transmission (PMTCT) programme is the most recent and perhaps the most controversial health intervention for children in South Africa. The programme requires the provision of anti-retroviral therapy to pregnant mothers and their newborn babies, to reduce the transmission of HIV from pregnant or breastfeeding mothers to their babies. Well-implemented PMTCT programmes can potentially reduce current estimated transmission rates by 50% or more. Given the current prevalence rates amongst pregnant women, this would mean saving thousands of South African babies from acquiring HIV-infection during the peri-natal period. The PMTCT programme thus has the potential to impact dramatically on children's health status and represents a critical programme for the advancement of child health rights in South Africa.

The introduction of a comprehensive, universal PMTCT programme in South Africa has been the basis for extensive advocacy for several years. PMTCT interventions are estimated to cost considerably less than treating and caring for HIV-positive babies. The costs of non-provision far outweigh the costs of provision. This is true even if the provision of formula feedings are factored in, as well as the required follow-up (Gaffen *et al* 2003).

Yet, despite the well-documented advantages of PMTCT programmes in international trials, the introduction of such a programme in South Africa followed a tortuous and controversial course. Following much public pressure, especially from the Treatment Action Campaign, government announced the establishment of 18 pilot sites (two per province) at the end of 2000. The aim of the pilot sites was to test and iron out the logistical requirements for the introduction of a PMTCT programme, before it was to be made universally available.

There were significant delays in extending the PMTCT programmes from the pilot project phase to universal roll-out. This formed the basis of a landmark 2002 court case, in which the TAC filed against the national Department of Health in an attempt to get a judicial directive that would force government to provide universal coverage for the PMTCT programme. The key issue regarding the pilot sites was that the PMTCT programme was accessible only to children who lived in or had access to the pilot site facilities, thus leaving large sections of the child population without access to this potentially life-saving intervention. The undue prolonging of the roll-out from pilotsite to universal coverage thus placed thousands of unborn and newborn children at risk of acquiring HIV infection.

Inadequate infrastructure and cost were the two main reasons given by government for not providing immediate universal coverage. In addition, they felt that the pilot programmes had not been adequately evaluated and that it would not be responsible to grant universal coverage in the absence of demonstrating the effectiveness of the programme in a routine health care setting. Several rights-based arguments emerged in the battle around the PMTCT programme. The health rights of children were fundamental to the argument of civil society, while differing opinions existed around the rights of the child to treatment in the absence of according the same right to mothers.

The Constitutional Court ruled in favour of the TAC and required the South African government to provide Nevirapine or similar anti-retroviral medicines to clinics that request them. In addition, the court required that counsellors be trained and any further obstacles to the roll-out of the PMTCT programme be removed. On the basis of TAC's appeal through the Constitutional Court, the Department of Health was ordered to make the PMTCT programme universally available with immediate effect. Thus all provinces were expected to accommodate the roll-out of the PMTCT within their current and future budgets.

## 3.2 THE IMPLEMENTATION PROCESS

Prior to the Constitutional Court ruling in the *TAC* case, the Department of Health had endorsed the establishment of two pilot sites per province to implement the PMTCT under "test" conditions, before it was to be rolled out to the rest of the country. Even before this national pilot site initiative and in contrast to the national stance, provinces such as the Western Cape and Gauteng had already implemented PMTCT programmes in selected areas. In the Western Cape for example, a pilot project had been run in a large urban informal settlement area, with the view to extending the programme across the entire province. By March 2002, the Western Cape released a full protocol on how to implement the PMTCT programme with a pledge to have the programme universally available by March 2003.

Around the same time, in February 2002, the Health Systems Trust released the findings of an evaluation it had conducted on behalf of the Department of Health, focusing on the 18 national PMTCT pilot sites. The Health System Trust pilot site evaluation showed that:

- Coverage through the pilot sites represented only nine percent of all women using public sector antenatal facilities;

- Voluntary counselling and testing varied between 17% and 90% across provinces, but that there was a generally positive increase in take-up; and

- Numerous logistical problems existed around the capacity of health facilities to provide the programme in its proper format. Many of these problems were due to underlying systemic problems that had escalated over time.

The report made many recommendations for addressing the clinical and service-specific aspects of the intervention. The report did, however, warn against under-estimating the challenge of implementing the PMTCT programme. At the same time it recognised that using logistical challenges as an excuse for non-delivery was unacceptable. Having considered the systemic challenges within health services and the requirements for the universal implementation of the PMTCT programme, the report concluded that, with political and senior management commitment, all provinces should be able to commence implementation of the PMTCT programme at additional sites by the middle of 2002.

On 5 July 2002, the Constitutional court ruled that: "The Constitution requires government to devise and implement within its available resources a comprehensive and co-ordinated programme to realise progressively the rights of pregnant women and their newborn children to have access to health services to combat mother-to-child transmission of HIV". This ruling was to be implemented without delay by all provinces.

In March 2003, the Western Cape became the first province to offer universal coverage of Nevirapine as a means to prevent HIV transmission from mothers to their babies. In a press statement, the Western Cape Department of Health announced a further expansion of the PMTCT programme that would include a period of treatment for mothers as well as the introduction of additional drugs to further reduce transmission rates from mothers to children.

Table 4.2 presents the status at the time of writing of current coverage and plans for further roll-out of the PMTCT programme in each of the nine provinces.

**TABLE 4.2 IMPLEMENTATION OF THE PMTCT PROGRAMME PER PROVINCE (2003)**

| Province | Implementation date of first PMTCT pilot sites | Coverage by 2003 | Plans for further roll-out |
|---|---|---|---|
| Eastern Cape | The national pilot site initiative started in September 2001, involving two hospitals with 12 and 47 feeder clinics respectively. | The programme was expanded to two further hospitals in September 2002, in response to the Constitutional Court order. | The health department aimed to have at least one fully functioning PMTCT site (hospital and feeder clinics) per district council by March 2003. This was partially achieved, with one site per district council, but not all feeder clinics are operational. |

| Province | Implementation date of first PMTCT pilot sites | Coverage by 2003 | Plans for further roll-out |
|---|---|---|---|
| Free State | Two pilot sites were initiated in July and August 2001 as part of the national initiative. | Two additional facilities were implemented between May 2002 and February 2003, based on their deemed eligibility against a set of criteria developed in this province. | Plans call for the expansion of at least one facility per district by March 2003. |
| Gauteng | Pilot sites were initiated in July 2001 in three hospitals and one community health centre. | Coverage extends to 100% of hospitals and 60% of midwife obstetric units. | Plans are to expand the PMTCT programme to the remaining midwife obstetric units and all feeder clinics. |
| KwaZulu-Natal | Two pilot sites were initiated in July 2001. | The programme currently covers all district hospitals and two feeder clinics per district hospital. Coverage in 2003 extended to 100% of hospitals, 44% of clinics and 33% of community health centres. | The province is in the process of rolling the programme out to attain universal coverage. |
| Limpopo | The programme was implemented by August 2001 in one pilot site and by November 2001 in a second pilot site. | Roll-out was extended to 42 facilities (hospitals and community health centres) and 81 feeder clinics (including the 36 attached to the two pilot sites). | Universal coverage is scheduled for completion by 2005. |
| Mpuma-langa | Two pilot sites commenced in July 2001 and October 2001 as part of the national initiative. | The PMTCT programme was expanded to 8 hospitals in December 2002, but with no operational feeder clinics and with no lay counsellors at the hospitals. | To date no plans are in place to expand the programme so as to achieve universal coverage. |
| Northern Cape | Two pilot sites became part of the national initiative in August 2001. | Currently only two pilot sites exist. | Plans exist for further roll-out to four of the largest hospitals and related facilities in the province. Time-frames and plans for universal roll-out remain unclear. |
| North West | One pilot site commenced services in June 2001 and a second pilot site was added in October 2002. | The programme was expanded to 88 new facilities by January 2003 (most of these being feeder clinics). | Plans exist for further roll-out and training. |

| Province | Implementation date of first PMTCT pilot sites | Coverage by 2003 | Plans for further roll-out |
|---|---|---|---|
| Western Cape | In January 1999, two years before the national initiative, a provincial PMTCT project was implemented in a large urban informal settlement area. Two further pilot sites were initiated as part of the national initiative in January 2001 and May 2001. | Coverage is universal. | Plans include the introduction of additional drugs to the current Nevirapine regime and extending antiretroviral therapy to adults. |

**Sources:** PMTCT National Steering Committee 2002; PMTCT National Steering Committee 2003; and oral presentations at the *First National Conference on HIV/AIDS*, Durban, 5-7 August 2003.

## 3.3 IMPLEMENTATION CHALLENGES

In the first pilot site evaluation conducted by the Health Systems Trust and in a subsequent analysis, major challenges were highlighted in relation to the broader health systems context in which the PMTCT programme is delivered. Given the difficulties and challenges in current health service infrastructure, current staff complements and the overall quality of child health services, the addition of a major and somewhat complex programme such as the PMTCT programme requires careful planning. Addressing the infrastructural requirements that are needed to implement the PMTCT programme would, however, not only allow for the successful implementation of the programme: it would also have many beneficial spin-offs for the overall development of the health system. While more detailed and longer-term evaluations of the programme are needed, this point is borne out by preliminary results from provinces such as the Western Cape.

A second and much more detailed evaluation of the implementation and challenges of the PMTCT programme in all provinces has recently been conducted by the Health Systems Trust on behalf of the national HIV programme. At the time of writing, the results from this evaluation were not yet publicly available. Hence it is not possible to comment fully on the current implementation status of the PMTCT programme in this publication. Once available, the evaluation is expected to provide very valuable insights into the implementation challenges at this stage of the programme and should provide a very useful set of recommendations for how to address these challenges.

The key challenge that has been highlighted thus far is the need to strengthen existing primary level clinics, as well as the related perinatal and support services. This includes services for the follow-up and support of mothers and babies for at least 18 months post-delivery for HIV-negative babies and for as long as is required for HIV-positive babies. A key aspect of strengthening service delivery is the appropriate resourcing for such facilities. In particular, it is necessary to ensure adequate and specific budgetary allocations for the aspects of the PMTCT programme that require resources over and above those that are normally required to deliver health services. The next section examines budgetary provisioning for the PMCT programme.

## 3.4 BUDGETING FOR AND SPENDING ON THE PMTCT PROGRAMME

This section provides:

- an overview of the budgetary framework of the PMTCT programme;

- information on how much government has allocated and spent on the PMTCT programme from its inception to the end of the 2003/04 MTEF period, focusing on conditional grant funding;

- an analysis of the budgetary allocation to this programme (through the conditional grants) in relation to other government expenditure items and programmes. This includes an analysis of real growth (annual percentage growth adjusted for inflation) in conditional grant allocations from programme inception until the end of the 2003/04 MTEF period;

- an analysis of expenditure data for the programme (limited to conditional grant data) in order to ascertain whether the funds allocated to the PMTCT programme are indeed spent; and

- preliminary suggestions about whether the funding of the PMTCT programme is sufficient.

It would be useful to consider how provinces are budgeting for the full-scale roll-out of the PMTCT programme, taking into account limitations associated with conditional grant sufficiency and formalities. However, provincial health departments may have allocated either more or less than these projected funds for the roll-out of the PMTCT programme, and data on the exact PMTCT budgets was not available for all provinces.

### 3.4.1 THE BUDGETARY FRAMEWORK FOR THE PMTCT PROGRAMME

The PMTCT programme is funded through two sources:

- a conditional grant is provided to provinces by national government; and

- allocations are made by provinces themselves out of their provincial revenue, that is, monies derived mainly from the equitable share allocated to them by national government through the so-called equitable share (ES) formula.

When the PMTCT programme was introduced in 2001, funding for the programme started out as a separate component to the HIV/AIDS conditional grant, which was provided to every provincial Department of Health. Conditional grant funding provided by national Treasury and the national Department of Health was allocated to the two pilot sites in each of the country's nine provinces.

Historically, health sector conditional grants for HIV/AIDS have generally been allocated to the provincial HIV/AIDS units, which have statutory responsibility for HIV/AIDS activities in the health sector. All provincial HIV/AIDS-related health department activities are co-ordinated and funded by these units. The units receive funding in the form of the HIV/AIDS conditional grant from the national health department and may receive funds from the provincial health departments as well. In 2001/02, at the initiation of the PMTCT pilots, PMTCT funds constituted a separate flow of funds from the general HIV/AIDS conditional grant going to the provinces. This meant that the PMTCT conditional grant allocation could only be spent on activities related to the PMTCT pilot programme. The provinces however under-spent on the PMTCT conditional grants.

Since 2002/03, the PMTCT conditional grant allocation has been included as a component in the general HIV/AIDS conditional grant allocation transferred to the provinces. This means that the provinces have flexibility regarding how much of the HIV/AIDS conditional grant allocation they will spend on the PMTCT programme rather than other "approved" HIV/AIDS-related activities (Department of Health 2002b:8, 11). The allocations for 2003/04 to 2004/05 can thus not be interpreted as indications of projected provincial expenditure on the PMTCT programme, as provinces will not necessarily plan for expenditure of the exact "PMTCT component" of HIV/AIDS-related activities. In other words, they could spend more (using equitable share or HIV/AIDS conditional grant funds) or less than the projected amount on PMTCT.

The formula for determining how much each province receives in their HIV/AIDS conditional grant is based on prevalence rates from the 2001 *Antenatal HIV Prevalence Survey*, the provincial estimated share of HIV-positive births, the share of reported rapes and the estimated share of AIDS cases (National Treasury 2003b:87). This approach has been criticised – particularly by the provinces themselves – for being too simplistic, thus failing to account for the intricacies of the HIV/AIDS epidemic in the particular socio-economic settings of individual provinces. For example, Eastern Cape treasury officials proposed that a "costed norms approach"[9] would be more suitable for channelling HIV/AIDS funds, as departments would have more flexibility in the choice of appropriate programmes and budgeting, taking projected actual costs of service delivery into account, which may differ per province.

In *Budget Review 2002*, National Treasury (2002b) introduced an additional mechanism for funding government's response to HIV/AIDS. The new funds transfer mechanism became known as the "targeted increase in provincial equitable share". In the 2003/04 budget, R1.1 billion of the R1.952 billion set aside for HIV/AIDS was sent to the provinces via the equitable share. The equitable share funds are intended to ensure the general strengthening of health services and to allow provinces to fund care and treatment options, including anti-retroviral drugs, once policy is finalised and approved (National Treasury 2003c:329).

The primary motivation for the introduction of the new transfer mechanism was to provide a response to the impact of HIV/AIDS on the health sector. Given that provincial departments are the prime means of delivering social services to the population, Treasury's decision to shift allocations to provinces is logical. This is particularly so because provinces will incur the majority of expenses in relation to HIV/AIDS. By providing provinces with more control over how and when these funds are spent, it is hoped that provinces will be able to support the most cost-effective programmes and those interventions that are most needed in each province. As indicated above, provinces have been using the equitable share to a varying extent to fund PMTCT activities since the inception of the programme in 2001/02.

There are however several pitfalls associated with using the equitable share as a funding mechanism for the PMTCT programme. First, both national Treasury and the national Department of Health have no legal means of ensuring that provinces spend the funds on the purpose for which they are intended. The allocation of the funds over all the competing provincial votes and functions is left to the discretion of the Provincial Treasuries (as with other equitable share funds). There is thus no guarantee that the funds will be allocated for health – or any HIV/AIDS-related purposes – let alone that they will be spent on the PMTCT programme.

Hickey (2001) suggested that by shifting the funding decisions regarding HIV/AIDS allocations to provinces, government appeared to be reacting to the concern that provinces have been under-spending on their conditional grants because of the complicated processes attached to conditional grants. To put PMTCT spending in context, Hickey (2002) calculated actual expenditure records on HIV/AIDS conditional grants for 2000/01, 2001/02 and 2002/03 (based solely on public spending data from National Treasury). The results suggested that spending on HIV/AIDS conditional grants was low because spending on conditional grants generally is low. Hickey (Ibid) furthermore presented evidence that spending on the HIV/AIDS conditional grants had significantly improved and that average spending for HIV/AIDS conditional grants for 2001/02 (77%) was higher than spending on conditional grants in general (70%).

The PMTCT programme has also been funded through a conditional grant system because HIV/AIDS is a national priority and "[the] distribution of [the] epidemic differs from equitable share distribution" (Department of Health 2003:8). Moreover, in relation to the PMTCT intervention in South Africa, imbalances and inequities exist both between provinces and within provinces. For example, as a result of historical policies, provinces and regions differ in terms of resources and infrastructure. Provinces and regions also differ in terms of demand for services as a result of various factors, including population density, the provincial prevalence rate and the percentage of the population who require access to public versus private sector health care. Hickey (2002) describes more fully the economic theory upon which this argument is based. Suffice it to say that the presence of such factors in the social sector in South African provinces, particularly in combination, warrants the need for conditional grants to fund the implementation of the PMTCT programme (Ibid:4).

In order to be able to monitor progress with regard to the PMTCT programme and other HIV/AIDS-related interventions, the Department of Health has developed a set of output indicators to provide the "primary monitoring condition" for the HIV/AIDS grant. The primary monitoring conditions in relation to the PMTCT programme are the number of mothers receiving voluntary counselling and testing and the number of mother/baby pairs receiving the PMTCT prohylaxis (National Treasury 2003b:87). However, the national and provincial health budgets and strategic plans for 2003/04 do not provide measurable output indicator targets in terms of mother-child pairs to be offered PMTCT counselling or to be treated.[10]

Starting from the financial year 2003/04, all provincial health budgets were required to include a dedicated sub-programme for HIV/AIDS. This was intended to improve departmental reporting abilities (to the national department), as well as the external assessments of provincial budgetary and expenditure trends in relation to HIV/AIDS-related activities. Most provinces provide budgetary information relating to the total amount spent on HIV/AIDS within the District Health Services programme in their 2003/04 budget statements. Other budget documentation in the public domain may provide insight into the total national HIV/AIDS conditional grant amounts allocated to each province, but do not specify what proportion of these conditional grant amounts is intended for PMTCT activities.

Due to the limited availability of financial data, the analysis below is limited to national conditional grant allocations for the PMTCT programme to provinces, which excludes substantial amounts allocated to the PMTCT programme from the provincial equitable share. This is due to the fact that provincial health departments generally do not report separately on how much of the equitable share amount allocated to the health vote has been used for PMTCT services.

## 3.4.2 BUDGET DATA FOR THE **PMTCT** PROGRAMME

The amount allocated for the PMTCT programme in 2001/02 was R20.298 million (National Treasury 2001:80), to be allocated through the conditional grant system for the pilot phase. In 2002/03, R25 million was allocated. According to National Treasury (2002:141), the conditional grant amount budgeted for the PMTCT pro-gramme was set to increase to R79 million in 2003/04 and to R156 million in 2004/05. This increase mirrors the expectation that provinces would roll out the PMTCT programme beyond the pilot projects in agreement with the Constitutional Court requirement that PMTCT services be expanded to achieve national implementa-tion. The exact amounts budgeted by the provinces for the PMTCT programme in 2003/04, however, could not be obtained. The budget figures for 2003/04 and 2004/05 in Table 4.3 below are MTEF estimates of conditional grant allocations for PMTCT purposes to the provinces made by the national department at the tabling of the 2002/03 budget.[11] The 2005/06 MTEF estimate is the conditional grant amount requested by the national Department of Health in September 2002 for the further roll-out of the PMTCT programme (Department of Health: 2002b).

Table 4.3 shows these budget allocations as a proportion of consolidated national and provincial expenditure, the latter as given by the National Treasury (2002b:148; 2003a:155). It shows how the proportion of the consolidated conditional grant budg-et allocated to the PMTCT programme was set to double between 2002/03 and 2003/04, and projected to double again by 2004/05. The PMTCT allocation consti-tutes a rather insignificant proportion of the consolidated national and provincial budget, at 0.022% in 2003/04. However, the doubling of this proportion in 2004/05 signifies the priority that government assigns to the roll-out of the PMTCT pro-gramme.

TABLE **4.3** CONSOLIDATED CONDITIONAL GRANTS FOR **PMTCT** PILOTS **(2001/02 & 2002/03)** AND FOR **PMTCT** ROLL-OUT **(2003/04 - 2005/06)**

| R'000 / % | PMTCT pilots Revised Estimates | Budget | MTEF | MTEF | PMTCT roll-out Requested by DOH |
|---|---|---|---|---|---|
| | 2001/02 | 2002/03 | 2003/04 | 2004/05 | 2005/06 |
| PMTCT conditional grant expenditure/ budget (R'000) | 20 298 | 25 000 | 79 125 | 155 693 | 182 817 |
| Consolidated provincial and national expenditure (R'000) | 271 941 000 | 310 230 000 | 351 338 000 | 380 778 000 | 415 012 000 |
| Programme budget as a % of consolidated provincial and national expenditure | 0.007 | 0.008 | 0.022 | 0.041 | 0.044 |

**Sources:** National Treasury (2002a:141) for PMTCT conditional grant expenditure/budget 2001/02 - 2004/05; Department of Health (2002b) for 2005/06 PMTCT conditional grant requested amount; National Treasury (2003a:155) for consolidated national and provincial expenditure 2002/03 - 2005/06; National Treasury (2002b:148) for consolidated national and provincial expenditure 2001/02; and own calculations.

The strong proportional growth of the PMTCT conditional grant (from 0.007% of consolidated provincial and national expenditure in 2001/02 to 0.022% in 2002/03 and 0.041% in 2003/04) is caused by substantial projected real annual growth in 2003/04 and 2004/05 (see Table 4.10), resulting in an average annual growth rate over the 2003/04 MTEF of nearly 100%. This budget growth comes from a rather small base, which initially only provided for the operational costs of the 18 PMTCT pilot sites.

TABLE **4.4** REAL ANNUAL GROWTH IN CONSOLIDATED CONDITIONAL GRANT **PMTCT** PROGRAMME BUDGETS **(2001/02 - 2005/06)** AND REAL ANNUAL AVERAGE GROWTH **(2002/03 - 2005/06)**

| | PMTCT pilot | | | PMTCT roll-out | |
|---|---|---|---|---|---|
| | 2001/02- 2002/03 | 2002/03- 2003/04 | 2003/04- 2004/05 | 2004/05- 2005/06 | Annual average 2003/04 - 2005/06 |
| Real growth (%) | 11.06 | 196.44 | 88.24 | 11.72 | 98.80 |

**Source:** Own calculations based on budget and expenditure figures in Table 4.3 above
**Note:** 2002/03 is the base year.

Given the substantial programme costs occurring at the beginning of a programme (start-up costs), provinces were often compelled to use provincial funding to get the PMTCT programme off the ground.[12] For example, KwaZulu-Natal incurred costs of R131 million in relation to the PMTCT programme in the 2001/02 financial year

(Green-Thompson in PMG 2002a). Some of the provincial health departments have also allocated funds from their provincial equitable share amount in order to top-up funding for the roll-out of the PMTCT programme. For example, for 2003/04 KwaZulu-Natal has allocated an additional amount of R126 million from the provincial equitable share, over and above the conditional grant amount of R11.6 million projected for the roll-out of the PMTCT programme in the province by the national Department of Health (2002b).[13] This implies that the PMTCT conditional grant amounts significantly understate the amount that is actually budgeted for and spent on the PMTCT programme in the provinces. Unfortunately, however, not all provinces specify the amounts they have added to the conditional grant amount for PMTCT purposes in their budget statements. Idasa's Health and HIV/AIDS research team has identified the need for further research on the provincial allocations to the PMTCT programme, in order to monitor whether and how this programme is prioritised in terms of funding commitments.

It is important to consider the question of under-spending of the conditional grant funding for the PMTCT programme and to show provincial variations in budget allocations and spending on the programme. Table 4.5 shows that in the first year of implementing the PMTCT programme pilots (2001/02), on aggregate about 72% of the allocated funds were spent. This could perhaps be seen as reasonable compared to government spending on other conditional grants in the first year of that grant. It was also more than was spent of other HIV/AIDS conditional grants in the same year (Malumba cited in PMG 2002b). Nevertheless, it means that some of the conditional grant funds allocated to the PMTCT programme were left unspent and that more mother-child pairs could perhaps have been treated in the pilot projects than was in fact the case. A partial explanation of under-spending on the PMTCT conditional grant in the provinces would be the late transfer of funds (the grant amount was only received in November 2001), as well as the lack of infrastructure and skills (Ibid). In 2002/03, the provinces together spent over 100% of the PMTCT conditional grant allocations on aggregate. This indicates a substantial improvement in PMTCT conditional grant spending.

**TABLE 4.5 ALLOCATED VERSUS ACTUAL EXPENDITURE FOR THE SUM OF THE PROVINCES' PMTCT CONDITIONAL GRANT**

| R'000 Year | Budget allocation | Estimated expenditure | Estimated expenditure as % of budgeted expenditure |
|---|---|---|---|
| 2001/02 (revised) | 20 298 | 14 631 | 72% |
| 2002/03 | 25 000 | 36 797 | 101% |

**Sources:** National Treasury (2002:141) for the PMTCT conditional grant budget allocations; Department of Health (2002c) for percentage spent of PMTCT amount received in 2001/02; and own calculations.

Table 4.6 shows the PMTCT conditional grant allocations to the provinces in 2001/02 and 2002/03 for the implementation of the PMTCT pilot programmes. Table 4.7 then shows how real growth in the PMTCT conditional grant component between 2001/02 and 2002/03 varies per province. After adjusting for inflation, it can be seen that all provinces received an increased budget for the continuation of the pilot programme. Particularly strong positive growth (above 20%) can be seen for the North West and Northern Cape PMTCT pilot budgets.

## TABLE 4.6 PMTCT CONDITIONAL GRANT ALLOCATIONS TO THE PROVINCES FOR PMTCT PILOTS (2001/02 & 2002/03), IN R '000

| Province | Revised Estimate 2001/02 | Budget 2002/03 |
|---|---|---|
| Eastern Cape | 2 341 | 2 906 |
| Free State | 865 | 1 056 |
| Gauteng | 2 130 | 2 722 |
| Limpopo | 1 705 | 2 098 |
| KwaZulu-Natal | 9 424 | 11 317 |
| Mpumalanga | 1 309 | 1 669 |
| Northern Cape | 815 | 1 112 |
| North West | 791 | 1 128 |
| Western Cape | 828 | 992 |
| **Total** | **20 298** | **25 000** |

**Sources:** Department of Health (2002c) for 2001/02 figures of PMTCT conditional grant amount received by each province; Department of Health, HIV/AIDS Chief Directorate for 2002/03 budget figures for PMTCT conditional grants.

**Note:** The provincial conditional grant amounts as provided for 2001/02 do not add up to the total as provided.

## TABLE 4.7 REAL ANNUAL GROWTH IN PMTCT CONDITIONAL GRANT ALLOCATIONS (2001/02 - 2002/03)

| Province | Real % growth 2001/02 – 2002/03 |
|---|---|
| Eastern Cape | 11.9 |
| Free State | 10.1 |
| Gauteng | 15.2 |
| Limpopo | 11.0 |
| KwaZulu-Natal | 8.3 |
| Mpumalanga | 15.0 |
| Northern Cape | 23.0 |
| North West | 28.6 |
| Western Cape | 8.0 |
| **Total** | **11.1** |

**Source:** Table 4.6 above and own calculations.

**Note:** 2002/03 was the base year. CPIX deflators were used to adjust for inflation (for 2001/02: 0.9017 and for 2002/03: 1.0000).

Table 4.8 shows great variation between the provinces in PMTCT conditional grant spending as a proportion of the budget in 2001/02. KwaZulu-Natal and Northern Cape recorded 100% spending of the allocated amount. Mpumalanga, North West and Western Cape recorded 1% spending or less, while Limpopo spent just above a quarter of the allocated funds.

**TABLE 4.8 ALLOCATED VERSUS ACTUAL EXPENDITURE OF PMTCT PROVINCIAL CONDITIONAL GRANT ALLOCATIONS (2001/02 & 2002/03)**

| Province | 2001/02 | | | 2002/03 | | |
| --- | --- | --- | --- | --- | --- | --- |
| | Actual (revised) budget allocation (in R '000) | Estimated expenditure (in R '000) | Estimated expenditure as % of budgeted expenditure | Actual budget allocation transferred, including roll-overs (in R '000) | Estimated expenditure (in R '000) | Estimated expenditure as % of budgeted expenditure |
| Eastern Cape | 2 341 | 1 545 | 66 | 2 906 | 1 158 | 40 |
| Free State | 865 | 649 | 75 | 1 056 | 1 067 | 101 |
| Gauteng | 2 130 | 1 747 | 82 | 2 772 | 2 722 | 100 |
| Limpopo | 1 705 | 443 | 26 | 2 098 | 4 183 | 199 |
| KwaZulu-Natal | 9 424 | 9 424 | 100 | 22 609 | 24 737 | 109 |
| Mpumalanga | 1 309 | 0 | 0 | 1 669 | 474 | 28 |
| Northern Cape | 815 | 815 | 100 | 1 112 | 1 002 | 90 |
| North West | 791 | 8 | 1 | 1 128 | 786 | 70 |
| Western Cape | 828 | 0 | 0 | 992 | 668 | 67 |
| **Total** | **20 298** | **14 631** | **72** | **36 292** | **36 797** | **101** |

**Sources:** Department of Health (2002c) for 2001/02 figures of PMTCT conditional grant amounts received and estimated percentage spent by each province; Department of Health, HIV/AIDS Chief Directorate for 2002/03 PMTCT conditional grant budget and estimated expenditure figures; and own calculations.

**Notes:** 1. The percentages giving estimated expenditure as a percentage of budgeted expenditure were provided without decimal figures.

2. The 2003 conditional grant amount transferred to KwaZulu-Natal includes a roll-over amount of R11 292 446.

3. Please note that the provincial conditional grant amounts for 2001/02 as provided do not add up to the total as provided.

One reason for the under-spending of funds could be the late arrival of PMTCT funds in November 2001, which resulted in delays in provincial departments' access to the funds (Malumba cited in PMG 2002b). The Western Cape funded their PMTCT programme out of another budget, hence recording 0% spending on the PMTCT conditional grant (Tswala cited in PMG 2002d). It is not clear whether the province has been able to reclaim the amount from the conditional grant, or whether the amount has been rolled over to the next financial year. In contrast, low spending on the PMTCT grant in the North West in 2001/02 was attributed to the fact that "the North West is a rural province, and lacked the requisite skills base...there were simply insufficient numbers of appropriately qualified trainers" (Ntshipale cited in PMG 2002c).

No clarity could be obtained regarding Mpumalanga's under-spending on the PMTCT grant in 2001/02 and the province continued to under-spend on the PMTCT conditional grant in 2002/03. Spending on the PMTCT pilot grant in the Eastern Cape deteriorated between 2001/02 and 2002/03. Other provinces fared generally much better in 2002/03, and notably North West and Limpopo drastically improved their PMTCT conditional grant spending. This is reflected in increases in the proportion of the budget spent, while their PMTCT budget increased in real terms (compare Tables 4.7 and 4.8). Limpopo spent nearly double the amount originally budgeted for the PMTCT conditional grant in 2002/03.

The spending results in Table 4.8 seem to suggest that despite growth in national conditional grant allocations to support progressive roll-out, the progressive realisation of child rights in terms of achieving the objectives of the PMTCT programme could vary per province. It should, however, be noted that expenditure results for a pilot programme cannot readily be applied to the roll-out phase of the same programme. In other words, spending patterns for the roll-out of a programme need not be similar to those of the pilot phase. This is because many problems typically encountered in the pilot phase that may hamper efficient spending of funds can be expected to be ironed out during the roll-out phase of the programme. Furthermore, provinces could use funds from other sources such as the provincial equitable share and donor-funding in order to roll out the programme (as happens for example in the Western Cape and KwaZulu-Natal). This is not reflected in the above analysis of conditional grant allocations.

Table 4.9 shows conditional grant allocations to the provinces for the roll-out of the PMTCT programme in 2003/04 and 2004/05, as projected by the national Department of Health in 2002. It should be noted here that since 2002/03, these amounts for the PMTCT programme are incorporated in the general HIV/AIDS grant. Provinces thus have flexibility with regard to how much of the HIV/AIDS grant they will spend on the PMTCT programme as opposed to other HIV/AIDS-related activities. In order to access the HIV/AIDS grant, provinces need to submit business plans that specify on what activities the funds will be spent. The figures in Table 4.9 are thus projections made in September 2002 by the national Department of Health regarding funds that would be required for the roll-out of the PMTCT programme in each of the provinces in 2003/04 and 2004/05, as a component of the HIV/AIDS conditional grant. The figures should not be interpreted as actually budgeted provincial conditional grant allocations that the provinces have to spend on the PMTCT. Rather, they give us some indication of the national Health Department's intentions in 2002 to progressively roll out the PMTCT programme.

**TABLE 4.9  PMTCT** CONDITIONAL GRANT AMOUNTS PROJECTED IN **2002** BY THE NATIONAL **DEPARTMENT OF HEALTH** FOR THE ROLL-OUT OF THE **PMTCT** PROGRAMME IN THE PROVINCES (IN **2003/04 & 2004/05**), IN R '000

| Province | 2003/04 | 2004/05 |
|---|---|---|
| Eastern Cape | 9 076 | 21 920 |
| Free State | 3 775 | 9 116 |
| Gauteng | 7 999 | 19 318 |
| Limpopo | 840 | 2 029 |
| KwaZulu-Natal | 11 582 | 27 972 |
| Mpumalanga[14] | 4 019 | 9 707 |
| Northern Cape | 4 707 | 11 361 |
| North West | 7 408 | 17 892 |
| Western Cape | 3 596 | 8 685 |
| **Total PMTCT roll-out** | **52 999** | **128 000** |
| Conditional grant amount requested for PMTCT infrastructure strengthening | 26 125 | 27 693 |
| **Total PMTCT conditional grant amount requested** | **79 125** | **155 693** |

**Source:** National Treasury, obtained from the Idasa research unit on AIDS and Public Finance.

Table 4.10 shows that growth in the PMTCT roll-out allocation between 2003/04 and 2004/05 was projected at about 130% in real terms for all provinces. This indicates the intent of the South African government to progressively roll out the PMTCT programme.

**TABLE 4.10: REAL ANNUAL GROWTH IN PROJECTED PMTCT CONDITIONAL GRANT ALLOCATIONS (2003/04 - 2004/05)**

| Province | 2003/04 – 2004/05 Real % growth |
|---|---|
| Eastern Cape | 130.23 |
| Free State | 130.20 |
| Gauteng | 130.22 |
| Limpopo | 130.26 |
| KwaZulu-Natal | 130.23 |
| Mpumalanga | 130.25 |
| Northern Cape | 130.09 |
| North West | 130.24 |
| Western Cape | 130.24 |
| **Total PMTCT roll-out** | **130.23** |
| Conditional grant amount requested for PMTCT infrastructure strengthening | 0.86 |
| **Total PMTCT conditional grant amount** | **87.22** |

**Source:** Own calculations based on figures in Table 4.9

**Note:** 2002/03 is the base year.

## 3.4.3 IS FUNDING FOR THE PMTCT PROGRAMME SUFFICIENT?

Table 4.11 shows that only 50% of the amount requested by the national Department of Health for the PMTCT programme in September 2001 was granted by National Treasury for 2002/03 and about 40% for 2004/05. This was partly due to National Treasury's uncertainty regarding costing information. The national Department of Health (2002b) states that:

> "...significant additional funds were allocated in the [2002/03] MTEF to fund the expansion of the PMTCT programme for...[2003/04 and 2004/05]. These cover drugs, formula, testing, salaries of counsellors, and compensation for nurse time spent on testing, administration of drugs and provision of infant feeding advice. [The funds] assume an expansion to 50% population coverage for 2003/04, and achievement of full coverage by 2004/05. The GOALS[15] analysis indicates that these amounts are broadly adequate to cover the recurrent costs of the PMTCT programme as it expands towards full coverage."

The "allocated" amounts for the PMTCT conditional grant component are reflected in Table 4.11, together with the amounts requested in September 2002.

**TABLE 4.11: ALLOCATED AMOUNTS FOR ROLL-OUT OF THE PMTCT PROGRAMME COMPARED TO AMOUNTS REQUESTED BY THE NATIONAL DEPARTMENT OF HEALTH (2003/04 – 2005/06)**

|  | 2003/04 | 2004/05 | 2005/06 |
|---|---|---|---|
| Requested by National Department of Health for 2002/03 MTEF (in R '000) | 156 921 | 389 950 | N/A |
| Requested by National Department of Health for 2003/04 MTEF (in R '000) | 108 785 | 200 162 | 182 817 |
| Allocated (in R '000) | 79 125 | 155 893 | N/A |
| Allocated amount as % of amount requested for 2002/03 MTEF | 50.42% | 39.88% | N/A |
| Allocated amount as % of amount requested for 2003/04 MTEF | 72.74% | 77.88% | N/A |
| Projected level of PMTCT coverage with amount allocated | 50% | 100% | N/A |

**Sources:** Department of Health (2001: 9) for 2002/03 MTEF requested amounts; Department of Health (2002b:11) for 2003/04 MTEF requested amounts; National Treasury (2002b:141) for allocated amounts.

Despite the requested amounts not being fully granted, the national Department of Health (2002b:5) maintains that 100% PMTCT coverage could be achieved by 2004/05 with the funds allocated over the 2002/03 MTEF. This could arguably be interpreted as sufficient funding for the progressive realisation of children's right to be protected against HIV transmission. However, the department adds that the achievement of full coverage by 2004/05 would be subject to revision "in the light of the results of the forthcoming evaluation of costs at four of the PMTCT pilots, and clear confirmation by provinces of the expected pace of implementation of PMTCT expansion" (Ibid).

It is possible that the provincial aggregate of spending 101% of the PMTCT conditional grant in 2002/03 will be reflected in the spending patterns regarding allocated PMTCT budgets in future. If so and if the Department of Health's cost assumptions are correct, it would indeed be feasible to realise 100% PMTCT coverage by 2004/05. However, inequities in the PMTCT roll-out amongst provinces and amongst regions within provinces could result in varying degrees of access to PMTCT treatment for HIV-positive pregnant women in different parts of the country.

Furthermore, as discussed above, the nationally projected PMTCT allocations may not be spent entirely on the PMTCT programme itself, due to discretion on the side of the provinces to spend parts of the amount on other activities. This may occur if the PMTCT amount is included in the HIV/AIDS conditional grant. In their 2002/03 and 2003/04 budget statements, some provincial Departments of Health already refered to the roll-out of the PMTCT programme as an "unfunded mandate" (Provincial Treasury of the Free State 2003:200; Provincial Treasury of KwaZulu-Natal 2003:195). This is despite the national Department of Health's statement (in National Treasury 2003c:329) that "increased baselines provide specifically for the faster roll-out of mother-to-child transmission prevention programmes".

Moreover, the inclusion of the PMTCT component in the broader HIV/AIDS grant since 2002/03 seems to have resulted in a decrease in available information on PMTCT budgets and expenditure. This places constraints on national and civil society monitoring of government's budgeting for the PMTCT programme, as witnessed by the limited availability of data on allocated funds for the PMTCT programme in the 2003/04 MTEF.

## 3.5 CONCLUDING COMMENTS ON THE PMTCT PROGRAMME

It is commendable to note the progress that has been made in the provision of the PMTCT programme since 2002 – albeit it is primarily due to the pressure from the Constitutional Court ruling. Similar progress can be noted in the budgetary alloca-tions to the PMTCT programme. The doubling of the PMTCT conditional grant allocations as a percentage of consolidated national and provincial expenditure and the positive real growth in actual and requested PMTCT conditional grant allocations, indicates that the national Health Department has prioritised the PMTCT pilots, and intends to support the progressive roll-out of the PMTCT programme.

Improvements in PMTCT pilot conditional grant expenditure as a proportion of the budgeted conditional grant amount, show that most provincial health departments are progressing with the PMTCT pilots.  Some of the provinces – Mpumalanga in partic-ular – seem to have experienced more difficulties than other provinces – such as the Free State, Gauteng, Limpopo and KwaZulu-Natal – in spending their PMTCT pilot conditional grant amounts.

Based on the available financial data (which does not reveal provincial equitable share allocations to the PMTCT programme for all provinces) and given the type of fund-ing mechanism used (that is, the flexible HIV/AIDS conditional grant), it cannot be concluded with certainty whether South Africa is budgeting sufficient funds to pro-gressively roll out the PMTCT programme.

Inequity in the benefits of the PMTCT programme for babies and children in differ-ent provinces could arise in future. Provincial health departments might spend com-paratively more or less on the implementation of the PMTCT programme, as condi-tional grant funding for the roll-out of the PMTCT programme is included in the more flexible HIV/AIDS conditional grant. This could be aggravated as some provin-cial health departments may be more successful than others in securing and spending additional funds for PMTCT programme implementation from their provincial equi-table shares.

Despite the obvious progress over the last year, it is of concern that despite the Constitutional Court ruling, there are still delays in the roll-out of the programme. It is also likely that, were it not for the strong direction given by the Constitutional Court ruling, the programme might not have received the priority attention in provinces that it was accorded as a result of the ruling. This suggests that stronger consideration might have to be given to litigation as a tool for ensuring the prioritisa-tion of children's health programmes within government.

At the same time, it is important to recognise that roll-out is not yet complete and that many implementation challenges remain. It has been suggested that the implementation challenges ahead relate not only specifically to the PMTCT programme, but also involve the need to strengthen existing primary level clinics, as well as the related peri-natal and support services. Universal roll-out requires careful monitoring and a sustainable commitment on the part of provincial health departments. To allow for effective monitoring of PMTCT programme prioritisation and transparency in the funding of the programme, there is a need for national and provincial Departments of Health to provide updated financial information regarding PMTCT programme funding, as well as measurable output targets for the PMTCT programme in their budgets.

# 4. CONCLUSIONS

The CRC, ACRWC and the South African Constitution place an obligation on South Africa as a country to ensure follow-through of our commitment to upholding children's right to health. This demands that policy, legislation, programme design, programme implementation and resource allocation all operate in accordance with this commitment. It also requires that South Africa is able to produce objective evidence as to whether the CRC obligations have been met.

The key to the universal implementation of good quality child health programmes lies in a multiplicity of factors that have been alluded to in earlier parts of the chapter. The current challenge is to provide a clear link between political commitment to children's rights and child health outcomes. Current evaluation and monitoring systems do not allow for following the links between the political commitment to rights, the interpretation of the right, the subsequent policies and programmes that have been developed, the outcomes of such policies and/or programmes and the decisions around resource allocation to child health programmes and services. A deliberate and well-constructed system is required to follow through the variables that will enable the measurement of child health outcomes against child rights and provide links to the steps that come in-between. One of the key shortcomings in current monitoring data on children is the predominant emphasis on child survival as opposed to a comprehensive assessment of child well-being. Currently available child health outcome data, programme and policy evaluations, as well as resource allocation frameworks, allow only for broad assumptions and face-value interpretations of the relationship, for example, between child rights and health outcomes.

From the limited financial information on child health programmes available, it is not possible to conclude whether government is indeed following through on its political commitment to the realisation of children's right to health, with firm implementation and resource support efforts. More detailed and disaggregated budget and expenditure information and programme implementation analyses would be required.

Nonetheless, the data presented in this chapter highlight a number of issues:

- Firstly, child health survival indicators, as measured by child mortality and morbidity data, show that the health status of South African children is worsening, primarily as a result of the HIV-epidemic. Given the emphasis placed on reducing child mortality and morbidity in article 24 of the CRC, this reflects a failure on the part of South Africa to adequately respond to this requirement of the article. Multiple factors contribute to this situation: it is not simply a failure in the health system to put good quality, well-functioning programmes and services in place. It also lies in the political stance around HIV/AIDS, the subsequent discourse and delayed programme response, financial allocation processes, failure of essential services such as water, housing and sanitation programmes and indeed aspects of the health system that are not functioning adequately.

- However, the chapter also shows that the national Department of Health has made concerted efforts to try and ensure children's right to the highest level of health possible within their policy and programme development. The overview of child-related health programmes demonstrates that there are good policies and programmes in place and that policy-makers and programme managers are cognisant of the obligations placed on them by the CRC. Indeed all the major areas of child health are covered by good policies and programmes that are globally recognised and endorsed. Further, the programmes that are highlighted in this chapter do strive to provide universal coverage for all children and contain provisions for children who are particularly at risk of ill-health and who are made vulnerable through poverty.

- At the same time, the discussions in this chapter draw attention to a number of gaps in translating constitutional obligations into good quality child health services. One of the key gaps is the lack of legislative follow-through for the protection of children's health rights, as the current National Health Act makes only limited provision for the protection of children's health rights. Although it is anticipated that the forthcoming Children's Bill will make further legislative provisions relating to child health, significant gaps in legislative provision for child health are likely to remain.

- Focusing on the PMCT programme, the analysis in section three of the chapter illustrates the progress that has been achieved in extending children's right to be protected from HIV infection. However, it also highlights a number of weaknesses in the implementation of this critical child health programme. The evaluation of the PMTCT programme reveals delays in the achievement of universal coverage, as well as significant disparities in implementation across provinces. It is of concern that a Constitutional Court order was required to spur provinces into action around the roll-out of the programme.

- This demonstrates a need to ensure that the constitutional obligations with regard to children are understood at all levels of decision-making and service provision, especially the levels at which financial and other resource allocation decisions are made. Dedicated child health structures such as the Maternal, Child and Women's Health sub-directorates attempt to translate children's rights into tangible child health programmes. However, parallel systems within the Department of Finance, as well as those relating to drug provisioning, monitoring and evaluation do not seem to prioritise children consistently and explicitly.

- While the current conceptualisation of programmes such as the PMTCT programme make provision for universal access, the challenge remains to ensure that health care facilities are adequately resourced and that health workers are fully equipped and trained. The inevitable discrepancies between health care access in richer versus poorer communities and between urban and rural areas might see the programme being available to some and yet perhaps not to the children that are most disadvantaged through poverty. The programme must thus pay careful attention to strengthening its implementation, specifically in those areas that are currently disadvantaged in terms of all forms of health care.

- It is difficult to assess from the available PMTCT evaluations whether government is rolling out the programme as fast as administrative capacity allows. The most recent evaluation conducted by Health Systems Trust is not yet available publicly and would presumably be able to answer many of the questions posed at the outset of this chapter.

- A further finding of this chapter is that financial management systems at national and provincial level are still not set up to adequately monitor budgetary resource allocations to child health programmes and services. Thus, in the absence of a prospective study of resource allocation to child health programmes, it will always be difficult to provide exact accounts. Analyses such as the ones attempted in this chapter would always have to rely on proxy data.

The rights of children to basic health services, as afforded in Section 28 (1)(c) of the Constitution, are as yet unfulfilled. Many challenges remain in the conceptualisation, planning and resourcing of health services for children. This is borne out by the unacceptably high levels of child mortality and morbidity and the concerning rise in these parameters. It requires an urgent inter-sectoral response and prioritisation of child health. This is a function that calls for priority attention from the parliamentary committees responsible for monitoring children's issues, government departments charged with service delivery responsibility to children and health service providers at all levels.

Key recommendations would thus include the following:

- There is a need for careful auditing as a critical component of conceptualising child health programmes. This will help programme designers to identify the resource requirements for implementation and to ensure that those resources are adequately planned for and made available from new or existing budgets.

- It is of concern that provinces now have more leeway to decide how much of the funds allocated by national government for spending on the PMTCT programme they will actually allocate to the programme. Priority child health programmes should be ring-fenced within budgetary and other resource allocation processes.

- It is essential to develop a well-functioning monitoring process to allow the tracking of child rights through to implementation, by using carefully selected child health and well-being indicators as outcome measures; and

• Government's obligations in terms of child rights need to be translated into practical guidelines for decision-makers and service providers. This would enhance their understanding of their obligations to children when making decisions around the development, resourcing and implementation of key child health programmes and services.

# REFERENCES

African National Congress. (1994) *A National Health Plan for South Africa.* Prepared by the ANC with technical support from WHO and UNICEF. Johannesburg: African National Congress.

Bradshaw, D. (2003) *Initial estimates from the South African National Burden of Disease Study 2000.* MRC Policy Brief, 1. Cape Town: Medical Research Council.

Burrows, S., B. Bowman, R. Matzopoulos & A. van Niekerk. (2001) *A profile of fatal injuries in South Africa 2000.* Second annual report of the national injury mortality surveillance system. Cape Town: Medical Research Council.

Cape High Court. (1999) *Grootboom v Oostenberg Municipality and Others.* Case No.6826/99, BCLR 2000(3) 277.

Constitutional Court of South Africa. (2000) *Government of the Republic of South Africa and Others v Grootboom and Others.* 2001 (1) SA 46 (CC); 2000 (11) BCLR 1169 (CC).

Constitutional Court of South Africa. (2002) *Minister of Health and Others v Treatment Action Campaign and Others.* 2002 (5) SA 721, 2002 (10) BCLR 1033 (CC).

Creamer, K. (2002) *The impact of South Africa's evolving jurisprudence on children's socio-economic rights on budget analysis.* Budget Information Service Occasional Paper. Cape Town: Idasa.

Department of Health. (1997) *White Paper for the Transformation of the Health System in South Africa.* Published in the Government Gazette, 382 (17910), Notice 667 of 1997. Pretoria: Government Printer.

Department of Health. (1998a) *South African Demographic and Health Survey.* Pretoria: Medical Research Council.

Department of Health. (1998b) *Vitamin A Deficiency.* Pretoria: Government Printer.

Department of Health. (1999) *Epi Comments.* March. Pretoria: Government Printer.

Department of Health. (2000) *The Primary Health Care service package for South Africa: A set of norms and standards.* Pretoria: Government Printer.

Department of Health. (2001) *An Enhanced Response to HIV/AIDS and Tuberculosis in the Public Health Sector – Key Components and Funding Requirements: 2002/03-2004/05.* Available at http://196.36.153.56/doh/aids/docs/response.html.

Department of Health. (2002a) *HIV/AIDS Funding for the Health Sector in Budget 2002: Comparison of funds allocated and funds requested in the Department of Health's "Enhanced Response" Budget Submission.* 26 March. Available under "Reports 2002" at http://www.doh.gov.za/aids/index.html.

Department of Health. (2002b) *Revising the enhanced response to HIV/AIDS and Tuberculosis in the Public Health Sector: Funding Requirements 2003/04 - 2005/06.* Draft 1, September.

Department of Health. (2002c) Unpublished document handed out at Health Portfolio Committee Budget Hearings. Available at http://www.pmg.org.za/docs/2002/appendices/020429simelela.ppt.

Department of Health. (2003) *Public Hearings of the Select Committee on Finance,* 13 March 2003.

Doherty, J. & H. McCleod. (2002) "Medical Schemes". In *South African Health Review.* Durban: Health Systems Trust.

Financial and Fiscal Commission. (2000) *Recommendations 2001-2004 MTEF cycle.* May.

Gaffen, N., N. Nattrass & C. Raubenheimer. (2003) *The cost of HIV prevention and treatment interventions in South Africa.* CSSR Working Paper, 28. Cape Town: University of Cape Town.

Giese, S., H. Meintjies, R. Croke & R. Chaimberlain. (2003) *Assessing the health and social needs of children in the context of HIV/AIDS.* Unpublished document commissioned by the Department of Health, Pretoria.

Giese, S. & G. Hussey. (2002) *Rapid appraisal of primary level health care services for HIV-positive children at public sector clinics in South Africa.* Cape Town: Children's Institute, University of Cape Town.

Hendriks, A. (1999) "The close connection between classical rights and the right to health with special reference to the right to sexual and reproductive health". In *Medicine and Law,* 18:225 - 227.

Hickey, A. (2001) *Extent of provincial underspending of HIV/AIDS conditional grants.* Budget Brief, 85. Cape Town: Budget Information Service, Idasa.

Hickey, A. (2002) "HIV/AIDS Spending Policy and Intergovernmental Fiscal Relations". In *South African Journal of Economics,* 70(7):4.

Hickey, A. & N. Ndlovu. (2003) *What does Budget 2003/04 allocate for HIV/AIDS?* Budget Brief, 127. Cape Town: Budget Information Service, Idasa.

Liebenberg, S. (2002) *South Africa's Evolving Juridprudence on Socio-Economic Rights.* Unpublished paper prepared for a research project on socio-economic rights and transformation in South Africa.

McCoy, D. (1996) *Free health care for pregnant women and children under 6: An impact assessment.* Durban: Health Systems Trust.

Mpumalanga Department of Health. (2003) *Strategic plan for the 2003/04 MTEF.* Available at http://www.treasury.gov.za/documents/budget/2003/provincial/Strategic%20Plans/MPU/MPU%20-%20Vote%2011%20-%20Health.pdf.

National Treasury. (2001) *Adjusted Estimates 2001.* Pretoria: Government Printer.

National Treasury. (2002a) *Budget Review.* Pretoria: Government Printer.

National Treasury. (2002b) *Budget Review:* Erata. Pretoria: Government Printer.

National Treasury. (2003a) *Budget Review.* Pretoria: Government Printer.

National Treasury. (2003b) *Division of Revenue Bill.* Pretoria: Government Printer.

National Treasury. (2003c) *Estimates of National Expenditure.* Pretoria: Government Printer.

Organisation of African Unity. (1981) The *African Charter on Human and Peoples' Rights.* OAU Document CAB/LEG/67/3.Rev.

Organisation of African Unity. (1990) *The African Charter on the Rights and Welfare of the Child.* OAU Document CAB/LEG/24.9/49.

Parliamentary Monitoring Group (PMG). (2002a) Comments made by R.W Green-Thompson on behalf of the KwaZulu-Natal Department of Health. In the minutes of the *Health Portfolio Committee Provincial Budget Hearings: KwaZulu-Natal, Gauteng and Mpumalanga.* 15 May 2002. Accessed at http://www.pmg.org.za/docs/2002/viewminute.php?id=1712 on 14/07/2003.

Parliamentary Monitoring Group (PMG). (2002b) Comments made by R. Malumba on behalf of the national Department of Health. In the minutes of the *Health Portfolio Committee Provincial Budget Hearings: Limpopo and Eastern Cape.* 15 May 2002. Accessed at http://www.pmg.org.za/docs/2002/viewminute.php?id=1712 on 14/07/2003.

Parliamentary Monitoring Group (PMG). (2002c) Comments made by Mr/Ms Ntshipale in the minutes of the *Health Portfolio Committee Provincial Budget Briefings: National Treasury, North West Province, Western Cape and Free State.* 13 May 2002. Accessed at http://www.pmg.org.za/docs/2002/viewminute.php?id=1630 on 14/07/2003. Parliamentary Monitoring Group (PMG). (2002d) Comments made by Mr/Ms Tswala in the minutes of the *Health Portfolio Committee Provincial Budget Hearings.* 15 May 2002. Accessed at http://www.pmg.org.za/docs/2002/viewminute.php?id=1712 on 14/07/2003.

PMTCT National Steering Committee. (2002) *Minutes of National Steering Committee meeting.* Unpublished document, 20 September.

PMTCT National Steering Committee. (2003) *Minutes of National Steering Committee meeting.* Unpublished document, 21 February.

Provincial Treasury of the Free State. (2003). *Budget Statement.* Available from Provincial Treasury of the Free State, Bloemfontein.

Provincial Treasury of KwaZulu-Natal. (2003). *Budget Statement.* Available from Provincial Treasury of KwaZulu-Natal, Pietermaritzburg.

Proudlock, P. & M. Shung-King. (2003) *Submission on the National Health Bill to the Portfolio Committee on Health.* August.

Republic of South Africa. (1994) *White Paper on Reconstruction and Development: Government's Strategy for Fundamental Transformation.* Pretoria: Government Printer.

Saitowitz, R., M. Hendricks, J. Fiedlier, I. Le Roux, G. Hussey & B. Makan. (2001) "A proposed vitamin A supplementation programme for South Africa: Design, coverage and cost." In *South African Medical Journal,* 91(9): 755-760.

Sloth-Nielson, J. (2001) "The child's right to social services, the right to social security, and primary prevention of child abuse: Some conclusions in the aftermath of Grootboom". In *South African Journal for Human Rights,* 17(2).

Streak, J. (2000) "Are children being put first in the health and nutrition sector?" In Cassiem, S., H. Perry, M. Sadan & J. Streak, *Child Poverty and the budget 2000: Are poor children being put first?* Cape Town: Idasa.

Vennekens-Poane, A. (2003) *Comparative provincial health budget brief.* Budget Brief, 131. Cape Town: Budget Information Service, Idasa.

United Nations. (1948) *Universal Declaration of Human Rights.* UN GA Res.217 A (II).

United Nations. (1966). *International Covenant on Economic, Social and Cultural Rights, Article 12.* UN Document A/6316.

Western Cape Department of Health. (2003) *Draft Strategic and Delivery Improvement Plan.* Available from: http://www.westerncape.gov.za/health/policy_planning/chapter_05.asp.

Wigton, A., B. Makan & D. McCoy. (1997) "Health and nutrition". In Robinson, S. & L. Biersteker (eds), *First Call: The South African Children's Budget.* Cape Town: Idasa.

World Health Organisation. (1981) *Basic Documents of the World Health Organisation* (32nd edition). Geneva: WHO.

World Health Organisation. (1998). *Resolution by the Executive Board.* Adopted 22 January. Res.EB/101.R2(1918).

## PERSONAL COMMUNICATION

The following people provided information through personal communication:

H. de Klerk, Department of Health, Pretoria, in 2003.

Dr A. Goga, Department of Health, in 2003.

P. Jeena, King Edward VIII Hospital, Durban, in May 2002.

R. Mohlabi, Department of Health, Pretoria, in August 2003.

# ENDNOTES

1   Discussions are underway to revise the World Health Organisation's definition of health. The proposed new draft reads: "Health is a dynamic state of complete physical, mental, spiritual and social well-being and not merely the absence of disease or infirmity". See the resolution by the Executive Board of the WHO (World Health Organisation 1998).

2   The Constitution of the World Health Organisation was adopted on 22 July 1946 and entered into force on 7 April 1948. It is reprinted in World Health Organisation (1981).

3   The Universal Declaration of Human Rights was adopted on 10 December 1948 (United Nations 1948).

4   The International Covenant on Economic, Social and Cultural Rights, article 12, was adopted on 16 December 1966 and entered into force on 3 January 1976 (United Nations 1966).

5   The African Charter on Human and Peoples' Rights was adopted on 27 June 1981 and entered into force on 21 October 1986 (Organisation of African Unity 1981).

6   The CRC was adopted on 20 November 1989 and entered into force on 2 September 1990. South Africa ratified and signed the convention in 1995, making this instrument and its principles an obligatory commitment from the South African government to the children of the country. Government has to give regular reports to the United Nations in terms of its performance in meeting the obligations spelt out in the convention, the next report being due in 2004.

7   The African Charter on the Rights and Welfare of the Child was adopted in 1990 and entered into force on 29 November 1999 (Organisation of African Unity 1990).

8   The specific programmes outlined in this section of the table are all part of the overall Integrated Nutrition Programme, which is discussed in more detail in chapter three of this book.

9   For more information on the costed norms approach, as proposed by the Financial and Fiscal Commission, see Financial and Fiscal Commission 2000.

10  The Western Cape Department of Health comes closest to the required indicators with its measurable target for the PMTCT programme for the 2003/04 financial year. The target was to ensure that the PMTCT programme was available at 75% of obstetric facilities and that 75% of pregnant mothers were offered PMTCT programme counselling. However, it did not provide the percentage or number of HIV-positive mother-child pairs that the province was planning to treat.

11   The MTEF estimates were obtained from the Idasa research unit on AIDS and Public Finance, sourced from the National Treasury.

12   The observation that provinces were often compelled to use provincial funds to cover the start-up costs of the PMTCT programme derives from notes of a speech by the Minister of Health at the health plenary session of the World Summit on Sustainable Development, 26 August 2002.

13   For 2004/05, KwaZulu-Natal has allocated an additional R135 million on top of the R28 million national conditional grant for the PMTCT programme, and a similar pattern can be observed for 2005/06 (Provincial Treasury of KwaZulu-Natal 2003:16).

14   According to the strategic plan of the Mpumalanga Department of Health (2003: 35), the PMTCT budgets over the 2003/04 MTEF are:

| Sub-programme ** R'000 | 2001/ 02 (Actual) | 2002/03 (Estimate) | 2003/04 (Budget) | 2004/05 (MTEF Projection) | 2005/06 (MTEF Projection) |
|---|---|---|---|---|---|
| Prevention of Mother to Child Transmission | ---- | R 294 | R 9 000 | R 11 555 | R 12 710 |

** **Please note:** original text incorrectly reads "R million". No distinction is made between conditional grant and discretionary funds.

15   The GOALS resource allocation model "combines demographic, epidemiological, cost, effectiveness, and likely effectiveness and cost-effectiveness of different strategies and intervention packages in the field of HIV prevention, AIDS care and TB control". The GOALS model was used in order to identify major gaps in the currently funded HIV/AIDS and TB control programmes (Department of Health 2002b).

# CHAPTER FIVE

Budgeting and service delivery in programmes targeted at the child's right to social services: The case of the Child Support Grant

Shaamela Cassiem and Lerato Kgamphe

# INTRODUCTION

This chapter monitors the measures taken by government to give effect to children's constitutional right to social services. Within the ambit of social services, the focus is specifically on children's right to social assistance. Section 28(1)(c) of the Constitution affords every child the right "to social services". In addition, section 27(1)(c) affords everyone the right to have "access to... social security, including, if they are unable to support themselves and their dependants, appropriate social assistance". To date, South Africa's jurisprudence has provided no clarity about whether the right to social services afforded to children in section 28(1)(c) includes the right to social assistance (Budlender in Creamer 2002; Liebenberg in personal correspondence). The attainment of children's rights would be enhanced if the right to social services afforded in section 28(1)(c) does in fact include the right to social assistance. This is due to the higher level of obligation placed on the state to give effect to section 28(1)(c) and 29(1)(a) rights (see chapter two and section one below).

The *White Paper for Social Welfare in South Africa* refers to social security as "a wide range of public and private measures that provide cash or in-kind benefits, or both" (Department of Welfare and Population Development 1997). Social security includes social assistance and social insurance. Social assistance is provided by the state, non-contributory and usually means-tested; benefits include cash transfers and vouchers (Child Health Policy Institute & the South African Federal Council on Disability 2001). Social insurance includes private and contributory schemes, for example work retirement insurance (ibid).

In South Africa, it is critical for government to provide social assistance to poor children and their parents or alternative care-givers. This is firstly because of the high level of poverty, including child poverty. The extent and depth of child poverty is illustrated in chapter one of this publication. The Committee of Inquiry into a Comprehensive System of Social Security for South Africa (hereafter referred to as the Taylor Committee) found that approximately 18 million people lived on less than R450 per month. Children make up roughly 70% of this group (Department of Social Development 2002). Secondly, access to a minimum income (the right to social assistance) is important for facilitating access to the other rights of children. For example, the accounts from poor children themselves, presented in chapter one, clearly demonstrate that for some poor children getting a minimum income (for example, by means of a grant) is a necessary condition for realising the right to education. Thirdly, government provision to realise the right to social assistance is further made critical by the fact that South Africa is suffering from a structural unemployment crisis with little prospects for millions of unskilled workers to find employment in the market economy.

The South African government touts its social security programmes as its most successful "fight against poverty" (National Treasury 2003c:110). South Africa has seven (statutory) social security grants. These are the State Old Age Pension, War Veteran's Grant, Disability Grant, Grant in Aid, Foster Care Grant, Care Dependency Grant and the Child Support Grant. As at March 2003, five and a half million people in South

Africa were receiving a social security grant. Of these beneficiaries, 45% were receiving a Child Support Grant (ibid). This represents the highest percentage share of the total number of social security beneficiaries. The second highest share (36%) goes to those receiving the Old Age Pension.

However, the coverage of social security remains a highly contentious area of government's response to extensive poverty and poverty-related problems in South Africa. The "coverage of social security grants" is understood to depend not only on who is eligible for social security grants, but also on their ability to access the grants. It is thus a product of both the design and the implementation of social security programmes. Factors such as the high prevalence of child poverty[1] and HIV/AIDS infection, as well as increasing numbers of orphans[2] have galvanised civil society and government to investigate different practices to better respond to social security and, in turn, the needs of vulnerable groups.

This chapter follows the monitoring method as set out in chapter two. Section one reviews what is known about the meaning and scope of the child's constitutional right to social services (and particularly to social assistance), as well as the associated state obligations to deliver this right. Drawing from evolving jurisprudence and expert opinion, the discussion in this section relates to government's constitutional obligations with respect to sections 27(1)(c), 27(2) and 28(1)(c) of the Constitution. It highlights the lack of clarity about what exactly children are entitled to under the right to social services and social assistance afforded by the Constitution, particularly the implications of section 28(1)(c). Moreover, it calls attention to the urgent need for consensus-building on what social assistance (and other social service benefits) poor children can claim from the state under sections 28(1)(c) and 27(1)(c). Section two identifies and describes the most important programmes introduced by government in order to give effect to the child's right to social services, and in particular social assistance.

Section three analyses the sufficiency of one of the main programmes that government has put in place to give effect to the child's right to social assistance, namely the Child Support Grant (CSG) programme. It considers whether the programme is sufficient both in terms of its conceptualisation and its implementation. This section provides the following:

- A description of the programme, with due consideration of whether it is conceptualised in such a way as to facilitate all children getting access to social assistance, particularly the most vulnerable, and in such a way as to enable the rapid roll-out of services;

- Information on the budget of the programme in the past and for the Medium-Term Expenditure Framework (MTEF) period 2003/04 - 2005/06;

- An analysis of the level of under-spending or over-spending on the CSG programme on the part of provincial governments in the recent past;

- Commentary on the extent to which the implementation of the programme is such that services have been, and are being, rolled out to all children in need, particularly those whose needs are most urgent, as a matter of urgency and as quickly as administrative capacity permits;

- An overview of the (financial and non-financial) implementation problems undermining universal access to the CSG for all children in need; and

- A review of what government is doing to overcome the hurdles identified above and a discussion on how these planned measures might be adjusted to improve the conceptualisation and implementation of the programme.

The conclusion summarises the main findings and arguments of the chapter and presents a set of recommendations relating to the further advancement of the child's right to social assistance.

# 1. THE MEANING AND SCOPE OF THE CHILD'S RIGHT TO SOCIAL SERVICES AND SOCIAL ASSISTANCE

## 1.1 THE BASIS OF THE CHILD'S RIGHT TO SOCIAL SERVICES AND SOCIAL ASSISTANCE

The child's right to social services and social assistance in South Africa is drawn from sections 28(1)(c), 28 (1)(b) and 27(1)(c) of the Constitution (Republic of South Africa 1996). The rights are explicitly afforded in sections 28(1)(c) and 27(1)(c). In the *Grootboom* case, the Constitutional Court (2000) held that section 28(1)(c) must be read in conjunction with section 28(1)(b) of the Constitution.

Section 28 (1)(c) states that:
"Every child has the right to...social services."

Section 28(1)(b) states that:
"Every child has the right...to family care and parental care or to appropriate alternative care when removed from the family environment."

Section 27(1)(c) states that:
"Everyone has the right to have access to...social security, including, if they are unable to support themselves and their dependants, appropriate social assistance."

The latter section is qualified by section 27(2):
"The state must take reasonable legislative and other measures, within its available resources, to achieve the progressive realisation of each of these rights."

The right to social assistance for children in South Africa is also entrenched in the African Charter on the Rights and Welfare of the Child (ACRWC), the United Nations Convention on the Rights of the Child (CRC) and the International Covenant on Economic, Social and Cultural Rights (ICESCR):

> "States Parties to the [African Charter on the Rights and Welfare of the Child] shall ensure, subject to available resources, to a disabled child and to those responsible for his (sic) care, of assistance for which application is made and which is appropriate to the child's condition..."
> *ACRWC, article 13(2)*

> "States Parties to the [African Charter on the Rights and Welfare of the Child] shall in accordance with their means and national conditions [take] all appropriate measures; (a) to assist parents and other persons responsible for the child and in case of need provide material assistance and support programmes..."
> *ACRWC, article 20(2)(a)*

> "For the purpose of guaranteeing and promoting the rights set forth in the [Convention on the Rights of the Child], States Parties shall render appropriate assistance to parents and legal guardians in the performance of their child-rearing responsibilities and shall ensure the development of institutions, facilities and services for the care of children."
> *CRC, article 18(2)*

> "A child temporarily or permanently deprived of his or her family environment, or in whose own best interests cannot be allowed to remain in that environment, shall be entitled to...assistance provided by the State...Such care could include, inter alia, foster placement..."
> *CRC, article 20(1)(3)*

> "States Parties recognize the right of the disabled child to special care and shall encourage and ensure the extension, subject to available resources, to the eligible child and those responsible for his or her care, of assistance for which application is made and which is appropriate to the child's condition and to the circumstances of the parents or others caring for the child."
> *CRC, article 23(2)*

> "States Parties shall recognize for every child the right to benefit from social security...and shall take the necessary measures to achieve this right in full realization of this right in accordance with their national law. The benefits should, where appropriate, be granted, taking into account the resources and the circumstances of the child and persons having responsibility for the maintenance of the child..."
> *CRC, article 26(1)(2)*

> "The States Parties to the present Covenant recognize the right of everyone to social security, including social insurance."
> *ICESCR, article 9*

# 1.2 CHILDREN'S ENTITLEMENTS UNDER THE RIGHT TO SOCIAL SERVICES

While children are afforded the right to social services[3] and social assistance under these legal instruments, it is not clear what exactly children can claim from the state through their social service and social assistance rights. Current interpretations of what South African children are entitled to by virtue of these rights derive from the evolving jurisprudence of the Constitutional Court and from expert opinion.

Sloth-Nielsen (2001) points out that a broad interpretation of section 28(1)(c) includes rights that fall under the category of "social spending", as evidenced in the *World Development Reports* released by the World Bank. A narrow view of social services places emphasis on developmental social welfare programmes and services such as those normally provided by South Africa's Department of Social Development.[4] In a similar vein, social assistance provision is the responsibility of the Department of Social Development.

The *White Paper for Social Welfare in South Africa* (Department of Welfare & Population Development 1997:Chapter 7, paragraph 1) defines the scope of social security to cover:

> "[a] wide range of public and private measures that provide cash or in-kind benefits, or both, first, in the event of an individual's earning power permanently ceasing, being interrupted, never developing, or being exercised only at acceptable social cost and such person being able to *avoid poverty*. And secondly, in order to *maintain children*" (emphasis added by authors).

The white paper therefore seems to suggest that government accepts that the objective of social assistance should be to ensure a decent standard of living for all people, and in particular, for children.

A concern that requires attention is whether children's socio-economic rights under sections 28 are limited or attenuated versions of the fuller rights afforded under sections 26 and 27 (Creamer 2002). According to Brand (in Creamer 2002 and in chapter 3 of this publication), a plain reading of the sections themselves seems to indicate that the rights entrenched in section 28 are of a more basic nature. In *Grootboom*, however, the Constitutional Court (2000) appeared to decide otherwise. Budlender (cited in Creamer 2002:27) describes the current situation as follows:

> "[T]here is a logical symmetry in the argument that s26 and s27 provide everyone with broad rights qualified by 'progressive realisation' and available resources etc., whereas sec 28(1)(c) provides children with unqualified rights to the more basic or attenuated forms of those rights. But the court would not buy that argument, partly because it wanted to escape the conclusion reached by the Cape High Court. It did not expressly reject the argument outside the context of shelter, but this is a logical conclusion from what it said...the issue will one day have to be re-argued in a different context. For the moment, though, I do

> not think one can say with any confidence that the sec 28(1)(c) rights are the attenuated form of the sec 26 and 27 rights – except of course where 28(1)(c) says so expressly, that is, 'basic' nutrition and 'basic' health care services."

As relayed in chapter two, the Constitutional Court has not yet pronounced on the exact nature and scope of government's obligations in relation to children's section 28(1)(c) rights. There has, however, been a great deal of debate amongst legal experts, child rights activists and researchers around how the court would be likely to interpret the scope of section 28(1)(c) rights, given its judgements in other matters involving socio-economic rights. Within this context, it remains unclear exactly which children are covered by the right to social services (and by inference to social assistance) given in section 28(1)(c). In section 27, the right of access to social assistance – that is, to non-contributory forms of support provided from public funds – is limited to those "*unable* to support themselves and their dependents" (Liebenberg 2002a:155, emphasis added). Liebenberg suggests that a broad interpretation of this right is preferable because the "vital interest that this right protects is an adequate standard of living for everyone" (ibid). The Cape High Court in the *Grootboom* case took a progressive view of the scope of section 28(1)(c) rights, implying that all children in need – and even indigent parents through their children – are covered by the rights. Liebenberg (2003:12) summarises as follows:

> "While [the Cape High Court accepted]…that the primary obligation to maintain a child rests on its parents, [the court] held that the state incurs an obligation to provide rudimentary shelter for children when their parents are unable to do so…[The court] went on to hold that the parents enjoyed a derivative right to be accommodated with their children in the aforesaid shelter, based on a joint reading of sections 28(1)(b), 28(1)(c) and 28(2)."

This broad view of the scope of the rights was rejected by the Constitutional Court when the case went on appeal. In this case (Constitutional Court 2000), the court took what seemed to be a conservative view: that only children living without parental care are covered by the rights given in section 28(1)(c). However, in the subsequent *Treatment Action Campaign* (TAC) judgment (Constitutional Court 2002)[5] the narrow view of the scope – that would exclude indigent children living with their parents – was rejected in favour of a definition that includes children living in poor households. Creamer (2002), drawing on the views of Brand and Budlender, concludes that the scope of the unqualified socio-economic rights (including that to social services) in section 28(1)(c) includes all indigent children, not only those without family care. It seems then, as Liebenberg suggests, that it can currently be assumed that it is *all* children in need that have a claim against the state for their right to social services under section 28(1)(c).

While the scope of children's right to social services under section 28(1)(c) may be more certain, the question of what children can claim from the state by virtue of this right is yet to be answered. In the various Constitutional Court cases relating to socio-economic rights, little direction has been given on the nature of the entitlements implied by section 28(1)(c). It is crucial for more clarity to be established around what exactly the rights to social security and social services in the Constitution entitle children to.

The Bill of Rights in the Constitution articulates that the state has a duty to "respect, protect, promote and fulfil"[6] all the rights afforded by the Constitution and that these rights affirm the values of human dignity, equality and freedom (sections 7(2); 9; 10; 12). Against this background, the following key elements are proposed for a rights-based approach to social assistance for children (see Liebenberg 2002a:156):

- **Universality:** All children in need of social assistance should be able to gain access to it.

- **Comprehensiveness:** The social security system should provide comprehensive coverage against all contingencies and life circumstances that threaten the income-earning ability of adults and their ability to support themselves and their dependants. This includes unemployment, disability and old age, as well as child support for impoverished care-givers.

- **Just administration:** The administration system should be publicly adminis-tered or regulated. The system must be in accordance with the administrative jus-tice rights set out in section 33 of the Constitution. The requirements governing eligibility for, and the termination of, benefits must be reasonable and procedu-rally fair. The system as a whole should also be efficient and accessible to users.

- **Adequacy and appropriateness:** The level of benefits afforded under the social assistance schemes must meet a minimum standard. For example, the bene-fit provided should at least be sufficient to ensure that the recipient does not fall below an accepted poverty line or minimum substance level for South Africa. An accepted minimum level of social assistance for children and adults must be established with due consideration of other social services available to children and adults that advance children's rights to (basic) social services.

- **Equality:** The social assistance system must not discriminate directly or indirect-ly against any person or group on grounds such as race, sex, gender, sexual orien-tation, ethnic or social origin or other grounds in terms of sections 9(3) and 9(4) of the Constitution.

The suggestion is then that the right to social assistance in the Constitution implies that all children are entitled to a level of income that ensures they do not "fall below an accepted poverty line". If this is accepted, the critical challenge is to establish an "accepted poverty line" and then to decide on grant values that will ensure that chil-dren are kept above this poverty line.

## 1.3 STATE OBLIGATIONS

As noted in chapter two, a distinction must be drawn between the *level* of the obliga-tion placed on the state by section 28 of the Constitution, as compared to the *level* of the obligation incurred by section 27. This is because children's socio-economic rights in section 28 are unqualified: the formulation used in this section does not include any limitations on how or how quickly government is expected to realise section 28 rights. On the other hand, the right to social security given in section 27(1)(c) is qualified: the formulation of this section stipulates that government has an obligation to take *reasonable measures* to ensure the *progressive realisation* of section 27 rights, within its *available resources.*

As alluded to above, section 27(1)(c) does not afford a direct claim on the state and must be read with section 27(2). The Bill of Rights expressly allows the state to realise the rights entrenched in section 27(1)(c) "progressively" (gradually) and "within its available resources". In order to give effect to the right, the state must adopt reasonable[7] legislation and other measures (for example financial, administrative and educational measures) that clearly and directly advance and improve access to social security. Because the entitlement in section 27(1)(c) is limited in this way, children cannot claim that the state must provide them with immediate and direct access to social security on the basis of section 27 rights.[8] Thus, although children are included in the right of access to social security in section 27(1)(c), vulnerable children especially hold a higher claim to the right to social security by virtue of their section 28 (1)(c) rights (Creamer 2002). As Liebenberg (cited in Creamer 2002:5) explains:

> "The clear implication of the Constitutional Court's reasoning in Grootboom relating to children's socio-economic rights in s 28(1)(c) is that children who are orphans, abandoned or not in the care of their families for other reasons have a direct claim against the state to be provided with shelter, basic nutrition, basic health care services and social services."

Brand (in Creamer 2002) however cautions against this, pointing out that in the *Grootboom* case, the court did not make it explicit that children who are not in the care of their families will have access to "unqualified" rights. In the light of this, Brand (Ibid:5) suggests:

> "[S]hould the notion of an unqualified right for such children come to be accepted, it would most likely be interpreted as conferring a duty on the state to provide the services and goods which comprise the right as a matter of 'absolute priority'."

Creamer (Ibid) offers some guidance in relation to the state's obligation to advance children's socio-economic rights. He proposes that the state's obligation to advance children's socio-economic rights can be read as an obligation to:

- provide legal and administrative infrastructure fulfilling the children's rights as set out in section 28; and
- provide families, and thereby children, with access to land (section 25), adequate housing (section 26), as well as health care, food, water and social security (section 27) on a programmatic and co-ordinated basis, subject to available resources.

Furthermore, these rights should be regarded as imposing an obligation on government to absolutely prioritise the basic rights of children.

Budlender (in Creamer 2002:27) suggests that the question of whether section 28(1)(c) rights are available in an unqualified way to children in need, or whether such rights must be progressively realised, remains a "fundamental unresolved issue".

Thus the precise state obligations associated with children's rights to social assistance are still unclear. The unqualified nature of the rights in section 28 implies an absolute priority on budget allocation. However, "a right cannot place a duty on the state to do that which is practically impossible" (Brand in Creamer 2002:41). At a practical level, it is impossible to immediately realise children's socio-economic rights. However, it can be stated unequivocally that children's socio-economic rights should be afforded a high priority in budgeting and service delivery: "[P]rogrammes devised to advance the socio-economic rights of children should be characterised by *accelerated and comprehensive* service delivery to all children in need" (Creamer 2002:27, emphasis added). Creamer (Ibid) goes on to suggest:

> "[T]he reasonable time period which should be regarded as concomitant with the states' obligations to absolutely prioritise these rights, will be measured in terms of the period required for the urgent marshalling of the real administrative capacity, rather than any delay justified in terms of a constraint on financial resources".

The attainment of the child's right to social assistance depends, in part, on an understanding of the precise entitlements that accompany the child's right to social security. As illustrated above, the exact nature of these entitlements remains unclear. In addition, the fulfilment of the right to social security must be related to the fulfilment of other children's rights including, *inter alia*, the right to basic education, the right to basic nutrition and the right to protection from abuse.

## 2. GOVERNMENT PROGRAMMES AIMED AT ADVANCING THE CHILD'S RIGHT TO SOCIAL SERVICES AND SOCIAL ASSISTANCE

Focusing on measures adopted by the Department of Social Development, Box 5.1 lists the main programmes that government has set in place to advance the child's right to social services and social assistance.

---

**BOX 5.1  MAIN PROGRAMMES AIMED AT ADVANCING THE CHILD'S RIGHT TO SOCIAL SERVICES AND SOCIAL ASSISTANCE**

1. Child Support Grant programme
2. Care Dependency Grant programme
3. Foster Care Grant programme
4. Social Relief of Distress programme
5. The HIV/AIDS programme (Home/Community-based Care programme)

---

6. Poverty Relief programme
7. Transformation of the Child and Youth Care programme
8. Secure Care programme
9. Child and Youth Justice Diversion programme
10. State Old Age Pension programme

The conceptualisation and implementation of these programmes are mainly the responsibility of the Department of Social Development. The national department is responsible for policy formulation and monitoring, the implementation of social security, including social assistance, assessing the social, economic and fiscal impact of social security programmes, the design of strategies and operating systems for service provision, facilitating the transformation of welfare service delivery and finally, the development of strategies for poverty reduction and community development (National Treasury 2003b). Provincial social development departments have largely been responsible for implementation and service delivery, including budgeting – in some cases with the assistance of other departments and organisations.[9] Provincial social development departments take responsibility for the implementation of social assistance programmes and have contracted private agencies to deliver payments of the grants.

Table 5.1 gives a broad overview of the main programmes that government has in place that give effect to the child's right to social services. It sets out who the programmes are targeted at, what the eligibility criteria are, what services are offered by each programme and what the implementation time-frame is.

Three programmes represented in Table 5.1 take the form of social assistance targeted specifically at children, namely the Child Support Grant (CSG), the Foster Care Grant (FCG) and the Care Dependency Grant (CDG). However, it is important to note that the adult-specific social assistance programmes also help in this regard. For example, the majority of elderly and disabled people living in poverty share a household with three or more generations. The grants they receive are largely pooled as household income (Department of Welfare & Population Development 1996). Poorer households tend to have more members: 20% of the poorest household in South Africa contain 20% of the population. Thus older household members' pensions tend to "trickle down" to many more people than the individual beneficiary (Ibid). Nonetheless, the broad overview of interventions above signals that there are gaps in programme coverage.

**TABLE 5.1  MAIN GOVERNMENT PROGRAMMES GIVING EFFECT TO CHILDREN'S RIGHT TO SOCIAL SERVICES**

| Programme title | Targeted beneficiaries and eligibility criteria | Services offered | Implementation time-frame |
|---|---|---|---|
| Child Support Grant (CSG) | The programme is targeted at children who pass a means test. The parent or care-giver applying for the grant on the child's behalf must supply identity documents and the child's birth certificate. See implementation time-frame for targeted age-groups. | The CSG takes the form of a monthly payment of R160, claimed by the care-giver on behalf of a child. | • The CSG was extended to all eligible children under 9 years old on 1 April 2003.<br>• It extends to all eligible children under 11 years old as from 1 April 2004.<br>• By April 2005, it will extend to all eligible children under 14. |
| Care Dependency Grant (CDG) | This grant is targeted at poor children who have severe mental or physical disabilities and are in need of full-time care. The child must be under 18 years, or up to 21 years if s/he is still in secondary school. | The CDG takes the form of a monthly payment of R700, claimed by the care-giver for a child who proves, through a medical assessment, severe disability. | There is little information on the number of eligible children. Government has no explicit time-frame for the roll-out of the grant to all eligible children. |
| Foster Care Grant (FCG) | This programme is targeted at children who are placed in foster care by a social worker on behalf of the children's court. | This grant takes the form of a monthly payment of R500, claimed by the care-giver with a court order indicating their foster care status. | The number of eligible children remains unclear. Government has no explicit time-frame for roll-out. |
| Secure Care programme | This programme is aimed at neglected, abused and exploited children. | The programme provides shelter for children who have been removed from their homes. | There are no official estimates of eligible children, nor a time-frame for roll-out. |
| National Integrated Strategy for children affected by HIV/AIDS (Home Care/ Community-based Care programme) | This programme has two target groups of beneficiaries:<br>• Families and children affected by and infected with HIV and AIDS; and<br>• Orphans and vulnerable groups. | The programme facilitates:<br>• access to social grants and material assistance, for example food, clothing and shelter;<br>• the establishment of alternative care or child care communities; and<br>• counselling, support and training for care-givers and volunteers. | No time-frame for implementation is provided. |

| Programme title | Targeted beneficiaries and eligibility criteria | Services offered | Implementation time-frame |
|---|---|---|---|
| Child and Youth Justice Diversion programme | This programme targets all children that are in conflict with the law, with the aim of keeping them out of the criminal justice system. | Different types of interventions are applied for different offences. These are in line with the Child Justice Bill, as well as the Probation Services Act. | These services have been offered since the early 1990s and have recently been formalised through legislation. |
| Transformation of the Child and Youth Care programme | This programme is also targeted at children in conflict with the law, as well as children in need of protection. | The programme provides transformation homes and places of safety as well as quality assurances from these places that the programmes are being implemented and are working. | The goal is for the programme to extend to all children in need of transformation. Inception was in 1995 and services offered are inter-ministerial. |
| Social Relief of Distress | This grant is a temporary provision for persons unable to meet their needs or the needs of their family, particularly persons and families experiencing a crisis period. | This grant takes the form of a specific monthly amount limited to three payments, while the persons are either being registered on the welfare system, or are altering their state of distress. | 2003 was the initial year of roll-out. The programme is inter-departmental and functions for all beneficiaries in need of distress at any one time. |
| Poverty Relief Programme | This programme is targeted at:<br>• the poorest parts of provinces;<br>• rural areas; and<br>• households where single women are the main breadwinners. | The programme aims to:<br>• relieve poverty in the poorest provinces;<br>• provide infrastructure;<br>• assist in human development and capacity-building;<br>• provide jobs;<br>• produce food and provide access to markets; and<br>• ensure project sustainability. | The programme began implementation in 1997, with no clear indication of the number of beneficiaries to be targeted. |
| State Old Age Pension Programme | This programme targets South African older persons (65 years and older if male, 60 years and older if female) subject to a means test and not living in a state institution or receiving any other grant. | The grant takes the form of a monthly payment of R700, subject to passing a means test. | This programme was initiated pre-democracy and has since been extended to include all older persons who pass the means test. |

**Sources:** National Department of Social Development, personal communication.

While CSG policy has changed to include children above seven years old, this still excludes all children over 14 years from eligibility. The current child grant system excludes children living on the streets, as applications must be brought by an adult care-giver. The means-testing for the CSG also fails to take child-headed households into consideration. In addition, there is no grant available for those with chronic illnesses associated with HIV/AIDS. No social assistance provision is made for adults between 18 and 60 years of age (only a disability grant, where appropriate). These gaps in programme design and delivery for the right to social assistance – both for children and adults – are well known. There has been extensive advocacy around the need for programmes such as the CSG to include all children (particularly those living on the streets and without adult care-givers) and for the introduction of a Basic Income Grant (BIG). Government has argued that it is not feasible to implement, manage and sustain a BIG and has opted to use other measures to alleviate poverty.

Against this background, there is a need to re-examine social security grants for children in South Africa. Demand for the FCG is likely to increase in the foreseeable future due to growing numbers of orphans in the wake of the HIV/AIDS epidemic. In addition, no provision has currently been made for the "vulnerabilities that children commonly face prior to the death of their parent(s) [and caregivers]" (Giese *et al* 2003). It can also be expected that demands on the social security system will increase as children infected with or affected by HIV/AIDS become eligible for CSGs, due to deepening child poverty as parents or care-givers become sick, are rendered unable to take care of their households and eventually die. One option to improve social security for children affected by HIV/AIDS is to afford the CSG to all children and to scrap the means test that remains an obstacle to receiving this grant.

The attainment of the right to social services depends on a comprehensive package of social services for all children. This includes direct cash transfers (the CSG, for example) and indirect benefits (community-based care, for example). Concerns regarding the sufficiency of social assistance for children derive, in part, from the difficulty in deciding whether the value of the CSG is adequate. This must be assessed in conjunction with an analysis of the other programmes that are in place to deliver other socio-economic rights to children, as well as careful measurement of the extent to which lack of income prevents children from realising their basic rights.

# 3. ANALYSIS OF THE CHILD SUPPORT GRANT PROGRAMME

This section of the chapter examines government's CSG programme, the primary means of social assistance for children. It is divided into five parts. First, the discussion looks into the conceptualisation of the programme and asks whether the programme design ensures that all children in need are covered, particularly the most vulnerable, and whether it caters for the rapid roll-out of benefits to all children in need. The chapter then puts the spotlight on budget allocations to the CSG programme and analyses the extent to which these allocations have been under- or over-spent. The third part of this section uses data on the take-up rates for the CSG to shed light on the roll-out rate of the grant. Fourthly, the analysis highlights the nature of the obstacles that need to be overcome to facilitate a more rapid roll-out of the grant to all children who are currently eligible for the grant and all children in need of the grant. The section concludes with an overview of government's current plans to extend the grant and some comments in this regard.

## 3.1 CONCEPTUALISATION OF THE CSG PROGRAMME

### 3.1.1 BACKGROUND

In 1996, the Welfare MinMec (Committee of the Minister of Welfare and the Provincial Members of the Executive Council) appointed the Lund Committee to review the problems of achieving racial equity in the State Maintenance Grant (SMG).[10] The SMG was a means-tested grant administered to a mother who was not receiving financial support from her partner or the father of her children or if she was widowed or "deserted". In 1997, the MinMec approved the recommendations made by the Lund Committee, including that the SMG be phased out. A moratorium was to be placed on new applications for the SMG. At the same time, a new programme of child support benefits was to be phased in, with poor children receiving R75, subject to a means test. Children's rights activists heavily contested the amount of R75. Although the CSG programme was first introduced in 1997 as the replacement of the SMG, it was only after lengthy discussions between government, NGOs and policy-makers, that the programme was implemented in 1998 with an agreed R100 for each benefici-ary. The Department of Social Development had three years to complete the phasing-out of the SMG.

The CSG was originally limited to children under seven years old and targeted the poorest 30% of South Africa's children. An application for the CSG is validated by the care-giver supplying his or her South African bar-coded Identity Document (ID), as well as the birth certificate of the child (that is, the potential beneficiary). Thereafter a means test is applied based on three criteria: the personal income of the primary care-giver and his/her spouse, their location (urban or rural) and the type of dwelling (informal or formal) in which the child lives. An applicant (acting on behalf of the child beneficiary) passes the means test if:

- S/he lives in an urban area, in a formal dwelling and has a personal income of below R9600 per annum; or

- S/he lives in an urban area, in an informal dwelling and has a personal income of below R13200 per annum; or

- S/he lives in a rural area in a formal or informal dwelling and has a personal income of below R13 200 per annum.

Table 5.2 details the provincial breakdown of the number of recipients that were tar-geted at the inception of the CSG in 1998. Government has acknowledged that this information is out-dated and that 3.6 million children under 7 years are eligible for the CSG (National Treasury 2003a). Table 5.3 provides updated information on the number of recipients for the CSG, using data from the Financial and Fiscal Commission (FFC).

**TABLE 5.2 PROVINCIAL BREAKDOWN OF OFFICIAL CSG ROLL-OUT TARGETS TO CHILDREN UNDER 7 (AS DEVISED IN APRIL 1998)**

| Provinces | Recipients to be reached by 31 March 2003 |
|---|---|
| Eastern Cape | 780 000 |
| Free State | 300 000 |
| Gauteng | 90 000 |
| KwaZulu-Natal | 600 000 |
| Mpumalanga | 210 000 |
| Northern Cape | 30 000 |
| Limpopo | 600 000 |
| North West | 330 000 |
| Western Cape | 90 000 |
| **Total** | **3 030 000** |

**Source:** Streak & Wehner 2002.

**TABLE 5.3 FFC ESTIMATES OF THE NUMBER OF CHILDREN UNDER 7 ELIGIBLE FOR THE CSG**

| | FFC | Difference between FFC estimates and official targets |
|---|---|---|
| Eastern Cape | 828 254 | 48 254 |
| Free State | 222 338 | -77 662 |
| Gauteng | 371 308 | 281 308 |
| KwaZulu-Natal | 862 696 | 262 696 |
| Limpopo | 787 159 | 187 159 |
| Mpumalanga | 310 089 | 100 089 |
| North West | 337 391 | 7 391 |
| Northern Cape | 128 260 | 98 260 |
| Western Cape | 183 715 | 93 715 |
| **Total** | **4 031 210** | **1 001 210** |

**Source:** Streak & Wehner 2002.

Government's decision to reduce the SMG amount and limit the new CSG to children under 7 and to the poorest 30% of children, was informed by the impending fiscal problems outlined by Servaas van der Berg, John Kruger and Pieter le Roux in the Lund Committee Report (Department of Welfare & Population Development 1996). According to this report, in 1990 it would have taken more than R20 billion per annum to make the existing SMG available to all eligible children under 18. This was not a feasible option at a time when government had implemented tight macro-economic policies as a means towards reducing the budget deficit and facilitating sustainable growth and poverty reduction. The introduction of the CSG must be seen in the context of the democratic government's introduction of a whole package of programmes to assist poor children, especially young children. This "package" could be seen to include, for example, the Primary School Nutrition Programme (now known as the Primary School Feeding Scheme) and the free health care policy.

From the beginning of April 1998, the CSG was phased in with support from a Child Support Implementation Grant (CSIG), totalling R75 million to be used between 1998/99 and 2000/01 (National Treasury 2003b:422). This amount was appropriated for the establishment and introduction of the CSG. This conditional grant would later be managed within the equitable share of the CSG because they served a simultaneous function – that is, for the improvement of social security and securing a basic income for the most impoverished children in South Africa (Hlatshwayo 2003:personal communication).

The decision to budget for the implementation of the CSG by means of a conditional grant took the following factors into consideration:

- The 1994 democratic government inherited diverse financial and administrative systems, which posed challenges in terms of amalgamations, efficiency and effectiveness;

- The (then) Department of Welfare & Population Development was responsible for the third largest national budget. It was tasked to manage large sums of money without adequately skilled personnel who could devote time to improving the financial management systems;

- There was an urgent need for improvements in management information systems, in order to support policy development and decision-making; and

- There was a lack of equipment to enable and to sustain tasks at all levels, especially service delivery (Ibid).

The CSG programme, like other social assistance programmes, has been and still is implemented by the provincial social development departments. Implementation responsibility includes budgeting for the grant. The national Department of Social Development has the responsibility to facilitate its implementation and to assist in monitoring the programme. The national department is also responsible for policymaking (such as changes in CSG eligibility or means-testing) and broad implementation plans (such as designing operating systems).

Since the introduction of the CSG in April 1998, the value of the grant has changed four times. The initial R100 remained unchanged until July 2001, when the grant was increased to R110. It was again increased to R130 in April 2002, to R140 in October 2002 and to R160 as from April 2003.

Table 5.4 shows the value of the grant and how it has changed over time, both in real and nominal terms.

**TABLE 5.4  NOMINAL AND REAL VALUE OF THE CSG (1998-2003), IN R**

| CSG | 1998 | 1999 | 2000 | 2001 | April 2002 | Oct 2002 | 2003 |
|---|---|---|---|---|---|---|---|
| Nominal | 100 | 100 | 100 | 110 | 130 | 140 | 160 |
| Real | 100 | 94.25 | 87.49 | 89.5 | 96.16 | 103.56 | 109.89 |

**Source:** National Department of Social Development, personal communication 2003.

**Note:** Real values were calculated with 1998 as the base year. The following deflators were applied: 1998/99=1, 99/00=1.061, 00/01=1.143, 01/02=1.229, 02/03=1.3519, 03/04=1.4559963. The CPIX as sourced from the *Budget Review* for each year in question was used to calculate the deflators.

Figure 5.1 gives a graphical representation of the changing CSG payment amount over time and how this has impacted on the real value of the grant. In real terms in 2003, the value of the CSG was just a little over the 1998 figure of R100.

**FIGURE 5.1 NOMINAL VS REAL VALUE OF THE CSG**

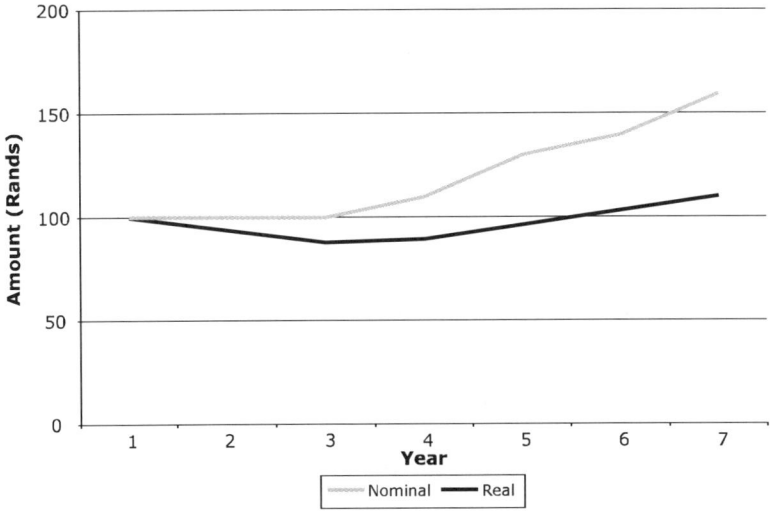

In 2003, the CSG programme was affected by a policy change. This must be seen in the context of extensive lobbying and advocacy by civil society and the recommendations made by the Taylor Committee. In February 2003, government announced that children under 9 years would now be targeted to receive the CSG from 2003/04, children under 11 years would be targeted from 2004/05 and children under 14 years would be targeted from 2005/06. The eligibility of the CSG would still be subject to the same means test, developed in 1998.

**TABLE 5.5 PLAN TO IMPLEMENT THE EXTENSION OF THE CSG (2003/04 - 2005/06)**

| Year | Age cohort | Number eligible | New beneficiaries month | New beneficiaries per |
|---|---|---|---|---|
| 2003/04 | 7 & 8 years | 929 336 | 1 597 759* | 133 147 |
| 2004/05 | 9 & 10 years | 1 306 335 | 1 306 335 | 108 861 |
| 2005/06 | 11, 12, 13 years | 1 271 506 | 1 271 506 | 105 959 |

**Source:** National Department of Social Development 2003.

**\*Note:** This figure includes the remainder of initial targets – that is the number of beneficiaries under 7 years not reached by 1 April 2003.

According to the national Department of Social Development (2003), the cost estimate of the extension is approximately R10 billion over the MTEF period 2003/04 to 2005/06. The conditional grant to fund the extension is R1 100 million in 2003/04, R3 435 million in 2004/05 and R6 464 million in 2005/06. This includes administration and disbursement costs at R29 per grant payment per month (Ibid).

## 3.1.2 DOES THE DESIGN OF THE CSG PROGRAMME FACILITATE ACCESS FOR ALL (PARTICULARLY THE MOST NEEDY) AND RAPID ROLL-OUT?

The conceptualisation of the CSG programme raises some concern, when considered in relation to the Constitution's promise of delivering social services to all children in need – and particularly to the most vulnerable children. First, the age eligibility of the grant remains problematic. The CSG fails to provide for all children, defined in section 28 of the Constitution as any person under the age of 18 years. Only children under 11 years will be eligible to benefit from this grant during the 2004/05 financial year and only children up to the age of 13 will have access to the CSG as from the financial year 2005/06. The South African government had a national target of reaching 3 030 000 children by the end of March 2003. However, there are an estimated 3.6 million children under the age of 7 currently already eligible for the child support grant (National Treasury 2003b:417). Government has also estimated that a further 3.2 million beneficiaries under 14 will have accessed their grants over the next three years (National Treasury 2003a). This policy means that children who are currently between the ages 12 and 14 will never benefit from the CSG. It also translates into approximately 7 million poor children between the ages 14 to 18 years who will never have a right to access social security through the CSG.

The Taylor Committee challenged the age policy of the CSG and recommended an "extension of the CSG to all children 0-18 years" (Department of Social Development 2002:81). The *Fourth Annual Economic and Social Rights Report,* released by the South African Human Rights Commission (2003:215), states that "it is unconstitutional for children between the ages of 8 and 18 to be denied access to social security". Streak and Wehner, in chapter two of this publication, point out that the state is obliged to fulfil the rights of children (as espoused in sections 28(1)(c) and 29(1)(a)) when parents are unable to fulfil their primary obligation. As illustrated in section one of this chapter, according to legal expert opinion, the state is obliged to prioritise basic services to children in its budgeting.

The second concern regarding the conceptualisation of the CSG programme relates to the application process involved in accessing the grant. As described above, children can only apply for the CSG via a parent or alternative care-giver, who must verify their own identity and produce the birth certificate of the intended beneficiary. The problems associated with accessing birth certificates are also experienced most acutely in poor families, where the CSG is most needed. Furthermore, the means test for the CSG has not been changed since 1998 and this has some implications for the poor and vulnerable. Failing to adjust the means test for inflation means that government has not taken into account the fact that the decided poverty level or line identified at the time of programme inception has increased since 1998, due to inflation.

Another important factor to consider is that the current means test does not take into account the number of children per household. Children living in larger families are indirectly excluded from eligibility, even though their need for the grant (defined in terms of access to resources) is as great as those in small families. Box 5.2 below illustrates this point, using the hypothetical example of Siya, a child of 12 months, living in two different circumstances.

## Box 5.2 The CSG means test and household size

| Household A | Household B |
|---|---|
| Siya lives with his mother in an urban area, in an informal dwelling. He is the only child in the household. His mother earns R1 000 per month. Assuming he and his mother share the benefits of her monthly income equally, he will have access to the benefits of about R500 per month. Siya's mother's income would be low enough for him to qualify for the CSG. | Siya lives with his mother and his three siblings, aged 10, 12 and 16 respectively. His mother earns R1 500 per month. Working on the assumption that the benefits flowing from the mother's income of R1 500 are divided equally amongst the individuals in the household, Siya would have access to only a R300 monthly share. At the same time, his mother's monthly income is too high for Siya to access the CSG. |

It is clear that household A will have far fewer expenses in terms of food, education and health care than household B. Yet in household B, Siya is excluded from benefiting from the CSG because the means test does not consider the number of children deriving benefit from a household's income.

Against this background, it was hoped that the long-awaited Social Assistance Bill would go some way towards addressing the gaps and concerns relating to social assistance for South African children. The Social Assistance Bill will play a pivotal role in the future development of programmes that give effect particularly to a child's right to social security. The objectives of the Social Assistance Bill (Department of Social Development 2003c:5) are to:

- provide for the financing of social assistance;
- provide for the administration of social assistance and the payment of social grants;
- make provision for social assistance and determine the qualification requirements in respect thereof;
- ensure that minimum norms and standards are set for the delivery of social assistance; and
- provide for the establishment of an inspectorate for social security.

However, the provisions being proposed in the Social Assistance Bill unfortunately appear inadequate to ensure that all children in need of social security will be more likely to access social security in future. For example, children living on the streets and in child-headed households would still not have access to a CSG under the new legislation. An adult primary care-giver would still be required before a child can qualify for a CSG. In terms of the bill, children would still have to be living in formal foster care to benefit from a Foster Care Grant (FCG). If community-based care is an alternative option for orphaned and vulnerable children, then the eligibility criteria for this type of care should match the circumstances of community-based care. Formal acknowledgement should also be afforded to institutions that give effect to community-based care, so that children living in these institutions are able to benefit from the FSG. According to government officials in National Treasury and the national Department of Social Development, the phased approach of extending the CSG programme is due to the lack of capacity and infrastructure for registration. According to officials, this approach was conceptualised to correspond with an administrative system that is only able to process a limited amount of applications per day. For example, only 929 000 children aged 7 to 8 years can be registered in 2003/04 (Hlatshwayo 2003:personal communication). Thus the planned roll-out rate is not so much constrained by lack of staff as by the inability of the computer soft- and hardware to process more grants. This may well be the case, but in the meantime, millions of children in need are denied their right to social assistance.

To conclude, considerable attention must be given to developing appropriate responses to the high incidence of child poverty and HIV/AIDS in South Africa. Moreover, consideration must be given to changing the CSG policy to improve access for all children to realise their rights as enshrined in sections 27(1(c) and 28(1)(c) of the Constitution.

## 3.2 BUDGET ANALYSIS OF THE CSG PROGRAMME

This sub-section firstly explains how government funds the CSG. The equitable share formula and conditional grant is examined in this respect. Secondly, it presents the budget allocations for the CSG since its inception on 1 April 1998, in absolute terms and as a percentage of consolidated provincial and national expenditure. Thirdly, it calculates real growth rates for the CSG programme budget allocations for the period 1998/99 to 2005/06. Finally, it presents actual expenditure data since programme inception and analyses the over- or under-spending in CSG budgets.

### 3.2.1 HOW DOES GOVERNMENT FUND THE CSG PROGRAMME?

Provincial governments and especially provincial social development departments had the predominant responsibility in rolling out the "first phase" of the CSG, which extended the grant to all eligible children age 0 to 6. Currently, they also have the primary responsibility for implementing the extended programme. This responsibility includes estimating the budget for the programme on an annual basis and allocating funds from the total provincial budget to the CSG programme.

As is well known, a large share of provincial budgets is made up of their equitable share revenue. Hence most of the money allocated to and spent on the CSG programme comes from the equitable shares of provincial governments. The equitable share is that share of funds in the National Revenue Account that each sphere of government is constitutionally entitled to. It is allocated to each province on the basis of a formula that considers indicators of relative need and past expenditure patterns. The provincial equitable share formula assigns relative weight to a number of components, as seen in Table 5.6.

**TABLE 5.6: PROVINCIAL EQUITABLE SHARE FORMULA (2003/04)**

| Component | Weighting (%) |
|---|---|
| Education | 41 |
| Health | 19 |
| Welfare | 18 |
| Basic share | 7 |
| Economic activity | 7 |
| Institutional | 5 |
| Backlog | 3 |
| Total | 100 |

**Source:** National Treasury 2003a: Table E-6.

Table 5.7 shows that the welfare weighting has two components: the target population for the main social grants ("all grants" column) and the population in the lowest two quintiles of income distribution ("income adjustment" column) (National Treasury 2003a).

**TABLE 5.7 CALCULATION OF THE WELFARE COMPONENT OF THE PROVINCIAL EQUITABLE SHARE**

| Percentage | Old age | Disability | Child care | All grants | Income adjustment | Weighted share |
|---|---|---|---|---|---|---|
| *Weighting* | *65* | *25* | *10* | *75* | *25* | *100* |
| Eastern Cape | 19.1 | 15.5 | 17.4 | 18 | 24.3 | 19.6 |
| Free state | 6.2 | 6.5 | 5.7 | 6.2 | 9.6 | 7.1 |
| Gauteng | 15.7 | 18.1 | 14.3 | 16.2 | 7.2 | 13.9 |
| KwaZulu-Natal | 19.8 | 20.7 | 21.7 | 20.2 | 17.6 | 19.6 |
| Limpopo | 13 | 12.1 | 14.8 | 13 | 15.8 | 13.7 |
| Mpumalanga | 5.9 | 6.9 | 7.3 | 6.3 | 7.1 | 6.5 |
| Northern Cape | 2.1 | 2.1 | 2 | 2.1 | 2.6 | 2.2 |
| North West | 7.8 | 8.3 | 8.4 | 8 | 10.7 | 8.7 |
| Western Cape | 10.4 | 9.7 | 8.4 | 10 | 5.2 | 8.8 |
| Total | 100 | 100 | 100 | 100 | 100 | 100 |

**Source:** National Treasury (2003a:262, Table E10).

The provinces have discretion to allocate their equitable share as they see fit. There is no legislation that obligates the provinces to allocate funds according to the national formulae. However, provinces are obliged to deliver according to their policy and legal contracts. Therefore, each of the provinces must plan for the payment of social security grants as a statutory obligation. Through monitoring of the CSG, attention has been drawn to the question of whether the amount allocated to the CSG through the equitable share formula is sufficient for provinces to finance the roll-out of the grant (see for example Streak & Wehner 2002). Arguments that the equitable share formula took insufficient account of the cost of rolling out the grant to all eligible children, led to an adjustment in weighting for social welfare from 17% to 18% in budget 2002 (National Treasury 2002c).

When the extension to the CSG programme was introduced concurrent with the 2003 budget, government increased the total amount to be disbursed to provinces through the equitable share. This was not only for the additional grants but also for associated functions of the CSG programme.

In addition to their equitable shares, provincial and local governments receive conditional grants from national government that are earmarked for a specific purpose. Conditional grants are introduced at the discretion of national government. Their function is not linked to the role of the equitable share, which is to ensure that provinces "are able to provide basic services and perform the functions allocated to them" (section 227(1) of the Constitution), including those services and functions that advance socio-economic rights (Streak & Wehner 2002). In other words, the equitable share formula funding is expected to be sufficient to enable provinces to perform their functions properly. However, some conditional grants have contributed to building administrative and financial management capacity in provinces, so as to enable them to properly implement such programmes. Current examples are the Financial Management and Quality Enhancement Grant from the national Department of Education, as well as the Financial Management and Improvement of Social Security System Grant from the national Department of Social Development.

The equitable share financing of the initial phase of the CSG programme (from April 1998 to April 2003) was supported and supplemented by conditional grant funding. A grant called the Child Support Implementation Grant (CSIG) was introduced for the period 1998/99 to 2000/01, to supplement the equitable share funding of the CSG. The implementation grant aimed to accommodate the increased number of beneficiaries by improving administration and infrastructure to deliver the CSG.

Currently, provinces are still expected to take the overwhelming responsibility for financing the extended CSG out of their own budgets (and hence their equitable shares). However, they also receive assistance by way of a new conditional grant, named the Child Support Extension Grant. This conditional grant was implemented from 1 April 2003 and spans the MTEF period 2003/04 to 2005/06. The grant allocation is for the actual grant amount paid to each beneficiary and for administration costs. As noted above, the grant amounts to R10.9 billion: R1.1 billion in 2003, increasing to R3.4 billion in 2004 and R6.4 billion in 2005. These estimates include allowance for administration and payment costs (calculated by the national Department of Social Development as being R29 per grant payment per month) and allows for a R10 increase in the value of the grant on 1 April 2004 (R160 to R170) and on 1 April 2005 (R170 to R180) (Department of Social Development 2003b).

## 3.2.2 TOTAL BUDGET ALLOCATIONS TO THE CSG PROGRAMME

Table 5.8 provides information on the consolidated provincial CSG budget allocations for 2002/03 and for the MTEF period 2003/04 to 2005/06. It also expresses these allocations as a proportion of consolidated provincial and national expenditure. Table 5.8 illustrates that the proportion of the CSG as a percentage of consolidated provincial and national expenditure peaks in 2004/05 and remains high for 2005/06 in relation to 2002/03 and 2003/04. Table 5.9 then shows the budget allocations to the CSG programme by province.

**TABLE 5.8 CSG BUDGET AND CSG BUDGET AS % OF CONSOLIDATED NATIONAL AND PROVINCIAL ALLOCATED EXPENDITURE (2002/03 & MTEF 2003/04 – 2005/06)**

| | 2002/03 | MTEF | | |
| --- | --- | --- | --- | --- |
| | | 2003/04 | 2004/05 | 2005/06 |
| CSG Budget* (in R) | 3 472 816 197 | 6 489 279 803 | 10 095 000 626 | 13379511870 |
| Consolidated provincial and national expenditure (in R) | 262 980 000 000 | 297 352 000 000 | 323 699 000 000 | 351 942 000 000 |
| CSG Budget as % of consolidated provincial and national expenditure | 1.32 | 2.18 | 3.12 | 3.80 |

**Source:** National Treasury 2003a; Provincial Estimates of Expenditure 2003; and own calculations.

**\*Note:** These figures include the CSG extension grant for the current MTEF period: R1.1 billion (2003/04), R3.4 billion (2004/05) and R6.4 billion (2005/06). The data on CSG budgets show the allocations, not actual expenditure.

**TABLE 5.9 PROVINCIAL BUDGET ALLOCATIONS TO THE CSG PROGRAMME (1998/99 - 2002/03 AS AT APRIL OF THAT YEAR), IN R**

| Province | 1998/99 | 1999/00 | 2000/01 | 2001/02 | 2002/03 |
| --- | --- | --- | --- | --- | --- |
| Eastern Cape | 58 646 000 | 39 655 000 | 141 600 000 | 690 716 119 | 857 529 000 |
| Free State | 20 880 000 | 56 481 000 | 40 321 000 | 78 132 000 | 153 398 000 |
| Gauteng | 28 000 000 | 26 441 000 | 75 469 000 | 225 420 000 | 402 178 000 |
| KwaZulu-Natal | 50 112 000 | 48 750 000 | 50 112 000 | 345 982 000 | 444 895 000 |
| Limpopo | 1 227 000 | 119 090 000 | 113 028 000 | 220 590 000 | 659 894 000 |
| Mpumalanga | 295 863 | 19 855 398 | 92 389 465 | 42 600 000 | 308 944 990 |
| North West | 1 989 038 | 15 932 628 | 93 542 920 | 186 619 727 | 348 578 271 |
| Northern Cape | | | 45 360 000 | 30 003 000 | 74 163 380 |
| Western Cape | 202 769 000 | 86 830 000 | 40 856 000 | 75 276 000 | 223 235 556 |
| Total | 363 918 901 | 413 035 026 | 692 678 385 | 1 895 338 846 | 3 472 816 197 |

**Sources:** Provincial Departments of Social Development (personal correspondence) for all provinces except KwaZulu-Natal; national Department of Social Development (personal correspondence) for KwaZulu-Natal figures.

Table 5.10 shows real growth rates in provincial CSG budget allocations for the period 1998/99 to 2003/04. The table shows that there has been a gradual decline in the growth of budget allocations for the overall CSG since the peak increase from 2000/01 to 2001/02, irrespective of the large nominal increases at provincial level. The highest real budget growth is recorded at 154% between 2000/01 to 2001/02. However, this growth declines to 67% between 2001/02 to 2002/03. The real budget growth increase of 73% between 2002/03 to 2003/04 is of considerable concern. There doesn't seem to have been monumental increases in real terms to provincial allocations, regardless of the change in policy and the inclusion of the conditional grant to assist with the extension of the CSG, which has been included in the final calculations for each province. For example, a 13% real increase in budget allocation for the Northern Cape in 2003/04 may not allow for the delivery of the CSG to the budgeted 51 000 children that government has set as a target for the province. This may prove to cause problems later when provinces' money reserves start depleting.

**TABLE 5.10 REAL BUDGET ALLOCATIONS AND REAL BUDGET GROWTH RATES FOR THE CSG (1998/99 – 2003/04)**

| Province | 1998/99 | 1999/00 | 2000/01 | 2001/02 | 2002/03 | 2003/04 |
|---|---|---|---|---|---|---|
| **Eastern Cape** | 58 646 000 | 39 655 000 | 141 600 000 | 690 716 119 | 857 529 000 | 1 704 957 000 |
| Real amount (in R) | 58 646 000 | 37 375 118 | 123 884 514 | 562 014 743 | 634 313 929 | 1 170 989 926 |
| Growth | | -36% | 231% | 354% | 13% | 85% |
| **Free State** | 20 880 000 | 56 481 000 | 40 321 000 | 78 132 000 | 153 398 000 | 332 617 000 |
| Real Amount (in R) | 20 880 000 | 53 233 742 | 35 276 465 | 63 573 637 | 113 468 452 | 228 446 322 |
| Growth | | 155% | -34% | 80% | 78% | 101% |
| **Gauteng** | 28 000 000 | 26 441 000 | 75 469 000 | 225 420 000 | 402 178 000 | 981 686 000 |
| Real Amount (in R) | 28 000 000 | 24 920 829 | 66 027 122 | 183 417 413 | 297 490 939 | 674 236 603 |
| Growth | | -11% | 165% | 178% | 62% | 127% |
| **KwaZulu-Natal** | 50 112 000 | 48 750 000 | 50 112 000 | 345 982 000 | 444 895 000 | 761 596 000 |
| Real Amount (in R) | 50 112 000 | 45 947 220 | 43 842 520 | 281 515 053 | 329 088 690 | 523 075 505 |
| Growth | | -8% | -5% | 542% | 17% | 59% |
| **Limpopo** | 0 | 119 090 000 | 113 028 000 | 220 590 000 | 659 894 000 | 1 036 320 000 |
| Real Amount (in R) | 0 | 112 243 167 | 98 887 139 | 179 487 388 | 488 123 382 | 711 760 050 |
| Growth | | 0% | -12% | 82% | 172% | 46% |
| **Mpumalanga** | 295 863 | 19 855 398 | 92 389 465 | 42 600 000 | 308 944 990 | 433 920 000 |
| Real Amount (in R) | 295 863 | 18 713 853 | 80 830 678 | 34 662 327 | 228 526 511 | 298 022 735 |
| Growth | | 6 225% | 332% | -57% | 559% | 30% |
| **North West** | 1 989 038 | 15 932 628 | 93 542 920 | 186 619 727 | 348 578 271 | 591 149 803 |
| Real Amount (in R) | 1 989 038 | 15 016 615 | 81 839 825 | 151 846 808 | 257 843 236 | 406 010 512 |
| Growth | | 655% | 445% | 86% | 70% | 57% |
| **Northern Cape** | | | 45 360 000 | 30 003 000 | 74 163 380 | 90 289 000 |
| Real Amount (in R) | 0 | 0 | 39 685 039 | 24 412 531 | 54 858 629 | 62 011 833 |
| Growth | | | | -38% | 125% | 13% |
| **Western Cape** | 202 769 000 | 86 830 000 | 40 856 000 | 75 276 000 | 223 235 556 | 556 745 000 |
| Real Amount (in R) | 202 769 000 | 81 837 889 | 35 744 532 | 61 249 797 | 165 127 270 | 382 380 779 |
| Growth | | -60% | -56% | 71% | 170% | 132% |
| **Total (in R)** | 363 918 901 | 413 035 026 | 692 678 385 | 1 895 338 846 | 3 472 816 197 | 6 489 279 803 |
| **Real total (in R)** | 363 918 901 | 389 288 432 | 606 017 835 | 1 542 179 696 | 2 568 841 036 | 4 456 934 268 |
| **Growth total** | | 7% | 56% | 154% | 67% | 73% |

**Sources:** Table 5.9 above; and own calculations.

**Note:** These figures were calculated with 1998 as the base year. The following deflators were applied: 1998/99=1, 99/00=1.061, 00/01=1.143, 01/02=1.229, 02/03=1.3519, 03/04=1.4559963. The CPIX given in the *Budget Review* for each year in question, was used to calculate the deflators.

## 3.2.3 UNDER- AND OVER-EXPENDITURE ON THE CSG PROGRAMME

Actual expenditure on a programme is not always the same as the expenditure that was budgeted for (budget allocations). Table 5.11 provides data on the provinces' estimated expenditure on the CSG programme for the years 1998/99 to 2002/03. Table 5.12 then applies the data from Tables 5.10 and 5.11 to show under- and over-spending on the CSG programme at the consolidated provincial level. Figure 5.2 compares the total average national estimated expenditure to the average actual expenditure.

## TABLE 5.11 ESTIMATED ACTUAL EXPENDITURE ON THE CSG PROGRAMME (1998/99 - 2002/03), IN R

| Province | 1998/99 | 1999/00 | 2000/01 | 2001/02 | 2002/03 |
|---|---|---|---|---|---|
| Eastern Cape | 4 800 000 | 56 400 000 | 198 874 800 | 295 826 400 | 857 529 000 |
| Free State | 469 924 | 7 485 487 | 42 272 537 | 104 400 342 | 227 528 124 |
| Gauteng | 756 000 | 22 886 000 | 112 566 000 | 209 640 000 | 427 693 000 |
| KwaZulu-Natal | 1 881 000 | 22 675 000 | 24 103 100 | 345 982 000 | 444 895 000 |
| Limpopo | 1 227 000 | 119 090 000 | 156 535 000 | 259 061 000 | 664 880 000 |
| Mpumalanga | 388 898 | 20 244 198 | 93 386 594 | 166 703 712 | 307 461 285 |
| North West | 1 016 000 | 1 575 000 | 22 410 000 | 74 511 000 | 120 146 000 |
| Northen Cape | | | 17 204 354 | 36 109 861 | 74 319 420 |
| Western Cape | 149 860 000 | 113 802 000 | 109 915 000 | 126 681 000 | 312 161 411 |
| **Total** | **160 398 822** | **364 157 685** | **777 267 385** | **1 618 915 315** | **3 436 613 240** |

**Source:** Data supplied by provincial Departments of Social Development in 2003 (personal correspondence).

## TABLE 5.12 CONSOLIDATED CSG ALLOCATED BUDGET VERSUS ACTUAL EXPENDITURE (1998/99 - 2002/03)

| Year | Initial budget | Estimated expenditure of initial budget allocation | Estimated expenditure as % |
|---|---|---|---|
| 1998/99 | 363 918 901 | 160 398 822 | 44% |
| 1999/00 | 413 035 026 | 364 157 685 | 88% |
| 2000/01 | 692 678 385 | 777 267 385 | 112% |
| 2001/02 | 1 895 338 846 | 1 618 915 315 | 85% |
| 2002/03 | 3 472 816 197 | 3 436 613 240 | 99% |

**Source:** Provincial Estimates of Expenditure; Tables 5.10 & 5.11 above; and own calculations

## FIGURE 5.2 CORRELATION OF ESTIMATED BUDGET EXPENDITURE AND ACTUAL

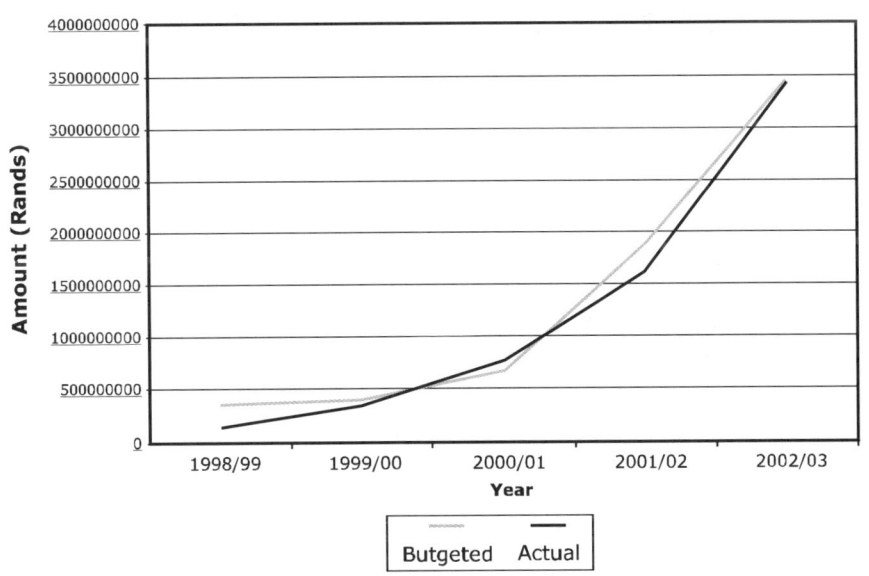

## EXPENDITURE ON THE CSG PROGRAMME (1998/99 – 2002/03)

TABLE 5.13 CSG UNDER- AND OVER-EXPENDITURE BY PROVINCE (1998/99 - 2002/03)

| Province | 1998/99 Over-/under-spending (in R) | % of budget spent | 1999/00 Over-/under-spending (in R) | % of budget Spent | 2000/01 Over-/under-spending (in R) | % of budget spent | 2001/02 Over-/under-spending (in R) | % of budget spent | 2002/03 Over-/under-spending (in R) | % of budget spent |
|---|---|---|---|---|---|---|---|---|---|---|
| Eastern Cape | -53 846 000 | 8% | 16 745 000 | 142% | 57 274 800 | 140% | -394 889 719 | 43% | 0 | 100% |
| Free State | -20 410 076 | 2% | -48 995 513 | 13% | 1 951 537 | 105% | 26 268 342 | 134% | 74 130 124 | 148% |
| Gauteng | -27 244 000 | 3% | -3 555 000 | 87% | 37 097 000 | 149% | -15 780 000 | 93% | 25 515 000 | 106% |
| KwaZulu-Natal | -48 231 000 | 4% | -26 075 000 | 47% | -26 008 900 | 48% | 0 | 100% | -368 433 000 | 55% |
| Limpopo | 0 | 100% | 0 | 100% | 43 507 000 | 138% | 38 471 000 | 117% | 4 986 000 | 101% |
| Mpumalanga | 93 035 | 131% | 388 800.5 | 102% | 997 129 | 101% | 124 103 712 | 391% | -1 483 705.42 | 100% |
| North West | -973 038 | 51% | -14 357 628 | 10% | -71 132 920 | 24% | -112 108 727 | 40% | -228 432 271 | 34% |
| Northern Cape | | | | | -28 155 646 | 38% | 6 106 861 | 120% | 156 040 | 100% |
| Western Cape | -52 909 000 | 74% | 26 972 000 | 131% | 69 059 000 | 269% | 51 405 000 | 168% | 88 926 411 | 140% |
| Total | -203 520 079 | 44% | -48 877 341 | 88% | 84 589 000 | 112% | -276 423 531 | 85% | -404 635 401 | 89% |

**Source:** Provincial Estimates of Expenditure 2003; Tables 5.9 and 5.11; and own calculations.

**Note:** Under-expenditure is indicated with negative figures and over-expenditure with positive figures, "0" shows no discrepancy.

As can be seen in the tables and figure, there has been a marked improvement on the part of provincial departments in the spending of their allocated CSG budgets. While the most recent results show no drastic under-spending, over-spending can also send signals of inadequate budgeting. As argued in section 3.2.2 of this chapter, this could be prompted largely by under-estimated beneficiary figures, and/or by constraints imposed by insufficient funding through the equitable share.

Using data from Tables 5.9 and 5.11, Table 5.13 presents data on which provinces have produced over-spending and which under-spending.

It is of concern that the Eastern Cape and the North West province – two of the poorer provinces – as well as KwaZulu-Natal remain poor spenders in comparison to other provinces. Figure 5.3 illustrates the distribution of expenditure over time. Mpumalanga shows the most excessive over-expenditure figures in comparison to other provinces. One of the main reasons for this is the lack of adequate data for proper budgeting of the CSG in relation to the take-up rates experienced, which were expected to have been less (but still remain below 100%). The North West in particular has fared badly, with reported actual expenditure never exceeding 50% of the allocated budget. The total CSG budget usage at a national level also remains just below the 100% mark.

**FIGURE 5.3 CSG UNDER- AND OVER-EXPENDITURE PER PROVINCE (1998/99-2002/03)**

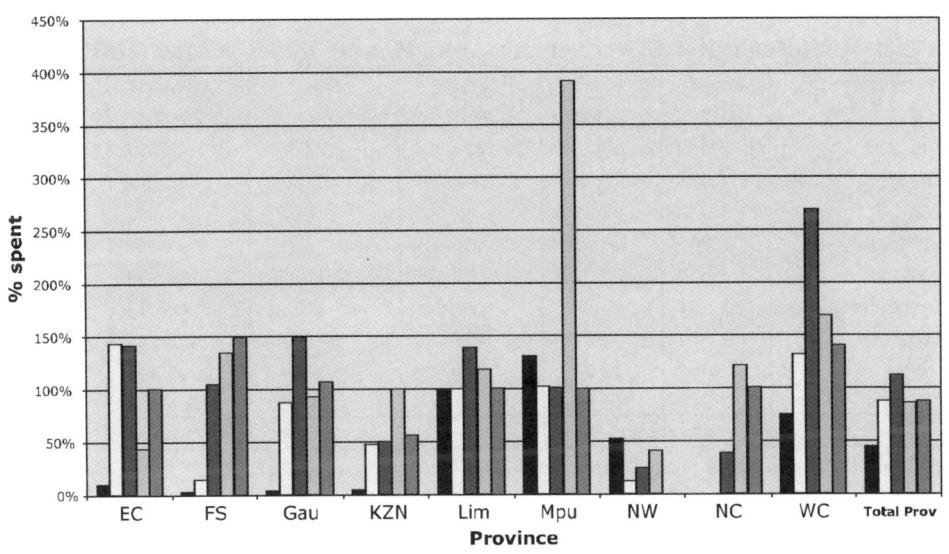

## 3.3 PROGRESS IN THE ROLL-OUT OF THE CSG PROGRAMME

This sub-section of the chapter provides an overview of the pace at which the CSG was rolled out to all eligible children between 1998 and 2003. It also examines whether the implementation of the CSG managed to reach the most vulnerable children. Finally, it considers the question of whether the pace of roll-out of the grant has been sufficiently rapid.

### 3.3.1 THE RATE OF EXPANSION OF ACCESS

It is difficult to illustrate government's success in rolling out the grant due to the fact that target beneficiary information is outdated and unreliable. To provide an overview of the pace at which the CSG has been rolled out by government, this sub-section of the chapter presents the following information:

- First, Table 5.14 gives data on the numbers of children accessing the CSG grant at different points in time during the period 1999 to 2003;

- Secondly, Table 5.15 provides information on take-up rates by comparing the number of actual beneficiaries receiving the CSG with government's own targets in this regard, as defined in April 1998; and

- Thirdly, Table 5.16 shows the take-up rates of the CSG by comparing the data on actual beneficiaries with the Financial and Fiscal Commission's more recent estimates of the number of eligible children under seven.

### TABLE 5.14 NUMBER OF CSG BENEFICIARIES (MARCH 1998 – MAY 2003)

| Province | March 1999 | March 2000 | Sept 2001 | May 2002 | 31 March 2003 | May 2003 |
|---|---|---|---|---|---|---|
| Eastern Cape | 5 670 | 55 717 | 206 394 | 277 939 | 405 815 | 480 728 |
| Free State | 1 675 | 13 753 | 71 240 | 107 242 | 150 480 | 163 291 |
| Gauteng | 1 872 | 47 910 | 149 843 | 209 399 | 315 897 | 356 599 |
| KwaZulu-Natal | 7 853 | 66 836 | 352 630 | 507 302 | 694 392 | 732 891 |
| Mpumalanga | 630 | 28 327 | 102 327 | 134 172 | 199 834 | 228 297 |
| Northern Cape | 2 255 | 12 805 | 24 824 | 35 505 | 46 412 | 50 815 |
| Limpopo | 2 384 | 53 815 | 159 989 | 301 289 | 407 041 | 456 882 |
| North West | 1 662 | 31 792 | 125 176 | 166 849 | 206 421 | 225 756 |
| Western Cape | 3 576 | 10 951 | 89 268 | 155 962 | 204 534 | 21 2363 |
| **Total** | **27 577** | **321 906** | **1 281 691** | **1 895 659** | **2 630 826** | **2 907 622** |

**Source:** National Department of Social Development 2003 (personal communication).[11]

**Note:** The figures for May 2003 are inclusive of the CSG extension to children under 9 years old.

Table 5.14 shows that the number of CSG beneficiaries increased from 27 577 in March 1999 to nearly 3 million by May 2003. By September 2003, the number of beneficiaries had increased to 3.1 million (Blecher 2003).

**TABLE 5.15 TAKE-UP RATES FOR THE CSG BASED ON OFFICIAL TARGETS (MARCH 1999 – MARCH 2003)**

| Province | Target numbers set for 31 March 2003 | Percentage of targeted beneficiaries actually reached by | | | | |
|---|---|---|---|---|---|---|
| | | March 1999 | March 2000 | Sept. 2001 | May 2002 | 31 March 2003 |
| Eastern Cape | 780 000 | 0.73% | 7.14% | 26.46% | 35.63% | 52.0% |
| Free State | 300 000 | 0.56% | 4.58% | 23.75% | 35.75% | 50.2% |
| Gauteng | 90 000 | 2.08% | 53.23% | 166.49% | 232.67% | 351.0% |
| KwaZulu-Natal | 600 000 | 1.31% | 11.14% | 58.77% | 84.55% | 115.7% |
| Mpumalanga | 210 000 | 0.30% | 13.49% | 48.73% | 63.89% | 95.2% |
| Northern Cape | 30 000 | 7.52% | 42.68% | 82.75% | 118.35% | 154.71% |
| Limpopo | 600 000 | 0.40% | 8.97% | 26.66% | 50.21% | 67.8% |
| North West | 330 000 | 0.50% | 9.63% | 37.93% | 50.56% | 62.6% |
| Western Cape | 90 000 | 3.97% | 12.17% | 99.19% | 173.29% | 235.96% |
| **Total** | **3 030 000** | **0.91%** | **10.62%** | **42.3%** | **62.56%** | **86.83%** |

**Source:** Tables 5.2 and 5.9; own calculations.

**Note:** i) The target numbers were set in April 1998 for the CSG policy aimed only at children under seven years.

ii) The data for March 1999 marks the percentage take-up since April 1998 – that is, from programme inception.

Table 5.15 illustrates the percentage take-up rates as from March 1999. Although not recorded as the weakest performing province in CSG delivery, the Eastern Cape remains a poor performer in CSG take-up rates. The delivery of social security grants in the Eastern Cape is a concern, especially due to the province's high share of poverty and poor record of service delivery.

**TABLE 5.16 TAKE-UP RATES FOR THE CSG BASED ON FFC ESTIMATES (MARCH 1999 – MAY 2003)**

| Province | FFC estimates of eligible children under 7 | Percentage of estimated beneficiaries actually reached | | | | |
|---|---|---|---|---|---|---|
| | | March 1999 | March 2000 | Sept. 2001 | May 2002 | May 2003 |
| Eastern Cape | 828254 | 1% | 7% | 25% | 34% | 58% |
| Free State | 222338 | 1% | 6% | 32% | 48% | 73% |
| Gauteng | 371308 | 1% | 13% | 40% | 56% | 96% |
| KwaZulu-Natal | 862696 | 1% | 8% | 41% | 59% | 85% |
| Mpumalanga | 310089 | 0% | 9% | 33% | 43% | 74% |
| Northern Cape | 128260 | 2% | 10% | 19% | 28% | 40% |
| Limpopo | 787159 | 0% | 7% | 20% | 38% | 58% |
| North West | 337391 | 0% | 9% | 37% | 49% | 67% |
| Western Cape | 183715 | 2% | 6% | 49% | 85% | 116% |
| **Total** | **4031210** | **1%** | **8%** | **32%** | **47%** | **72%** |

**Source:** Streak & Kgamphe 2002, updated in 2003 through personal correspondence.

Looking at the take-up rates using both the government targets and FFC estimates, the Eastern Cape and Limpopo appear to be the weakest performers. One area of particular concern is the Northern Cape. Using the government estimates to calculate progress in the Northern Cape, the take-up rate on 31 March 2003 was 154%. However, when the FFC data is used as a basis for calculating take-up, the Northern Cape's rate is a mere 40%. The tables also indicate that the Western Cape and Gauteng are strong performers, recording the highest take-up rates between March 2000 and September 2001. KwaZulu-Natal is rapidly improving its take-up rates.

To summarise the current situation in the roll-out of the CSG to children under seven, there were 2.6 million children in this age cohort benefiting from the CSG programme as at 31 March 2003. This translates into 86.8% of the target of 3.03 million beneficiaries, which government had set at the inception of the CSG in 1998. Between 31 March 2003 and 30 September 2003, an additional 490 422 children under seven years were benefiting from the CSG. This amounts to 3.1 million children under seven years since the inception of the CSG in 1998 (Blecher 2003). As regards the beneficiaries between the ages of seven and eight, a total of 447 179 children within this age cohort were benefiting from the CSG between 1 April 2003 and 30 September 2003 (Ibid). Over this same period, government recorded a total of over 900 000 new beneficiaries, which equates to approximately 156 000 new beneficiaries per month over that six-month period (Ibid). It is clear that government has succeeded in improving the roll-out of the CSG. However, concern still lies with the number of eligible children that are not benefiting from the grant.

## 3.3.2 HAS THE CSG BEEN REACHING THE MOST VULNERABLE CHILDREN?

This sub-section uses previous research on the CSG programme by other research institutions to consider whether the implementation of the CSG is reaching the most vulnerable children, or whether it is exclusionary in practice. Studies suggest that there have indeed been problems in reaching the most vulnerable and poor children in the CSG implementation process (Giese *et al* 2003; Ewing 2004). This has mainly been due to problems of accessibility, as well as a lack of infrastructure and means for the distribution of the CSG to those most in need. Ewing (2004) has shown that poor children in the Msinga/Weenen districts of KwaZulu-Natal, as well as children living in child-headed households in Pietermaritzburg, continue to struggle to access the CSG:

> "The children interviewed generally have no access to state welfare benefits and they rely on casual work, assistance from neighbours and relatives, begging, borrowing and donations from NGOs and welfare bodies to survive".

The children from child-headed households who were interviewed could not access any social security grant due to their lack of identification documents and the procedural requirements related to fostering.

Even though there is still a challenge in ensuring that the poorest of the poor in rural areas access the grant, progress is being made. This is well illustrated in a recent study, *The reach of the South African Child Support Grant: Evidence from KwaZulu-Natal* (Case *et al* 2003). This study focused on children under seven years resident in a demographic surveillance site in the Hlabisa district in KwaZulu-Natal. The area is "predominantly rural, very poor, and has high rates of migration…bearing a heavy death and disease burden, associated with the HIV/AIDS crisis. It is thus precisely the kind of area that the Child Support Grant is intended to reach" (Ibid:1). The study finds that 36% of all children under the age of seven years in this rural KwaZulu-Natal district had had some contact with the CSG system. Between 80% and 90% of children between one and six years who had had contact with the CSG system were receiving a grant in 2002 (Ibid). According to the authors (Ibid:10):

> "[the fact that] in the fifth year of the grant, it was reaching fully a third of age-eligible children in this remote rural area, half of whom received a grant within 3 months, shows a real commitment to implementation".

The study asked the question "Is the grant well-targeted for poverty?" In the absence of income data on all the children included in the study, parents' education, employment and household asset ownership was applied to assess the success of the CSG targeting (Ibid). Beneficiaries of the CSG in this geographical area had parents who are less well educated, and parents who are less likely to be employed (Ibid). The study found "households with greater numbers of children age-eligible to receive the grant report receiving a larger number of grants, on average" (Ibid:11).

The results of effective targeting were constrained by the fact that whether or not a child received a CSG depended in large measure on the presence of his or her mother:

> "Although a child who has lost a father is significantly more likely to receive a grant, this is not true for children who have lost a mother. In fact, children whose mothers are non-resident, or dead, or whose survival status is unknown, are significantly less likely to receive a grant, holding constant the child's father's status. Lack of widespread knowledge of the fact that primary caregivers need not be mothers provides a possible explanation of our finding. Alternatively, when a mother is absent, the child's primary care-giver may be less able to access the relevant documents necessary for registering the child's birth. The Child Support Grant is currently being extended to children aged 7 to 14, who are even less likely than younger children to be residing with their mothers. This makes a better understanding of this phenomenon essential" (Ibid).

Against this background, it would appear that the CSG is still exclusionary in its implementation and has not yet reached all of the most vulnerable, mainly due to the requirements of the means test. However, the research studies available, including those above, are not sufficient to make an absolute assessment of the extent of exclusion in the implementation of the CSG.

## 3.3.3  Is the roll-out rate of the CSG sufficient?

It is clear that the reach of the CSG programme is currently insufficient in light of the obligations on government to deliver the grant. Has the roll-out rate been sufficiently rapid? As pointed out in chapter two and in section one of this chapter, government is obliged to extend the right to social assistance to children, as a matter of urgency and as rapidly as administrative capacity allows. According to National Treasury officials (Plaatjies 2003:personal communication), the roll-out rate *is* in fact as rapid as administrative capacity facilitates. This may be the case, but in light of the desperate situation of many poor children (see chapter one), it is imperative for delivery capacity to be built quickly so as to facilitate more rapid roll-out – not only to all children currently eligible, but to all those in need.

Figure 5.4 depicts the roll-out rate of the CSG for different provinces. It illustrates graphically that Gauteng has the steepest growth incline and Northern Cape has the slowest roll-out, using government eligibility data and take-up rates.

**FIGURE 5.4 PROVINCIAL CSG ROLL-OUT RATES (MARCH 1999 – MARCH 2003)**

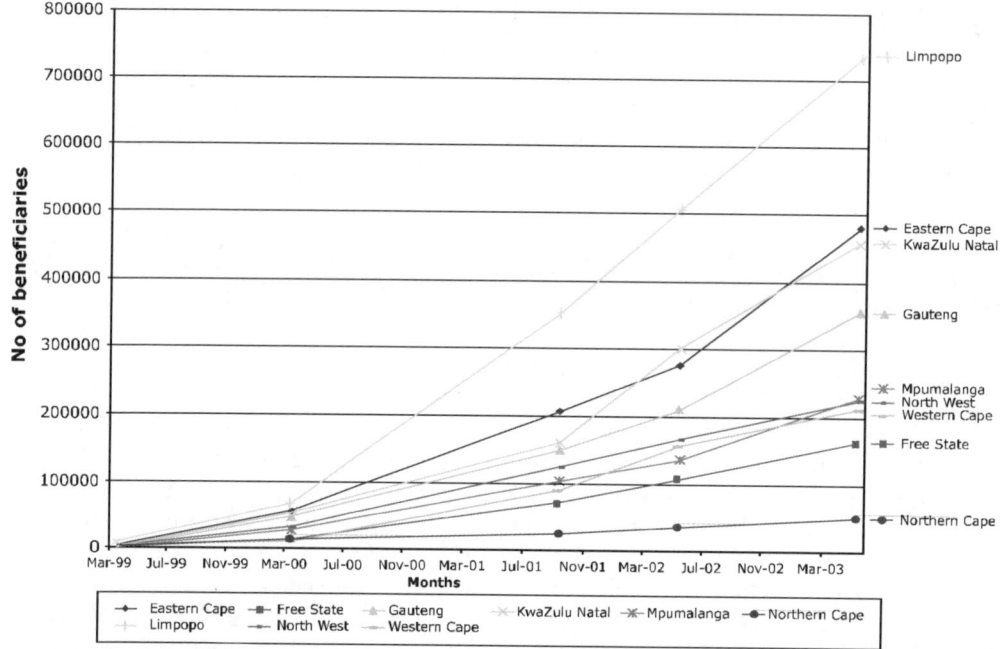

## 3.4 PROBLEMS CONSTRAINING THE ROLL-OUT OF THE CSG

It is clear from the discussion above that government has indeed made substantial progress towards advancing children's right to social assistance through the CSG in most provinces. At the same time, however, there is a decided need to re-consider the eligibility criteria for the grant so as to include all children in need. It is also essential for the rate of roll-out to be improved, particularly in the Eastern Cape, Northern Cape and Limpopo provinces. As a means to ensure that roll-out is accelerated in future, it is important to identify the set of (financial and non-financial) factors constraining the pace of roll-out and to consider how these obstacles may be overcome. This section describes the obstacles that have been raised by service providers and potential beneficiaries as constraints to the rate of expansion of access to the CSG for eligible children.

## 3.4.1 OBSTACLES RAISED BY SERVICE PROVIDERS

Since 1997, the administration and management of social assistance has been designated to provincial social development departments. These provincial departments are responsible for the administration, financing and payment of social grants. The problems experienced in the implementation of the CSG are not unique to this grant alone. The current social assistance system is beset by a number of administrative deficiencies, including poor management, weaknesses in the distribution and development of human resources, inadequate infrastructure and information technology support systems, high levels of fraud and long delays in grant approval (see Giese *et al* 2003; Nelson Mandela Foundation/HSRC 2002; School of Public Health *et al* 2002; NADEL 1999; Samson 2002).

According to Hlatshwayo (2003:personal communication), a key constraint to the implementation and delivery of the CSG lies with human resource capacity. This capacity problem has two dimensions. Firstly, officials in some instances do not understand the legislation, policies and procedures governing the CSG programme. Secondly, implementation is constrained by an inadequate ratio of beneficiaries to service providers.

Amongst officials working on the CSG programme, there appear to be different interpretations of the relevant legislation, policies and procedures. This can be categorised as follows:

- There is a lack of uniformity in the application of the means test within provinces and across provinces (Plaatjies 2003:personal communication). This results in some applicants conforming to the regulations (for example, having to provide all documentation for the means test), while other applicants are able to access the CSG without passing the means test.

- There is a lack of clarity regarding the execution of the new CSG policy of adding an additional age cohort for registration annually on 1 April, particularly as regards the inclusion of seven to eight-year-olds in the 2003/04 financial year. Despite clear directives from the national and provincial departments to social services offices, officials continue to display a lack of clarity on the phased-in extension of the CSG to children under 14 years. For example, would an eight-year old child who turns nine years before 1 April 2004 be de-registered and then have to be re-registered during that financial year? On enquiring after this concern, conflicting responses were offered from government officials within the national Department of Social Development. One official asserted that no child would be de-registered, while another was in agreement with the example posed above.

- Implementation is also constrained by a lack of uniformity in administrative procedures. Poor or absent control mechanisms have meant that the CSG has quite often been accessed by persons not eligible for the grant (Department of Social Development 2003b). Because of the poor uniformity of administrative processes and procedures, access to the CSG continues to be unequal.

Service providers also drew attention to administrative overload in the processing of the CSG, highlighting the large numbers of applications processed compared to the small numbers of administrative staff employed for this task (Plaatjies 2003:personal communication). The slow processing of grant applications causes delays in the speedy delivery of grants.

Any single grant application can take anywhere between 20 to 90 days to process! (Department of Social Development 2003b). A survey of the implementation and service delivery of social security grants indicates that due to high take-up rates, especially of the CSG, staff members are unable to cope with the workload (Van der Westhuizen & Van Zyl 2002). An additional problem identified by this survey is a lack of adequate staff training. In the same survey, the national Department of Social Development highlighted the fact that provincial social development staff members do not have the necessary skills to budget adequately for grants.

Government's main reason for not increasing the age eligibility of the CSG more quickly is that SOCPEN (government's grant administration system) can only process 133 000 new beneficiaries per month for 2003/04. However, the actual number of beneficiaries added to the system between April and September 2003 exceeded 159 000 new beneficiaries per month, as noted above. It would thus appear that it is not the data management system itself that slows down the processing of CSG applications, but rather that the administrative system is a major hurdle to rapidly increasing CSG access to more children.

Implementation and service delivery also continues to be impeded by claimants who lack the requisite documentation and physical access to government offices, especially in remote areas (Plaatjies 2003:personal communication).

### 3.4.2 OBSTACLES RAISED BY BENEFICIARIES, POTENTIAL BENEFICIARIES AND CARE-GIVERS

In the child participation study conducted for this publication (see Ewing 2004), women in Msinga/Weenen in northern KwaZulu-Natal, described their experiences of applying for a CSG. Married parents had to provide the social development (welfare) office with their identification documents, their marriage certificate, the birth certificate of the child or children, as well as providing proof of income or, more commonly, an affidavit declaring no income. Most people in Msinga/Weenen were however not married, or were not married in a court and therefore did not have a marriage certificate. Unmarried mothers were expected to come to the application office with the father of the child. Many of the Msinga/Weenen men were in Johannesburg or working elsewhere on farms and were only home for the December holidays, when the offices are closed.

Similarly, children living in child-headed households around Pietermaritzburg also cited the absence of their identity documents as an obstacle to receiving the CSG (Ewing 2004). Only one of the children participating in the study was receiving a CSG, despite the fact that ten children were eligible. The 2002 child participation study of the Alliance for Children's Entitlement to Social Security (ACESS) concurs.

Children cited lack of identity documents and birth certificates as an obstacle to accessing grants. The ACESS study concluded that the need to produce birth certificates in order to apply for a CSG was a definite problem. For example, out of a group of 25 children who should otherwise have had access, only nine children had birth certificates:

> "The problem will be birth certificates. I don't have one – I cannot get an ID book. I don't know even know where my mother is – what can I do?" (ACESS 2002:66).

Lack of knowledge of the existence of the CSG was cited by some care-givers as an obstacle to accessing it (Ewing 2004; Ibid). The women from Msinga/Weenen also identified transport costs as an obstacle to accessing the grant. Such costs were incurred firstly to apply for all the necessary documents, secondly to apply for the grant and then subsequently to collect the grant payments on a monthly basis. They relied on community workers to transport them to apply for the CSG. The trade-offs involved in accessing the grant were apparent in many children's responses in the ACESS study. The amount of money available in a household would very often either just cover food or transport to town:

> "It is a problem of money because Home Affairs is far from here – we cannot go all the time to try and get a birth certificate" (Ibid).

The key obstacles to implementation and service delivery in the CSG programme, as identified by service providers, beneficiaries, potential beneficiaries and their care-givers, can be summarised as:

- Limitations in human resource capacity;
- Lack of uniformity in the application of legislation, policies and procedures guiding the CSG;
- Lack of birth certificates on the part of beneficiaries;
- Lack of identification documents on the part of parents and care-givers;
- The limited capacity of SOCPEN to register applications; and
- Prohibitive transport and travel costs associated with the application and collection of the CSG.

## 3.5 GOVERNMENT MEASURES TO OVERCOME IMPLEMENTATION OBSTACLES

This section provides information about the steps taken by government between 2002 and 2003 to overcome the obstacles children have experienced in gaining access to the CSG. It also reviews government's future plans to improve implementation and service delivery for the CSG programme.

### 3.5.1 RESPONSES BY GOVERNMENT

Between 2002 and 2003, government focused on improving information systems and human capacity for the implementation and service delivery of the CSG.

### Improvement of information systems

With the help of the conditional grant of over R200 million, provinces have been purchasing computers and upgrading their information systems to improve administration and take-up (Department of Social Development 2003b). This has proved particularly effective in the poorer and rural provinces. The national department has initiated the upgrading and enhancement of the SOCPEN system, as well as the improvement of management information (Ibid).

### Improvement of human resource capacity

During 2002, particular attention was given to improve the competency of officials (Ibid). In order to improve uniformity in the way government officials process CSG applications, training has focused both on social security legislation and on corresponding work procedures. Additional staff members were hired to increase processing capacity and bring it more in line with the existing demand for CSGs, but this has still proved insufficient (Ibid).

### Registration of birth certificates and identity documents

The national Department of Social Development embarked on a marketing strategy to encourage people to apply for identity documents and to register the birth of their child(ren). A registration campaign was initiated in June 2002, co-ordinated by the national Department of Social Development and the Department of Home Affairs, aimed at registering adults with identity documents and children with birth certificates. At a national level, radio and newspaper media were used to spread the message, while provincial promotion efforts included *imbizos* and home visits by politicians and volunteers. To complement this initiative, the national Department of Social Development planned to interface with the Department of Home Affairs information system in 2003 (as regards the age of grant beneficiaries and birth registration). This was intended to improve efforts in ensuring that the right beneficiaries access the grants.

## 3.5.2 GOVERNMENT'S FUTURE PLANS TO IMPROVE THE ROLL-OUT OF THE CSG

Since 1994, the South African government has been grappling with social security-related problems of poor service delivery and inequitable access inherited from the former system. In 1996, government appointed the Committee for the Restructuring of Social Security (CRSS). This committee was to make recommendations on the improvement of the social security system. The main recommendation of the CRSS was the establishment of a nationally-organised social security system with uniform management, budgeting and communication systems.

The *Intergovernmental Fiscal Review* (National Treasury 2003c) identifies the challenges for the improvement of the social security grant system as follows:

- The efficient implementation of policy changes concerning grants and the extension of access to grants. Administrative and information systems capacity must be reinforced; and

- The upgrading of grant service delivery, partly through the enhancement of current practices and, in the medium-term, also establishing an appropriate institutional framework, including a public entity for grant administration and delivery.

A key priority for government – and a requirement for the further extension of the safety net – is to improve service delivery to beneficiaries (National Treasury 2003b). Subsequent to the review of social assistance administration and an audit of pay points in provinces, the national Department of Social Development has launched a comprehensive grant administration improvement programme (Ibid).

The grant improvement initiative aims to apply national norms and standards in the following areas:

- applications and other grant administration processes;
- communication and customer care;
- pay point infrastructure and facilities; and
- information technology.

The replacement of SOCPEN remains a priority and the national department is currently exploring options for acquiring a new system. Until a new system is in place, the current system will be upgraded.

The move towards a dedicated national public entity to administer and pay grants could see full responsibility for the social grant function moved to national government. Anticipated improvements include the standardised, more effective and more economical administration of grants, extended equitable access, as well as consistent supervision and management of the system (Ibid). These plans could go a long way to improving access and service delivery for the beneficiaries of the CSG.

Government has proposed that a National Social Security Agency (hereafter referred to as the Agency) be established and tasked with the delivery of social assistance, as well as taking responsibility to resolve the problems experienced by the current social assistance delivery system. The functions of the Agency as described in the Social Security Agency Bill are to ensure the effective provision of social security services. This is seen to require:

> "... uniform norms and standards, standardised delivery mechanisms and a national policy for the efficient, economic and effective use of the limited resources available for social security and for the promotion of equal access to government services" (Department of Social Development 2003d:6).

Cabinet has, in principle, approved the establishment of the South African Social Security Agency as a Schedule 3A Public Entity in terms of the Public Finance Management Act. This new body would be a national government agency tasked with the management and administration of the grant delivery system: this would no longer be a function of the public service. The business principles of the Agency must comply with the norms and standards set by government and ensure equitable access.

The Social Security Agency Bill proposes that the Agency would take on the role of service provider – that is, in terms of grant management, administration and payment. This translates into the removal of these associated functions from the national department and provincial executives. The accountability for the payment of social assistance grants would remain with the national Department of Social Development, but its role would change to that of service assuror rather than provider (Hlawatshayo 2003:personal communication). The national department would retain the functions, inter alia, of funding and costing national policies, policy reform, regulation, monitoring and evaluation, as well as the establishment of service delivery agreements. The anticipated roles of provincial Departments of Social Development remain unclear.

The thinking behind the establishment of a private entity to run a public concern is directly linked to the issue of capacity and the quality of service delivery. The process of implementing the Agency is planned to be a gradual process to ensure that current service provision is not interrupted. The agency should be established in such a way as to enable broader service delivery (in the long term) than is the case with current functions. All provinces are to be included in the process and the Agency is to ensure that its delivery is sustainable and grows in line with the policies and plans for grants as set by the national Department of Social Development.

From the proposed plans for the Agency, the following are of concern:

- A lack of clarity regarding the nature of the relationship between the Minister of Social Development, the Agency and other inter-governmental departments (for example, the Department of Home Affairs); and

- The Social Security Agency Bill does not demand anything more stringent, in terms of financial management, accountability and transparency, than is currently already expected from provincial departments. It therefore offers no innovation to counter existing concerns relating to corruption.

To fulfil the right to social security, the social security system must be efficient and accessible to users. It is thus vital for the conceptualisation of the Agency to develop in such a way as to give effect to "administrative justice", as set out in section 33 of the Constitution:

> "(1) Everyone has the right to administrative action that is lawful, reasonable and procedurally fair.
>
> (2) Everyone whose rights have been adversely affected by administrative action has the right to be given written reasons.
>
> (3) National legislation must be enacted to give effect to these rights and must - ....
>
>     (b) impose a duty on the state to give effect to the rights in subsections (1) and (2); and
>
>     (c) promote an efficient administration" (authors' emphasis).

In conclusion, it is clear that government's plans to overcome implementation obstacles relating to social security, as described above, do not currently include the extension of the CSG to all children in need. While the age limit for access to the CSG will increase to 14 in the not-too-distant future, the application requirements for the grant remain unchanged. These will continue to function as barriers to access, reinforcing the already existing gaps in CSG coverage amongst children aged 0 to 9. These factors undermine the ability of the CSG programme to impact more effectively on child poverty, especially given the current exclusion of many adults from the social security net and government's hesitancy to broaden the social security net to include all adults living in poverty.

# 4. CONCLUDING SUMMARY AND RECOMMENDATIONS

The aim of this chapter has been to contribute to monitoring government's performance in taking measures to give effect to the child's right to social services, and in particular, to social assistance in South Africa. It has placed the spotlight primarily on government's actions (in budgeting and service delivery) to give effect to these rights through the CSG programme. To set the scene, the chapter first considered what children are entitled to claim from the state under their right to basic social services and social security. It also provided a description of government programmes that have been put in place to give effect to these rights.

Section one looked into the nature and scope of the entitlements given to children in the Constitution and the associated obligations thereby placed on the state. The following crucial points emerged from this section:

- There is a need for greater clarity about what exactly children are entitled to by virtue of their right to social services and social assistance. It is clear that children, along with everyone, have a *qualified* right to social assistance under section 27 of the Constitution. At the same time, the formulation of section 28 appears to give children an unqualified right to social services, which may or may not be understood to include the right to social assistance.

- Current interpretations of children's constitutional rights in South Africa suggest that children must be afforded a higher priority than all citizens in government's programme design, budgeting and service delivery, in order to actualise their right to social assistance. Moreover, government is obliged to prioritise the most vulnerable of children.

- Acknowledging that it is practically impossible to realise children's rights to social security immediately, it is important to stress that children's socio-economic rights must be afforded a high priority in budgeting and service delivery. This implies an obligation to roll-out programmes to deliver children's right to social services as a matter of urgency and as rapidly as administrative capacity allows, and to build capacity which can accelerate the delivery of children's rights.

- The attainment of the right to social security cannot be seen in isolation from the attainment of the right to other social services and other children's rights. Therefore, sound programmes, improved budgeting and service delivery for all children's rights provide an opportunity also to advance the child's right to social security.

- The state has an obligation to provide the legal and administrative infrastructure required to fulfil children's rights as set out in section 28 of the South African Constitution.

Section two provided an overview of the programmes government has put in place to give effect to the right to social services, focusing primarily on those of the Department of Social Development. This section highlighted the following points:

- Adult social assistance programmes help give effect to children's right to social assistance.

- There are gaps in the coverage of existing social assistance programmes. The phased-in extension of the CSG to include all eligible children under 14 still excludes children between 14 and 18 years old. This exclusion affects approximately 7 million children. There is as yet no plan by government to change the CSG policy to afford all children access to the CSG.

- There is no clear policy on ensuring that all children affected by HIV/AIDS are able to realise their right to social assistance.

- Existing social assistance programmes, by way of their design, exclude particularly vulnerable children, for example those living on the streets and/or in child-headed households.

- The CSG programme must be understood as part of a "package" of government services aimed at children. Thus the sufficiency of the monthly CSG payment can only be assessed by looking at its value in conjunction with other government programmes that are in place to deliver other socio-economic rights. More detailed information on the depth of child poverty would also be needed.

Section three presented an analysis of the CSG programme. The discussion drew attention to the following critical points:

- The CSG programme was conceptualised to ensure that more South African children in need would gain access to social assistance, than was the case with the racially-based State Maintenance Grant.

- However, the design of the CSG programme places a great deal of emphasis on the means-testing of care-givers before access can be gained to the benefits of the programme. It also requires that an adult care-giver applies for and receives the CSG on a child's behalf and that certain official documents must be produced before a CSG application can be processed.

- As such, the CSG has been conceptualised with very specific access barriers built into the basic workings of the programme. While these barriers were probably intended to discourage misuse of the CSG programme, the effect has been to place obstacles in the way of especially vulnerable children accessing the grant.

- Since the introduction of the CSG, the nominal value of the grant has changed four times. When adjusted for inflation to 2003 rands, the value of the CSG in 2003 is just above the value set at its inception in 1998.

- The means test has remained unchanged since 1998 and does not take household size into account. This excludes children living in larger families, whose need for the grant (in terms of access to resources) is as great as those in small families.

- For the most part, provincial social development departments have been under-spending or over-spending on their CSG budgets. Of particular concern are the under-expenditures in the Eastern Cape for 2001/02 and drastic over-expenditure in the Western Cape and Mpumalanga in 2002/03. Considering the high poverty share and rate of the Eastern Cape, drastic steps need to be taken to improve social assistance delivery in this province.

- The take-up rate of the CSG is weakest in the Eastern Cape, Limpopo and the Northern Cape. KwaZulu-Natal is rapidly improving its take-up rate. While certain progress has been made – both in terms of the rate of roll-out and in reaching vulnerable children – it is imperative that both improve. Too many eligible children, particularly very vulnerable children, such as those living in remote areas and without care-givers, do not benefit from the CSG to which they are entitled.

- Obstacles experienced in the implementation and service delivery of the CSG include limitations in human resource capacity and administrative overload within the provincial Departments of Social Development, together with the constraints imposed by the SOCPEN system itself. From beneficiaries' and their care-givers' point of view, hurdles to accessing the CSG include not having birth certificates or identity documents, as well as the transport costs involved in gaining copies of these and then applying for and collecting the CSG.

- Government has plans in place to improve the computer system for administering grants. It has also attended to the training of government officials and increasing the number of staff in order to respond to the increasing volume of applications. A registration campaign was further co-ordinated to increase awareness of the CSG and to register children with birth certificates and adults with identity documents. Moreover, government plans to improve the efficiency of the entire social assistance system by establishing a national Social Security Agency to deliver grants throughout the country.

Against this background, this chapter concludes with the following recommendations regarding government's measures to advance the child's right to social services:

- The scope and nature of the child's right to social security remain unclear. Efforts to monitor the realisation of children's right to social security would be much more effective if improved indicators could be developed. Such indicators would provide benchmarks against which to measure the extent to which children are attaining their right to social security.

- In order for progress to be measured, there is a need for the national Department of Social Development to provide a transparent plan of action for realising this right. This plan of action should include benchmarks (including targets) tied to specific time-frames.

- If the level of benefits provided under the CSG should meet a defined minimum standard, it would follow that a defined minimum be established for the CSG, taking into account other social assistance programmes and the actual situation of children.

- Children who are primary care-givers in households affected by HIV/AIDS should be able to apply (as primary care-givers) for the CSG for children in that household.

- There is a need for better planning on the part of provincial social development departments to deliver the CSG. This calls for better budget planning (over- and under-expenditure are concerns) and improving administrative capacity.

- The means test is in need of adjustment so as to ensure that children in larger households are not discriminated against and those without necessary documents are not excluded.

- All children under 18 years should be eligible for the CSG.

More specifically, to improve the implementation of the CSG, urgent attention is required in the following areas:

- The CSG policy and strategy should be marketed as widely as possible, particularly to care-givers, parents and government officials.

- Efficiency can be increased by bringing about improvements in the CSG registration system. In other words, once a child has been registered for a CSG, the system should maintain their data until they reach 14 years. This would also avoid the unnecessary process of registering a child three times before they reach 14 years. This will affect all children aged eight who turn nine before 1 April 1 2004.

- It is essential for the national Department of Social Development to ensure that its projection of potential beneficiaries is adequately reflected in the budget allocations made by provincial governments for the CSG programme. Poor projections lead to the persistent under-estimation of the provincial budgets required to roll the CSG out. This pressure on provincial budgets is at the root of many of the implementation problems alluded to above.

- There is an urgent need to establish the number of children who are eligible for the CSG in South Africa. While the number of CSG-eligible children remains in contention, as evidenced above, negative impacts will be felt at the level of budg-eting and service delivery. Some provinces exceeded their target for the CSG (as at 31 March 2003, Gauteng had exceed its target by 350%) and other provinces under-performed (as at the same date, Free State had under-performed by 50%). It is difficult to interpret this apparent over- or under-performance without clari-ty around the number of eligible children in each province.

- Increased administrative support is required for those provinces that continue to perform badly in their take-up rates of the CSG.

# REFERENCES

ACESS. (2002) *Children's Voices on Social Security.* Available at http://www.acess.org.za.

ACESS. (2003) *ACESS Newsletter,* March. Available at http://www.acess.org.za.

ACESS. (2003a) *Child Support Grant: Case Alert.* 18 April.

ACESS. (2003b) *Child Support Grant: Case Alert.* 29 April.

Bilchitz, D. (2003) "Towards a reasonable approach to the minimum core: laying the foundations for future socio-economic rights jurisprudence". In *South African Journal of Human Rights,* 19(2). Cape Town: Juta.

Blecher, M. (2003) *Contemporary issues affecting budgeting.* Paper presented at the Idasa national training course "Strengthening capacity in budget analysis to foster pro-poor budgeting in South Africa", on 17 October 2003. Available at www.idasa.org.za/bis.

Cape High Court. (2000) *Grootboom v Oostenberg Municipality and Others.* 2000 (3) BCLR 1169 (CC).

Case, A., V. Hosegood & F. Lund. (2003) *The reach of the South African Child Support Grant: Evidence from KwaZulu-Natal.* CDS Working Paper, 38, October.

Cassiem, S., Proudlock, P. and Streak, J. (2002) *Child Support Grant and Budget 2002.* Budget Brief 95 Cape Town: Budget Information Service, Idasa.

Child Health Policy Institute and the South African Federal Council on Disability. (2001) *Social Security Policy Options for People with Disabilities in South Africa: an International and Comparative Review.* Available at http://web.uct.ac.za/depts/ci/index.htm.

Cockerell, A. (1996) "The Law of Persons and the Bill of Rights". In *Bill of Rights,* 3E-13.

Constitutional Court of South Africa. (2000) *Government of the Republic of South Africa and Others v Grootboom and Others.* 2001 (1) SA 46 (CC); 2000 (11) BCLR 1169 (CC).

Constitutional Court of South Africa. (2002) *Minister of Health and Others v Treatment Action Campaign and Others.* 2002 (5) SA 721, 2002 (10) BCLR 1033 (CC).

Creamer, K. (2002) *The impact of South Africa's evolving jurisprudence on children's socio-economic rights on budget analysis.* BIS Occasional Paper, 5, November. Cape Town: Idasa Budget Information Service.

Department of Social Development. (2002) *Transforming the Present – Protecting the Future: Draft consolidated report of the Committee of Inquiry into a Comprehensive System of Social Security for South Africa.* Pretoria: Government Printer.

Department of Social Development. (2003a) *Children's Bill.* Pretoria: Government Printer.

Department of Social Development. (2003b) *Extension of the Child Support Grant to Children up to 14 years of Age: Draft Business Plan for Implementation.* Unpublished document.

Department of Social Development. (2003c) *Social Assistance Bill.* Pretoria: Government Printer.

Department of Social Development. (2003d) *South African Social Security Agency Bill.* Pretoria: Government Printer.

Department of Social Development. (2003e) *You and your grants 2003.* Accessed at http://www.welfare.gov.za/services.

Department of Welfare and Population Development. (1996) *Report of the Lund Committee on Child and Family Support.* Pretoria: Government Printer

Department of Welfare and Population Development. (1997) *White Paper for Social Welfare in South Africa.* Pretoria: Government Printer.

Ewing, D. (2004) *Report on the children's participation component of monitoring child socio-economic rights in South Africa.* Cape Town: Idasa Budget Information Service.

Giese, S., H. Meintjies, R. Croke & R. Chamberlain. (2003) *Health and social services to address the needs of orphans and other vulnerable children in the context of HIV/AIDS: Research report and recommendations.* Cape Town: Children's Institute/National Department of Health.

Guthrie, T. (2002) *Analysis of the national social security payments of the Child Support Grant for children in South Africa for the period Dec 2001 to Oct 2002.* Unpublished paper. Available at http://web.uct.ac.za/depts/ci/index.htm.

Himes, J. (2000) "Resource Mobilisation for the Realisation of Children's Rights". In *Children's Rights: Turning Principles into Practice.* Sweden: Save the Children Sweden/ UNICEF.

Liebenberg, S. (2001) "The right to social assistance: the implications of Grootboom for policy reform in South Africa". In *South African Journal of Human Rights,* 17(2). Cape Town: Juta.

Liebenberg, S. (2002a) "The right to social security: A response". In Brand, D. & S. Russell (eds), *Exploring the core content of socio-economic rights.* Pretoria: Protea Book House.

Liebenberg, S. (2002b) *South Africa's Evolving Jurisprudence on Socio-economic rights.* Conference paper. Available from the Community Law Centre, University of the Western Cape, or available at http:// www.communitylawcentre.org.za/ser.

Liebenberg, S. (2003) "South Africa's evolving jurisprudence on socio-economic rights: An effective tool in challenging poverty?". Forthcoming in *Law, Democracy and Development.* United Kingdom: Butterworths.

Mgijima, C. (1999) "South African situation analysis - South African Government: Department of Health". In *International Consultative Conference on Food Security and Nutrition as Human Rights.* Report of conference proceedings. Johannesburg: South African Human Rights Commission.

NADEL. (1999) *Old Age Pensions and the Challenges posed to the State: South Africa's Dilemma.* Cape Town: NADEL.

National Treasury. (2002a) *Medium Term Budget Policy Statement.* Pretoria: Government Printer.

National Treasury. (2002b) *Division of Revenue Act.* Pretoria: Government Printer.

National Treasury. (2002c) *Budget Review.* Pretoria: Government Printer.

National Treasury. (2002d) *Workshop outcomes for the Department of Social Development regarding the establishment of the Social Security Agency.* Unpublished document.

National Treasury. (2003a) *Budget Review.* Pretoria: Government Printer.

National Treasury. (2003b) *Estimates of National Expenditure.* Pretoria: Government Printer.

National Treasury. (2003c) *Intergovernmental Fiscal Review.* Pretoria: Government Printer.

Nelson Mandela Foundation / Human Sciences Research Council. (2002) *HIV/AIDS study.* Accessed at http://www.mandela-children.com/english/worddoc/HIVReport.pdf.

Organisation of African Unity. (1990) *African Charter on the Rights and Welfare of the Child.* OAU Document CAB/LEG/24.9/49.

Republic of South Africa. (1996) *The Constitution of the Republic of South Africa.* Act 108 of 1996. Pretoria: Government Printer.

Resolve Group. (2002) *Workshop outcome report for the Department of Social Development regarding the Establishment of a Specialist Grant Payment Agency.* Unpublished document. Available from the national Department of Social Development.

Samson, M. (2002) *Changes in caregivers, due to poverty shocks or HIV/AIDS-related deaths, complicate the documentation required for successful application for the Child Support Grant.* Cape Town: EPRI.

School of Public Health (University of the Western Cape), Social Disadvantage Research Centre (University of Oxford) & the Economic Research Institute. (2002) *Social security transfers, poverty and chronic illness in the Eastern Cape: An investigation of the relationship between social security grants, the alleviation of rural poverty and chronic illnesses including those associated with HIV/Aids – a case study of Mount Frere in the Eastern Cape.* Publisher unknown.

Sloth-Nielsen, J. (2001) "The child's right to social services, the right to social security, and primary prevention of child abuse: some conclusions in the aftermath of Grootboom". In *South African Journal of Human Rights,* 17(2). Cape Town: Juta.

South African Human Rights Commission. (2003) *4th Annual Economic and Social Rights Report: 2000-2002.* Johannesburg: SAHRC.

Streak, J. (2002) *Provincial child poverty rates and numbers based on poverty lines of R400 and R200 and October Household Survey data.* Child Poverty Monitor, 1. Cape Town: Idasa Budget Information Service.

Streak, J. & J. Wehner. (2002) *Budgeting for socio-economic rights in South Africa.* Applied Fiscal Research Centre (AFReC) Research Monograph, 24. Cape Town: AFReC, University of Cape Town.

Streak, J. (2003) *Child poverty, child rights and Budget 2003: The right thing or a step in the right direction?* Budget Brief, 125. Cape Town: Idasa Budget Information Service.

Streak, J. & L. Kgamphe. (2002) *Government's recent performance in budgeting for the child's right to social assistance in South Africa.* Budget Brief, 107. Cape Town: Idasa Budget Information Service.

Tilley, A. (2000) "Social Welfare Rights". In Liebenberg, S. & K. Pillay (eds), *Socio economic rights in South Africa: A resource book.* Cape Town: Socio-economic Rights Project, University of the Western Cape.

Van der Westhuizen, C. & A. van Zyl. (2002) *Obstacles to the delivery of social security grants?* Budget Brief, 110. Cape Town: Idasa Budget Information Service.

## PERSONAL COMMUNICATION

The following people provided information through personal communications between March and September 2003:

Mr Bukhosini, Director of Social Security, Kwa-Zulu Natal Department of Social Development

A. Coleridge, Director of Social Security, Northern Cape Department of Social Development

H. de Graas, Director of Social Security, Western Cape Department of Social Development

Ms Fhatuwane and Ms Lekina, Administrative officers, Northern Province Department of Social Development

R. Hlawatshwayo, Director: Social Security and Social Assistance, National Department of Social Development

R. Leshotho, Director of Social Security, Free State Department of Social Development

R. Mokoena, Director of Social Security, Mpumalanga Department of Social Development

K. More, Director of Social Security, North West Department of Social Development

D. Plaatjies, Director: Social Security and Social Assistance, National Treasury

J. Sofika, Director of Social Security, Eastern Cape Department of Social Development

J. Tebeila, Senior Administrative Clerk, Finance and Economic Directorate, National Department of Social Development

A. Wagener, Senior Administrative Officer, Social Security Directorate, Gauteng Department of Social Development

# ENDNOTES

1   In chapter one of this publication, Streak shows that according to the 2000 *Income and Expenditure Survey* and an income poverty line of R430/month per capita for a child in 2000 rands, 74.8% of South Africa's children are income poor. This translates into 13 million income poor children in 2000.

2   See for example Nelson Mandela Foundation/HSRC 2002; Giese *et al* 2003.

3   On examination of the inclusion of the right to social services, it would appear that there are no direct corresponding articles in treaty law (Sloth-Nielsen 2001). Sloth-Nielsen proposes articles 10(1) and (3) have some relevance (Ibid).

4   In the Cape High Court (2000:paragraphs 75 & 78) judgement in the *Grootboom* matter, these are referred to as social *welfare* programmes (Sloth-Nielsen 2001).

5   The TAC and others challenged the South African government over the reasonableness of its programme to provide anti-retroviral drugs to pregnant women to prevent mother-to-child transmission of the human immunodeficiency virus (HIV), on the grounds of sections 27 and 28 of the Constitution. The Constitutional Court found in favour of the applicants for two reasons. First, the court held that government's measures to realise the right to health could not be regarded as reasonable in so far as the provision of the anti-retroviral drug, Nevirapine, was limited to a number of pilot sites when latent capacity already

existed elsewhere for administering the drug. Secondly the court held that government had not sufficiently provided for a broadening of the prerequisite programme capacity (Constitutional Court 2002:135).

6   All children's rights bear an obligation on government. With regard to the obligation to "respect", government is obliged to improve mechanisms so that children are able to access their rights. The obligation to "promote" requires, *inter alia*, that government raises public awareness of children's rights within civil society and amongst government officials themselves. Under the obligation to "protect", government is obliged to pass laws that protect the violation of children's rights. The obligation to "fulfil" means that government is obliged to create programmes that give effect to the rights of the child including raising public awareness of children's rights (see South African Human Rights Commission 2003).

7   In *Grootboom* (Constitutional Court 2000), the court set out the criteria it would use to assess the reasonableness of government measures in relation to socio-economic rights. It specified that reasonableness calls for a consideration of the urgency of the need to be met. It also requires balance and flexibility and must take account of short-, medium- and long-term needs. It must not exclude a significant segment of society, and must consider those who cannot pay for the services. Bilchitz (2003) agrees in part with this notion of reasonableness. However, he argues that the condition to "take account of urgent interests, for example, seems more likely to arise from a consideration of the right itself and the obligations it entails rather than from the notion of reasonableness alone" (Ibid:9).

8   The Department of Social Development refers to the legal obligation to deliver the CSG as a an obligation as referenced by section 27(1)(c).

9   For example, in the case of the Child and Youth Diversion Programme, the Department of Social Development collaborates with the Department of Justice, faith-based organisations as well as non-government organisations in order to implement the programme.

10  The SMG provided a parent allowance of R430 and a child allowance of R135. White and Indian mothers were the primary beneficiaries of the grant.

11  Ms Naiker supplied data on the targets set in 1998 – see Idasa (2002) *Budget Brief*, 95. Ms Jooste provided data for the years 2000 to 2002 and Jeremia Tebeila those for 2003.

# CHAPTER SIX

## The child's right to basic education

By Mandla Seleoane[1]

# INTRODUCTION

This chapter considers the child's right to basic education and attempts to monitor government's implementation of the right. To that end, section one first examines the meaning and scope of the child's right to basic education. This section unpacks, inter alia, how the concept of "the child's right to basic education" is to be understood in the South African legal context and considers the question of whether basic education for children is free in South Africa. Section two then identifies and briefly discusses the programmes that government has called into existence to give effect to the child's right to basic education, namely General Education and Training (GET), Early Childhood Development (ECD) and Education for Learners with Special Needs (ELSEN). The third section analyses government's budgeting for the child's right to basic education. The budget analysis covers the period 1999/00 to 2005/06, but gives particular attention to the years 2002/03 to 2005/06. Finally, section four draws together the main points to have emerged in the chapter, with a particular focus on government's policy, programme conceptualisation and budgeting to advance the child's right to basic education.

The right to basic education is provided for in section 29 of the Constitution as part of the right to education generally. Therefore, in trying to unpack the right, reference will be made to the constitutional text on the matter. Reference will also be made to judicial decisions that have a bearing on the right. Some of the decisions do not have a *direct* bearing on the right to basic education or education as such, but convey legal principles that should be taken into account when thinking about the right to basic education.

Article 5 of the Vienna Declaration states, *inter alia,* that "all human rights are universal, indivisible, and *interdependent and interrelated*" (emphasis added). Therefore, although the right to education, and thus to basic education, is set out in section 29 of the Constitution, there is a need to read this right in conjunction with other constitutional provisions that have a bearing on the right. Some of the provisions, although not dedicated to education as such, will nevertheless impact on the right to education.

Section 28 of the Constitution, for example, deals with the rights of children generally. There is only one stipulation within the section that makes direct reference to the child's education. It is suggested, however, that all or most of the other stipulations in section 28 also have a bearing on the child's right to education to the extent that, if they are not fulfilled, the child's education is likely to be affected negatively. Therefore, if the rights afforded specifically to children in section 28 are not given effect to – for example, the right to family or parental care, to basic nutrition, shelter, basic healthcare and social services, to protection against maltreatment, neglect, abuse, degradation and exploitative labour practices[2] – then his or her right to education is more than likely to suffer as a result.

It is thus important, for analytical as well as fiscal purposes, to keep the inter-relationship between rights in mind when considering the child's right to basic education. This consideration is reflected in the way this publication monitors government measures to give effect to multiple children's rights, emphasising throughout the inter-connection between these measures.

# 1. THE MEANING AND SCOPE OF THE CHILD'S RIGHT TO BASIC EDUCATION

Box 6.1 sets out the provisions relating to the right to education as set out in section 29 of the Constitution.

## BOX 6.1 SECTION 29 OF THE CONSTITUTION

(1) Everyone has the right –
    (a) to basic education, including adult basic education; and
    (b) to further education, which the state, through reasonable measures, must make progressively available and accessible.

(2) Everyone has the right to receive education in the official language or languages of their choice in public educational institutions where that education is reasonably practicable. In order to ensure the effective access to, and implementation of, this right, the state must consider all reasonable educational alternatives, including single medium institutions, taking into account –
    (a) equity;
    (b) practicability; and
    (c) the need to redress the results of past racially discriminatory laws and practices.

(3) Everyone has the right to establish and maintain, at their own expense, independent educational institutions that –
    a) do not discriminate on the basis of race;
    b) are registered with the state; and
    c) maintain standards that are not inferior to standards at comparable public educational institutions.

(4) Subsection (3) does not preclude state subsidies for independent educational institutions.

## 1.1 THE MEANING OF THE RIGHT TO BASIC EDUCATION

This chapter is not concerned with all the education rights set out in section 29, including the right to adult basic education, but with the right of the child to basic education. However, a number of important insights emerge from a reading of the provisions in section 29. Firstly, it is clear that the child has a right to basic education. The scope of this right is considered in more detail in section 1.2 below. The child's right to basic education is direct. He or she is promised, not the right of *access to* basic education, but basic education itself. Therefore the state is under a constitutional obligation to provide basic education to the child, rather than merely refraining from interference with his or her acquisition of this right. In the words of Judge Mahomed (Constitutional Court 1996), when he served as Deputy President of the Constitutional Court:

> "[Section 32(a) of the interim constitution[3]] creates a positive right that basic education be provided for every person and not merely a negative right that such a person should not be obstructed in pursuing his or her basic education."

The child's right to basic education therefore imposes a positive duty on the state, rather than the negative duty to refrain from impeding children from access to the right (Bekker 2000:7).

Secondly, unlike other social and economic rights, and like the section 28 child socio-economic rights, the state's obligation to provide basic education to the child is not subject to reasonable legislative and other measures. Therefore the state cannot argue, in the face of a demand to provide basic education to the child, that such a demand is unreasonable.

A third important point emerging from the provisions in section 29 is that, unlike other social and economic rights and like section 28 child socio-economic rights, the child's right to basic education is not subject to progressive realisation. In other words, it is immediate.

Fourthly, unlike other social and economic rights, and as is the case for section 28 child socio-economic rights, the child's right to basic education does not depend on resources that may or may not be available to the state. In other words, the right is unconditional. The Cape High Court (1997) judgment in *B and Others v Minister of Correctional Services and Others*[4] provides guidance on how a right that is articulated in unconditional terms should be approached. The case involved an application brought by prisoners under section 35(2)(e) of the Constitution, which articulates their right to medical treatment at the state's expense in unconditional terms. The court stated that, once it is established that any other medicine than AZT would be inadequate for the purpose of treating an HIV-positive prisoner or detainee, it is no defence for the state to argue that it does not have the money to provide the AZT.

It could, of course, be argued that the Cape High Court judgment is not conclusive on the matter, and that finality on how to approach section 35(2)(e) must await a Constitutional Court judgment. Until then, however, it is suggested that the Cape High Court judgment does provide guidance on the question and that it cannot be brushed aside too lightly. Attention is also drawn to another Cape High Court judgment in *Grootboom v Oostenberg Municipality and Others*.[5] In this judgment, the court suggested that budgetary limitations are not relevant to the construction to be placed on the right of a child to have shelter in terms of section 28(1)(c) of the Constitution.[6]

I have argued elsewhere (Seleoane 2003:141) that while the Constitutional Court overruled Davis J in the *Grootboom* case, the reversal was not based on an incorrect apprehension of the nature of the duty imposed by the right, but of its *locus* in the first place. Therefore it is suggested that the view expressed by Davis, referred to above, has not been rendered irrelevant by the Constitutional Court's later judgment.

It was suggested that the view argued above is open to criticism in that it conveys that a child living in an area where there is no school, may demand that a school be built in the area. It was suggested, moreover, that reliance couldn't be placed on the two Cape High Court judgments cited above without further ado in order to support the notion of an unconditional right to basic education, since section 36 of the Bill of Rights was not explored in those cases.[7]

The suggestion that children in an area where there is no school might not be entitled to demand of the state to build one is reminiscent of the manner in which the Constitutional Court handled the question of the state's minimum core obligation with reference to social and economic rights. It opined that any minimum core obligation that might exist would not entitle the bearer of the right to demand that the state should deliver the content envisaged by that right. The minimum core responsibility resting on the state, so the Constitutional Court held, means only that such obligation must be taken into account in evaluating whether the measures introduced by the state to give effect to the right are reasonable.[8] It stated further that in practice it would in any event be impossible to afford everyone the services entailed in the minimum core responsibility created by social and economic rights.[9]

I have suggested elsewhere (Seleoane 2003:153-154) that the Constitutional Court's opinion on the state's minimum core responsibility is problematic in the light of *General Comment Number 3* of the United Nations' Committee on Economic, Social and Cultural Rights (1990:5th Session). *This General Comment* states quite clearly that there is an obligation on the state to provide "minimum essential levels" of the rights protected by the International Covenant on Economic, Social and Cultural Rights (ICESCR). One of those rights is the right to basic education. The *General Comment* says the state fails in its obligations if it leaves a significant number of individuals under its jurisdiction without the benefit of the contents of those rights.

Therefore, the view that there is no obligation on the state to deliver the content of a social and economic right – such as the child's right to basic education – is not supportable in the face of *General Comment Number 3*. One cannot embrace the *General Comment* and then assert that there is no obligation on the state to deliver the content of the right. If one holds the opinion that the state is under no obligation to deliver the content of the right, one must abandon *General Comment Number 3* quite clearly as a necessary condition for holding the opinion under consideration.

In principle, therefore, there should be no obstacle to children of a sufficient number demanding not only that the state must build a school in their area if there were none, but also that it should provide teachers and whatever else is necessary in order to give effect to their right to basic education. If the children were of an insufficient number to justify the demand, it is hard to see a principled objection to a demand by them that the state should introduce such measures as may be reasonably necessary in order to enable them to attend the nearest school in pursuance of their right to basic education. Such measures may include, for instance, state provision of transport to ferry them to and from the nearest available school. But the notion that such children might have no remedy at all simply as a result of their locale, seems constitutionally suspect, viewed against their right to basic education.

The limitation of the right of children to basic education in terms of section 36 of the Constitution would require, in the language of that section itself, that there should exist a law of general application purporting to do exactly that. The present chapter is written at a time when no such law exists. In trying to understand what the Constitution means when it proclaims the right in unconditional terms, guidance must be sought from court judgments. They convey that resource constraints should not be lightly implied into the construction of the right where the Constitution has excluded them. Therefore it is suggested that, at this moment, section 36 of the Bill of Rights is not relevant to the interpretation of the right to basic education.

I have argued that, in any event, interpreting the right to basic education and limiting it under section 36 should that be necessary, would have been conceptually different exercises. When one interprets a right, one does something fundamentally different from what one does when limiting it. I have argued, indeed, that interpreting the right precedes limiting it, for otherwise we do not know what we are limiting (Seleoane, 2003:140-141).[10] Therefore it is suggested that the possibility of limiting the right of children to basic education under section 36 is not germane to developing an understanding of what that right, as it is formulated in section 29, means.

In summary then, the thrust of this section is that the right of the child to basic education is unconditional. It is not subject to resources that may or may not be available to the state. The resources may well be a factor to take into account in assessing whether the state is acting reasonably in giving effect to the right, but should not have the effect of limiting the right. Further, the state is constitutionally bound to provide basic education for the child, and not merely to refrain from taking measures that hamper the child in obtaining basic education. That means the state bears the constitutional obligation, among others, to provide the things that are necessary in order for the child to receive basic education, including buildings and personnel.

## 1.2 THE SCOPE OF THE RIGHT TO BASIC EDUCATION

There is a need in this context to define the notion of "basic education". The term "basic education" is not defined in the Constitution. The Interim Constitution did not define it either. In recognition of this fact, the *White Paper on Education and Training* (Department of Education 1995:paragraph 14) argues that the meaning of basic education must therefore be "settled by policy in such a way that the intention of the Constitution is affirmed". The white paper further states (Ibid:paragraph 13) that:

> "Appropriately designed education programmes to the level of the proposed General Education Certificate (GEC) (one year reception class plus 9 years of schooling), whether offered in school to children, or through other forms of delivery to young people and adults, would adequately define basic education for purposes of the constitutional requirement."

The white paper (Ibid:paragraph 14, supra note 33) cites article 1 of the World Declaration on Education to the effect that:

- Every child, youth and adult shall be able to benefit from educational opportunities designed to meet their needs;

- The said needs comprise tools such as literacy, oral expression, numeracy problem-solving, knowledge, skills, values and attitudes, which human beings require in order to survive, develop their full capacities, live and work with dignity, participate fully in development, improve the quality of their lives, make informed decisions, and continue learning.

The education ministry associates itself with the sentiments expressed in the declaration and states that "basic education must be defined in terms of learning needs appropriate to the age and experience of the learner...." (Ibid).

Useful as the World Declaration on Education might be, it remains rather vague in defining basic education. Different people might apprehend the needs and tools required by human beings in order to get along the journey of life differently. Kriel (1996:38) argues that such vagueness allows "the courts a wide latitude to determine what standard of education is prescribed by the Constitution" in relation to "basic education". Implicit in the argument is the suggestion that the Constitution envisaged a standard of education in laying down the right to basic education. If that is so, it is suggested that it would have been better not to leave the question open, even if it is supposed that the courts thereby acquire wide latitude to determine the matter. The judicialisation of human rights is not necessarily an uncontested matter. As Roux (undated: 8) argues, nothing stops a politically conservative judge from reading down rights whilst deploying the progressive language of the Constitution.[11]

Relevant international instruments (to be discussed in more detail in section 1.4) suggest that "basic education" might be the same thing as "primary" or "fundamental" education. The South African Schools Act makes school attendance compulsory between the ages of 7 and 15 years or up to the ninth grade, whichever happens first. The Department of Education (2001a:17) states that "we defined general education and training ... to span Grades 1-9". Therefore it could be inferred that "basic education" is education from grade 1 to grade 9. The same inference can be drawn from the definitions given in the Further Education and Training Act and those of the National Qualifications Authority Act (see also Liebenberg & Pillay 2000:351).

Accepting the above, the point can be made that the educational levels that people need in order to survive, develop their full capacity and work with dignity are a matter of context framed in time and space. The time appears to have receded to grade 9, implying that adequate education would have taken place by then to allow an individual to face the challenges of life and to work with dignity. There may well be a point to expanding our notions of basic education so that, at the very least, grade 12 forms a part of that definition.

To sum up, then, it would appear that both international human rights instruments and South African law favour the view that basic education is from grade 1 to grade 9. Whereas it is possible to argue plausibly for the inclusion of grade 12 in the definition of basic education, it would seem that such a project belongs to the future (even though we can start the debate now).

## 1.3 THE DEFINITION OF A CHILD

The focus of this chapter is on the child's right to basic education. Having considered above the meaning of "basic education", it is now necessary to clarify what is meant by a "child". The Constitution does not itself define a "child" for educational purposes since, presumably, it is concerned with education for all, rather than education for the child as such. However, where it deals with the rights of children generally, the Constitution defines a child as "a person under the age of 18 years" (section 28(3)). The audit of early childhood development (ECD) provisioning (Williams *et al* 2001:16) speaks about children spanning the ages of 0 to 18 years.

The Adult Basic Education and Training Act (Department of Education 2000a: section 6) defines an adult as a person who is sixteen years or older. As noted above, the South African Schools Act (Department of Education 1996) makes school attendance compulsory between the ages of 7 and 15 years or up to the ninth grade, whichever happens first. Since the section 28(3) definition of the child is explicitly meant for the operation of section 28 of the Constitution, it is suggested that, for the purposes of the child's right to basic education, a child be defined as a person who is younger than sixteen years of age.

A number of arguments may be made against the suggestion above. It may be argued that in defining a "child" for the purposes of his or her right to basic education, account must be taken of section 39(2) of the Bill of Rights. The section provides that, "when interpreting any legislation ... every court, tribunal or forum must promote the spirit, purport and objects of the Bill of Rights". It can further be contended that the section 28(3) definition of a child, previously referred to, is normative in that all legislation and policy must comply with it. Finally, it may well be argued that it is unacceptable to define children between 16 and 18 years of age out of the right of the child to basic education.

The view that children between 16 and 18 years of age should not be defined out of the right to basic education has political and social merit. A lot can be said for fixing the cut-off point at 17 rather than 15 years, for purposes of the right of the child to basic education, a proposal that is compatible with the one that basic education should be extended to include grade 12, referred to previously. However the proposition that it is constitutionally wrong to have a lower cut-off point is debatable. It is by no means certain that section 39(2) of the Bill of Rights can be relied on without further ado in order to catch children between 16 and 18 years of age within the "net" of basic education rights. In order to rely on section 39(2) for this purpose, it would first be necessary to show that "the spirit, purport and objects" of the Bill of Rights suggest that such children should be covered. Deriving this spirit from section 28(3) by according it normative status on the issue, seems to have no textual support in section 28(3) itself. The latter section states clearly that it is defining a child for the purpose of the rights conferred in section 28, and not for the entire Bill of Rights.

Bentley (2002:4-10) discusses some of the boundary problems related to defining "childhood". She indicates that for different considerations, the cut-off point is fixed differently. When the Constitution lays down the minimum voting age as 18 years (in section 46(1)(d)), it seems to convey a lower childhood threshold for voting purposes. When, by contrast, South African marriage laws lay down the minimum marriageable age as 21 years, they convey a higher childhood threshold for purposes of marriage. None of these definitions, it is submitted, are obviously vulnerable to attack for want of promoting the spirit, purport and objects of the Bill of Rights.

⌐ her definitions (Rule, undated: 2)[12] may factor in the question whether the person contemplated is in formal schooling or not, in addition to his or her age. It is suggested that for current purposes the question whether the person is in formal schooling or not should not affect his or her status as a child. This is because the question under consideration here is, at least in part, whether his or her right to basic education is not affected adversely by the very fact that he or she is not in formal schooling at that age.

In any event, since our concern is the child's right to basic education in South Africa, the question of who a child is must be resolved on the basis of South African legislation – unless it is less favourable than international instruments. Since South African legislation on education suggests that a person is a child until he or she attains the age of 16, the fact that he or she may be outside the formal schooling system at an earlier age is precisely what the law suggests should not happen. Therefore if such a person is outside the formal schooling system, he or she is not defined out of the child's right to basic education. To the contrary, in such circumstances, efforts must be made to get him or her back into the system so that his or her right to basic education can be restored.

In conclusion, it would seem that in South Africa the authorities suggest that, for purposes of basic education, the cut-off point for childhood is 15 years. This view appears to enjoy the support of international instruments on human rights. As was the case in respect of the expansion of the meaning of "basic education" to include grade 12, expanding the meaning of "child" for the purposes of basic education seems to be a project for the future.

## 1.4 FREE BASIC EDUCATION FOR THE CHILD

Malherbe (1997:85-86) points out that during the negotiation process preceding the Interim Constitution, one of the constitutional drafts placed before the negotiators by the South African Law Commission contained a clause on free primary education. Yet neither the Interim Constitution nor the 1996 Constitution includes a clause on free education. From a constitutional standpoint, there is therefore no free education in South Africa at any level and the child is thus not entitled to any free education.

However, section 5(3)(a) of the South African Schools Act (Department of Education 1996) provides that no child may be denied access to a public school on the basis that their parents are unable to pay prescribed school fees. It also provides for the partial or complete exemption from school fees for children whose parents cannot afford them. The Department of Education's Admission Policy for Ordinary Public Schools provides that no learner should be suspended from class, denied access to cultural, sporting or social activities of the school, denied a school report or transfer certificate or be victimised in any other way, on the basis that his or her parents are unable to pay school fees.

The fact that learners cannot officially be turned away from public schools or otherwise disadvantaged for their parents' inability to pay school fees can however not be a substitute for the right to free basic education for the child. First, the reality on the ground does not conform to legislation and policy. Children do in fact get sent away, their reports do in fact get withheld and they are in fact subjected to various forms of humiliation and embarrassment as a result of their parents' inability to pay school fees (Ministry of Education 2003b). But if basic education were offered for free to the child as a constitutional right, none of these might be possible.

In the current situation, as Vally (2001:6) points out, parents can also be sued for non-payment of school fees. The Deputy Minister of Education, Mosibudi Mangena, does not dispute that these deviations do occur. Indeed, a press statement drawn up for the Minister of Education, dated 18 February 2003, indicates that the minister is "extremely concerned" about reports he had received about such deviations. Mangena (2003:personal interview) argues, however, that part of the problem is that parents do not attend meetings and therefore are unfamiliar with their rights. Of even more interest, he cites the right of school governing bodies to sue for payment of owing monies as a reason why there is no need to turn learners away. His reasoning is that the fees have nothing to do with the department but are an agreement that parents themselves make for purposes agreed by them. Presumably, therefore, if a parent fails to pay the fees, this is a contractual matter among the parents and the learner should not be affected by it.

However one looks at the matter, it seems quite clear that South Africa falls short of the requirements of international human rights instruments on the right to basic education for the child. The Convention on the Rights of the Child (CRC) in Article 28 provides that member states must "make primary education compulsory and available free to all". Article 4(a) of the Convention Against Discrimination in Education contains a similar provision. The Universal Declaration of Human Rights (UDHR), in Article 26(1), says that "elementary" or "fundamental" education should be free and compulsory.

The rights enshrined in the UDHR are given effect, *inter alia,* by the International Covenant on Economic, Social and Cultural Rights (ICESCR) (Alston 1998:2; Bekker 2000:130). The ICESCR (in Article 13(2)(a)) states that, in order to achieve "the full realisation" of the right to education, states parties must make primary education compulsory and free. The ICESCR further provides that a member state which, at the time of becoming a party, has as yet not secured free and compulsory primary education for those under its jurisdiction, must produce a detailed plan of action for the progressive implementation, within two years of the principle of compulsory education free of charge for all (Article 14).

It could be argued in favour of South Africa that it is not, strictly speaking, bound to give effect to the ICESCR. South Africa signed the ICESCR on 3 October 1994, but has to date not ratified the covenant (Department of Foreign Affairs, undated:1). It is clear, however, that South Africa drew up its own Bill of Rights, including the right to education, using terminology that is ostensibly borrowed from the ICESCR. Furthermore, in terms of the non-ratification argument, there was no obligation on South Africa, in drawing up the National Action Plan for the Promotion and Protection of Human Rights (NAP) in December 1998, to include social and economic rights in that plan. But it did – and included, indeed, the right to education in that plan. However it studiously side-stepped the issue of free basic education completely (NAP Project Steering Committee 1998:122-127).

Therefore South Africa's conduct is not always compatible with its non-ratification of the ICESCR, and its failure to provide free basic education cannot consistently be justified on the basis of non-ratification. The force of this argument becomes even stronger when consideration is given to the fact that South Africa is failing to comply even with those treaties that it has ratified. The CRC, for example, similarly enjoins on states parties to provide primary education for free. South Africa also falls short when it comes to regional human rights instruments on the child's right to basic education. The African Charter on the Rights and Welfare of the Child provides, in article 11 (3) (a), that basic education must be free and compulsory.

Deputy Minister Mangena argues that even though basic education might not be legally free in South Africa, it is *in fact* free. He argues that the state provides educators, classrooms, textbooks and stationery for free to learners. If there are learners who do not receive learning materials, that is because of human failure at the distribution points. He points out, moreover, that government is reviewing the idea of user fees for learners and might introduce a dispensation where 40% of learners whose parents are amongst the poorest of the poor are automatically exempted from user fees. How will the poorest of the poor be identified so that their children might be exempted from user fees? The Deputy Minister responds that the government might identify, say, a place like Sekhukhune as a depressed area and then direct that all learners there must be exempt from user fees. Further, children who receive child grants from the state would be automatically exempted from user fees even if they fall outside of an area targeted by the directive (Mangena 2003:personal interview). The Minister of Education, Kadar Asmal, was quoted as setting the percentage of children who would benefit from this dispensation at 60. The formulation attributed to him is slightly different in terms of how the dispensation is meant to work. He is reported to have said 60% of children at poor schools will be exempted from user fees (*Sowetan* 2003: 4).

Whereas such a move would represent some forward movement, it would be far from satisfactory. First, it is hard to see why, in reason, 40% or 60% of the poorest of the poor should be part of such a scheme. If the scheme is meant for the benefit of the poorest of the poor, howsoever defined, it is suggested that the scheme can only work well if they all benefit from it, and not only an arbitrarily pre-determined percentage of the poorest of poor children. Secondly, it is possible to think of numerous "depressed" areas in South Africa. At some point, in trying to fit them into the 40% or 60% envisaged, the arithmetic is simply bound to break down, forcing the authorities to fall back on arbitrary choices once again. Thirdly, even if agreement is reached on which areas may be defined as "depressed" and therefore deserving of the exemption, the fact would remain that not everyone living in such an area is among the poorest of the poor. Since the exemption is a blanket exemption, learners whose parents are able to pay user fees in the area will have the benefit of free education for the sheer reason that government has looked favourably on their area. Learners whose parents might well qualify under the label "poorest of the poor", but who live in an area that has not been chosen by government as a "depressed area", will be locked out of the benefit.

It is suggested that all the complicated calculations implicit in the Department of Education's approach to this issue can simply be avoided by providing basic education to the child free of charge. All the manoeuvring that accompanies the effort to avoid free basic education is not worth the administrative headaches, which must necessarily be occasioned by the proposed dispensation.

To summarise this sub-section, the reality is that there is no free basic education in South Africa. South Africa is out of line with international human rights instruments in this regard. But it is also out of line with its own laws, which make attendance of school compulsory up to the end of grade 9. Countries that have succeeded in making schooling compulsory up to that level, have also made it free. It is a contradiction in terms to make schooling compulsory but not free, since in some instances this compels people to do what is impossible for them to carry out in practice.

# 2. GOVERNMENT PROGRAMMES TO GIVE EFFECT TO THE CHILD'S RIGHT TO BASIC EDUCATION

This section of the chapter sets out to identify those programmes put in place by government to provide for the child's right to basic education. This task is not as straightforward as it might seem, for three reasons. Firstly, the broad strategic framework of the Department of Education includes several focal areas that are crucial to furthering children's basic education rights. However, these focal areas cut across the education and training terrain, and are not defined in terms of the basic education of children per se. Secondly, when it comes to selecting those programmes that only or primarily impact on children, some ambiguity remains around the parameters of "basic education" in practice, and whether Early Childhood Development (or a component thereof) should be included in the analysis. Thirdly, the names used by the national and provincial education departments to describe their work programmes (for example, General Education and Training) do not always correspond with the names of their budget programmes (for example, Public Ordinary Schools). These three issues are addressed briefly below before proceeding with the overview of programmes.

The Department of Education's strategic plan, devised in 2000, is called *Tirisano*. The term means, literally, "working together". The nine priority areas identified in this implementation plan are listed in Box 6.2.

## BOX 6.2 *TIRISANO* PRIORITY AREAS

- Making provincial systems work by making co-operative government work;
- Breaking the back of illiteracy among adults and the youth in five years;
- Making schools centres of community life;
- Ending the condition of physical degradation in South African schools;

- Developing the professional quality of teachers;

- Ensuring the success of active learning through outcomes-based education;

- Creating a vibrant further education and training system to equip the youth and adults to meet the social and economic needs of the 21st century;

- Implementing a rational, seamless higher education system that grasps the intellectual and professional challenges facing South Africa in the 21st century; and

- Dealing urgently and purposefully with the HIV/AIDS emergency in and through the education and training system.

The Department of Education considers the nine priority areas of *Tirisano* to constitute five over-arching programme areas, namely:

- HIV/AIDS;

- School effectiveness and teacher professionalism;

- The fight against illiteracy;

- Further education and training and higher education; and

- Organisational effectiveness of national and provincial educational systems.

Of the five programme areas, three have obvious relevance to this chapter. These are school effectiveness and teacher professionalism, the fight against illiteracy and the organisational effectiveness of national and provincial educational systems. Therefore the Department of Education has three over-arching programmes that have an obvious bearing on the right of the child to basic education, even if they are not very clearly articulated.

Against this background, the next step is to consider which, if any, more specific programmes government has set in place to provide children with basic education. In terms of the international and South African legal framework, section one above illustrated that "basic education" is most strongly associated with formal schooling from grade 1 to grade 9. However, education policy-makers, researchers and practitioners in South Africa often include early childhood development within their understanding of "basic education". This ambiguity is borne out by the perspectives emanating from the Department of Education itself. For example, officials of the department could not give pointers to any departmental programmes specifically designed to realise the child's right to basic education, with the possible exception of Early Childhood Development. It is also noteworthy that the Grade R year of Early Childhood Development is included with the nine years of "basic education" in the national curriculum statement. The inclusion of Grade R in this core policy document would seem to suggest that at least this component of Early Childhood Development should be understood as either forming part of basic education, or being very closely tied to basic education. Either way, it is broadly recognised that the provision of Early Childhood Development has a significant positive impact on what happens from grade 1 onwards.

This suggests that programme conceptualisation, budgeting and implementation of Early Childhood Development represents an important area to focus on in monitoring government's measures to advance the child's right to basic education. For the purposes of this chapter, Department of Education programmes and budgets relating to early childhood development have therefore been included in the overviews and analyses to follow.

This section of the chapter offers brief descriptions of General Education and Training, Early Childhood Development and Education for Learners with Special Needs. According to the Deputy Minister of the Department of Education, these programmes can broadly speaking be identified as the most important for giving effect to the right to basic education. This is followed, in section three, by an overview and analysis of government's budgeting for the child's right to basic education. It should be noted, as will become clear in section 3.1, that the budget programmes of provincial education departments do not correspond exactly with the education programmes identified in this section. Provincial education budgets, for example, provide for "Ordinary Public Schools". However, there does not appear to be a programme within the department with the same name. Upon questioning a number of officials at the Department of Education, they reported that there was no such programme. A deputy director explained that the reference to "Public Ordinary Schools" in the budget serves only to distinguish those schools from other types of schools that the state may be funding, but does not imply the existence of a programme with that name. She said that Public Ordinary Schools have no programmatic existence outside of general education and training (Obeke 2003:personal interview).

## 2.1 GENERAL EDUCATION AND TRAINING (GET)

General education and training is not perceived as a programme in itself. It is most often referred to by the department itself in the context of *Curriculum 2005*. It would appear, though, that a number of concepts are seen to be central to general education and training: these include a "learner-centred" approach and "outcomes-based" education, as well as continuous assessment for judging the learner's performance (Department of Education 2001a:17-18).

The Department of Education (2001b: 16) considers itself bound by the Constitution to provide all learners with "ten years of compulsory school education, including one year of early childhood development". Therefore General Education and Training is concerned with children from grade R to grade 9 or age 15, whichever happens first. To provide for this, the South African Schools Act was promulgated and the Department of Education adopted an Admission Policy for Ordinary Public Schools. These instruments provide, inter alia, that:

- No learner may be denied access to a public school on the basis that their parents are unable to pay prescribed school fees;

- Learners whose parents cannot afford school fees can be partially or fully exempted from payment; and

- No learner should be suspended from class, denied access to cultural, sporting or social activities of the school, denied a school report or transfer certificate or victimised in any other way, on the basis that its parents are unable to pay school fees.

As indicated earlier, the department understands its constitutional obligation to also include the provisioning of classrooms, teachers and learning materials, including books and stationery. Table 6.1 shows the shift in learner/classroom ratios across provinces between 1996 and 2000. Table 6.2 illustrates the change in learner/educator ratios over the same period.

### TABLE 6.1 NUMBER OF LEARNERS TO A CLASSROOM BY PROVINCE (1996 AND 2000)

| Province | 1996 | | | 2000 | | | Change between 1996 and 2000* |
|---|---|---|---|---|---|---|---|
| | Learners | Classrooms | Learners per classroom | Learners | Classrooms | Learners per classroom | |
| Eastern Cape | 2 226 408 | 40 489 | 55 | 2 113 387 | 52 222 | 40 | -15 |
| Free State | 785 217 | 20 583 | 38 | 744 627 | 22 841 | 33 | -5 |
| Gauteng | 1 424 360 | 41 721 | 34 | 1 527 698 | 46 324 | 33 | -1 |
| KwaZulu-Natal | 2 612 235 | 58 423 | 45 | 2 646 126 | 68 031 | 39 | -5 |
| Mpumalanga | 898 210 | 19 996 | 45 | 857 241 | 17 766 | 48 | 3 |
| Northern Cape | 199 603 | 6 265 | 32 | 174 497 | 6 772 | 26 | -6 |
| Northern Province | 1 902 732 | 38 958 | 49 | 1 722 869 | 45 649 | 38 | -9 |
| North West | 954 907 | 23 928 | 40 | 896 141 | 26 680 | 34 | -6 |
| Western Cape | 871 708 | 26 461 | 33 | 916 115 | 29 545 | 31 | -2 |
| National | 11 875 380 | 276 824 | 43 | 11 598 701 | 315 830 | 37 | -6 |

**Source:** Department of Education 2000b: 21, 29.

**\* Note:** A negative value in the right-hand column shows improvement in the learner/ classroom ratio.

### TABLE 6.2 LEARNER/EDUCATOR RATIOS BY PROVINCE (1996 AND 2000)[13]

| Province | 1996 | | | 2000 | | | Change between 1996 and 2000* |
|---|---|---|---|---|---|---|---|
| | Learners | Educators | Ratio | Learners | Educators | Ratio | |
| Eastern Cape | 2 226 408 | 62 773 | 35 | 2 113 387 | 66 702 | 32 | -3 |
| Free State | 785 217 | 24 869 | 32 | 744 627 | 24 305 | 31 | -1 |
| Gauteng | 1 424 360 | 51 031 | 28 | 1 527 698 | 52 568 | 29 | 1 |
| KwaZulu-Natal | 2 612 235 | 75 723 | 34 | 2 646 126 | 77 039 | 34 | 0 |
| Mpumalanga | 898 210 | 25 175 | 36 | 857 241 | 22 179 | 39 | 3 |
| Northern Cape | 199 603 | 7 487 | 27 | 174 497 | 6 798 | 26 | -1 |
| Northern Province | 1 902 732 | 57 145 | 33 | 1 722 869 | 55 912 | 31 | -2 |
| North West | 954 907 | 32 682 | 29 | 896 141 | 30 589 | 29 | 0 |
| Western Cape | 871 708 | 33 714 | 26 | 916 115 | 29 873 | 31 | 5 |
| National | 11 875 380 | 370 599 | 32 | 11 598 701 | 365 965 | 32 | 0 |

**Source:** Department of Education 2000b: 21.

**\* Note:** A negative value in the right-hand column shows improvement in the learner/ educator ratio.

According to Deputy Minister Mangena, there are some 300 000 children who should be at school but are not (this amounts to roughly 3% of children of school-going age). This figure is arrived at using deductive logic: the number of children enrolled at schools in South Africa is simply subtracted from the number of children that Statistics South Africa reports there are in the country. He surmises that these might largely consist of so-called street children and children in farming communities. While the existence of out-of-school children is recognised as a serious challenge, the department has no pronounced programme to ensure that these children find their way back to school.

## 2.2 EARLY CHILDHOOD DEVELOPMENT (ECD)

Early childhood development is articulated more fully and coherently in its programmatic import with regard to the child's right to education, than is the case with general education and training. It is concerned with children from birth up to grade R – that is, the Reception Year. The *Education White Paper 5: Early Childhood Education* (Department of Education 2001b:12-13) asserts that:

- South Africa is committed in terms of section 28 of the Constitution as well as the World Declaration on the Survival, Protection and Development of Children, to the advancement of the rights of children;

- The early years of a child's life are critical for the development of the potential of the human being, and the first seven years are characterised by the rapid development of the physical, emotional, intellectual, social and moral character of the child; and

- Unless the conditions of poverty under which many children grow up are addressed, some 40% of South Africa's children face the prospect of irreversible brain damage and stunted physical growth.

The department points out that the needs and indivisible rights of children, implied in any early childhood development programme, span the areas of health, nutrition, a safe environment, as well as psycho-social and cognitive development. Therefore efforts to advance early childhood development has to cut across departments (Ibid:15). Against this background, the department then defines *its* role in early childhood development partly with reference to the constitutional obligation to "provide all learners with ten years of compulsory school education, including one year of early childhood development called the Reception Year" (Ibid:16).[14] It acknowledges the formative importance of the first three years of the child's life, but states that its policy priority is "the implementation of the pre-school Reception Year (grade R) for five year olds turning six in the year of admission" (Ibid).

An audit commissioned by the Department of Education in 2001 suggested that there were approximately six million children in the age group 0 to 6 years in South Africa. Of these, just over a million were enrolled at an ECD centre (Department of Education 2001b:18). Unfortunately, the ages of the six million children between birth and six were not disaggregated. While the White Paper (Ibid:21) indicates that there is a tendency to enrol children at an ECD facility around the age of 3 years, it remains unclear exactly what proportion of the six million could be expected to be at an ECD facility. It is safe to hypothesise, though, that a vast majority of those who should have been at an ECD facility, were not there.

The audit found that there were 23 482 ECD sites countrywide. Table 6.3 shows how these are distributed amongst the nine provinces.

**TABLE 6.3  ECD SITES IN SOUTH AFRICA BY PROVINCE**

| Province | Number of sites | % of national number |
|---|---|---|
| Eastern Cape | 3 231 | 14 |
| Free State | 1 665 | 7 |
| Gauteng | 5 308 | 23 |
| KwaZulu-Natal | 5 684 | 24 |
| Mpumalanga | 1 367 | 6 |
| Northern Cape | 422 | 2 |
| Northern Province | 1 987 | 8 |
| North West | 1 174 | 5 |
| Western Cape | 2 644 | 11 |
| **Total** | **23 482** | **100** |

**Source:** Williams *et al* 2001.

The table reflects that KwaZulu-Natal and Gauteng have the highest number of ECD centres (24% and 23% respectively), while the Free State, Mpumalanga, Northern Cape, Northern Province and North West have the lowest ECD centre figures (on average 5.6% of the national figure). With the possible exception of Mpumalanga, these are also the poorer of the nine provinces making up South Africa. This reality should drive home the need for the state to get more meaningfully involved in ensuring the establishment of sufficient ECD facilities and their equitable distribution across provinces.

The White Paper notes that approximately 82% of ECD services that are available cater for children between 3 and 5 years of age and expresses concern that "children from birth to 2 years, the most critical stage in terms of children's growth and development" are neglected (Ibid). It would appear that, from the department's standpoint, the ideal would have been for ECD services to be provided for children from birth until, at the very least, they enrol at a school. If this is accepted, then all the six million or so children previously referred to should have some access to ECD services. Against this background, the current national ratio of ECD sites to children of 1 / 256 seems clearly inadequate.

Table 6.4 illustrates the different types of ECD sites identified in the audit, which collected information from 21 892 ECD facilities.

**TABLE 6.4 TYPES OF ECD SITES**

| Type | Number | % of all ECD sites audited |
|------|--------|----------------------------|
| School-based | 3 623 | 17 |
| Community-based | 10 816 | 49 |
| Home-based | 7 453 | 34 |
| **Total** | **21 892** | **100** |

**Source:** Williams *et al* 2001.

Thus, some 83% of the ECD services that are available in the country are not school-based and probably also not state-funded. However, even where it is said that the ECD sites are school-based, it is not clear whether the school being referred to is a public or private school. It is therefore not obvious that the school-based services are funded by the state in their entirety. Even if they were public school-based, it would not necessarily follow that the services are entirely state-funded. The audit (Williams *et al* 2001: 20) significantly stated:

> "Despite the various official pronouncements, policy development and pilot programmes detailed above, the [ECD] sector has yet to receive a clear indication of priority status and direction. Consequently Departments of Education in some of the more disadvantaged provinces are directing resources away from ECD provision. Funding to the NGO sector is diminishing, which may eventually hamper the sector's capacity to make meaningful contributions to ongoing developments…The financial and resource constraints pose difficult challenges for the development of a national ECD programme."

Table 6.5 indicates the number of ECD practitioners and child-minders and their ratio to the numbers of children enrolled at ECD sites by province.

**TABLE 6.5 NUMBER OF PRACTITIONERS/CHILD-MINDERS AND THEIR RATIO TO THE CHILDREN**

| Province | Practitioners | Children | Child-practitioner ratio |
|----------|---------------|----------|--------------------------|
| Eastern Cape | 6 354 | 15 2451 | 24:1 |
| Free State | 3 964 | 7 5493 | 19:1 |
| Gauteng | 15 052 | 23 6523 | 16:1 |
| KwaZulu-Natal | 10 603 | 21 3950 | 20:1 |
| Mpumalanga | 2 658 | 5 2626 | 20:1 |
| Northern Cape | 844 | 2 0278 | 23:1 |
| Northern Province | 3 615 | 8 2582 | 23:1 |
| North West | 2 910 | 5 3554 | 18:1 |
| Western Cape | 8 503 | 14 3016 | 17:1 |
| **Total** | **54 503** | **103 0473** | **19:1** |

**Source:** Williams *et al* 2001.

While these ratios may seem encouraging, it has to be borne in mind that they are based on a less than ideal situation, as the Department of Education itself would say. The ideal situation would have been for all six million or so children of the relevant age in South Africa to have access to these practitioners. Then the national practitioner-child ratio would be 110:1.

## 2.3 EDUCATION FOR LEARNERS WITH SPECIAL EDUCATION NEEDS (ELSEN)

According to *Education White Paper Number 6: Special Needs Education* (Department of Education 2001c:14), there are close to three million people in South Africa (that is, approximately 8% of the population) who have some form of disability. The prevalence of different kinds of disabilities can be broken down as follows:

- Sight          41.05%.
- Hearing        14.43%.
- Physical       20.99%.
- Mental         7.25%.
- Multiple       5.8%.
- Not specified  10.49%.

The South African Schools Act (Department of Education 1996) directs Ordinary Public Schools to admit learners with special education needs wherever this is practicable. The Admission Policy for Ordinary Public Schools states that the rights and wishes of learners with special needs must be taken into account upon admission (Ibid:paragraph 22). Schools must, as far as possible, make their facilities accessible to such learners. It would therefore not be enough to merely admit the learners. The physical surroundings and infrastructure of the school must make the necessary accommodation for learners with special needs.

The Admission Policy implies that an effort should be made to integrate learners with special educational needs in the educational context prevailing at the school (Ibid:paragraph 23). Where the necessary support for the integration cannot be provided, the principal of the school must apply to the head of department to have the learner admitted to a suitable public school in the same province and, if necessary, a different province. Before the contemplated transfer can take effect, the head of department must consult with the parents of the learner and such other support personnel as may be necessary (Ibid:paragraph 24).

# 3. GOVERNMENT BUDGETING FOR THE CHILD'S RIGHT TO BASIC EDUCATION

This section begins by defining the relative roles of provincial and national government in financing and implementing programmes that give effect to the child's right to basic education. It also explains the education budget classification system. The programme classification that emerges from the consideration of the official budget documents (National Treasury 2003a, 2003b, 2003c & 2003d; Provincial Treasury 2003) reinforces the point that government has no official programme dedicated to delivering the child's right to basic education. In the absence of this, the budget analysis focuses on the four programmes that can be identified as together providing the best indicator (proxy) of government's financing of the child's right to basic education. These are Public Ordinary Schooling (POS), Independent School Subsidies (ISS), Early Childhood Development (ECD) and Special Schools Education (SSE).

## 3.1 RESPONSIBILITIES OF SPHERES OF GOVERNMENT AND THE BUDGETING SYSTEM

Constitutionally, education is a concurrent function of provincial and national government, with the exception of tertiary education. This means that the responsibility for transforming and improving the education system, including progress in giving effect to children's right to basic education, is shared between national government and the provinces.

The national education department is responsible for formulating all aspects of education policy and setting norms and standards relating to all levels of education. It is also responsible for funding higher education institutions through subsidies to universities and technikons, as well as giving financial support to students through the National Student Financial Aid Scheme. Provincial government education departments are responsible for all aspects of school education and Further Education and Training (FET), as well as important additional programmes such as Adult Basic Education and Training (ABET) and Early Childhood Development (National Treasury 2003a:294; National Treasury 2003b:52; Motala 1997:125). Thus, while basic education provision is primarily the responsibility of provinces, national government also has a role to play in the form of policy development, programme conceptualisation and monitoring.

In order to finance school education, further education and the other education programmes it is responsible for, each provincial education department has to draw on the total amount of revenue available to the province for the relevant financial year. The majority of each province's revenue (about 95%) is comprised of its equitable share, which is the amount of money allocated to the province by national government from the national revenue fund (Streak and Wehner 2002:17). The process whereby each province is allocated its equitable share every financial year involves a vertical and horizontal division of revenue. Firstly, nationally-collected revenue is split amongst the three spheres of government (the vertical division). Once the envelope for each sphere has been determined, the provincial total is then divided amongst the nine provinces and the local government share of revenue is divided amongst the various municipalities (the horizontal division) (Ibid). Thus, the amount of revenue each province has available for allocating to education (including basic education) is influenced both by how much is made available to all provinces through the vertical split and by how much is given to each province through the horizontal split.

The vertical division of revenue is based on a political judgement made by Cabinet (Ibid:18). The division of the aggregate pool of provincial funding amongst provinces is determined by a formula that considers indicators of relative need and past expenditure patterns. More specifically, the provincial equitable share formula assigns relative weighting to a number of components, as listed in Box 6.3. The greatest weighting is given to the three expenditure areas relating to key socio-economic rights: education, health and welfare.

**Box 6.3: PROVINCIAL EQUITABLE SHARE FORMULA IN 2003/04**

| _COMPONENT_ | _WEIGHTING (%)_ |
| --- | --- |
| Education | 41 |
| Health | 19 |
| Social Security | 18 |
| Basic share | 7 |
| Backlog | 3 |
| Economic output | 7 |
| Institutional | 5 |

**Source:** National Treasury (2003d:259).

The education share (41%) in the equitable share formula is based on the size of the school-age population (6-17) and the average number of learners enrolled in Ordinary Public Schools. It is important to note that the fact that education has a weight of 41% in the equitable share formula does not mean that each province has to allocate 41% of its total revenue to education each year. The decision about exactly how much to allocate to the various education programmes is left largely to each provincial government, with some input being made by National Treasury through a consultation process when budgets are being decided upon.

The financing of ECD is the responsibility of provinces and hence funding for ECD has come mainly via provincial allocations from the equitable shares. However national government has over the recent past played a role in ECD financing through conditional grant funding. An early childhood development conditional grant was introduced in 2001/02, primarily to assist in the development and implementation of a compulsory Reception Year of schooling (Grade R). On the introduction of the ECD conditional grant, its purpose was defined as follows:

- To continue with the pilot projects for the implementation of a compulsory Reception Year as part of the 10 years of compulsory schooling; and

- To develop the capacity of the national and provincial education departments to ensure the expansion of a compulsory Reception Year (Grade R) for learners turning six years old (National Treasury 2001:267).

The conditional grant for ECD for all provinces amounted to R21 million in 2001/02, R52 million in 2002/03 and R88 million in 2003/04. Appendix A shows the distribution of the grant across provinces for each of the relevant years. The year 2003/04 was the last year of this conditional grant and it will be incorporated into the equitable share in 2004/05. The continued roll-out of the Grade R early childhood development programme is therefore in future to be funded only from provincial equitable shares (National Treasury 2003d:266).

Tables 6.6 and 6.7 below illustrate the spending programmes of national and provincial education departments, providing a corresponding description of the purpose of each "budget programme" as presented in the national and provincial budgets (see National Treasury 2003a, 2003b & 2003c; Provincial Treasuries 2003).

**TABLE 6.6 CLASSIFICATION OF NATIONAL EDUCATION BUDGET INTO PROGRAMMES**

| Programme number | Budget programme title | Purpose of programme (objective) |
|---|---|---|
| Programme 1 | Administration | To provide for policy formulation and conduct and the overall management of the department. |
| Programme 2 | Planning and Monitoring | To provide information analysis and support in the development, implementation and monitoring of education policies, programmes and projects, as well as ensuring quality. |
| Programme 3 | General Education | To manage the development, implementation, evaluation and maintenance of national policy, programmes and systems for general education. |
| Programme 4 | Further Education and Training | To provide strategic direction to the Further Education and Training (FET) sector and manage the planning, development, evaluation and maintenance of national policy, programmes and systems for Further Education and Training, including national assessments and quality assurance systems. |
| Programme 5 | Higher Education | To provide strategic direction and to develop policy for an effective and efficient higher education system that contributes to fulfilling the human resource, research and knowledge needs of South Africa. |

**Source:** National Treasury (2003 a:293-294).

To recall, it was suggested above that basic education for children in South Africa can be defined as compulsory schooling from grade 1 to grade 9. It was further motivated that ECD be included in any analysis of government measures to advance children's right to basic education. From the description of national programmes in Table 6.6 above, it follows that the national Department of Education is primarily involved in the provision of basic education to children through policy development and monitoring. This is captured in the description of Programme 3 – General Education and Training (GET).[15]

**TABLE 6.7 CLASSIFICATION OF PROVINCIAL EDUCATION BUDGETS INTO PROGRAMMES**

| Programme number | Budget programme title | Purpose of programme (objective) |
|---|---|---|
| Programme 1 | Administration | To provide overall management and support to the education system. |
| Programme 2 | Public Ordinary Schools | To provide public ordinary school education from grades 1-12 in accordance with the South African Schools Act of 1996. Also to ensure funding in line with the national norms and standards for school funding. |
| Programme 3 | Independent School Subsidies | To provide a subsidy to all independent schools that qualify in terms of the criteria as provided for in the South African Schools Act and to monitor these schools' performance. |
| Programme 4 | Public Special School Education | To provide public education in special schools in accordance with the South African Schools Act of 1996 and White Paper 6 on inclusive education. |
| Programme 5 | Further Education and Training | To provide further education and training at public FET colleges, in accordance with the Further Education and Training Act of 1998. |
| Programme 6 | Adult Basic Education and Training | To provide adult basic education and training, in accordance with the Adult Basic Education and Training Act of 2000. |
| Programme 7 | Early Childhood Development | To provide early childhood education at the Grade R and earlier levels in accordance with White Paper 5. |
| Programme 8 | Auxiliary and Associated Services | To provide education institutions as a whole with support. |

**Note:** The descriptions of the purpose of programmes in the table above are very brief and do not represent an exact reflection of the purpose as stated in the different provincial budget books by each education department. This is because of the length of the list of objectives stipulated by different provinces and slight differences in detailed objectives across provinces.

**Source:** National Treasury (2003b:B7.5); Gauteng Provincial Government Budget 2003; Western Cape Provincial Government Budget 2003.

Table 6.7 includes four programmes that call for attention in order to track government's budgeting for the child's right to basic education, namely POS, ECD, SSE and ISS. However, the table also suggests that tracking expenditure on these programmes can only provide a rough guide to government's funding of the child's right to basic education. This is because the four programmes together do not capture all the funding from government that is spent on basic education for children and include some funding that is not spent on basic education for children. For example, over and above these four programmes, some of the funds allocated to GET in the national education budget are also spent on providing basic education to children. In addition, the four programmes are not limited to basic education for children: POS and ISS funds are also spent on schooling for grades 10, 11 and 12, which is not currently included in the definition of basic education in South Africa.

Sections 3.2 and 3.3 now take a more detailed look at government budgeting to advance the child's right to basic education, with a specific focus on the four provincial budget programmes identified above. The key points that emerge from the budgets are pulled out in the course of the analysis. These are then integrated into the concluding summary of government's programming for the right to basic education in section four.

## 3.2 MACRO VIEW: BUDGETS OF NATIONAL AND PROVINCIAL EDUCATION DEPARTMENTS

This section provides a broad overview of the education budgets of both spheres of government that are involved in financing and delivering education. To this end, Tables 6.8, 6.9 and 6.10 present information on:

- National government programme expenditure on education for 1999/00 to 2005/06;

- Consolidated provincial government programme expenditure for 1999/00 to 2005/06;

- Total consolidated national and provincial education expenditure for 1999/00 to 2005/06, including:

  * the expression of these figures as a share of consolidated national and provincial allocated expenditure (total expenditure less contingency reserve and interest payments) for the years 2002/03 to 2005/06; and

  * Real growth rates in national and consolidated provincial education expenditure for the years 2002/03 to 2005/06.

**TABLE 6.8 EDUCATION SPENDING OF NATIONAL EDUCATION DEPARTMENT BY PROGRAMME (1999/00 - 2005/06), IN R '000**

| Programme | Expenditure outcome | | | Revised estimate | Medium-term expenditure estimate | | |
|---|---|---|---|---|---|---|---|
| | 1990/00 | 2000/01 | 2001/02 | 2002/03 | 2003/04 | 2004/05 | 2005/06 |
| Administration | 48 823 | 49 851 | 61 694 | 63 688 | 81 090 | 105 859 | 112 521 |
| Planning & monitoring | 330 061 | 271 251 | 289 199 | 326 456 | 379 131 | 324 288 | 342 622 |
| GET | 29 048 | 86 247 | 136 896 | 291 110 | 357 107 | 222 565 | 235 446 |
| FET | 83 030 | 65 900 | 72 714 | 94 799 | 111 012 | 129 216 | 142 005 |
| Higher education | 6 619 640 | 7 084 975 | 7 543 343 | 8 045 318 | 8 954 500 | 9 702 596 | 10 328 868 |
| Total including conditional grants: | 7 111 602 | 7 557 954 | 8 103 846 | 8 821 351 | 9 882 840 | 10 484524 | 11 161 462 |
| ECD conditional grant | | | 21 000 | 53 000 | 88 000 | | |
| HIV/AIDS conditional grant | | 26 930 | 62 896 | 144 605 | 120 474 | 125 579 | 136 293 |
| Financial management conditional grant | 192 000 | 204 049 | 213 000 | 228 320 | 234 414 | 248 479 | 263 388 |
| **Total less conditional grants** | 6 919 602 | 7 326 975 | 7 806 950 | 8 395 426 | 9 439 952 | 10 107 466 | 10 761 781 |

**Source:** National Treasury (2003a:296, 320); Kuben Naidoo, National Treasury Budget Office (personal communication).

**TABLE 6.9 CONSOLIDATED PROVINCIAL EDUCATION SPENDING BY PROGRAMME (1999/00 - 2005/06), IN R MILLION**

| Programme | 1999/00 Actual | 2000/01 Actual | 2001/02 Actual | 2002/03 Estimated actual | Medium-term estimates 2003/04 | 2004/05 | 2005/06 |
|---|---|---|---|---|---|---|---|
| Administration | 2 644 | 2 472 | 3 479 | 3 780 | 4 328 | 4 574 | 4 832 |
| Public ordinary school education | 33 653 | 36 966 | 39 213 | 44 306 | 48 804 | 52 702 | 56 083 |
| Independent school subsidies | 176 | 206 | 187 | 196 | 235 | 245 | 253 |
| Public special school education | 1 116 | 1 134 | 1 356 | 1 446 | 1 595 | 1 665 | 1 764 |
| Further education and training | 754 | 827 | 869 | 1 082 | 1 201 | 1 276 | 1 360 |
| Adult basic education and training | 362 | 410 | 401 | 512 | 551 | 595 | 637 |
| Early childhood development | 199 | 197 | 248 | 449 | 510 | 538 | 591 |
| Auxiliary and associated services | 657 | 653 | 844 | 1 199 | 1 519 | 1 701 | 1 784 |
| Other programmes | 266 | 359 | 293 | 132 | 154 | 151 | 161 |
| **Total** | **39 828** | **43 223** | **46 889** | **53 102** | **58 897** | **63 447** | **67 465** |

**Source:** National Treasury (2003b:55).

**TABLE 6.10 CONSOLIDATED PROVINCIAL AND NATIONAL EDUCATION SPENDING – AMOUNT, REAL GROWTH AND AS A % CONSOLIDATED NATIONAL AND PROVINCIAL ALLOCATED EXPENDITURE (2002/03 - 2005/06)**

| | 2002/03 Estimated actual | Medium-term estimates 2003/04 | 2004/05 | 2005/06 |
|---|---|---|---|---|
| Consolidated national and provincial allocated expenditure (R million) | 262 980 | 297 352 | 323 699 | 351 942 |
| Consolidated national and provincial education expenditure (R million) | 61 497 | 68 336 | 73 554 | 78 226 |
| National (excluding conditional grants) | 8 395 | 9 439 | 10 107 | 10 761 |
| Provincial (including conditional grants) | 53 102 | 58 897 | 63 447 | 67 465 |
| Consolidated education expenditure as % of consolidated provincial and national allocated expenditure | 23.3% | 22.9% | 22.7% | 22.2% |
| **Real growth** (%) in: | | | | |
| National budget (excluding conditional grants) | | 5.4% | 2.0% | 1.4% |
| Provincial budgets (including conditional grants) | | 4.0% | 2.6% | 1.3% |

**Note:** To calculate the real values, GDP inflation rates given in Budget Review 2003 (National Treasury 2003c) were used, with 2002/03 as a base year. Deflator for 2002/03=1; 2003/04=1.066; 2004/05=1.118234; 2005/06=1.173027.

**Source:** Tables 6.6 and 6.7 above; National Treasury (2003c:155); and own calculations.

The following main points emerge from the macro view on education spending as presented in the tables above:

- Government expenditure on education represents a large proportion of total non-interest spending (allocated expenditure). More specifically, education absorbed 23.3% of consolidated national and provincial allocated spending in 2002/3. While the proportion declines slightly over the medium term, it remains high at 22.2% in 2005/06.

- Within consolidated national and provincial education spending, provincial education spending is by far the greatest.

- Over the MTEF period 2003/04 to 2005/06, both national and consolidated provincial spending are expected to grow in real terms, at first at a relatively rapid pace (5.4% and 2.0% respectively in 2003/04) and then at a slower pace.

## 3.3 ANALYSIS OF THE FOUR BUDGET PROGRAMMES MOST IMPORTANT FOR GIVING EFFECT TO CHILDREN'S RIGHT TO BASIC EDUCATION

This section undertakes a more detailed budget analysis of the four programmes that together provide the best indicator of budgeting for the right to basic education – namely POS, ECD, ISS and SSE. The section presents information on the following:

- Consolidated provincial expenditure on the four programmes as a share of consolidated national and provincial allocated and education expenditure for the years 2002/03 to 2005/06;

- Estimated real growth rates in the consolidated provincial expenditure on each of the four programmes and the four together for the period 1999/00 to 2005/06;

- Estimated expenditure and estimated real growth rate in expenditure on the four programmes for each province for the period 1999/00 to 2005/06; and

- Estimated expenditure on each of the programmes in each province as a percentage of the total estimated education expenditure in that province for the period 2002/03 to 2005/06.

### 3.3.1 CONSOLIDATED PROVINCIAL SPENDING ON POS, ISS, ECD AND SSE

Table 6.11 shows consolidated provincial estimated expenditure on POS, ISS, ECD and SSE for the period 2002/03 to 2005/06, expressed as a percentage of:

- Consolidated national and provincial education spending; and
- Consolidated national and provincial allocated expenditure.

The purpose of this exercise is to show the level of prioritisation attached to each of these four programmes, as well as the priority being enjoyed by the four programmes together as a proxy for spending on basic education as a whole in the near future.

**TABLE 6.11 SPENDING ON POS, ECD, ISS AND SSE AS A % OF CONSOLIDATED PROVINCIAL AND NATIONAL EDUCATION AND ALLOCATED EXPENDITURE (20002/03 - 2005/06)**

| | 2002/03 | Medium-Term | | |
| --- | --- | --- | --- | --- |
| | 2002/03 | 2003/04 | 2004/05 | 2005/06 |
| **Public Ordinary Schooling** | | | | |
| Amount (R million) | 44 306 | 48 804 | 52 702 | 56 083 |
| % of consolidated allocated expenditure | 16.85% | 16.41% | 16.28% | 15.94% |
| % of consolidated education expenditure | 72.05% | 71.42% | 71.65% | 71.69% |
| **Early Childhood Development** | | | | |
| Amount (R million) | 449 | 510 | 538 | 591 |
| % of consolidated allocated expenditure | 0.17% | 0.17% | 0.17% | 0.17% |
| % of consolidated education expenditure | 0.73% | 0.75% | 0.73% | 0.76% |
| **Independent School Subsidies** | | | | |
| Amount (R million) | 196 | 235 | 245 | 253 |
| % of consolidated allocated expenditure | 0.07% | 0.08% | 0.08% | 0.07% |
| % of consolidated education expenditure | 0.32% | 0.34% | 0.33% | 0.32% |
| **Special School Education** | | | | |
| Amount (R million) | 14 46 | 15 95 | 16 65 | 17 64 |
| % of consolidated allocated expenditure | 0.55% | 0.54% | 0.51% | 0.50% |
| % of consolidated education expenditure | 2.34% | 2.33% | 2.25% | 2.26% |
| **All four programmes** | | | | |
| Amount (R million) | 46 397 | 51 144 | 55 150 | 58 691 |
| % of consolidated allocated expenditure | 17.64% | 17.20% | 17.04% | 16.68% |
| % of consolidated education expenditure | 75.45% | 74.84% | 74.98% | 75.03% |

**Source:** Tables 6.6, 6.7 and 6.8 above; and own calculations.

From the data in Table 6.11, the following important points can be noted:

- Aggregate provincial expenditure on the four programmes that offer the best rough indicator of spending on basic education for children, constitutes a large proportion of consolidated national and provincial education expenditure for the years 2002/03 to 2005/06. There is a slight decline in the share – from 75.45% to 75.03% – between 2002/03 and 2005/06, but it is marginal. The share of spending on these four programmes in consolidated allocated expenditure is also relatively high across the period, though it declines from 17.64% to 16.68%. The high share of spending on these programmes within the total education budget and in consolidated national and provincial allocated expenditure suggests that government attaches priority to spending on the realisation of the right to basic education for children in South Africa.

- The large share of "spending on basic education for children" as indicated in the table above, is largely due to the size of spending on public ordinary schools and, to a lesser extent, on independent school subsidies.

- Special school education spending and early childhood development spending constitute a very small share of both consolidated national and provincial allocated expenditure and of education expenditure for the years 2002/03 to 2005/06. The share of aggregated provincial spending on ECD within consolidated national and provincial education expenditure is to increase slightly over the period 2002/03 to 2005/06. However, it still remains tiny, at less than 1% (0.76% to be exact). While the importance of ECD spending has thus been increasing, the data suggest that it is still not a key spending priority of government. This is of concern given the need to expand access to ECD facilities, as identified in section two above.

Figure 6.1 illustrates the real growth rate trend in the four programme budgets at the consolidated provincial level for the period 1990/00 to 2005/06.[16] The data on which this figure is based reveal the following important trends in the near future:

- For public ordinary schooling budgets, the real growth rates for 2003/04, 2004/05 and 2005/06 are 3.3%, 2.9% and 1.4% respectively;

- Special school education budgets show real growth rates of 3.5% for 2003/04, -0.5% for 2004/05 and 0.9% for 2005/06;

- For 2003/04, 2004/05 and 2005/06, the budgets for independent school subsidies show real growth rates of 11.9%, -1.02% and -0.7% respectively; and

- ECD budgets[17] reveal real growth rates of 6.79% in 2003/04, 0.75% in 2004/05 and 4.3% in 2005/06.

The data on the real growth in spending on the four programmes by all nine provinces together illustrate that of the four programmes, POS and ECD are expected to see the fastest and most consistent real growth in the near future. It can also be noted that the consolidated ECD provincial budget grew very rapidly in 2001/02. This reflects the introduction of the conditional grant to finance the implementation of the compulsory Grade R in 2001/02. There is a dip in the real growth rate of consolidated provincial ECD spending in 2004/05. This probably reflects failure by provinces to fill the gap left by the termination of the grant and adequately budget for ECD in 2004/05. The increase in the growth rate in 2005/06 implies that by that year, provinces may better rise to the challenge of filling the ECD funding gap left by the termination of the ECD Grade R conditional grant.

**FIGURE 6.1: REAL GROWTH RATES IN POS, ISS, SSE AND ECD BUDGETS SINCE 2000/01**

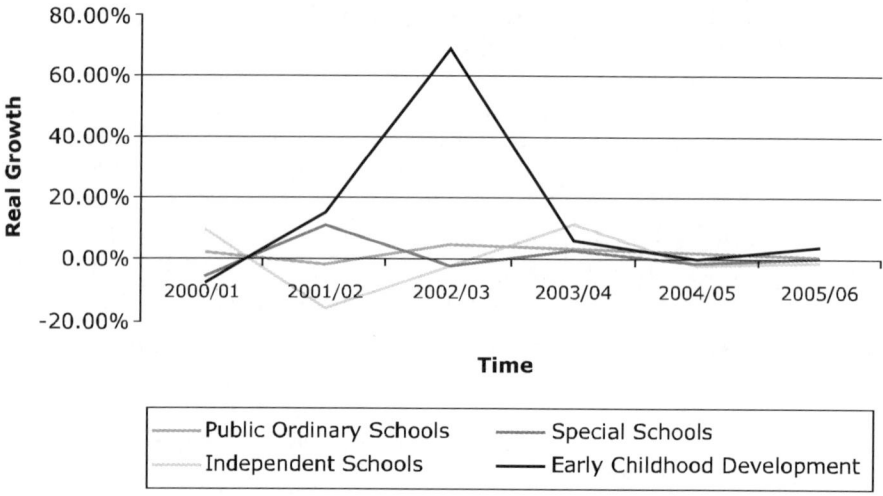

## 3.3.2 INTER-PROVINCIAL ANALYSIS: POS, ECD, ISS AND SSE BUDGETS IN EACH PROVINCE

In this sub-section, Tables 6.12 to 6.15 provide data on:

- The real growth rate[18] in spending on POS, ECD, SSE and ISS in each of the nine provinces for the period 1999/00 to 2005/06; and

- The prioritisation of each of the four programme budgets in each province, as reflected by estimated programme expenditure as a percentage of the estimated total provincial education expenditure for the period 2003/04 to 2005/06.

The four tables below present the relevant budget information for each of the four programmes in turn. The aim of this analysis is to tease out any significant differences in the real growth rate trend of all four programme budgets across provinces and in the proportion of POS, ECD, ISS and SSE in education spending in each province.

**TABLE 6.12 EXPENDITURE ON POS: TOTAL (IN R MILLION), REAL GROWTH RATE AND AS % OF ESTIMATED EDUCATION EXPENDITURE IN EACH PROVINCE**

| Province | 1999/00 | 2000/01 | 2001/02 | 2002/03 | 2003/04 | 2004/05 | 2005/06 |
|---|---|---|---|---|---|---|---|
| | Actual | Actual | Actual | Estimated actual | Medium-term estimates | | |
| **Eastern Cape** | 5904 | 6357 | 7078 | 8019 | 8441 | 9376 | 10126 |
| % of EC education expenditure | | | | 86.3% | 86.16% | 86.0% | 86.2% |
| Real growth | | 0.44% | 3.57% | 5.19% | -1.25% | 5.89% | 2.95% |
| **Free State** | 2312 | 2505 | 2611 | 2958 | 3271 | 3522 | 3780 |
| % of FS education expenditure | | | | 81.3% | 81.1 | 79.1 | 78.9 |
| Real growth | | 1.07% | -3.04% | 5.19% | 3.73% | 2.64% | 2.31% |
| **Gauteng** | 4967 | 5647 | 5438 | 6383 | 6823 | 7250 | 7627 |
| % of GT education expenditure | | | | 77.9 | 77.1 | 77.5 | 77.8 |
| Real growth | | 6.05% | -10.42% | 8.99% | 0.28% | 1.29% | 0.29% |
| **KwaZulu-Natal** | 6287 | 7177 | 7841 | 8890 | 10167 | 10862 | 11510 |
| % of KZN education expenditure | | | | 85.7 | 85.6 | 85.6 | 85.5 |
| Real growth | | 6.49% | 1.63% | 5.27% | 7.28% | 1.85% | 1.02% |
| **Limpopo** | 4835 | 5220 | 5553 | 6141 | 7014 | 7502 | 7867 |
| % of LMP education expenditure | | | | 83.1 | 82.4 | 82.8 | 82.8 |
| Real growth | | 0.71% | -1.04% | 2.68% | 7.14% | 1.96% | -0.03% |
| **Mpumalanga** | 2468 | 2660 | 2898 | 3368 | 3844 | 4155 | 4550 |
| % of MPL education expenditure | | | | 85.2 | 84.9 | 84.4 | 84.6 |
| Real growth | | 0.54% | 1.35% | 7.91% | 7.07% | 3.04% | 4.39% |
| **Northern Cape** | 781 | 841 | 864 | 883 | 992 | 1069 | 1159 |
| % of NC education expenditure | | | | 76.2 | 75.9 | 75.9 | 74.4 |
| Real growth | | 0.45% | -4.43% | -5.11% | 5.39% | 2.73% | 3.35% |
| **North West** | 2938 | 3229 | 3385 | 3746 | 4071 | 4501 | 4811 |
| % of NW education expenditure | | | | 86.4 | 85.3 | 85.8 | 86..1 |
| Real growth | | 2.52% | -2.48% | 2.75% | 1.95% | 5.40% | 1.89% |
| **Western Cape** | 3160 | 3330 | 3545 | 3917 | 4180 | 4465 | 4652 |
| % of WC education expenditure | | | | 81.5 | 81.4 | 81.9 | 81.9 |
| Real growth | | -1.70% | -0.97% | 2.59% | 0.11% | 1.83% | -0.68% |
| **All provinces** | **33652** | **36966** | **39213** | **44305** | **48803** | **52702** | **56082** |
| % of all provincial education expenditure | | | | 83.4 | 82.8 | 83.0 | 83.0 |
| Real growth | | 2.47% | -1.32% | 4.91% | 3.33% | 2.94% | 1.44% |

**Note:** To convert the nominal amounts into real amounts for the growth rate calculations, GDP inflation figures presented in the 2003 *Budget Review* (National Treasury 2003c) were used, with 1999/00 as a base year.
**Source:** National Treasury (2003b:Annexure A, Table A2.3 - A2.3.9); and own calculations.

Table 6.12 reveals a small variation in the exact proportion of POS spending in total education expenditure in each province. However, in all provinces POS is the main driver of education spending, with no province having less than 74% of its education spending dedicated to POS. There is hardly any movement in the share of POS in education spending in all of the provinces over the MTEF. The almost 2% decline in the Free State and Northern Cape appears as the most noteworthy shift. It is difficult to make general statements about the real growth rate trend in POS spending over the entire period 1990/00 to 2005/06 in each of the nine provinces. It is most important to highlight which of the provinces' POS budgets are expected to see the slowest real growth over the MTEF period 2002/03 to 2005/06. In this regard, the negative real growth rate in POS spending in the Eastern Cape in 2003/04 is cause for concern. The rate of real growth in POS spending in the Western Cape and Gauteng also appears to be lower than that of other provinces when the MTEF period is considered as a whole. In the Western Cape, the growth is barely positive in 2003/04 and negative in 2005/06. In Gauteng, it is barely positive in 2003/04 and 2005/06.

**TABLE 6.13 EXPENDITURE ON SSE: TOTAL (IN R MILLION), REAL GROWTH RATE AND AS % OF ESTIMATED EDUCATION EXPENDITURE IN EACH PROVINCE**

| Province | 1999/00 Actual | 2000/01 Actual | 2001/02 Actual | 2002/03 Estimated actual | 2003/04 Medium-term estimates | 2004/05 | 2005/06 |
|---|---|---|---|---|---|---|---|
| **Eastern Cape** | 92 | 82 | 129 | 173 | 197 | 184 | 196 |
| % of EC education spending | | | | 1.8 | 1.9 | 1.6 | 1.6 |
| Real growth | | -16.86% | 46.34% | 24.52% | 6.82% | -10.96% | 1.55% |
| **Free State** | 82 | 89 | 94 | 103 | 118 | 127 | 137 |
| % of FS education spending | | | | 2.8 | 2.9 | 2.8 | 2.8 |
| Real growth | | 1.25% | -1.75% | 1.74% | 7.47% | 2.60% | 2.84% |
| **Gauteng** | 329 | 321 | 413 | 406 | 421 | 442 | 464 |
| % of GT education spending | | | | 4.9 | 4.7 | 4.7 | 4.7 |
| Real growth | | -8.98% | 19.68% | -8.72% | -2.73% | 0.08% | 0.07% |
| **KwaZulu-Natal** | 145 | 155 | 191 | 211 | 235 | 250 | 266 |
| % of KZN education spending | | | | 2.0 | 1.9 | 1.9 | 1.9 |
| Real growth | | -0.28% | 14.63% | 2.57% | 4.48% | 1.41% | 1.43% |
| **Limpopo** | 74 | 77 | 87 | 97 | 119 | 126 | 133 |
| % of LMP education spending | | | | 1.3 | 1.4 | 1.3 | 1.4 |
| Real growth | | -2.93% | 5.10% | 3.52% | 15.08% | 0.94% | 0.62% |
| **Mpumalanga** | 46 | 51 | 53 | 50 | 69 | 73 | 77 |
| % of MPL education spending | | | | 1.2 | 1.5 | 1.4 | 1.4 |
| Real growth | | 3.42% | -3.33% | -12.41% | 29.46% | 0.86% | 0.55% |
| **Northern Cape** | 25 | 24 | 31 | 38 | 43 | 46 | 49 |
| % of NC education spending | | | | 3.3 | 3.2 | 3.2 | 3.1 |
| Real growth | | -10.45% | 20.16% | 13.82% | 6.15% | 1.98% | 1.55% |
| **North West** | 55 | 59 | 66 | 68 | 76 | 80 | 84 |
| % of NW education spending | | | | 1.5 | 1.5 | 1.5 | 1.5 |
| Real growth | | 0.07% | 4.06% | -4.34% | 4.84% | 0.35% | 0.10% |
| **Western Cape** | 267 | 276 | 294 | 301 | 319 | 338 | 358 |
| % of WC education spending | | | | 6.2 | 6.2 | 6.2 | 6.3 |
| Real growth | | -3.57% | -0.91% | -4.94% | -0.58% | 1.01% | 0.97% |
| **Total** | **1115** | **1134** | **1358** | **1447** | **1597** | **1666** | **1764** |
| % of total provincial education expenditure | | | | 2.7 | 2.7 | 2.6 | 2.6 |
| Real growth | | -5.13% | 11.40% | -1.06% | 3.53% | -0.55% | 0.94% |

**Note:** To convert the nominal amounts into real amounts for the growth rate calculations, the GDP inflation figures presented in the 2003 *Budget Review* (National Treasury 2003c) were used, with 1999/00 as a base year.

**Source:** National Treasury (2003b:Annexure A, Table A2.3 - A2.3.9); and own calculations.

As regards real growth rates in spending on SSE at the level of each province, two particular concerns emerge from the data in Table 6.13. These are the large real decrease in
spending on SSE in the Eastern Cape in 2004/05, as well as the real decrease in the
Western Cape in 2003/04. Aside from this, SSE budgets are generally expected to grow
at a slow but positive pace. The slow pace of growth in 2004/05 at the aggregate provincial level is largely attributable to the large contraction in spending on SSE in Eastern
Cape. The table reveals quite substantial variation in spending on SSE as a proportion of
spending on education. For example, Western Cape plans to spend a 6.3% share of its
education resources on SSE in 2005/06, while the Eastern Cape, Mpumalanga and
Limpopo have shares of only 1.6%, 1.4% and 1.4% respectively. This in part reflects the
distribution of special schools across provinces. For example, Western Cape is home to
the largest school for the visually impaired, located in Worcester.

**TABLE 6.14 EXPENDITURE ON ISS: TOTAL (IN R MILLION), REAL GROWTH RATE
AND AS % OF ESTIMATED EDUCATION EXPENDITURE IN EACH PROVINCE**

| Province | 1999/00 | 2000/01 | 2001/02 | 2002/03 | 2003/04 | 2004/05 | 2005/06 |
|---|---|---|---|---|---|---|---|
| | Actual | Actual | Actual | Estimated actual | Medium-term estimates | | |
| **Eastern Cape** | 9 | 11 | 11 | 19 | 17 | 17 | 18 |
| % of EC education spending | | | | 0.2 | 0.1 | 0.1 | 0.1 |
| Real growth | | 14.01% | -6.98% | 60.38% | -16.07% | -4.67% | 0.94% |
| **Free State** | 12 | 13 | 14 | 9 | 17 | 19 | 21 |
| % of FS education spending | | | | 0.2 | 0.4 | 0.4 | 0.4 |
| Real growth | | 1.06% | 0.18% | -40.31% | 77.19% | 6.54% | 5.36% |
| **Gauteng** | 98 | 117 | 102 | 103 | 117 | 117 | 117 |
| % of GT education spending | | | | 1.2 | 1.3 | 1.2 | 1.1 |
| Real growth | | 11.37% | -18.90% | -6.24% | 6.56% | -4.67% | -4.67% |
| **KwaZulu-Natal** | 17 | 24 | 17 | 20 | 26 | 28 | 30 |
| % of KZN education spending | | | | 0.1 | 0.2 | 0.2 | 0.2 |
| Real growth | | 31.69% | -34.11% | 9.24% | 21.95% | 2.66% | 2.14% |
| **Limpopo** | 6 | 6 | 8 | 9 | 14 | 15 | 17 |
| % of LMP education spending | | | | 0.1 | 0.1 | 0.1 | 0.1 |
| Real growth | | -6.72% | 24.03% | 4.46% | 45.92% | 2.14% | 8.04% |
| **Mpumalanga** | 8 | 11 | 5 | 3 | 9 | 9 | 10 |
| % of MPL education spending | | | | 0.08 | 0.2 | 0.1 | 0.1 |
| Real growth | | 28.26% | -57.72% | -44.29% | 181.43% | -4.67% | 5.92% |
| **Northern Cape** | 3 | 3 | 4 | 4 | 5 | 5 | 5 |
| % of NC education spending | | | | 0.3 | 0.3 | 0.3 | 0.3 |
| Real growth | | -6.72% | 24.03% | -7.15% | 17.26% | -4.67% | -4.67% |
| **North West** | 3 | 4 | 4 | 4 | 5 | 6 | 6 |
| % of NW education spending | | | | 0.09 | 0.1 | 0.1 | 0.1 |
| Real growth | | 24.38% | -6.98% | -7.15% | 17.26% | 14.39% | -4.67% |
| **Western Cape** | 19 | 17 | 22 | 26 | 25 | 28 | 30 |
| % of WC education spending | | | | 0.5 | 0.4 | 0.5 | 0.5 |
| Real growth | | -16.54% | 20.38% | 9.73% | -9.80% | 6.77% | 2.14% |
| **Total** | 175 | 206 | 187 | 197 | 235 | 244 | 254 |
| % of total provincial education spending | | | | 0.37 | 0.39 | 0.38 | 0.37 |
| Real growth | | 9.81% | -15.56% | -2.18% | 11.90% | -1.02% | -0.76% |

**Note:** To convert the nominal amounts into real amounts for the growth rate calculations, the GDP inflation figures presented in the 2003 *Budget Review* (National Treasury 2003c) were used, with 1999/00 as a base year.
**Source:** National Treasury (2003b:Annexure A, Table A2.3 - A2.3.9); and own calculations.

It is difficult to make any general statements about the real growth rate in expenditure on ISS at the provincial level for the period 1990/00 to 2005/06. Even if we consider only expected real expenditure growth for the years 2003/04 to 2005/06, it can be seen that growth rates vary substantially across provinces and years. In the aggregate, the average real expected growth rate in expenditure across provinces is positive but marginal, at less than 1% for the years 2003/04 to 2005/06. However, this does not say much about actual expected growth rates in each province. The expected proportion of spending on ISS in total provincial education spending is rather similar – at around 0.1 to 0.2% for the years 2003/04 to 2005/06 – across provinces. The exception seems to be the Western Cape and in particular Gauteng, which spend a larger proportion of their education budgets on ISS. For example, in Gauteng the share of ISS spending in provincial education spending is expected to be 1.3%, 1.2% and 1.1% respectively for the years 2003/04, 2004/05 and 2005/06.

Table 6.15 on the following page presents the provincial expenditure data on ECD. The first thing to note about the data on ECD expenditure is the zero spending recorded for 2001/02 in two provinces, namely Gauteng and Limpopo. As explained in endnote 19, the data in Table 6.15 apparently includes the ECD conditional grant funding from national government. Data on the allocation of the ECD conditional grant across provinces (see Appendix A) show that allocations were made to every province in the years 2001/02, 2002/03 and 2003/04. In light of this, the zero spending recorded in Limpopo and Gauteng appears peculiar. According to Kuben Naidoo (personal communication) from the Budget Office at the National Treasury, the zero for the two provinces may be explained by lack of spending in 2001/02 on the ECD funds allocated through the conditional grant mechanism.

The second important point to note from the data on ECD spending in each province is the low level of prioritisation generally given to ECD in provincial education budgets. This is reflected in the small size (on average just under 1%) of the proportion of ECD spending in total provincial education spending. Thirdly, however, there is also variation in the precise proportion of ECD spending in total education spending at the provincial level. For example in the Eastern Cape, the share is only 0.38% for 2005/06, whereas in North West, it is 2.72% and in Gauteng 1.05% for the same year. In general, ECD spending is to grow at a slow positive rate across provinces over the years 2003/04 to 2005/06, with a dip in the middle year (reflective of the termination of the ECD conditional grant). At the same time, there is also substantial variation in the precise growth rate in ECD spending expected in each province. For example, the Eastern Cape has negative growth in ECD spending for two of the years, as does the Western Cape and Mpumalanga. On the other hand, Free State has very high positive growth rates for the years 2004/05 and 2005/06. The negative growth rates in ECD spending in some provinces for some of the years are cause for concern in light of the need to expand access to ECD facilities across provinces and children's right to have access to these facilities.

**TABLE 6.15: EDUCATION EXPENDITURE ON ECD: TOTAL (IN R MILLION), REAL GROWTH RATE AND AS % OF ESTIMATED EDUCATION EXPENDITURE IN EACH PROVINCE[19]**

| Province | 1999/00 | 2000/01 | 2001/02 | 2002/03 | 2003/04 | 2004/05 | 2005/06 |
|---|---|---|---|---|---|---|---|
| | Actual | Actual | Actual | Estimated actual | Medium-term estimates | | |
| **Eastern Cape** | 4 | 6 | 3 | 39 | 40 | 43 | 45 |
| % of EC education spending | | | | 0.42 | 0.40 | 0.39 | 0.38 |
| Real growth | | 39.93% | -53.49% | 1107.06% | -3.79% | 2.48% | -0.24% |
| **Free State** | 9 | 11 | 10 | 22 | 18 | 35 | 57 |
| % of FS education spending | | | | 0.61 | 0.45 | 0.79 | 1.19 |
| Real growth | | 14.01% | -15.43% | 104.27% | -23.25% | 85.36% | 55.25% |
| **Gauteng** | 0 | 0 | 0 | 92 | 103 | 100 | 103 |
| % of GT education spending | | | | 1.12 | 1.16 | 1.07 | 1.05 |
| Real growth | | 0 | 0 | 0 | 5.02% | -7.45% | -1.81% |
| **KwaZulu-Natal** | 27 | 22 | 42 | 65 | 67 | 79 | 87 |
| % of KZN education spending | | | | 0.63 | 0.56 | 0.62 | 0.65 |
| Real growth | | -23.99% | 77.59% | 43.70% | -3.30% | 12.40% | 4.98% |
| **Limpopo** | 0 | 0 | 0 | 13 | 18 | 18 | 19 |
| % of LMP education spending | | | | 0.18 | 0.21 | 0.20 | 0.20 |
| Real growth | | 0 | 0 | 0 | 29.89% | -4.67% | 0.62% |
| **Mpumalanga** | 27 | 31 | 29 | 30 | 61 | 55 | 55 |
| % of MPL education spending | | | | 0.76 | 1.35 | 1.12 | 1.02 |
| Real growth | | 7.10% | -12.98% | -3.95% | 90.74% | -14.05% | -4.67% |
| **Northern Cape** | 7 | 6 | 8 | 11 | 12 | 13 | 16 |
| % of NC education spending | | | | 0.96 | 0.92 | 0.92 | 1.03 |
| Real growth | | -20.04% | 24.03% | 27.67% | 2.34% | 3.27% | 17.33% |
| **North West** | 98 | 93 | 128 | 127 | 137 | 141 | 152 |
| % of NW education spending | | | | 2.93 | 2.87 | 2.69 | 2.72 |
| Real growth | | -11.48% | 28.03% | -7.87% | 1.20% | -1.89% | 2.77% |
| **Western Cape** | 27 | 28 | 26 | 49 | 54 | 55 | 56 |
| % of WC education spending | | | | 1.02 | 1.05 | 1.01 | 0.99 |
| Real growth | | -3.26% | -13.62% | 74.99% | 3.38% | -2.91% | -2.94% |
| **Total** | **199** | **197** | **246** | **448** | **510** | **539** | **590** |
| % of total provincial education spending | | | | 0.84 | 0.86 | 0.84 | 0.87 |
| Real growth | | -7.65% | 16.16% | 69.09% | 6.79% | 0.75% | 4.35% |

**Note:** To convert the nominal amounts into real amounts for the growth rate calculations, the GDP inflation figures presented in the 2003 *Budget Review* (National Treasury 2003c) were used, with 1999/00 as a base year.

**Source:** National Treasury (2003b:Annexure A, Table A2.3 - A2.3.9); and own calculations.

# 4. CONCLUDING SUMMARY AND RECOMMENDATIONS

This part of the chapter recaps the main points that have emerged in sections 1 to 3 above. General education and training, early childhood development and education for learners with special needs are discussed in turn in sections 4.1 to 4.3 below. Finally, section 4.4 draws out the most important conclusions that can be highlighted across these programmes, focusing on policy and programme conceptualisation, as well as budgeting to advance the child's right to basic education.

## 4.1 GENERAL EDUCATION AND TRAINING (GET)

### 4.1.1 LEGAL AND POLICY FRAMEWORK

The legal and policy framework for the implementation of the right of the child to basic education exists and is, generally, satisfactory. It is not articulated, as previously indicated, in a manner that distinguishes the *child's right to basic education* from the right to education broadly, and generally collapses the child's right to basic education into general education and training.

This chapter has argued that the current legal framework identifies basic education as schooling from grades 1 to 9 – or between the ages of 7 and 15. Without conceding the view that it is constitutionally wrong to fix the cut-off point at age 15 for giving effect to the child's right to basic education, it remains nevertheless true that it would be better to fix it at age 17. Similarly, it would be better to extend the notion of basic education so as to include grade 12, rather than fix the outer line at grade 9. Furthermore, there is a need to clarify whether ECD (or at least the Grade R year) can be regarded as part of "basic education". While the guiding legislation seems to suggest grade 1 as the starting point, the Department of Education itself appears to understand ECD as a component of basic education. ECD is broadly accepted as a vital intervention for young children, at the same time enhancing their capacity to participate effectively in education once they begin formal schooling. From a child rights perspective, there is thus a strong motivation to focus on ECD in any efforts to advance children's right to basic education.

In terms of giving effect to the child's right to basic education, a principal weakness of the legal and policy framework is the failure to provide for free education. As previously argued, not only does this failure represent non-compliance with international and regional human rights instruments, it is also a contradiction in terms of South Africa's own legislation, which makes school attendance compulsory between ages 7 and 15 or up to grade 9, whichever occurs first. Education cannot be compulsory if it is not free since the law might then be commanding something that may well be impossible.

Both law and policy provide for exemptions and prevent learners from being excluded on the basis that their parents cannot pay user fees. However, this simply does not address the concern that basic education is not free in South Africa. Various studies show that the protection entailed in law and policy does not work in the intended way and learners are treated in ways that render the protection rather nugatory.

## 4.1.2 LEARNER/CLASSROOM RATIOS

The information in Table 6.1 suggests that there is a tolerable number of learners per classroom, with a national average of 37 learners per classroom. It suggests also that, with the exception of Mpumalanga, there has been some improvement, moving from the base year, 1996, through to 2000, with a national average drop of 6 learners per classroom.

I have argued elsewhere (Seleoane 2003:160-161) that the fact that there is an improvement in the learner/classroom ratio appears to be a lucky combination of contradictory factors. These are, on the one hand, the failure by parents to avail their children of the education opportunities that are present and on the other hand, the sheer will to receive education. These factors are indicated respectively by the fact that, in the year of the survey, school enrolment was 300 000 students lower than the base year (1996), and that a good number of students used shelters for classrooms. Some 2.6% of the structures that were counted as classrooms in the survey were not proper classrooms, but mere shelters.

Therefore, the fact that the national average number of students per classroom was satisfactory at the time of the survey should not lead to relaxation. If all children who should be in school were induced to go to school, as they should, the picture would change. It is suggested that planning should be premised on the assumption that children who should be at school, will be. There is therefore room for improvement in this area.

## 4.1.3 LEARNER/EDUCATOR RATIOS

Table 6.2 indicates an acceptable learner/educator ratio, with a national average of 1:32. It shows that, with the exception of Gauteng, Mpumalanga and the Western Cape, the ratio improved in the six other provinces over the period surveyed. As argued in section 2.1, the healthy learner/educator ratio is partly attributable to the fact that there was a whooping drop in enrolment figures and that, had the enrolment figures increased in line with demographic projections at the rate of 3%, the situation might be less colourful. It would appear, therefore, that while the situation is not disconcerting, there is yet room for improvement both in the provisioning of classrooms and of educators. Moreover, this does not even speak to the quality of educators and school buildings, but merely to the numbers.

## 4.1.4 BUDGETING FOR GET (AND THE RIGHT TO BASIC EDUCATION IN GENERAL)

Budgeting for GET and the child's right to basic education, it was argued above, takes place largely through allocations to and spending on POS, ISS, SSE and ECD. From the analysis of government's budgeting for basic education above, it became clear that basic education provision for children is prioritised in government's budgeting – even if there is no explicit linking of allocations to a programme to give effect to the child's right to basic education in the budget process. The prioritisation of spending on the child's right to basic education was reflected in the high proportion of spending on the four programmes, POS, ISS, ECD and SSE, in provincial and national consolidated allocated and education expenditure. It also emerged that in general, the programmes that are most important for delivering the child's right to basic education are to see positive but slow growth in the near future. In light of the large share of education spending – particularly on POS and ISS – in total government spending, it is unrealistic to expect the pace of real growth in spending on these programmes to grow much more quickly in the future. However, the low level of priority currently being afforded to ECD in education spending, and the need for ECD to reach more children in need, indicates that there is a real need for ECD spending to increase at a faster rate. Perhaps part of the extra allocations to ECD will have to be found through efficiency gains in other education programmes.

It is important to acknowledge that for some children, their inability to access schooling (and realise the right to basic education) is linked to a failure to realise other socio-economic rights – such as basic nutrition or social security (minimum income). Thus policy-makers and budgeters seeking to advance children's participation in basic education, face the critical challenge of developing a system that offers a remedy to this problem. This will probably involve a more explicit consideration of child rights in programming and budgeting by policy-makers and budgeting officials, as well as efforts to link spending on basic education to spending on the other socio-economic rights of children and their parents.

## 4.2 EARLY CHILDHOOD DEVELOPMENT (ECD)

It is clear from government pronouncements that early childhood development is crucial for the intellectual development of the child and therefore for the child's ability to derive full benefits from the constitutional guarantee of the right to education. This sub-section considers whether existing ECD programmes compare favourably with the importance assigned to this stage of the child's development.

### 4.2.1 LEGAL AND POLICY FRAMEWORK

Outside of general education and training, the state takes explicit responsibility for one year only of the child's early development, namely, the fifth or sixth, as the case might be, depending on when the child turns six or seven. What about the remainder of the period that the department itself recognises as being crucial to the development of the child's potential? The department's own definition of early childhood development gives a clue as to what its thinking on the matter might be:

> "Early childhood development ... refers to a comprehensive approach to policies and programmes for children from birth to nine years of age *with the active participation of their parents and care-givers.* Its purpose is to protect the child's rights to develop his or her full cognitive, emotional, social and physical potential.

> Consistent with our White Paper I on Education and Training ... and our Interim Policy for early Childhood Development ... we define early childhood development ... as an umbrella term that applies to the processes by which children from birth to at least 9 years grow and thrive, physically, mentally, emotionally, morally and socially" (emphasis added) (Department of Education 2001b:14-15).

The department repeatedly emphasises the role of the family and the community in early childhood development. It also refers to the importance of community-based services for early childhood development (Ibid:15).

It says, then, in effect, that the remainder of the period in early childhood development is at least in part the responsibility of the parent, care-giver or the community.[20] It cannot, in fairness, be expected that the family and the community be exonerated from their responsibility for the upbringing of the child and ensuring its balanced development and that the state must bear all the responsibility. However, the "integrated approach" that the department speaks about has to be spelled out more clearly if it must deliver the results envisaged in the White Paper.

As pointed out before, the department fears that, unless progress is made in addressing the conditions of poverty under which many children are raised, 40% of South Africa's children might suffer irreversible brain damage and stunted physical growth. In 1999, the South African Catholics Bishops' Conference issued a pastoral statement under the title *Economic Justice in South Africa*. The statement indicated that some 53% of the population of South Africa lives in conditions of poverty. A study undertaken by the South African Institute of Race Relations (1999:296) suggested that 36.6% of South African households lived on a monthly income of below R900 per month in 1999, whilst another 14.7% lived on a monthly income of less than R1400. The latter study also suggested that some 49.5% of South Africans of working age were unemployed. A SANGOCO study (1997) arrived at a similar figure.

These figures suggest that approximately at the time when the *White Paper on Early Childhood Development* was drawn up, many of the beneficiaries it targeted were indeed living in abject poverty. This fact is acknowledged by the White Paper itself. It must be considered whether the parents, care-givers, or even the community in which children grow up, has the resources to fulfil the role the White Paper envisages. The question therefore arises whether sufficient community-based services for early childhood development, as envisaged by the White Paper, exist for the majority of children in South Africa.

The department's assertion that the approach to early childhood development ought to be an integrated one that uses parents in the community is supportable, but it has implications for the conceptualisation of the problem that early childhood development programmes seek to solve. The problem itself must be conceptualised in an integrated way. It is not only a question of the development of the children themselves, but of their milieu as well, and this much the department itself asserts. In other words, if the early development of children is assigned in part to their parents, care-givers and communities, the question must arise whether they have the wherewithal to do the job. Motala *et al* (1999:8) indicate that there are "between 9 million and 12.5 million adults in South Africa who are functionally illiterate" and that in "the poorest provinces illiteracy rates top 70%".

The question must arise, therefore, as to what it means to acknowledge, as the department does, that the first seven years of the child's life are critical to its intellectual formation, and then resign itself to five or six of those being left in the hands of some 12.5 million adults who themselves often did not enjoy the right to education. It seems clear that, without external intervention, many families have limited banked knowledge and experience to play an active role in some dimensions of early childhood development and often lack the more formal literacy skills to prepare children for schooling from Grade R onwards.

One year does not seem to be sufficient to reverse the intellectual damage that the department itself points out children in poor surroundings are exposed to. Therefore, the education department's policy to make only one year in this period its priority seems to present difficulties that, in effect, militate against what it seeks to achieve. If the department wishes to have parents, care-givers and the community play a meaningful role in the intellectual formation of children, it has to recognise the extent of adult literacy in South Africa. It has to empower parents, care-givers and the community to play the role it envisages for them. Motala *et al* write:

> "[O]nly a very small portion of the national education budget is spent on Adult Basic Education and Training... – in [the] 1998/1999 financial year, 0.8% of the national education budget was allocated to ABET. Furthermore, ABET is one of the first areas to face cuts when provinces face a financial squeeze. In the Eastern Cape, for example, 432 ABET centres were closed down in 1998. In 1999 ABET funding has declined in Mpumalanga, Northern Cape and KwaZulu-Natal. The intermittent provision of ABET in the state system, and the increasing financial burden placed on learners – increasingly learners are obliged to pay for tuition, learning materials and examination fees – make it particularly difficult for adults who live in rural areas, and for women and the unemployed, to take part in literacy education."

With reference to the 1997/98 education budget, Fair Share (1997) wrote that the state projected an annual expenditure of 31c per illiterate person in South Africa. If the arguments above are accepted, it seems to follow not only that an overwhelming number of parents, care-givers and members of the community are ill-equipped for the role the state envisages for them, but also that this state of affairs is likely to define South African society for many years to come. It also suggests that the state is not doing nearly enough to remedy the situation and that, therefore, the expectation it has of parents, care-givers and the community is not well founded.

It is suggested that two options are open to the state. The Constitution binds it to give effect to the right to basic education for adults, and the right is not encumbered by resource constraints. The state expects adults to fulfil an important function in respect of the right of children to basic education, which the state itself acknowledges is contingent on what happens to children in the first seven years of their lives. It would therefore not be unreasonable to expect that the state would facilitate ABET fully. It is not unreasonable to suppose that the state's integrated approach to early childhood development would entail equipping those it expects to help advance the development of children with the tools required to do the job. Towards this end, it is not only important for government to become more actively involved in creating opportunities for adults to develop their literacy. Job creation (or direct income support) in poor communities is also crucial.

Although it is doubtful that, from the standpoint of the Bill of Rights, adult and children's education should be conceived of as alternatives, another option for the state would be to substantially expand its role in the advancement of early childhood development. It is certainly not an option, within the South African context, for the Department of Education to take express responsibility for only 14% of the period when the child's intellectual formation is most critical.

## 4.2.2 EARLY CHILDHOOD DEVELOPMENT FACILITIES

The audit of early childhood development sites (Williams *et al* 2001) indicated that there were approximately six million children in the age group 0 to 6 years in South Africa in 2001. Of these, approximately one million, or 17%, were enrolled at an ECD centre. Clearly the situation is far from satisfactory, with 83% of children who should be in an ECD centre being left out of the loop.

Proceeding on the basis that there are six million children who should be at an ECD centre, and that there are 23 842 ECD centres countrywide, this means that the ratio of candidates to centres is, as previously stated, 256:1. This seems to clearly indicate that there aren't nearly enough ECD facilities in South Africa.

It has also been noted that some 83% of the ECD centres in South Africa are not school-based. This raises the question whether the educators providing ECD services are qualified for the job they do. The audit surveyed 48 561 ECD service providers and found that:

- 5 620 (12%) were qualified;
- 7 563 (15%) were under-qualified;
- 3 615 (7%) were non-ECD qualified;
- 20 730 (43%) were NGO-trained; and
- 11 033 (23%) had no training.

Therefore only 12% of those who provide ECD services nationally are qualified for the job. It is suggested that this is incompatible with the role the state envisages for ECD service providers and, as previously argued, that the state ought to equip them with the tools to do the job it envisages for them.

### 4.2.3 BUDGETING FOR EARLY CHILDHOOD DEVELOPMENT

The main point that emerged from the analysis of ECD spending in section 3 above is the need for all provinces, but particularly poorer ones such as the Eastern Cape, to step up funding of ECD facilities. This should be done in a way that not only ensures that funds can be spent, but also does not focus on Grade R to the exclusion of younger children. Furthermore, future plans to extend more financial resources to ECD would ideally have to take into account that often it is failure to realise other basic rights – such as the right to basic nutrition and parents and children's right to a minimum income – that prevents access to basic education and ECD.

## 4.3 LEARNERS WITH SPECIAL NEEDS

### 4.3.1 LEGAL AND POLICY FRAMEWORK

A reading of section 2.3 will indicate that there is a well-developed legal and policy framework in respect of learners with special needs. There is also a well-articulated plan of action.

### 4.3.2 SCHOOLS FOR LEARNERS WITH SPECIAL NEEDS

According to the *White Paper on Special Needs Education* (Department of Education 2001c:13), there are 380 special schools in South Africa, catering for some 64 603 learners.[21] According to the *Report on the School Register of Needs* (Department of Education 2000b:89):

- The 1996 census revealed that only 14.8% of children of school-going age with disabilities attended school. Although there might be other explanations for the high number of such children not being in school, the possibility cannot be discounted that many are out of school because of learning facilities not being readily available. For instance, throughout the country, there are only three schools for visually disabled learners, one for the deaf and blind, two for the hard of hearing and three for children suffering from epilepsy.

- Of the existing schools for learners with special needs, 36.4% cater for learners that have mental disabilities. Such children, however, comprise only 6.7% of children with disabilities in South Africa. Children who are visually impaired, on the other hand, make up 37.9% of children with disabilities and yet only 2.3% of the schools registered for learners with special needs are dedicated to them.

If these facts are examined against the directive of the Constitutional Court in *Grootboom*, it becomes clear that there is a problem. The court ruled that it is not enough to have policies and programmes in place – the policies and programmes must be *well-directed*. It seems quite clear in this case that the schools that are registered to serve learners with special needs are not well-directed, since their distribution by type does not seem to take into account the demographics of the population they are designed for.

## 4.4 GENERAL CONCLUSION AND RECOMMENDATIONS

### 4.4.1 POLICY AND PROGRAMME CONCEPTUALISATION

The available information on government measures to advance the child's right to basic education seems to suggest that, while the programming, policy and legislation framework is satisfactory in some respects, there is still scope for improvement. There is, for instance, a clear need to make basic education available free of charge. Government itself appears to appreciate this need. As noted in this chapter, Deputy Minister Mangena argues that, while basic education might not be free as a matter of law, it is in fact free in the light of all the services that the state provides and pays for. The department's recognition of the need for free basic schooling is further manifest in the legal and policy measures that bar learners from being sent away or otherwise treated unfavourably as a result of their parents being unable to pay user fees at public schools. It is also reflected in the department's policy that provides for full or partial exemption from user fees for those learners whose parents are poor.

Against this background, it is hard to see why government resists providing basic education for free. This resistance becomes even more difficult to understand when one considers that some of South Africa's neighbours that are much less well-endowed, are in fact doing so — Mozambique being but one example.

Further, government's laws and policies on the right of the child to basic education do not always seem consistent with one another. The laws and policies dictate that basic education shall be compulsory. Government itself suggests that approximately 40% of South Africa's children are raised in poverty and this percentage may well be substantially higher (see chapter one of this book). The point is that government realises that there is a high proportion of learners in South Africa who live and grow up in poverty. It stands to reason that for these children, compulsory education must remain meaningless. Their parents are in all probability unable to pay for their education, even if they had the inclination to obey the policy and legislative directive to ensure that their children are at school up to the prescribed age or grade. Providing basic education for free would resolve the contradiction.

Government recognises as a serious challenge the fact that over 300 000 children who should be in school are not accessing their right to education. Yet it is another striking misfortune that the Department of Education has no pronounced programme to ensure that these children find their way back to school.

As argued in this chapter, there is also a need to clarify whether the right to basic education includes the right to participate in early childhood development, and if so, from what age. While the importance of ECD is acknowledged at a policy level, it remains unclear what exactly children are entitled to in terms of this fundamental stage of educational development.

A recommendation that flows from this chapter and the poverty analysis in chapter one is the need for government to design and implement inter-sectoral strategies or programmes that consider more than budget allocations and spending in the education sector itself in an effort to assist those children prevented from realising their right to basic education due to poverty. If all children in South Africa are to be in a position to claim their right to basic education, then strategies must be put in place to ensure that children who cannot go to school due to lack of sufficient income at the household level – for basic goods such as food, transport and clothing – get access to these goods. In order to remain true to its obligation to deliver basic education to all children in South Africa, there is thus a need for government to consider the extension of further programmes giving effect to other basic child socio-economic rights and to the basic socio-economic rights of parents, such as the right to a minimum income.

At the level of programme conceptualisation and policy, a final recommendation that emerged from this chapter is the need for government to focus more on the early years of ECD in its conceptualisation of ECD. In addition, it is essential for government's Adult Basic Education and Training and job creation strategies to be linked more explicitly to its strategy for providing ECD in poor communities. Effective provision of ECD, particularly pre-Grade R, is heavily dependent on adult literacy and children living in communities where income is sufficient to meet basic needs.

## 4.4.2 BUDGETING

The budget analysis found that it is difficult to rigorously track government spending on the child's right to basic education. This is because there is no explicit system or programme for linking a particular programme, budget allocations and spending to the state's constitutional obligation to realise the right to basic education. Nevertheless, a consideration of spending on the four programmes, POS, ECD, SSE and ISS, can provide a good rough indicator of government's spending on the child's right to basic education.

Spending on the child's right to basic education was found to be prioritised in government spending. At the same time, the budget analysis showed that in the allocation of funds to programmes giving effect to the child's right to basic education, there is a need to give more emphasis to ECD, and not only Grade R. Increased provincial allocations to ECD are needed, particularly in light of the termination in 2003/04 of the conditional grant for ECD from national government. The challenge of stepping up investment in ECD is greater in some provinces, for example in the Eastern Cape. Additional funds for ECD must not come at the cost of fewer funds being available for spending on other education programmes that are important for giving effect to the child's right to basic education unless of course, they are released through efficiency gains.

A final need identified in this chapter is for government – perhaps National Treasury in conjunction with the National Department of Education – to think about formulating a system in the official budget documentation to facilitate keeping a better track record of government's programming and budgeting for the child's right to basic education.

# REFERENCES

Alston, P. (1998) "Economic and Social Rights in the International Arena". In *Economic and Social Rights Review,* 1(2), June.

Bekker, G. (2000) "The Right to Education in the South African Constitution". In Mashavha, L.V. (ed), *A Compilation of Essential Documents on the Right to Education: Volume 2.* Pretoria: Centre for Human Rights.

Bentley, K. (2002) *Can there be any universal children's rights? Some considerations concerning relativity and enforcement.* Unpublished paper available from Human Sciences Research Council.

Cape High Court. (1997) *B and Others v Minister of Correctional Services and Others.* 1997(6) BCLR 789 (C).

Cape High Court. (1999) *Grootboom v Oostenberg Municipality and Others.* Case No.6826/99, BCLR 2000(3) 277.

Constitutional Court. (1996) *Ex parte Gauteng Provincial Legislature: In re Dispute Concerning the Constitutionality of Certain Provisions of the Gauteng School Education Bill of 1995.* 1996 (3) SA 165 (CC).

Constitutional Court. (2000) *Government of the Republic of South Africa and Others v Grootboom and Others.* 2001(1) SA 46 (CC) 2000(11) BCLR 1169 (CC).

Constitutional Court. (2002) *Minister of Health and Others v Treatment Action Campaign and Others.* 2002(5) SA 721 (CC), 2002 (10) BCLR 1033.

Craven, M.C.R. (1995) *The International Covenant on Economic, Social and Cultural Rights.* Oxford: Clarendon Press.

Department of Education. (1995) *White Paper on Education & Training.* Published in the Government Gazette, 357 (16312), General Notice No 196 of 1995. Pretoria: Government Printer.

Department of Education. (1996) *South African Schools Act.* Act No 84 of 1996. Pretoria: Government Printer.

Department of Education. (2000a). *Adult Basic Education and Training Act.* Act No 52 of 2000. Pretoria: Government Printer.

Department of Education. (2000b) *Report on the School Register of Needs Survey.* Pretoria: Government Printer.

Department of Education. (2001a) *Education in South Africa: Achievements since 1994.* Pretoria: Government Printer.

Department of Education. (2001b) *Education White Paper 5: Early Childhood Education.* Published in the Government Gazette (436) 22756, 17 October. Pretoria: Government Printer.

Department of Education. (2001c) *Education White Paper 6: Special Needs Education.* Pretoria: Government Printer.

Department of Foreign Affairs. (Undated) *Position with Regard to Human Rights Treaties.* Unpublished document distributed on the occasion of the 50th anniversary of the UDHR on 10 December 1998.

Fair Share. (1997) *Key Concepts about the 1997/98 Budget and the Macro-economic Plan (GEAR).* Cape Town: Fair Share.

Kriel, R.R. (1996) "Right to Education". In Chaskalson, M. *et al, Constitutional Law of South Africa.* Cape Town: Juta.

Liebenberg, S. & K. Pillay (eds). (2000) *Socio-Economic Rights in South Africa: A Resource Book.* Cape Town: Community Law Centre, University of the Western Cape.

Malherbe, E.F.M. (1997) *Reflections on the background and contents of the education clause in the South African Bill of Rights.* TSAR 1997 (1).

Meyerson, D. (1997) *Reading the Constitution through the Lens of Philosophy.* Cape Town: University of Cape Town.

Ministry of Education. (2003a) *Media briefing by Minister Kader Asmal on Education Department Budget Vote 2003/2004.* 20 May.

Ministry of Education. (2003b). *The Review of the Financing, Resourcing and Costs of Education in Public Schools.* Press release dated 18 February.

Motala, S., S. Vally & M. Modiba. (1999) "A Call to Action: A Review of Minister K. Asmal's Education Priorities". In *Quarterly Review,* 6 (3), 15 September.

National Treasury. (2001) *Budget Review.* Pretoria: Government Printer.

National Treasury. (2003a) *Estimates of National Expenditure.* Vote 15: Education. Pretoria: Government Printer.

National Treasury. (2003b) *Intergovernmental Fiscal Review.* Pretoria: Government Printer.

National Treasury. (2003c) *Budget Review.* Pretoria: Government Printer.

NAP Project Steering Committee. (1998) *The National Action Plan for the Promotion & Protection of Human Rights.* Pocket-size version.

Provincial Treasuries. (2003) *Provincial Estimates of Expenditure.* The estimates of expenditure for each province are available from the relevant provincial treasury.

Republic of South Africa. (1996) *The Constitution of the Republic of South Africa Act.* Act 108 of 1996.

Roux, T. (Undated) *Understanding Grootboom – A Response to Cass R Sunstein.* Unpublished paper available from the Centre for Applied Legal Studies, University of the Witwatersrand.

Rule, P. (Undated) *"The time is burning":* *The Right of adults to basic education in South Africa.* Unpublished draft paper available from the Education Rights Project, Wits University.

Seleoane, M. (2003) "The Right to Education: Lessons from Grootboom". In *Law, Democracy & Development,* 7(1). Lexis Nexis Butterworths.

South African Institute for Race Relations. (1999) *South African Survey 1999: Millennium Edition.* Johannesburg: SAIRR.

South African National Coalition of Non-governmental Organisations (SANGOCO). (1997) *NGO Matters,* 2(9), August.

*Sowetan.* (2003) "Fees plan is a ploy". 20 June.

Streak, J and Wehner, J. (2002) *Budgeting for Socio-economic Rights in South Africa: The Case of the Child Support Grant Programme.* Applied Fiscal Research Centre Research Monograph Series, 24. Available from AFReC at the University of Cape Town.

Vally, S. (2001) "Fundamentals of Education and the Right to Basic Education". In *Quarterly Review,* December. Johannesburg: Education Policy Unit, University of the Witwatersrand.

Williams, T. *et al.* (2001) *The Nationwide Audit of ECD Provisioning in South Africa.* Pretoria: Department of Education.

Wilson, S. & B. Ramadiro. (2002) *Report on the Education Rights Project workshop with the Soweto Electricity Crisis Committee.* Unpublished document. 5 December.

Wildeman, R. (2003) *Reviewing provincial education Budgets 2003.* Budget Brief. Cape Town: Idasa Budget Information Service. Available at http://www.idasa.org.za/bis/.

## APPENDIX A

### TABLE 6.16 CONDITIONAL GRANT FOR ECD BY PROVINCE (2001/02 - 2003/04), IN R '000

| | 2001/02 | 2002/03 | 2003/04 |
|---|---|---|---|
| Eastern Cape | 3 885 | 9 620 | 16 280 |
| Free State | 1 323 | 3 276 | 5 544 |
| Gauteng | 2 583 | 6 396 | 10 824 |
| KwaZulu-Natal | 4 641 | 11 492 | 19 448 |
| Mpumalanga | 1 533 | 3 796 | 6 424 |
| Northern Cape | 399 | 988 | 1 672 |
| Northern Province | 3 297 | 8 164 | 13 816 |
| North West | 1 680 | 4 160 | 7 040 |
| Western Cape | 1 659 | 4 108 | 6 952 |
| **All provinces** | **21 000** | **52 000** | **88 000** |

**Source:** National Treasury (2001:267); National Treasury (2003d:17).

## ENDNOTES

1   I am grateful to Professor Sandy Liebenberg for kindly allowing me to borrow from data that were gathered for a study commissioned by the Community Law Centre, UWC. The budget analysis section of this chapter, section 3, was conducted by Judith Streak with assistance from Lerato Kgamphe and written by Judith Streak. I would also like to thank Faranaaz Veriava for comment on an early draft of this chapter.

2   The child's right to family or parental care is given in section 28(1)(b) of the Constitution. The child's rights to basic nutrition, shelter, basic health care and social services are afforded in section 28(1)(c). Children are protected against maltreatment, neglect, abuse and degradation by section 28(1)(d). Section 28(1)(e) sets out the child's right to be protected from exploitative labour practices.

3   *Ex parte Gauteng Provincial Legislature: In re Dispute Concerning the Constitutionality of Certain Provisions of the Gauteng School Education Bill of 1995* 1996 (3) SA 165 (CC). Although this judgment related to the right to basic education in section 32 of the Interim Constitution (Act 200 of 1993), it is equally apposite to a construction of section 29(1)(a) of the 1996 Constitution, owing to similar drafting.

4   1997(6) BCLR 789 (C).

5   2000(3) BCLR 277 (C).

6   *Ibid* 290G – J – 291A – C.

7   Section 36 is the general limitations clause. It provides that any right mentioned in the Bill of Rights may be limited by a law of general application, provided the conditions stipulated in section 36 are satisfied.

8   *Government of the Republic of South Africa and Others v Grootboom and Others* 2001(1) SA 46 (CC) 2000(11) BCLR 1169 (CC) par 33.

9   *Minister of Health and Others v Treatment Action Campaign and Others* 2002(5) SA 721 (CC), 2002 (10) BCLR 1033, pars 26-39.

10   It may be noted that the text referred to in this footnote also canvasses the propriety of burdening the right to basic education with resource constraints through a process of interpretation, whilst the Constitution has not encumbered the right with such constraints.

11   See also Meyerson (1997:1-3) where she discusses the problem of subjectivity in the context of rights limitation.

12   The relevant part of the paper is concerned with defining "an adult", but it should follow that the obverse would apply to "the child".

13   The figures include both educators paid by the state and those paid by school governing bodies.

14   It may be noted in passing that the obligation as formulated by the department flows more from the South African Schools Act, than from the Constitution. It is the act, not the Constitution, which stipulates the number of compulsory school-going years.

15   According to Kuben Naidoo from the Budget Office in the National Treasury, the conditional grant for ECD is slotted under the allocation to the GET programme in the budget information provided in the *National Estimates of Expenditure* (see Table 6.8).

16   To convert the nominal budget data into real values, the GDP inflation estimate was used as provided by National Treasury in *Budget Review* 2002 for 2000/01 and *Budget Review* 2003 for the remaining years of the period analysed (see National Treasury 2002; National Treasury 2003c). 1999/00 has been used as the base year.

17   The ECD conditional grant funding is included in the ECD programme budget as portrayed in figure 6.1. The data are taken from the 2003 *Intergovernmental Fiscal Review* (National Treasury 2003b), which according to Kuben Naidoo from National Treasury Budget Office, includes conditional grant funding.

18   1999/00 was used as a base year for the conversion into real values. For an explanation of the inflation rates used for the conversion, see endnote 16.

19   This ECD programme spending data, which is from the 2003/04 *Intergovernmental Fiscal Review* (National Treasury 2003c), apparently includes the ECD conditional grant funding (Kuben Naidoo, Budget Office, National Treasury).

20   Early childhood development clearly not only involves the delivery of education services. In addition to interventions that promote intellectual and skills development in young children, ECD is seen to include measures that advance children's broad well-being, including health, nutrition, physical care, and cultural and social development. Besides the Department of Education, other government departments and institutions are therefore seen to play a crucial role in ECD programme development, budgeting and provisioning. The *White Paper on Early Childhood Development* (Department of Education 2001b: Section 5) identifies a number of critical role-players in ECD delivery before the Grade R year. These include the Department of Social Development, the Department of Health, local governments (which provide numerous childcare facilities and funding to NGOs who provide ECD services), as well as the ECD priority group of the National Programme of Action for Children, located in the office of the Presidency.

21   There appears to be a discrepancy between the White Paper and the *Report on the School Register of Needs 2000 Survey* (Department of Education 2000b). According to the report, there were 390 schools for learners with special needs in South Africa

in the year 2000 and 78 123 learners. It is tempting to put the discrepancy down to the data having been gathered at different times. However, when it is taken into account that the White Paper is dated July 2001, it seems it should be citing higher figures than the report.

# CONCLUSION

Judith Streak[1]

The immediate objective of this publication has been to evaluate government's progress in implementing child socio-economic rights, focusing on the unqualified rights afforded to children in the Constitution. Part of this task was to highlight challenges (primarily, but not only, for government officials and researchers) relating to the advancement of these rights. The ultimate objective is for the research presented in this book to work as a tool to advance child rights. Towards this end, this concluding summary draws together the main findings of the book, following the structure of the preceding chapters as follows:

- Section one reviews the main points relating to the child poverty crisis as presented in chapter one. It also recaps the inferences drawn out in this chapter regarding government's own strategy for reducing child poverty and realising children's socio-economic rights.

- Section two summarises the most critical insights derived from chapter two of the book. It briefly recounts the actors responsible for realising children's socio-economic rights, as well as the main strategies used by government to meet its socio-economic rights obligations from 1994 to 2003. The discussion then turns to our current understanding of the content and scope of unqualified constitutional child socio-economic rights, as well as the associated state obligations. Finally, section two recaps how the current understanding of child socio-economic rights and state obligations was used as a basis to derive a monitoring method for this publication.

- Section three of the conclusion presents the main findings of chapters three to six of the book. It looks across these four chapters to draw out important information and insights regarding the meaning of the child's right to basic nutrition, basic health care services, social services and basic education. It considers the programmes put in place by government to advance these rights, focusing specific attention on the sufficiency of the programmes selected for detailed analysis in each chapter.

# 1. THE CHILD POVERTY CRISIS AND ITS IMPLICATIONS FOR POLICY

To gain perspective on the child poverty crisis, chapter one uses quantitative indicators supported by household survey data (in the form of the 2000 Income and Expenditure Survey and 1999 National Food Consumption Survey). This picture of child poverty in South Africa is supplemented with qualitative information gathered from children living in poverty and/or difficult circumstances.

Two quantitative indicators are used to shed light on the scale and distribution of child poverty, namely income and food insecurity (hunger). Looking first at data on children who are poor in the sense that they lack sufficient income, the chapter found the following:

- When a high poverty line of R430/month per capita (in 2000 rands) was applied, 74.8% of South Africa's children were revealed as income poor in 2000. Of these income poor children, 60% were concentrated in three provinces, namely KwaZulu-Natal, the Eastern Cape and Limpopo.

- When a lower poverty line of R215/month per capita (in 2000 rands) was used, 54.2% of children emerged as income poor.

- A consideration of absolute income poverty lines used by other researchers suggests that the two poverty lines above may be a little on the high side. There is also known under-reporting of income in the 2000 Income and Expenditure Survey. These two factors imply that the estimates presented in chapter one may be a little inflated. Other money-metric-based measurements of child poverty in the recent past have found between 28% and 75.8% of children to be poor, depending on the poverty line and household survey data used in the analysis.

Having said this, the food insecurity indicator analysis found the scale and distribution of child poverty to be similar to the results presented in chapter one, based on the 2000 Income and Expenditure Survey. Looking at data on children who are poor in the sense that they lack sufficient food, the chapter reported the following:

- At the national level, 52% of children age 1 to 9 years (4.6 million children) experienced hunger in 1999. A further 23% were at risk of hunger.

- Therefore, if poor children are classified as those experiencing hunger and at risk of hunger, the food insecurity analysis suggests that 75% of South Africa's children are poor. Using Census 2001 estimates of children aged 0 to 17 in South Africa, this implies 13 million poor children.

The qualitative research presented in chapter one draws from the perspectives of four groups of children who were discriminated against or marginalised for a variety of reasons. Their views on their own experiences of poverty and their access to services remind us that poverty entails a complex mix of suffering, where basics such as education and adequate food often become luxuries. This research also revealed that poverty spans a range of different forms of suffering. These do not only include hardship linked directly to insufficient command over commodities and services – such as hunger, inadequate food and shelter, insufficient access to income, social assistance and health care services and an inability to attend school. While these aspects of poverty remain important, children experiencing poverty in South Africa tell us that it is also about suffering from discriminatory practices, social exclusion and vulnerability linked to their economic situation.

Critically from a policy perspective, the child participation research illustrates that most of the children understand their situation to be directly linked to the precarious economic situation of their parents (or alternative care-givers). This, in turn, relates directly to limited job opportunities (high unemployment) or in the case of farm children, the low wages of farm workers. It also shows that the inability of many poor children to access certain services and meet some basic needs (such as schooling), is linked to an inability to access other services and meet other basic needs (such as basic nutrition and/or social assistance). In other words, the non-realisation of one basic socio-economic right is linked to the failure to realise another. Some children who participated in the research, for example those living in a shelter in Cape Town, found themselves in a situation where they had to trade non-socio-economic rights – such as the right to parental care and a family life – in order to realise their basic socio-economic rights.

The perspective on child poverty gained through the dual lenses of indicators and participatory research made it clear that after ten years of democracy, there is still an urgent need for government to enhance the effectiveness of its strategy to eradicate child poverty and realise socio-economic rights. The following pointers emerged from the child participation research to inform the way government goes about conceptualising and implementing more effective programmes to give effect to child socio-economic rights:

- It is essential for government to continue implementing the set of programmes it has designed to deliver basic and other social services to children. However, due to the inter-dependence of different socio-economic rights, it is important for these measures to be conceptualised and implemented as an integrated set of programmes. For example, it is no use having a programme to provide compulsory basic education when children do not have the material means to access schooling due to income poverty.

- Even when good programmes are in place to realise particular children's rights and basic needs – such as health care services and education – insufficient income, and linked to this, transport, often prevents access to services. This highlights the importance of further investment in infrastructure, such as roads in remote poor areas, and of extending the reach of social assistance and job-creation programmes for poor children and their families.

- There is a need to re-consider the criteria of programmes directed at children, so as to ensure that all children in need are included and that discriminatory implementation practices are put to an end.

- Children should not have to realise their socio-economic rights at the expense of other rights given to children in section 28 of the Constitution. This implies a need for government to design and implement programmes to realise children's socio-economic rights in tandem with programmes to realise the socio-economic rights of their parents (or alternative care-givers).

- The majority of children participating in the research were not sufficiently informed about their rights or how to claim them. There is thus a need to include outreach and awareness-building elements in government's strategy to realise child socio-economic rights.

# 2. CHILD SOCIO-ECONOMIC RIGHTS IN THE CONSTITUTION AND A METHOD TO MONITOR IMPLEMENTATION

Chapter two of this book provides a conceptual and methodological framework to guide the analysis in the rest of the publication. The critical aim of the chapter is to derive a method for monitoring government's progress in meeting its obligations in relation to children's unqualified constitutional socio-economic rights.

In order to inform the framework, the chapter first gives an overview of children's socio-economic rights in South Africa and considers who is responsible for translating these rights into practice. The following key points emerge in this regard:

- The South African Constitution (1996) entrenches a comprehensive set of justiciable socio-economic rights for children.

- Sections 26 and 27 of the Bill of Rights give everyone rights relating to housing, health care, food, water and social security (including social assistance).

- Section 28, which deals specifically with children's rights, affords all children the rights to basic nutrition, basic health care services, shelter and social services.

- Section 29 affords everyone the right to basic and further education.

- The socio-economic rights in the Constitution are coupled with particular state obligations. The Constitution obliges the state to "respect, protect, promote and fulfil" constitutional rights. It also defines the roles of the different components that make up the state in advancing constitutional rights, including the legislature, the executive and the judiciary.

- With regard to the latter, the Constitutional Court plays a particularly important role in working to advance child socio-economic rights, by checking government compliance with socio-economic rights obligations, ensuring appropriate relief when a right has been breached and helping to clarify the scope and content of rights.

- The rights given to everyone in sections 26 and 27, as well as the right to further education, are qualified in that the state has to take reasonable legislative and other measures, within its available resources, to achieve the progressive realisation of each of these rights.

- The socio-economic rights of children in section 28(1)(c) and the right to basic education in section 29(1)(a) are unqualified.

- The socio-economic rights of South African children are further protected by the democratic government's ratification (in 1996) of the Convention on the Rights of the Child and the African Charter on the Rights and Welfare of the Child (in 2000).

- A number of actors have a legal or constitutional obligation to advance children's socio-economic rights: these include the state, parents and the Human Rights Commission.

- Several other actors play a significant role in advancing child socio-economic rights, even though they do not have a legal or constitutional obligation to do so. These include the private sector, rights-bearers (or children themselves) and their care-givers, civil society child rights researchers and child rights advocates, and international bodies such as the United Nations Committee on the Rights of the Child.

- The distinction between actors with legal obligations and those without implies that the efforts of the former should be measurable and subject to monitoring with reference to their legally defined obligations. This is a critical point that underpins the development and application of the kind of monitoring tool explored in this publication.

- Due to pervasive and severe poverty in South Africa, many parents are unable to meet their constitutional obligations to provide for their children's basic needs. In this context, government has an elevated role in advancing child socio-economic rights by conceptualising and implementing programmes that provide services to meet the basic needs of children and their care-givers.

## 2.1 GOVERNMENT'S BROAD APPROACH TO REALISING CHILD SOCIO-ECONOMIC RIGHTS BETWEEN 1994 AND 2003

Against the background above, the discussion in chapter two turns to a consideration of government's two leading development strategy statements since 1994 – namely the Reconstruction and Development Strategy (RDP) of 1994 and the Growth, Employment and Redistribution (GEAR) Strategy of 1996. The RDP was very ambitious and optimistic about the potential for government to reduce poverty quickly through financing and implementing a broad range of programmes to deliver basic and social services to the poor. The GEAR strategy also stressed the importance of spending on programmes delivering services to the poor as a means to alleviate poverty. However, it emphasised that for sustainability purposes, this channel had to play second fiddle to job-creation through private investment. The GEAR strategy linked rapid poverty reduction (and by implication, the realisation of socio-economic rights) to conservative macro-economic policy, in the form of budget deficit reduction and restrictive monetary policy. It also stressed the need for institution-building at the level of the state to enhance the efficiency of spending and delivery capacity.

The most important findings and recommendations flowing from this section can be summarised as follows:

- In spite of a heavy reliance on the market mechanism to reduce poverty and a conservative fiscal stance between 1996 and 2000, the democratic government has put an extensive array of direct measures in place to give affect to child socio-economic rights. These include many legal reforms relating to child rights and child poverty, as well as the financing and implementation of a broad range of programmes aimed at giving the poor (including poor children) services to meet their basic needs.

- At the same time, it is difficult to pin-point and keep a record of the plethora of programmes put in place to advance child socio-economic rights. An important challenge is therefore for government to develop and put in place a system linking its programming and budgeting to its constitutional obligations as regards children (and others). The Constitution sets up, through its rights articles, benchmarks against which government must direct and evaluate its programming and budgeting. In the 1990s, government put in place the National Programme of Action for children (NPA), an umbrella co-ordinating mechanism that aims to ensure that children and child rights are prioritised in policy, budgets and service delivery. However, there is as yet, in practice, no systematic process for prioritising child-specific and other socio-economic rights in government's policy formulation, budget allocation process or programme implementation. This is a crucial challenge for government budgeting, programme system design and monitoring in the future.

- To push the pace of realising child socio-economic rights in the future, it is important to focus on the opportunities and challenges left by the GEAR policy and economic legacy. As chapter one of this book illustrated, there can be no doubt that GEAR left extensive and deep poverty in its wake.

- Government has made remarkable progress in extending social assistance: by 2003, over half of those in need were estimated to be accessing a state grant. However, fiscal discipline and implementation problems meant that there were still huge gaps in the coverage of the social assistance network. Half of those people in need of income support still do not have access to any income from the state, mostly because of exclusion from eligibility for a grant, but also due to implementation failures.

- The further advancement of socio-economic rights, including those of children, is heavily dependent on government developing more direct measures (such as job-creation and social assistance programmes) in the near future. South Africa faces a structural unemployment crisis. Despite improved conditions for attracting private sector investment, this mechanism cannot be relied upon to generate many jobs for the poor.

- The public sector debt-reduction and budget deficit reform initiatives implemented in the late 1990s under the auspices of GEAR, have placed government in a better position to facilitate the realisation of child socio-economic rights as we move into the future. There are still complex administrative and human resource capacity constraints in the public sector. However, public sector administrative capacity has seen improvement and government's financial position is more conducive to raising the level of government spending.

- Finally, in the post-GEAR implementation period – since 2000 – government's development strategy has shown a number of new aspects, which are positive for the challenge of advancing child socio-economic rights more quickly. These include explicit reference to the realisation of socio-economic rights as a driving goal of development strategy, a more expansionary fiscal stance with priority being given to government spending on infrastructure and services for the poor, as well as greater commitment to expanding direct measures of support for the poor – including job-creation projects and social assistance programmes.

## 2.2 THE SCOPE AND CONTENT OF CHILDREN'S UNQUALIFIED SOCIO-ECONOMIC RIGHTS AND THE STATE'S OBLIGATIONS TO ADVANCE THEM: CURRENT UNDERSTANDING AND THE SEARCH FOR CLARITY

Perhaps the most important point emerging from this study is the current lack of clarity around scope and content of the unqualified child socio-economic rights in the Constitution. Linked to this, there is a corresponding need to clarify the precise details of the obligations on the state (including government) to deliver these rights. The precise details of what children can claim from the state under their unqualified constitutional socio-economic rights necessarily evolves over time. It is the outcome of a process of dialogue in society, led by national and international law and jurisprudence (particularly Constitutional Court jurisprudence) and augmented by the views of researchers, activists and policy-makers. It is imperative for the rapid advancement of child socio-economic rights that urgent attention is given to this matter. The lack of understanding about what which children are entitled to claim from government by way of sections 28(1)(c) and 29(1)(a) makes it difficult for government to formulate effective implementation  strategies. It is virtually impossible to deliver something satisfactorily if you do not know the exact specifications of what it is that you are expected to deliver. The lack of clarity also undermines the formulation of rigorous monitoring methods that are aimed at holding the state accountable for its actions.

In order to inform the development of a monitoring framework, chapter two seeks to provide a general view of the current status of understanding on the scope and content of constitutional child socio-economic rights, focusing on unqualified rights. There has recently been a lot of debate over the scope of the unqualified socio-economic rights given to children in the Constitution. Views have included the progressive stance (coming from the High Court's judgement in the *Grootboom* case) that poor children – and through them their parents – are covered by the unqualified right to shelter in section 28. From here, they have ranged to the conservative stance taken by the Constitutional Court in the *Grootboom* case, that only children living without their parents are covered by the rights in an unqualified manner. The dominant perspective (supported by the Constitutional Court in the *Treatment Action Campaign* case) currently is that the unqualified nature of children's section 28 socio-economic rights extends, at the very least, to cover all children in need (including poor children living with their parents). The problem with the latter interpretation is that it leaves the door open for poor children to be separated from their parents in order for their basic socio-economic rights to be met.

As regards the content of the unqualified socio-economic rights afforded to children in the Constitution – and associated state obligations – several key questions remain answered. These include the following:

- How does the level of the entitlement given to children by section 28 rights differ from the level of entitlements given to everyone (including children) in sections 26 and 27? Do the rights given to children in section 28 translate into only an attenuated or basic level of services? Linked to this, what constitutes the precise entitlements stipulated in the sections?

- When it comes to government's duty to deliver, what is the implication of the wording of the Constitution, whereby the socio-economic rights in section 28 are formulated as "rights to" and those in sections 26 and 27 are formulated as "rights to have access to"?

- Is social assistance included in the right to social services given in section 28? Is government under a higher level delivery obligation to provide children with social assistance under section 28 or is it only obliged to take reasonable and other measures, within available resources, to realise children's right to social assistance under section 27?

- What does it mean for the state's obligations that the rights in section 28(1)(c) and 29(1)(a) are unqualified? Does it mean that all children in need have a direct claim against the state for services to give effect to the rights immediately, regardless of (financial and administrative) resource constraints? Would such an interpretation be practical? If not, what then can litigators demand for children in need? How do we guard against government postponing the delivery of children's socio-economic rights on the basis of resource and time constraints?

- How do we relate government's obligations to child socio-economic rights in section 28(1)(c) and 29(1)(a) to the children's qualified socio-economic rights in the Constitution?

The Constitutional Court has yet to make a judgement on government's fulfilment of its obligations to realise any of the unqualified rights given to children in section 28(1)(c) and 29(1)(a). In the meantime, the search continues for clarity around what children in need can claim from the state under these rights. A view, which can be seen as the current dominant opinion, has recently been put forward by a group of human rights legal experts. It draws from the Constitutional Court's judgements (in the *Grootboom* and *TAC* cases) on government's performance in delivering the qualified socio-economic rights in the Constitution (see the 2002 report by Creamer).

In this view, government is obliged to deliver the rights given to children in sections 28(1)(c) and 29(1)(a) as a matter of priority. Furthermore, in testing government's compliance with its obligations, the Constitutional Court would in all probability apply the reasonableness review paradigm that it used to assess compliance with section 26 and 27 rights in the *Grootboom* and *TAC* cases. However, the unqualified nature of the state's obligations in relation to child socio-economic rights implies that the court would be likely to apply a *higher standard* of reasonableness in assessing programmes for the advancement of these rights. It suggests that the state should be held accountable for putting in place, as a matter of priority, programmes to realise the socio-economic rights given to children in sections 28(1)(c) and 29(1)(a). Moreover, government in this view also has the obligation to cater for *all children in need* in such programmes and to roll out services from relevant programmes as a matter of urgency and as quickly *as the building of administrative capacity permits* (irrespective of financial considerations).

Notwithstanding the merits of this view, chapter two highlights a number of concerns relating to this interpretation of the state's obligations to deliver unqualified child socio-economic rights:

- It implies that, instead of having a direct claim against the state for something tangible under their unqualified constitutional socio-economic rights, children can only claim a reasonable programme (that passes the higher level reasonable measures test), one that may or may not (in the face of real world administrative constraints) result in the short-term realisation of their relevant basic rights.

- It makes it very difficult and time-consuming to prove, through litigation, that government is not fulfilling its obligations to a particular child or group of children.

- The higher level reasonable measures test is not easily transported out of the court room and into a method that can be applied by researchers to evaluate government's achievements and shortcomings.

- It leaves open the important question of what level of services children can claim from the state, whether through a reasonable programme or a direct claim.

## 2.3 A METHOD FOR MONITORING GOVERNMENT'S IMPLEMENTATION

The monitoring method developed in chapter two was influenced by (though not exclusively based on) the three-step logical sequence suggested by Creamer in his report. It calls for a three-stage analysis of government's actions. Section five of chapter two presents Creamer's suggested sequence and sets out the monitoring framework used to guide the analyses in chapters three to six of this book.

The monitoring framework includes six questions for analysing the sufficiency of specific programmes government has put in place to advance a particular child socio-economic right. The selection of these questions was based on a consideration of the dominant, yet unclear, current view of government's legal obligations to give effect to unqualified child socio-economic rights (as put forward in the Creamer report). It was also informed by the need to generate information that is useful – that is, information that can help policy-makers and implementers to improve budgeting and programming for child socio-economic rights. Finally, it took into account what questions could practically be addressed by researchers in the face of capacity, data and time constraints. As pointed out in the introduction to this publication, it is crucial for the advancement of child socio-economic rights that such methods are developed further in future, guided by an improved understanding of state obligations, the needs of poor children, as well as the insights of child rights activists and policy-makers.

# 3. MONITORING GOVERNMENT'S MEASURES FOR ADVANCING UNQUALIFIED CHILD SOCIO-ECONOMIC RIGHTS: KEY FINDINGS

## 3.1 THE MEANING OF THE CHILD'S RIGHT TO BASIC NUTRITION, BASIC HEALTH SERVICES, SOCIAL SERVICES AND BASIC EDUCATION

In chapters three to six, the various authors grapple with the meaning of the child's right to basic nutrition, basic health services, social services and to basic education. Their discussions reflect the lack of clarity about the content and scope of unqualified child socio-economic rights, as well as the associated state obligations to deliver these rights. At the same time, they make important contributions to the debate by putting forward arguments, both about the current understanding of these rights and about how it could – or should – be expanded in future.

Three of the four chapters examine a right given to children both in section 27 and in section 28 of the Constitution. Chapters three, four and five all highlight, in diverse ways, the differences and tensions between children's section 27 and section 28 socio-economic rights. The following key points are made:

- An important finding emerging from these chapters is the need to understand children's entitlements and the state's obligations as operating on two levels: the entitlements and *qualified* obligation under section 27 and the entitlements and *unqualified*, higher level obligation under section 28. These two sections of the Constitution confer on children a range of different entitlements that intersect and overlap with each other.

- As regards the child's right to basic nutrition, chapter three draws attention to the fact that section 27(1)(b) affords children, along with everyone, the right to have access to sufficient food. This right, it argues, entitles children to require the state to take measures that are reasonably capable, within the resources that are available, which will allow them to gain access to food over time. This entitlement is limited in the sense that children cannot under this right claim immediate and direct access to food from the state. The right to basic nutrition in section 28 on the other hand, is much less attenuated. In terms of their section 28 rights, children can require the state to ensure that they receive at least that level of nutrition that enables dignified survival and basic physical and mental development.

- Likewise, the examination of child health rights in chapter four highlights the difference in formulation between sections 27 and 28. It calls for greater clarity on the meaning of the right to have access to health care services (as afforded in section 27), as opposed to the child's right to basic health care services (as given in section 28). The authors argue that the right of children to basic health care services in section 28(1)(c) was included in the Constitution for a purpose. The formulation of section 28 suggests that the intention was to afford special protection for children's rights. In resolving the tension between sections 27 and 28, chapter four proposes that preference should thus be shown for an interpretation that favours the promotion and protection of children's rights.

- When it comes to the right of the child to social security, the difference in formulation between section 27 and section 28 is even more stark and perplexing. Section 27 explicitly gives children, along with everyone, the right to social security and when appropriate, social assistance. As is the case above, this right is however subject to limitations and does not translate into children having an immediate claim for these services against the state. Section 28, on the other hand, while not subject to limitations, simply affords children the right to "social services". Chapter five stresses the importance of ascertaining whether the right to social assistance is included within the right to social services afforded to children in section 28(1)(c).

- The discussions in chapters three, four and five all echo the view, as expressed by Creamer, that there is a higher duty on the state to deliver children's section 28 socio-economic rights, as opposed to the (qualified) socio-economic rights of everyone as afforded in section 27.

Chapter six draws attention to the fact that the right to basic education as set out in section 29 of the Constitution, like the children's socio-economic rights in section 28, is similarly free of limitations. The child's right to basic education, it argues, should be understood as unconditional. Given then, that the state has a higher duty to realise the child's rights to basic nutrition, basic health care services, social services and basic education, what can this "higher duty" be understood to amount to? What are children entitled to by virtue of their section 28 rights and what can the state be expected to do in order to meet its obligations? The four monitoring chapters in this volume raise the following points in this regard:

- Chapter three suggests that the duty on the state to deliver children's section 28 right to basic nutrition does not only include taking steps to facilitate parents or family members realising the right. It also requires of the state to provide for the nutritional needs of those children whose parents or family members are unable to care for them. The latter duty is to be met by the state both by supporting parents and family members in their efforts to provide for the nutritional needs of their children and in appropriate cases, by providing food directly to children. However, the chapter cautions against interpreting the unqualified nature of the section 28 right as placing a duty on the state to deliver irrespective of resource constraints. This is because it is impossible to place a duty on the state that it is at times impossible to meet. Instead, it should be seen as a duty to prioritise the nutritional needs and rights of children in nutrition policies, programmes and budgetary allocations. Perhaps controversially, Brand argues further that by implication, children's basic survival nutritional needs should be given precedence over other broader societal, economic and political demands. He also suggests that at least children's basic survival nutritional needs should be given precedence over the food needs of other people.

- Against this background, chapter three goes a step further by identifying two critical areas of activity through which the state must fulfil its nutritional obligations: it must ensure both the availability of food, as well as access, or actual entitlement, to food. To create actual entitlement to food for children, the state must firstly facilitate access to food by making it possible for reasonably self-sufficient parents to obtain food for themselves and their families. In addition, in some circumstances, creating entitlement to food amongst children might include the direct provision of food or the resources with which to acquire food to children and/or their care-givers. Finally, children's food rights imply a need for the state to have measures to ensure that existing entitlement to food is in fact effective and that government's measures can be monitored.

- In discussing the nature of the entitlements and the duty on the state in relation to children's right to basic health care services, chapter four draws attention to the need to reach consensus on exactly what package of services could be seen to make up "basic health care services". While current policy documents tend to emphasise access to primary health care, the authors argue that basic health care should be seen as a broader concept than primary health care. Chapter four motivates for adopting a broad definition of the right to basic health care services, such as the one developed by the World Health Organisation, in order to define the meaning of the right enshrined in section 28(1)(c). This definition regards "health" as including all dimensions of children's lives and requires a comprehensive inter-sectoral approach to delivering services that advance children's health rights.

- Looking towards the child's right to social services, chapter five concurs that section 28 should be seen to place a duty on the state to prioritise the delivery of social services to children. Moreover, the authors suggest that the obligation should be understood in terms of the higher standard reasonable measures test. Crucially, Cassiem and Kgamphe point out that domestic law – and in particular the White Paper for Social Welfare in South Africa – suggests that government accepts that the objective of social assistance is to ensure a decent standard of living for all people, and in particular, for children. This implies that a key challenge for giving effect to children's right to social assistance is deciding what "a decent standard of living for children" consists of and what this implies about what level of income children with different needs should be entitled to from the state. Chapter five also points out that the derivation of services from children's constitutional right to social assistance must ensure that the following five rights-based criteria are met: universality, comprehensiveness, just administration, adequacy and appropriateness, as well as equality.

- As regards the child's right to basic education, chapter six looks towards South African legislation and international rights instruments to define what children are entitled to by virtue of this right. The chapter suggests that the unconditional nature of the child's right to basic education places a positive duty on the state. This means the state not only has a duty to refrain from taking measures that hamper the child in obtaining basic education, but furthermore is constitutionally bound to provide the things that are necessary in order for the child to receive basic education. Seleoane finds that the child's right to basic education is most appropriately understood, within the current legal context, to include schooling from grades 1 to 9. The chapter argues that an important project for the future is consider the expansion of this definition of basic education to include grades 10 to 12, as well as early childhood development (not only Grade R). The chapter also illustrates that while basic education has been made compulsory in South Africa, it is not free. This catch-22 situation seriously undermines the child's right to basic education as in many instances, poverty and the non-realisation of other rights – such as the rights to basic nutrition and a minimum income – prevents children from accessing basic education.

- Finally, in defining the level of entitlements implied by the unqualified child socio-economic rights, all four chapters draw attention to the importance of acknowledging the inter-dependence between the realisation of different child socio-economic rights. In the same vein, they also highlight the close correlation between realising children's socio-economic rights and those of their care-givers.

## 3.2 PROGRAMMES THAT GIVE EFFECT TO THE RIGHTS TO BASIC NUTRITION, BASIC HEALTH SERVICES, SOCIAL SERVICES AND BASIC EDUCATION

Government's unqualified obligations to give effect to children's constitutional rights to basic nutrition, basic health care services, social services and basic education include the duty to put in place programmes to advance the rights. The second step in the monitoring method called for researchers to ask whether programmes had indeed been put in place to realise these rights.

In all four chapters, the authors found that there were a range of government programmes in place to give effect to the child socio-economic rights examined in this book. These included programmes targeting the provision of services to children and to poor families or households (with the exception of children's right to basic education, where the programmes were all child-specific). The list of programme titles generated by the findings across all four chapters is too long to present here. However, to reflect the democratic government's achievements in this regard, the table below sets out the number of programmes delivering child-specific services and services for poor families, which were identified as effecting each of the rights. Due to the inter-dependence between the socio-economic rights of children, on the one hand, and on the other, between the socio-economic rights of children and adults, there was some overlap across the chapters in the programmes identified.

**NUMBER OF GOVERNMENT PROGRAMMES (PROVIDING SERVICES TO POOR CHILDREN AND TO POOR PEOPLE) IDENTIFIED AS EFFECTING UNQUALIFIED CHILD SOCIO-ECONOMIC RIGHTS**

| Unqualified constitutional child socio-economic right | Programmes targeted specifi- cally at children | Programmes targeted generally at poor families | Total programmes giving effect to the right |
|---|---|---|---|
| Basic nutrition | 5 | 10 | 15 |
| Basic health care services * | 9 | 10 | 19 |
| Social services | 6 | 4 | 10 |
| Basic education** | 3 | | 3 |
| **The four rights** | **23** | **24** | **47** |

Note:

\* In the identification of measures giving effect to children's right to health care services in chapter four, programmes and policies were identified. This count includes both.

\*\* In the education chapter, the author noted that according to national government officials, no pro-grammes have the specific objective of realising the right to basic education. Thus, the figures presented here must be seen as a count of the number of programmes that can be seen to give effect to the right – and not of programmes specifically designed to realise the right to basic education.

The high number of programmes identified is testimony to the positive contribution of government to the advancement of child socio-economic rights over the first ten years of democracy. However, when looking within and across the chapters at the range of programmes and services offered to children (and considering the poverty and structural unemployment crisis), it is also noteworthy that gaps emerge. In this regard, of most concern is the absence of a programme offering universal income support (either through a direct income transfer, food vouchers or public works) to adults who are unemployed and the failure of government's child-targeted social assistance programmes to cater for children of all ages who are in need. Another noteworthy absence is a programme aimed at implementing measures to ensure that out-of-school children are placed back into schools.

## 3.3 THE SUFFICIENCY OF SOME KEY PROGRAMMES GIVING EFFECT TO THE CHILD'S RIGHT TO BASIC NUTRITION, BASIC HEALTH SERVICES, SOCIAL SERVICES AND BASIC EDUCATION

This section of the conclusion mirrors the third step of the monitoring method derived in this publication to highlight achievements and challenges in government's measures to advance the unqualified constitutional socio-economic rights of children. This step involves analysing the sufficiency of a number of selected programmes that government has put in place to give effect to the rights. Broadly speaking, in addition to briefly describing the programme's objectives, services and target audience, the programme sufficiency analysis asks for the spotlight to be placed on the following:

• Asking whether the programme has been conceptualised and implemented in such a way that all children in need can be reached, further as a matter of urgency and as quickly as administrative capacity permits;

- Scrutinising programme budgets, focusing on real growth, the programme budget as a proportion of consolidated provincial and national government spending, as well as actual versus allocated expenditure; and

- Highlighting the challenges in the programme (both in its conceptualisation and its implementation) which need to be addressed to speed up service delivery, reach all children in need and hence maximise the impact of the programme on the relevant right.

The exact manner in which step three of the monitoring was conducted, differed across the four monitoring chapters, reflecting the authors' own specialist skills (be they legal, budget, and/or sector-specific) and data constraints. This part of the conclusion seeks to draw together the findings on programme sufficiency from the analyses in the four monitoring chapters. To this end, the summary below identifies the programme(s) interrogated in each of the chapters and highlights the key findings, focusing on achievements and the three aspects of the programme sufficiency analysis outlined above.

Chapter three provides a sufficiency analysis of the Primary School Feeding Scheme (PSFS) programme. The most important findings emerging from this exercise are as follows:

- The conceptualisation of the PSFS programme was found to be sound (including its targeting of poor children), even though it only has limited potential as a mechanism to realise children's right to basic nutrition. The programme is conceptualised with the primary objective of enhancing the ability of school-going children to participate effectively in education and has the secondary objective of improving children's nutrition status. It cannot, on its own, serve as vehicle to realise children's right to basic nutrition in any substantial way and is not conceptualised to do so.

- In terms of implementation achievements – including budgeting – government has expanded the reach of the programme by rolling out services (an early morning meal to children between the ages of seven and fourteen) to an increasing number of schools, across all provinces. When the programme was first implemented in 1994/95, it reached 15 911 schools. By 2002/03, 16 441 were being serviced by the programme. According to government officials, there are hardly any new schools applying for coverage in the programme which could meet the programme's criteria for access. In expanding the reach of the programme, efficiency has been enhanced in terms of targeting and reaching schools and children in need, and in terms of spending programme budget allocations. While 100% spending of funds across all provinces has yet to be achieved, there has been dramatic improvement over time across all provinces in spending the total amount allocated to the programme through the conditional grant that finances it.

- There are two main challenges for the PSFS programme on the implementation front. Firstly, in most provinces the type of meal provided to children does not match the list of menu options set by national government, which is meant to be

used as a guide by provincial health departments and non-governmental implementation agencies. A key challenge is thus for the meal offered to be brought
more in line with national government's criteria and to ensure that it realises the
objective of providing not less than 25% of the recommended daily allowance
(RDA) of energy for 7 to 10 year olds and not less than 20% of the RDA of
energy for 11 to 14 year olds. Secondly, there is a need to ensure that the efficiency and effectiveness of the programme are not compromised when the provincial education departments take over the management and implementation of the
PSFS in 2004/05.

- An important conceptualisation challenge for the PSFS programme is for the recording of budget allocation and spending data to change, so that its budget implementation can be tracked more efficiently. In 1997/98 the name of the programme
  changed from the Primary School Nutrition Programme (PSNP) to the PSFS. At
  the same time, the funding of the programme was no longer sent by national government through the PSNP-specific conditional grant. Instead, it is now sent as part of
  the funds allocated by national government to provinces through the more general
  Integrated Nutrition Programme (INP) conditional grant. This makes it difficult to
  track budget allocations and spending on the PSFS.

- Finally, in the context of endemic poverty at the household level, there is a need
  for government to pay more explicit attention to the limits of the PSFS programme (as well as the Department of Health's Programme for the In-patient
  Management of Severe Protein-Energy Malnutrition [PEM] Programme) in
  order to make sustainable inroads into improving children's nutrition and education status (the dual objectives of the programme). It is also essential for government to attend to the development of income support measures for poor children and adults in order to give effect to the child's right to basic nutrition.

Chapter four focuses its programme sufficiency analysis on the Prevention of Mother-
to-Child Transmission (PMTCT) programme. The authors present the following key
findings:

- In its initial stages, the conceptualisation and implementation of the PMTCT
  programme certainly did not meet the criteria of covering all those in need,
  rolling out services as a matter of urgency and as quickly as administrative capacity facilitates. The programme was first implemented at the end of 2000, when
  government, under pressure from the TAC, announced the establishment of 18
  pilot sites, two in each province. (Some provinces, notably Western Cape and
  Gauteng, had already at this stage begun the operation of such programmes.)
  The pilots were supposed to help iron out any implementation and other problems before making the programme universal. However, the latter was slow in
  coming. On the basis that the programme was not being rolled out rapidly
  enough, and excluded too many child-and-mother pairs not in close proximity to
  the pilot sites, the TAC took government to the Constitutional Court. In its
  landmark 2002 judgement, the Constitutional Court found in favour of the TAC
  that the programme was not sufficient in its coverage and speed of roll-out. The
  Department of Health was ordered to make the PMTCT programme universally

available with immediate effect. Provinces were expected to accommodate the roll-out of the PMTCT programme within their current and future budgets. Thus, the first key point to come out of the programme sufficiency analysis on the PMTCT is the power of advocacy, research and litigation action in facilitating the introduction of a programme to advance constitutional socio-economic rights and in pushing the scope and pace of the programme over time.

- Since 2002, the rate of roll-out of the PMTCT programme has varied substantially across all provinces. The three provinces that seem to have lagged behind are Mpumalanga, North West and the Northern Cape, while roll-out in Gauteng and Western Cape has been most rapid. It is clear, however, that the health rights of mothers and children are being advanced through the programme and that, even in remote areas, mother and child pairs are benefiting from the services it offers.

- The most important challenge facing the PMTCT programme is to strengthen existing primary level clinics, as well as the related peri-natal support services. This includes services for the follow-up and support of mothers and babies for at least 18 months post-delivery for HIV-negative babies and for as long as is required for HIV-positive babies.

- In terms of budget allocations and implementation, it is difficult to track the amount of money allocated to and spent on the PMTCT programme. This flows from the mode of financing the programme. Funding for the programme comes out of allocations from provincial equitable share funding and allocations from the HIV/AIDS conditional grant allocated to provincial HIV/AIDS units by national government. The analysis of actual spending of the conditional grant in provinces over the period 2000/01 to 2003/04 shows that provinces have made significant progress in improving their budget implementation. An important rec-ommendation is that allocations for the PMTCT programme be ring-fenced by national government for spending on the programme and sent through to provinces in the form of a PMTCT-specific conditional grant.

Chapter five interrogates the sufficiency of the Child Support Grant (CSG) pro-gramme. This programme was introduced in April 1998 as a social assistance pro-gramme for children under 7. It offered a monthly payment of R100 to the care-giver of a child, provided the care-giver passed an asset (income-driven) means test. By 2003, the grant value had been increased to R160 (which translates into an increase of R10 in real terms since 1998). The following key findings flow from the analysis of the CSG:

- The recent past has brought some positive achievement on the part of govern-ment relating to the conceptualisation of the CSG programme. In February 2003, government announced an expansion of the age coverage of the pro-gramme. It would extend its target to include children in need under 9 years in 2003/04, children under 11 years in 2004/05 and children under 14 years in 2005/06.

- The current conceptualisation of the CSG programme still reveals a number of important weaknesses. Firstly, the programme excludes children of all ages. Secondly, the administration procedure for accessing the grant continues to undermine the rapid roll-out of the programme and makes it difficult to reach particularly vulnerable groups. These include children living without adult care-givers and birth certificates, and children whose income poverty makes it difficult to travel to social development offices. Thirdly, the means test for the CSG does not take into account the number of children being supported by a care-giver applying for a grant on behalf of a child. As such, depending on the care-givers income, it often discriminates against children in households with many members. A final weakness may be the level of the CSG benefit amount (now R160 per beneficiary).

- These key concerns present challenges for government, civil society child rights activists and monitoring researchers. There is a need to revisit the means test and administrative criteria of the CSG programme to speed up delivery to all children in need, particularly those that are most vulnerable. Careful research is also required on the sufficiency of the value of the grant in the context of child poverty and children's right to a level of income that ensures that they can meet their basic needs.

- As far as implementation achievements and challenges are concerned (including budget allocations and implementation), the provincial government departments have made great strides in expanding access to the grant. While the chapter reveals a need for better eligibility data to be collected, it also suggests that all provinces have made dramatic progress, in particular the Western Cape and Gauteng. The Eastern Cape and Limpopo emerge as provinces where the challenge to extend the grant is the greatest.

- Chapter five also presents case study research to shed light on the achievements of the CSG programme in reaching the most vulnerable. The findings suggest that in remote areas, where the need for the CSG is greatest and outreach is most difficult, at least 30% of children in need are accessing the grant. While this reflects progress, it also illustrates the challenge left in extending the programme rapidly in future in a way that the most vulnerable of children under 14 will benefit.

- The authors explain the difficulty in answering the question of whether the roll-out of the CSG over the recent past and its planned roll-out in future has been/is as rapid as administrative capacity allows. According to National Treasury, the planned rate of future roll-out and the decision not to extend the grant to children of all ages was dictated by administrative constraints and in particular, an inability to add children at a quicker rate using the current computer hardware and SOCPEN system.

- The analysis of CSG programme budgets in the provinces between 1998/99 and 2005/06 showed a marked improvement on the part of provincial departments in spending their allocated budgets. Under-budgeting (over-spending) was emerging as a challenge in most provinces. However in 2002/03, KwaZulu-Natal and North West province failed to spend all funds allocated to the programme. The chapter also raises concern about the sufficiency of the size of 2003/04 CSG programme budgets, in light of the need to extend the grant to older eligible children in 2003/04.

- Finally, chapter five draws attention to the following implementation challenges for the CSG programme, which need to be addressed in order to push the pace of delivery and to make the programme more effective:

  * There is a need to improve costing of the roll-out of the programme so that the current problem of under-spending and over-spending is eliminated and, in particular, so that insufficient funding does not constrain the rate of delivery of social assistance to children. This in turn requires human resource capacity-building, better data on eligible children and knowledge of how delivery capacity will evolve over time.

  * There is a need to continue to implement the current outreach programme (including mobile clinics in remote and poor areas).

  * There is a need to improve knowledge amongst service providers and potential beneficiaries about the current eligibility criteria and, in particular, how the expanded age limit is to be implemented.

  * There is a need for the Department of Home Affairs to continue providing birth certificates to children who do not have them.

  * The possible transfer of the CSG to the National Agency for Social Assistance should be done in a way that does not undermine progress in the rate of expansion of access and efficiency of the programme.

  * The existing technological and administrative constraints associated with the SOCPEN system appear to be a major factor undermining the delivery of social assistance to all children in need. Urgent attention is therefore required around the financing and establishment of appropriate computer system capacity.

Chapter six does not undertake a detailed sufficiency analysis of a programme giving effect to the child's unqualified constitutional right to a basic education. Instead, it comments more broadly on government's conceptualisation and budgeting for programmes affecting this right. The emerging findings in this regard are as follows:

- The conceptualisation of government programmes to advance the child's right to basic education reveals several weaknesses. Firstly, it is of major concern that basic education in South Africa is compulsory, but not free. The failure to make education legally free undermines universality in the realisation of the child's right to basic education, as many children and their parents are too poor to acquire the goods and services (such as uniforms and transport) to attend school, let alone to pay school fees. Secondly, the chapter questions the legal definition of "basic education", which is seen to include schooling from grades I to

9, but excludes grades 10 to 12 and ECD. A third weakness in conceptualisation relates specifically to ECD programming and policy. Sufficient attention is not being paid to the design of strategies to deliver pre-Grade R early childhood development. Nor is adequate consideration being given to the impact of poverty and illiteracy in undermining the effectiveness of pre-Grade R ECD provision in poor communities.

- The analysis of government's budgeting for the child's right to a basic education highlights how difficult it is to identify and track programme budgets that provide a rigorous understanding of allocations and spending for the right to basic education. However, the chapter suggests that there are four programme budgets that together provide a good rough indicator of government's budgeting and spending on the right. These budget programmes are Public Ordinary Schools (POS), Independent School Subsidies (ISS), Early Childhood Development (ECD) and Special School Education (SSE).

- The budget analysis indicates that government has given priority to spending on basic education (as proxied by these four programmes). Spending on these four programmes constitutes a very large share of consolidated provincial and national allocated spending (for example 17.2% in 2003/04 ) and of consolidated national and provincial education spending (for example 74.8% in 2003/04). At the same time however, the chapter reveals a need for greater prioritisation of ECD in budgeting. In the context of the termination of the ECD conditional grant in 2003/04, the role of provincial education departments (together with provincial social development departments) will become more critical in financing the further development and delivery of ECD, as well as monitoring provincial progress in this regard.

- A number of important conceptualisation and implementation challenges can be identified in relation to government's measures to advance the child's right to basic education. There is a need for government to take legal action to make basic education free and to broaden the definition of basic education upwards, to include grades 10 to 12 and downwards, to include ECD. In order to track government's performance in budgeting for the child's right to basic education in a more accurate and useful way, changes are required to programme organisation and recording of data in the budget allocation and monitoring system. Further improvements are needed in classroom/learner and teacher/educator ratios.

- Finally, in the context of the structural unemployment and poverty crises that currently prevail in South Africa, there is a need for a progressive stance to be adopted by government in thinking about the types of programmes needed to ensure the delivery of the right to basic education to all children. Bringing about universal access to basic education requires not only spending on and provision of classrooms, teachers and learner materials (the traditional focus). It calls for a broader strategy and range of measures, cutting across a number of sectors and including initiatives that give effect to the other socio-economic rights of children in the Constitution (particularly to social assistance).

The ultimate objective of this publication has been to produce research findings that work to advance children's constitutional socio-economic rights. This in turn depends on a constructive response on the part of government to the general suggestions presented in chapter one, which emanate from the perspectives of poor children themselves. It further depends on active and open engagement between civil society and government around the more specific programme-related recommendations that flowed from the analysis in each of the four monitoring chapters. In addition, relevant actors in civil society (including researchers, activists and litigators) need to rise to the crucial challenge of making more explicit the precise level and range of entitlements children can claim from the state under their unqualified socio-economic rights and that we need to hold government accountable for. In this process, attention will have to be paid to the inter-dependence of the different child socio-economic rights, and of the socio-economic rights of children and adults. A dominant theme that flowed through this publication relates to the latter. This is that in order to advance children's socio-economic rights, it is crucial for government to make progress in realising the right of adults to a basic income. With this in mind, the new attention of the democratic government on designing and implementing programmes of job-creation for the poor is an important development that needs to be encouraged and monitored.

# ENDNOTES

I   The author thankfully acknowledges the assistance of Shaamela Cassiem and Christina Nomdo, of the Children's Budget Unit, Budget Information Service, Idasa and Erika Coetzee.

# INDEX

Please note: References to tables and figures are in italics.

# S